Nature–Inspired Computing Applications in Advanced Communication Networks

Govind P. Gupta
National Institute of Technology, Raipur, India

A volume in the Advances
in Computer and Electrical
Engineering (ACEE) Book Series

Published in the United States of America by
    IGI Global
    Engineering Science Reference (an imprint of IGI Global)
    701 E. Chocolate Avenue
    Hershey PA, USA 17033
    Tel: 717-533-8845
    Fax: 717-533-8661
    E-mail: cust@igi-global.com
    Web site: http://www.igi-global.com

Library of Congress Cataloging-in-Publication Data

Names: Gupta, Govind P., 1979- editor.
Title: Nature-inspired computing applications in advanced communication
  networks / Govind P. Gupta, editor.
Description: Hershey, PA : Engineering Science Reference, [2020] | Includes
  bibliographical references. | Summary: "This book explores the
  application of nature-inspired intelligence for solving various
  optimization problems of the advanced communication networks such as
  WSNs, VANETs, IoT, and DSNs"-- Provided by publisher.
Identifiers: LCCN 2019032854 (print) | LCCN 2019032855 (ebook) | ISBN
  9781799816263 (h/c) | ISBN 9781799816270 (s/c) | ISBN 9781799816287
  (eISBN)
Subjects: LCSH: Wireless communication systems--Technological innovations.
Classification: LCC TK5103.2 .N399 2020 (print) | LCC TK5103.2 (ebook) |
  DDC 004.6--dc23
LC record available at https://lccn.loc.gov/2019032854
LC ebook record available at https://lccn.loc.gov/2019032855

This book is published in the IGI Global book series Advances in Computer and Electrical Engineering (ACEE) (ISSN: 2327-039X; eISSN: 2327-0403)

British Cataloguing in Publication Data
A Cataloguing in Publication record for this book is available from the British Library.

All work contributed to this book is new, previously-unpublished material.
The views expressed in this book are those of the authors, but not necessarily of the publisher.

For electronic access to this publication, please contact: eresources@igi-global.com.

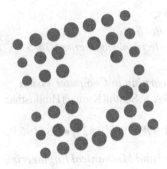

Advances in Computer and Electrical Engineering (ACEE) Book Series

ISSN:2327-039X
EISSN:2327-0403

Editor-in-Chief: Srikanta Patnaik, SOA University, India

MISSION

The fields of computer engineering and electrical engineering encompass a broad range of interdisciplinary topics allowing for expansive research developments across multiple fields. Research in these areas continues to develop and become increasingly important as computer and electrical systems have become an integral part of everyday life.

The **Advances in Computer and Electrical Engineering (ACEE) Book Series** aims to publish research on diverse topics pertaining to computer engineering and electrical engineering. **ACEE** encourages scholarly discourse on the latest applications, tools, and methodologies being implemented in the field for the design and development of computer and electrical systems.

COVERAGE

- Computer Architecture
- Chip Design
- Programming
- Computer Hardware
- Circuit Analysis
- Optical Electronics
- Power Electronics
- Electrical Power Conversion
- Qualitative Methods
- VLSI Fabrication

IGI Global is currently accepting manuscripts for publication within this series. To submit a proposal for a volume in this series, please contact our Acquisition Editors at Acquisitions@igi-global.com or visit: http://www.igi-global.com/publish/.

The Advances in Computer and Electrical Engineering (ACEE) Book Series (ISSN 2327-039X) is published by IGI Global, 701 E. Chocolate Avenue, Hershey, PA 17033-1240, USA, www.igi-global.com. This series is composed of titles available for purchase individually; each title is edited to be contextually exclusive from any other title within the series. For pricing and ordering information please visit http://www.igi-global.com/book-series/advances-computer-electrical-engineering/73675. Postmaster: Send all address changes to above address. ©© 2020 IGI Global. All rights, including translation in other languages reserved by the publisher. No part of this series may be reproduced or used in any form or by any means – graphics, electronic, or mechanical, including photocopying, recording, taping, or information and retrieval systems – without written permission from the publisher, except for non commercial, educational use, including classroom teaching purposes. The views expressed in this series are those of the authors, but not necessarily of IGI Global.

Titles in this Series

For a list of additional titles in this series, please visit:
https://www.igi-global.com/book-series/advances-computer-electrical-engineering/73675

Challenges and Applications for Implementing Machine Learning in Computer Vision
Ramgopal Kashyap (Amity University Chhattisgarh, India) and A.V. Senthil Kumar (Hindusthan College of Arts and Science, India)
Engineering Science Reference • ©2020 • 300pp • H/C (ISBN: 9781799801825) • US $195.00

Handbook of Research on Recent Developments in Electrical and Mechanical Engineering
Jamal Zbitou (University of Hassan 1st, Morocco) Catalin Iulian Pruncu (Imperial College London, UK) and Ahmed Errkik (University of Hassan 1st, Morocco)
Engineering Science Reference • ©2020 • 553pp • H/C (ISBN: 9781799801177) • US $255.00

Architecture and Security Issues in Fog Computing Applications
Sam Goundar (The University of the South Pacific, Fiji) S. Bharath Bhushan (Sree Vidyanikethan Engineering College, India) and Praveen Kumar Rayani (National Institute of Technology, Durgapur, India)
Engineering Science Reference • ©2020 • 205pp • H/C (ISBN: 9781799801948) • US $215.00

Handbook of Research on Advanced Applications of Graph Theory in Modern Society
Madhumangal Pal (Vidyasagar University, India) Sovan Samanta (Tamralipta Mahavidyalaya, India) and Anita Pal (National Institute of Technology Durgapur, India)
Engineering Science Reference • ©2020 • 591pp • H/C (ISBN: 9781522593805) • US $245.00

Novel Practices and Trends in Grid and Cloud Computing
Pethuru Raj (Reliance Jio Infocomm Ltd. (RJIL), India) and S. Koteeswaran (Vel Tech, India)
Engineering Science Reference • ©2019 • 374pp • H/C (ISBN: 9781522590231) • US $255.00

Blockchain Technology for Global Social Change
Jane Thomason (University College London, UK) Sonja Bernhardt (ThoughtWare, Australia) Tia Kansara (Replenish Earth Ltd, UK) and Nichola Cooper (Blockchain Quantum Impact, Australia)
Engineering Science Reference • ©2019 • 243pp • H/C (ISBN: 9781522595786) • US $195.00

For an entire list of titles in this series, please visit:
https://www.igi-global.com/book-series/advances-computer-electrical-engineering/73675

701 East Chocolate Avenue, Hershey, PA 17033, USA
Tel: 717-533-8845 x100 • Fax: 717-533-8661
E-Mail: cust@igi-global.com • www.igi-global.com

Table of Contents

Detailed Table of Contents

    Amanpreet Kaur, Jaypee Institute of Information Technology, India
    Govind P. Gupta, National Institute of Technology, Raipur, India
    Sangeeta Mittal, Jaypee Institute of Information Technology, India

In wireless sensor networks, localization is one of the essential requirements. Most applications are of no use, if location information is not available. Based on cost, localization algorithms can be divided into two categories, namely range-based and range-free. Range-free are cost-effective, but they lack accuracy. In this chapter, the role of nature-inspired algorithms in enhancing the accuracy of range-free algorithms has been investigated. Inferences drawn from exhaustive literature survey of recent research in this area establishes the importance of these algorithms in sensor localization.

    Ashish Yadav, Indian Institute of Information Technology Design and
        Manufacturing, Jabalpur, India
    Sunil Agrawal, Indian Institute of Information Technology Design and
        Manufacturing, Jabalpur, India

Growing interests from customers in customized products and increasing competition among peers necessitate companies to configure and balance their manufacturing systems more effectively than ever before. Two-sided assembly lines are usually constructed to produce large-sized high-volume products such as buses, trucks, automobiles, and some domestic products. Since the problem is well known as NP-hard problem, a mathematical model is solved by an exact solution-based approach and spider monkey optimization (SMO) algorithm that is inspired by the intelligent foraging behavior of fission-fusion social structure-based animals. In this chapter, the proposed mathematical model is applied to solve benchmark problems of two-sided assembly line balancing problem to minimize the number of mated stations and idle time. The experimental results show that spider monkey optimizations provide better results.

Chapter 3

Vrajesh Kumar Chawra, National Institute of Technology, Raipur, India
Govind P. Gupta, National Institute of Technology, Raipur, India

The formation of the unequal clusters of the sensor nodes is a burning research issue in wireless sensor networks (WSN). Energy-hole and non-uniform load assignment are two major issues in most of the existing node clustering schemes. This affects the network lifetime of WSN. Salp optimization-based algorithm is used to solve these problems. The proposed algorithm is used for cluster head selection. The performance of the proposed scheme is compared with the two-node clustering scheme in the term of residual energy, energy consumption, and network lifetime. The results show the proposed scheme outperforms the existing protocols in term of network lifetime under different network configurations.

Chapter 4

Mohamed Mounir, El-Gazeera High Institute (EGI) for Engineering and
*   Technology, Egypt*
Mohamed Bakry El Mashade, Al Azhar University, Egypt
Gurjot Singh Gaba, Lovely Professional University, India

OFDM is widely used in high data rate applications due to its ability to mitigate frequency selectivity. However, OFDM suffers from high PAPR problem. This degrades the system performance. PTS is a promising PAPR reduction technique. However, its computational complexity is large; to reduce it, different suboptimal solution (heuristics) were presented in literature. Heuristics PTS algorithms can be categorized into descent-heuristics and metaheuristics. In this chapter, descent-heuristics-based PTS and metaheuristics-based PTS are compared. Results showed that RS-PTS is the best one among descent-heuristics algorithms. Metaheuristics algorithms can also be classified into single solution-based methods and nature-inspired methods. Among metaheuristics algorithms, two natural inspired algorithms and one single solution-based methods, namely PSO, ABC, and SA, were selected to be compared with descent-heuristics algorithms. Results showed that PTS based on nature-inspired methods is better than PTS based on descent heuristics and PTS based on single-solution metaheuristics method.

Chapter 5
Hassan El Alami, National Institute of Posts and Telecommunications (INPT), Rabat, Morocco

Abdellah Najid, National Institute of Posts and Telecommunications (INPT), Rabat, Morocco

Energy consumption is a constraint in the design architecture of wireless sensor networks (WSNs) and internet of things (IoT). In order to overcome this constraint, many techniques have been proposed to enhance energy efficiency in WSNs. In existing works, several innovative techniques for the physical, the link, and the network layer of OSI model are implemented. Energy consumption in the WSNs is to find the best compromise of energy consumption between the various tasks performed by the objects, the detection, the processing, and the data communication tasks. It is this last task that consumes more energy. As a result, the main objective for the WSNs and the IoT is to minimize the energy consumed during this task. One of the most used solutions is to propose efficient routing techniques in terms of energy consumption. In this chapter, the authors present a review of related works on energy efficiency in WSNs and IoT. The network layer routing protocols are the main concerns in this chapter. The interest is focused on the issue of designing data routing techniques in WSNs and IoT.

Chapter 6
Padmapriya N., IFET College of Engineering, India

N. Kumaratharan, Sri Venkateswara College of Engineering, India

Aswini R., IFET College of Engineering, India

A wireless sensor network (WSN) is a gathering of sensor hubs that powerfully self-sort themselves into a wireless system without the use of any previous framework. One of the serious issues in WSNs is the energy consumption, whereby the system lifetime is subject to this factor. Energy-efficient routing is viewed as the most testing errand. Sensor organizes for the most part work in perplexing and dynamic situations and directing winds up repetitive assignment to keep up as the system measure increments. This chapter portrays the structure of wireless sensor network the analysis and study of different research works identified with energy-efficient routing in wireless sensor networks. Along these lines, to beat all the routing issues, the pattern has moved to biological-based algorithms like swarm intelligence-based strategies. Ant colony optimization-based routing protocols have shown outstanding outcomes as far as execution when connected to WSN routing.

Chapter 7

Many original ideologies are being applied as solutions to the problems of wireless sensor networks with the rigorous experimentation and advancement in technology and research. This chapter reviews various energy-efficient routing algorithms, classifying them based on methodology applied. The classification is based on design approach used to solve the basic problem arising in construction of transmission path between source and base station (BS) with minimum energy consumption. The pros and cons of routing algorithms for WSN are analyzed. The parameters to be considered in evaluation of all routing protocols are summarized.

Vehicular ad hoc networks (VANET) are networks that interconnect road and vehicles. The mobile nodes are used to connect themselves in self-organized manner. VANET is valuable that gives better performance and assures safe transportation system in prospect. Few of them are covered that helps in knowing the best protocol to be used in particular work. Initially, renewable energy is considered to be those sources that are derived either directly or indirectly from solar energy. Due to emission of harmful gases, in VANET, use of renewable resources come in existence. In another section of the chapter, various energy issues in VANET have been highlighted and added the concept of VANET-CLOUD. As cloud computing technologies have potential to improve the travelling experience and safety of roads by giving provision of various solutions like traffic lights synchronization, alternative routes, etc., VANET-CLOUD has been added at the end of the chapter.

Chapter 9

Saloni Dhiman, Dr. B. R. Ambedkar National Institute of Technology, Jalandhar, India

Deepti Kakkar, Dr. B. R. Ambedkar National Institute of Technology, Jalandhar, India

Gurjot Kaur, Dr. B. R. Ambedkar National Institute of Technology, Jalandhar, India

Wireless sensor networks (WSNs) consist of several sensor nodes (SNs) that are powered by battery, so their lifetime is limited, which ultimately affects the lifespan and hence performance of the overall networks. Till now many techniques have been developed to solve this problem of WSN. Clustering is among the effective technique used for increasing the network lifespan. In this chapter, analysis of multi-hop routing protocol based on grid clustering with different selection criteria is presented. For analysis, the network is divided into equal-sized grids where each grid corresponds to a cluster and is assigned with a grid head (GH) responsible for collecting data from each SN belonging to respective grid and transferring it to the base station (BS) using multi-hop routing. The performance of the network has been analyzed for different position of BS, different number of grids, and different number of SNs.

Preface

OBJECTIVE OF THE BOOK

Nature-inspired computing based meta-heuristic algorithms have become progressively more popular in solving the multi-objective optimization problems of different research fields. Practical applications of Nature-inspired computing techniques in solving various optimization problems of the advanced communication networks such as Wireless Sensor Networks, Vehicular AdHoc Networks, Internet of Things, Data Center network, are very challenging issues. The main aim of this book is to provide a unique collection of research works as well as review of research works in the area of application of nature-inspired computing in the optimization problems of advanced communication networks. There are various NP-hard problems in the field of Advanced Communication Networks that can be solve efficiently using nature-inspired intelligence such as localizations, routing, clustering, etc. This book provides basic understanding of nature-inspired computing and its applications in solving various multi-objective optimization problems of the advanced communication networks.

ORGANIZATION OF THE BOOK

This book contains nine chapters that mainly outline the application of nature-inspired computing in solving the different optimization problems such as localization, routing, node clustering in WSN, scheduling, energy optimization etc.

Chapter 1 covers application of nature-inspired computing and its impact in determining the node localization in WSNs. In this chapter, a brief overview of nature-inspired algorithms such as *PSO*, Cuckoo Search, Genetic Algorithm, and Grey Wolf Optimization (*GWO*) are discussed in detail. This chapter studied impact of nature-inspired computing in enhancing accuracy of range free algorithms.

Chapter 2 presents a detail study of spider monkeys optimization scheme and its application in two sided assembly line balancing problem. In this chapter, a new mathematical model of two-sided assembly line balancing problem is applied to solve benchmark problem P(16) with the objective of minimize idle time and the number of mated station.

Chapter 3 presents application of Salp meta-heuristic technique for selection of cluster Heads in Wireless Sensor networks and for unequal clustering. This chapter discusses a brief overview of Salp swarm optimization and a detail discussion in clustering problem. Performance of the proposed scheme is evaluated and compared with three schemes such as hybrid dolphin echolocation and crow search optimization (*DECSA*), *GA* and *LEACH*.

In Chapter 4, descent heuristics, such as, *IPTS, RS-PTS, and GD-PTS* were compared with meta-heuristics-based PTS techniques. Simulated annealing was selected as single solution meta-heuristics method and Particle Swarm Optimization (*PSO*), Artificial Bee Colony (*ABC*), were selected as a nature inspired meta-heuristics methods. Results showed that, PTS based on nature Inspired methods is better than PTS that based on descent heuristics and PTS based on single solution meta-heuristics method (i.e. SA).

Chapter 5 focuses on Optimization of Energy Efficiency in Wireless Sensor Networks and Internet of Things. This chapter presents a review of related works on energy efficiency in WSNs and IoT. The network layer routing protocols are our main concerns in this chapter. Our interest is focused on the issue of designing data routing techniques in WSNs and IoT.

Chapter 6 portrays the structure of wireless sensor network and its analysis and study of different research works identified with Energy Efficient Routing in Wireless Sensor Networks. This chapter discusses different Biological-based routing algorithms such as Swarm Intelligence based strategies; Ant Colony Optimization based routing protocols for WSNs.

Chapter 7 reviews on various energy efficient routing algorithms, classifying them based on methodology applied. The classification is based on design approach used to solve the basic problem arising in construction of transmission path between source and base station with minimum energy consumption. The pros and cons of routing algorithm for WSN is stated architectures are analyzed.

In Chapter 8, a various energy issues in VANET have been highlighted and added the concept of VANET-CLOUD. This chapter studied application of cloud computing technologies to improve the travelling experience and safety of roads by giving provision of various solutions like traffic lights synchronization, alternative routes, etc.

Chapter 9 presents multi-hop routing protocol based on grid clustering with different selection criteria. For analysis, the network is divided into equal-sized grids where each grid corresponds to a cluster and is assigned with a Grid Head (*GH*) which is responsible for collecting data from each sensor node belonging to respective grid and transferring it to the Base Station (*BS*) using multi-hop routing. The performance of the network has been analyzed for different position of *BS*, different number of grids and different numbers of sensor nodes.

Govind P. Gupta
National Institute of Technology, Raipur, India

Chapter 1
Impact of Nature-Inspired Algorithms on Localization Algorithms in Wireless Sensor Networks

Amanpreet Kaur
Jaypee Institute of Information Technology, India

Govind P. Gupta
National Institute of Technology, Raipur, India

Sangeeta Mittal
Jaypee Institute of Information Technology, India

ABSTRACT

In wireless sensor networks, localization is one of the essential requirements. Most applications are of no use, if location information is not available. Based on cost, localization algorithms can be divided into two categories, namely range-based and range-free. Range-free are cost-effective, but they lack accuracy. In this chapter, the role of nature-inspired algorithms in enhancing the accuracy of range-free algorithms has been investigated. Inferences drawn from exhaustive literature survey of recent research in this area establishes the importance of these algorithms in sensor localization.

DOI: 10.4018/978-1-7998-1626-3.ch001

INTRODUCTION

Wireless Sensor Networks (WSNs) is hot research area nowadays (Rawat, Singh, Chaouchi, & J.M.Bonnin, 2014). It is collection of sensitive and dedicated sensor nodes that sense some critical event such as heat, moisture, light, pressure, etc and processes this information and sends it to base station via multiple hops (Kaur, Kumar & Gupta, 2019). WSN can be used for many critical applications such as military, forest surveillance, and intrusion detection, civilian applications because of its rapid deployment, self organizing behavior and fault tolerant nature. In all these kinds of applications, main role of WSN is to detect an event and send it to base station for immediate action (Han, Xu, Duong, Jiang & Hara, 2013). But for immediate response, location of event is also required. This identification of location of event i.e. location of sensor that detected that vent is called Localization. This is most challenging problems in field of WSN. The technique makes use of few sensor nodes that are usually deployed uniformly in whole WSN and have knowledge of their locality. With the aid of these anchor nodes, remaining unknown nodes try to find their location. Localization contains two phases: Distance estimation and Position estimation as depicted in Figure 1 (Farooq-i-Azam & Ayyaz, 2016).

In localization process, firstly unknown nodes predict their distance from anchor nodes and then predict their location. Distance/Angle estimation process can be of two types depending upon measurement technique and are range-based or range-free (Zhao, Xi, He, Liu, Li & Yang, 2013). Range based attains distance/angle data among neighbour nodes and usually uses specialized equipment, whereas Range free applies connectivity data between neighbouring nodes without using any specialized equipment. Examples of range based include Received Signal Strength Indicator (RSSI) (Girod, Bychobvskiy, Elson & Estrin, 2002), Time of Arrival (TOA) (Harter, Hopper, Steggles, Ward & Webster, 2002), Time Difference of Arrival (TDOA) (Cheng, Thaeler, Xue & Chen, 2004) [8], Angle of Arrival (AOA) (Niculescu & Nath, 2003), etc. Examples of Range free are Centroid (Bulusu, Heidemann & Estrin, 2000), Distance Vector-Hop (DV-Hop) (Niculescu & Nath, 2001), Amorphous

Figure 1. Localization process

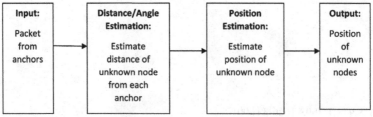

(Nagpal, Shrobe & Bachrach, 1999), Approximate Point in Triangle (APIT) (He, Huang, Blum, Stankovic & Abdelzaher, 2003), Multi Dimensional Scaling (MDS) (Ruml & Shang, 2004), etc. Range free is more popular due to its cost effectiveness as they do not require any expensive hardware unlike range based techniques. But range free has low accuracy. There have been so many proposals to improve its accuracy in last two decades. This paper surveys all these proposals that uses nature inspired algorithms for improvement.

NATURE INSPIRED ALGORITHMS

Nature could be a wealthy supply of ideas for optimization. Nature inspired algorithms that have been inspired from nature have become so popular now–a-days due to its accuracy and simplicity. They do not rely on any problem and can be used for extensive range of problems. They are generally preferred as they apply easy and simple concepts and can avoid local optima and gives results quite closer to global optima (Talbi, 2009)[15]. There are a range of nature inspired algorithm such as Particle Swarm Optimization (*PSO*) algorithm (Shi, 2001), Firefly Algorithm (*FA*) (Yang, 2010), Flower Pollination Algorithm (*FPA*) (Nabil, 2016)[18], Cuckoo Search (*CS*) (Yang & Deb, 2009), Ant Colony Optimization (*ACO*) algorithm (Dorigo & Birattari, 2006), Butterfly Optimization Algorithm (*BOA*) (Arora & Singh, 2017), Genetic Algorithm (*GA*) (Dasgupta, & Michalewicz, 1997), Grey Wolf Optimization (*GWO*) (Mirjalili, Mirjalili, & Lewis, 2014) which we will discussed as follows:

Particle Swarm Optimization

PSO is rooted on behavior of group of birds. This is based on following scenario where flock of birds is aimlessly exploring for the food in some particular area. The question is that if there is single piece of food in specific place, then how all birds will find the location of food. The best approach is to track that bird which is adjacent to foodstuff. PSO algorithm uses same strategy to find solution and is used for extensive variety of optimization problems. For PSO, each bird is called particle or single solution in the exploration space. All these particles compute their fitness value by using fitness function and have velocities to control speed and direction of flying.

PSO works in multiple iterations. Initially, there are group of random units. For each round, every unit updates itself by using two preeminent values. The former one called as pbest is the best solution it has achieved so far. Next one is called gbest that is global best acquired by any unit in the population.

After getting these two preeminent values, all units update its velocities and position according to following Equations (1) and (2) for iteration i+1 for unit u.

$$v_u^{i+1} = w \times v_u^i + c_1 \times rand_1^i \times \left(pbest_u^i - x_u^i\right) + c_2 \times rand_2^i \times \left(gbest_u^k - x_u^k\right) \qquad (1)$$

$$x_u^{i+1} = x_u^i + v_u^{i+1} \qquad (2)$$

where v_u^i is velocity vector of unit u, x_u^i is position vector of unit u, $pbest_u^i$ is individual preeminent value of unit u and $gbest_u^i$ is global preeminent value of all particles in entire search space, c_1 and c_2 are learning factors and $rand_1^i$ and $rand_2^i$ are both arbitrary values amid[0,1].

Cuckoo Search Algorithm

Cuckoos are birds that are famous for their lovely sounds and strange reproductive strategy. Some of classes of Cuckoo leave their eggs in other host bird's nest by replacing with host bird's egg in the nest. These cuckoo species have evolved in this way that their egg resembles host bird's egg. Thus host bird is not able to differentiate between her and cuckoo's eggs. If somehow, host bird finds about this thing, in that case either it heave unfamiliar eggs or abandon her nest and build its own nest in some other place.

For simplicity, CS algorithm follows three assumptions: First one is that each cuckoo produces single egg at an instance, and places it in randomly chosen nest. Second assumption is that next generations hold top nests with high superiority of eggs. Thirdly, the count of accessible host nests is set, and event that egg replaced by cuckoo is identified by host bird with likelihood (*pa*) whose value lies in the range of [0, 1]. In last assumption, the fraction likelihood (*pa*) of the n nests is replaced by new nests (with new arbitrary solutions). The pseudo code is described in Figure 2.

To generate new solution for cuckoo u, a Lévy flight is carried out as depicted in Equation (3):

$$x_u^{i+1} = x_u^i + \alpha \oplus L\grave{e}vy\left(\lambda\right) \qquad (3)$$

where $\alpha > 0$ is the step size. Usually the value of α is 1. The above equation is fundamentally the stochastic equation for arbitrary walk. In common, an arbitrary walk is a Markov chain whose subsequent position only relies on existing position (initial term in equation (3)) and the transition likelihood (next term).

Figure 2. Psuedo code of CS algorithm

```
Cuckoo Search via Lévy Flights
begin
Objective function f(x), x =(x1,...,xd)T
Generate initial population of host nests with size n, xi (i =1,2,...,n)
while (t < Max Generation) or (stop criterion)
Get a cuckoo randomly by Lévy flights
Evaluate its quality/fitness Fi
Choose a nest among n (say, j) randomly
if (Fi <Fj),
replace j by the new solution;
end
A fraction probability (pa) of worse nests are abandoned and new nest
(solution) is built;
Keep the best solutions (or nests with quality solutions);
Rank the solutions and find the current best nest;
end
Post process results and visualization
end
```

The Lévy flight basically assigns an arbitrary walk by drawing random step length from a Lévy distribution according to Equation (4).

$$Lèvy \sim u = i^{-\lambda}(1 < \lambda \leq 3) \tag{4}$$

that has an unbounded variance with an unbounded mean. New solutions can be formed by Lévy walk around the preeminent solution generated so far to speed up the local search.

Genetic Algorithm

This is an optimization approach obtained from concepts of evolutionary theory.
   It is based on following concepts:

1.   All individuals in population contend for resources and mate.
2.   Two fittest individuals then mate to produce more offspring compared with others.
3.   Better and fit genes transmit from parent to offsprings, and in most cases offsprings are better than parents.
4.   In this way, next generation is more suitable than previous generation.

Figure 3. Crosover operation

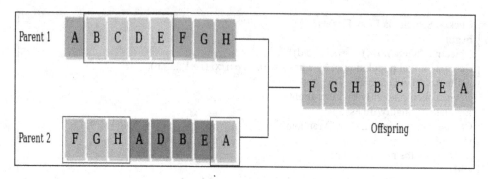

Figure 4. Mutation Operation

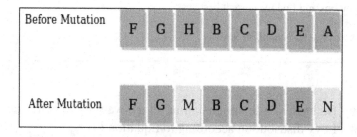

Major operations are selection, crossover and mutation.

a. **Selection Operator:** The idea is select individuals with good fitness score which will be used for next operator and their genes are used.

b. **Crossover Operator:** In this operation, two individuals that are selected from previous operation are allowed to mate. Then the genes at this crossover are exchanged thus creating a completely new individual (offspring). For example –

3. **Mutation Operator:** In this, some random genes are inserted in offspring to maintain the variety in population to avoid the premature convergence. For example –

The whole algorithm can be briefed as revealed in Figure 5.

Figure 5. Psuedo Code of GA

```
1) Randomly initialize populations p
2) Determine fitness of population
3) Untill convergence repeat:
      a) Select parents from population
      b) Crossover and generate new population
      c) Perform mutation on new population
      d) Calculate fitness for new population
```

Grey Wolf Algorithm

Grey Wolf optimization (GWO) is most popular meta-heuristic optimization technique proposed by S. Mijalali et al. GWO is motivated by social chain of command and hunting method of grey wolves. This optimization technique is quite flexible, simple and tries to search entire search space instead of local optima solution. It has been proved in this paper that GWO when tested with 28 standard functions and contrasted with other well recognized meta-heuristic algorithms, then it gives best results. According to social hierarchy, grey wolves can be classified into four categories. Alphas belong to top most category that act as decision makers of chasing, rest place and many more decisions. Second category is of betas that acts as assistant to alphas. Last one in this category is omegas and deltas.

In GWO, alpha (α) is best solution, then subsequently top solutions are beta (β) and delta ($'$). Other candidate solutions are omega ($\acute{E}$). The wolves surround prey during hunting technique that can be described using mathematical model given below:

$$D = C.X_p\left(i\right) - X\left(i\right) \tag{5}$$

$$X\left(i+1\right) = X_p\left(i\right) - B.D \tag{6}$$

where i is iteration number, B and C are coefficient vectors, Xp is location of prey and X is location vector of grey wolf. The vectors B and C are obtained as given below:

$$B = 2a, r_1 - a \tag{7}$$

$$C = 2, r_2 \tag{8}$$

where a is a vector which decrements linearly from 2 to 0 and r_1, r_2 are random vectors that lies in range from 0 to 1.

In GWO, location of prey is estimated by considering locations estimated by all alpha, beta and delta.

Assuming role of each type of wolf in determining location of prey, following formulas are considered to obtain location of prey:

$$D_\infty = C_1.X_\infty - X; D_\beta = C_2.X_\beta - X; D_8 = C_3.X_8 - X \tag{9}$$

$$X_1 = X_\infty - B_1.D_\infty; X_2 = X_2 - B_2.D_2; X_3 = X. - B_3.D. \tag{10}$$

$$X\left(\text{iteration} + 1\right) = \frac{X_{1+}X_2 + X_3}{3} \tag{11}$$

The pseudo code of GWO is given in Figure 6.

Figure 6. Psuedo Code of GWO

Algorithm: Psuedo Code of Grey Wolf Optimization algorithm

1: Initialize the population of grey wolf and value of the coefficients a, B ,C, max_iteration
    // max_iteration representa maximum number of iteration
2: Determine fitness function for each solution vector of population.
3: Let X_α= best solution, X_β= second best solution and X_δ = third best solution
4: while (iteration < max_iteration){
5:    for each solution particle {
6:       Update position of particle by applying Equation (11)
7:    }
8:    Update values of coefficients a, B ,C
9:    Again, determine fitness value for each particle of population
10:   Update X_α, X_β and X_δ according to fitness function
11:   iteration=iteration+1
12: }
13: return centroid of X_α, X_β and X_δ.

NATURE INSPIRED ALGORITHMS FOR WSN LOCALIZATION

3D DV-hop Localisation Scheme Based on Particle Swarm Optimisation in Wireless Sensor Networks (Chen & Zhang, 2014)

To get better localization accuracy of most popular algorithm (DV-Hop), an improvement is proposed by B.Zhang et al. in 2014 that mainly targets 3D WSN area and uses PSO algorithm with inertia weight. The algorithm works as following:

Initialize population- Each particle in population is coordinate of every unknown node. To improve accuracy, first initial candidate solutions of particles are randomly generated for node u by following equation (12).

$$X_u^1 = \begin{bmatrix} x_u + (-1)^{[r \times 10]} \times r \times \partial_x \\ y_u + (-1)^{[r \times 10]} \times r \times \partial_y \\ z_u + (-1)^{[r \times 10]} \times r \times \partial_z \end{bmatrix} \tag{12}$$

where (x_u, y_u, z_u) are estimated coordinates of node u obtained from previous proposal DV-Hop[11], $\partial_x = \dfrac{x_u}{2}, \partial_y = \dfrac{y_u}{2}, \partial_z = \dfrac{z_u}{2}$ and r is a random number from [0,1].

Compute the fitness value of each particle. The fitness is intended using following Equation (13).

$$\text{fitness}\left(X_u^i\right) = \sum_{j=1}^{n} \pm_j^2 \times \left(d_{uj} - \left|X_u^i - M_j\right|\right)^2 \tag{13}$$

where M_j is location of anchor node j, i is iteration number and α is value that contrariwise relative to number of hops involving unknown node u and anchor node j.

For every particle u, its fitness value is compared with pbest value and current position value (pbest) is updated with smaller value.

For every particle u, its fitness value is compared with gbest value and current global position value(gbest) is updated with smaller value.

Revise each particle's velocity and location by using following equation (14).

$$v_u^{i+1} = \left(\acute{E} \times v_u^i\right) + c_1 \times \left(\text{pbest}_u^i - X_u^i\right) + c_2 \times \text{rand}_u^i \times \left(\text{pbest}_u^i - X_u^i\right) \tag{14}$$

$$X_u^{i+1} = X_u^i + v_u^{i+1} \tag{15}$$

where v is velocity vector, X is current location vector, rand is arbitrary number amid 0 and 1, ω is inertia weight to maintain balance between gbest and pbest values and is obtained using Equation (16).

$$\acute{E} = \acute{E}_{max} - \left(\frac{\acute{E}_{max} - \acute{E}_{min}}{i_{max}} \right) \times i \tag{16}$$

where ω_{max}, ω_{min} are initial and final inertia weights, i_{max} is maximum amount of iterations and i is existing iteration number.

Repeat Steps (b) to (e) till maximum number of iterations are reached.

It is proved that application of PSO and inertia weight improves localization precision of proposed one when contrasted with DV Hop without increasing any additional hardware.

Improved DV-Hop Node Localization Algorithm in Wireless Sensor Networks using PSO (Chen, & Zhang, 2012)

This proposal is an improvement of DV-Hop. Initially, all anchor nodes are placed at boundary in WSN network. Secondly, average hop distance that is approximate distance in one hop is adapted and this modified average hop distance is used to compute approximate location of unknown node using 2D Hyperbolic method. Lastly, PSO is applied to correct position of unknown node obtained from previous step. This last step makes result closer than previous value. Simulation results confirm that proposed algorithm gives higher performance in terms of localization accuracy when contrasted with DV-Hop and some existing improved variants.

Wireless Sensor Network Localization Based on Cuckoo Search Algorithm (Goyal & Patterh, 2014)

S. Goyal et al., 2014 (**Goyal & Patterh, 2014**) proposed a novel approach based on cuckoo search algorithm to estimate sensor node location. Proposed algorithm is then compared with PSO and a variety of biogeography based optimization approaches (BBO) and gives superior results in terms of localization correctness. The approach works in following way:

Assuming, there are n unknown nodes and m anchor nodes in WSN area and every node has predetermined communication range(r) and nodes that are in communication range of three or more nodes can be localized. Each unknown node that can be localized estimates its distance from each one of its neighbouring anchors i using following Equation (17).

$$d_i' = d_i + n_i \qquad (17)$$

where di is actual remoteness of unknown node from anchor i obtained by using Equation (18).

$$d_i = \sqrt{\left(x - x_i\right)^2 + \left(y - y_i\right)^2} \qquad (18)$$

and distance estimation are affected with Gaussian noise ni due to surroundings consideration.

After this, each node executes CS algorithm to localize itself. The objective function is to reduce following function:

$$f(x, y) = \frac{1}{m} \sum_{j=1}^{m} \left(d_i' - d_i\right)^2 \qquad (19)$$

Where m >=3 is total count of anchors within transmission range of given node.

An Improved Localization Algorithm Based on Genetic Algorithm in Wireless Sensor Networks (Peng & Li, 2015)

This algorithm is an enhanced variation of DV-Hop that applies GA mainly to get better localization accuracy. The algorithm works in following steps:

Step 1: Computation of least hop-count value from every node to every anchor.

Step 2: Computation of average hop size by each anchor.

Step 3: Computation of distance of each unknown node from each anchor by multiplying minimum hop-count value with average hop size.

Step 4: Find population possible area of each unknown node and Initialize population.

Step 5: Assess fitness of each particle.

Step 6: Genetic operations (crossover, mutation, and selection) are applied to produce the next population. This process is recurring until the top criterion is fulfilled.

A Hybrid Algorithm of GA + Simplex Method in WSN Localization (Wang, Wang, Wang & Zhang, 2015)

In order to improve localization accuracy, in this proposal, F.Wang et al., 2015 uses combination of GA and simplex numerical method. This modifies last stage of DV-Hop which applies GA and simplex method to optimize position of unknown nodes. Simulation results show that localization accuracy and convergence rate is improved to large extent.

Nature Inspired Algorithm-Based Improved Variants of DV-Hop Algorithm for Randomly Deployed 2D and 3D Wireless Sensor Networks (Kaur, Kumar & Gupta, 2018)

This paper proposes Grey Wolf Optimization based algorithm that applies GWO in second phase of DV-Hop. Given proposal assumes that anchors have higher power compared with unknown node as extra computations are performed at anchor side. The modified second phase of proposed algorithm works as:

Phase 2: Obtaining Optimized Average Hop Distance by each anchor and Distance of unknown node from each anchor:

After first phase, all anchors calculate average distance in one hop (AvgHopSizei).

Then, each anchor computes actual distance d_{ij}^{true} by using Euclidean Distance Equation.

Thirdly, anchor nodes apply grey wolf optimization algorithm to optimize AvgHopSizei. Since anchors have higher power, thus these additional computations can be easily done at their side. The objective function (f1) used in GWO is as follows:

$$\text{Minimize } e_{ij} = \sum_{j=1, j \neq i}^{m} (d_{ij}^{true} - d_{ij}) \qquad (20)$$

where $0 < \text{AvgHopSize}_i \leq \max(d_{ij})$

The problem is to find better estimate of average hop distance of anchor i by minimizing eij.

These GWO steps performed by each anchor for obtaining optimized average hop size are given in Figure 7.

After refining Average Hop Size value by each anchor, each anchor sends another more packet containing refined AvgHopSize_i to its neighbours.

Figure 7. Psuedo Code for Phase 2 of grey wolf based algorithm

---

Algorithm : *Psuedo code of Phase 2 performed by each anchor*

Input: Beacon packets containing location and minimum hop count from each anchor i

Output: Optimized Average hop distance for each anchor

1. *Initialize a random population in space between 0 and max(d_{ij}), value of a, B , C, max_iteration //max_iteration represents maximum number of iteration*

2. *Compute value of the objective function for each individual particle of population using Equation (20).*

3. *Set initial best estimates of X_α, X_β and X_δ.*

4. *Initialize iteration=1. // iteration represents iteration number*

5. *While (iteration <=max_iteration) {*

6.   *for each particle in population*

7.   *Update its average hop distance by using Equation (11).*

8.   *Update values of coefficients a , B and C.*

9.   *Again determine objective function f_1 for all particles.*

10.   *Update X_α, X_β and X_δ according to fitness function*

11.   *iteration=iteration+1*

12. *}*

13. *Get the centroid of X_α, X_β and X_δ and return optimized average hop distance as this value.*

Receiving node (with id u) only keeps average hop size (AvgHopSize$_j$) from nearest anchor (assuming having id j). Nearest anchor will be one whose packet will reach given node first, thus first packet containing AvgHopSize$_j$ will form nearest anchor node.

After receiving packet, node calculates approximate distances (d_{iu}) from each anchor node i by multiplying AvgHopSize$_j$ of its nearest anchor j by hop count (hop$_{ui}$) obtained from its hop count table. This distance information is used in the next phase.

$$d_{ui} = \text{AvgHopSize}_j \times \text{hop}_{ui} \tag{21}$$

MAIN FINDINGS

The key purpose of all these proposals is to improve localization precision by applying nature inspired algorithms. The result findings of these proposals are discussed below:

1. B.Zhang et al., 2014 (Chen & Zhang, 2014) proposal was coded in Matlab and all nodes are arbitrarily deployed in 3D WSN area of size *100 X 100 X 100* metre³. Localisation error in this approach is reduced by 15-25% when contrasted with traditional 3D DV-hop technique. It is observed that if radio range of sensor nodes is small, then localisation error is excessively high. Thus it is required to pick realistic radio range. Also, PSO method enhances computational complexity.

2. **X.**Chen et al., 2012 **(Chen, & Zhang, 2012)** also applied PSO algorithm to perk up localization precision of DV-Hop [11] and J.Z.Lin et al.,2009[30]. To prove this fact, these entire algorithms were implementing in Matlab2009 and WSN area of 100 X 100 metre² was considered. It is proved from simulation results that given proposal are better than previous algorithms. It gives 11% higher accuracy when compared with DV-Hop[11] and 6% higher accuracy when compared with J.Z. Lin et al.,2009[30].

3. S. Goyal et al., 2014 (Goyal & Patterh, 2014) applied CS algorithm on localization algorithm and proved its superiority by using simulation over other evolutionary algorithms. For given simulation, sensor nodes were randomly deployed over a *10 X 10* metre² *WSN* area. 200 nodes were randomly deployed in which 10 are anchor nodes in *WSN* area. The proposal does not apply any weighted approach as used in previous algorithms that limits global search ability. If the given proposal is combined with weight coefficient, then it will improve accuracy to large extent. Still, the given proposal improves accuracy by 15-20% whwn compared with other evolutionary algorithms.

4. Bo.Peng et al., 2015 (Peng & Li, 2015) applied GA algorithm on DV-Hop in its third phase. Simulation results verify that this particular approach improves localization precision by 5-8% when contrasted with DV-Hop algorithm.

5. F. Wang et al., 2015 (Wang, Wang, Wang & Zhang, 2015) proposed hybrid approach of GA and simplex method in last phase of DV-Hop[11], Simulation results show that the accuracy is improved by at most 15% if comparison is done with DV-Hop algorithm.

6. A.Kaur in (Kaur, Kumar & Gupta, 2018) first analyzes main error caused due to rough calculation of average hop distances by each anchor in Phase 2 of *DV-Hop. T*o decrease localization error of *DV-Hop*, GWO is used to get better estimation of average hop distance. Based on GWO optimization technique, *GWOLA* and *Weighted-GWOLA* are proposed. *GWOLA* refines average hop

distance in second stage of *DV-Hop*. *Weighted-GWOLA* first refines average hop distance by each anchor in second phase and then weighted approach is enforced by unknown node in third phase in which weight is inversely proportional to minimum hops from each anchor. Simulation is performed and it is proved that both proposals perform superior to *DV-Hop* and its recent variants. Localization accuracy is improved upto 10% with slight increase in the computational complexity at anchor nodes only and no increase in computations at unknown nodes.

From above survey, it has been observed that nature inspired algorithms play a vital task in field of localization in *WSN*. If these optimization algorithms are applied with current existing algorithms, then it improves localization accuracy significantly.

CONCLUSION AND FUTURE SCOPE

In this chapter, Nature-Inspired range-free node localization algorithms have been surveyed.

All these proposals have improved accurateness and rapid convergence when contrasted with traditional algorithms. Inferences from these proposals prove that nature inspired algorithms can be applied to localization algorithm to get higher accuracy and these optimization algorithms play an important role in field of Localization in WSN.

REFERENCES

Arora, S., & Singh, S. (2017). An improved butterfly optimization algorithm with chaos. *Journal of Intelligent & Fuzzy Systems, 32*(1), 1079–1088. doi:10.3233/JIFS-16798

Bulusu, N., Heidemann, J., & Estrin, D. (2000). GPS-less low-cost outdoor localization for very small devices. *IEEE Personal Communications, 7*(5), 28-34.

Chen, X., & Zhang, B. (2012). Improved DV-Hop node localization algorithm in wireless sensor networks. *International Journal of Distributed Sensor Networks, 8*(8), 213980. doi:10.1155/2012/213980

Chen, X., & Zhang, B. (2014). 3D DV-hop localisation scheme based on particle swarm optimisation in wireless sensor networks. *International Journal of Sensor Networks, 16*(2), 100–105. doi:10.1504/IJSNET.2014.065869

Cheng, X., Thaeler, A., Xue, G., & Chen, D. (2004, March). TPS: A time-based positioning scheme for outdoor wireless sensor networks. In IEEE INFOCOM 2004 (Vol. 4, pp. 2685-2696). IEEE.

Dasgupta, D., & Michalewicz, Z. (Eds.). (2013). *Evolutionary algorithms in engineering applications*. Springer Science & Business Media.

Dorigo, M., & Birattari, M. (2010). *Ant colony optimization*. Springer.

Farooq-i-Azam, M., & Ayyaz, M. N. (2016). Location and position estimation in wireless sensor networks. In Wireless Sensor Networks: Current Status and Future Trends (pp. 179-214). CRC Press.

Girod, L., Bychkovskiy, V., Elson, J., & Estrin, D. (2002, September). Locating tiny sensors in time and space: A case study. In *Proceedings. IEEE International Conference on Computer Design: VLSI in Computers and Processors* (pp. 214-219). IEEE. 10.1109/ICCD.2002.1106773

Goyal, S., & Patterh, M. S. (2014). Wireless sensor network localization based on cuckoo search algorithm. *Wireless Personal Communications, 79*(1), 223–234. doi:10.100711277-014-1850-8

Han, G., Xu, H., Duong, T. Q., Jiang, J., & Hara, T. (2013). Localization algorithms of wireless sensor networks: A survey. *Telecommunication Systems, 52*(4), 2419–2436. doi:10.100711235-011-9564-7

Harter, A., Hopper, A., Steggles, P., Ward, A., & Webster, P. (2001). The anatomy of a context-aware application. *Wireless Networks, 1*(1).

He, T., Huang, C., Blum, B. M., Stankovic, J. A., & Abdelzaher, T. (2003, September). Range-free localization schemes for large scale sensor networks. In *Proceedings of the 9th annual international conference on Mobile computing and networking* (pp. 81-95). ACM. 10.1145/938985.938995

Kaur, A., Kumar, P., & Gupta, G. P. (2017). A weighted centroid localization algorithm for randomly deployed wireless sensor networks. *Journal of King Saud University-Computer and Information Sciences*.

Kaur, A., Kumar, P., & Gupta, G. P. (2018). Nature inspired algorithm-based improved variants of DV-Hop algorithm for randomly deployed 2D and 3D wireless sensor networks. *Wireless Personal Communications*, *101*(1), 567–582. doi:10.100711277-018-5704-7

Lin, J. Z., Chen, X. B., & Liu, H. B. (2009). Iterative algorithm for locating nodes in WSN based on modifying average hopping distances. *Journal of Communication*, *30*(10), 107–113.

Mirjalili, S., Mirjalili, S. M., & Lewis, A. (2014). Grey wolf optimizer. *Advances in Engineering Software*, *69*, 46–61. doi:10.1016/j.advengsoft.2013.12.007

Nabil, E. (2016). A modified flower pollination algorithm for global optimization. *Expert Systems with Applications*, *57*, 192–203. doi:10.1016/j.eswa.2016.03.047

Nagpal, R., Shrobe, H., & Bachrach, J. (2003, April). Organizing a global coordinate system from local information on an ad hoc sensor network. In *Information processing in sensor networks* (pp. 333–348). Berlin: Springer. doi:10.1007/3-540-36978-3_22

Niculescu, D., & Nath, B. (2001, November). Ad hoc positioning system (APS). In *GLOBECOM'01. IEEE Global Telecommunications Conference (Cat. No. 01CH37270)* (Vol. 5, pp. 2926-2931). IEEE.

Niculescu, D., & Nath, B. (2003, March). Ad hoc positioning system (APS) using AOA. In *IEEE INFOCOM 2003. Twenty-second Annual Joint Conference of the IEEE Computer and Communications Societies (IEEE Cat. No. 03CH37428)* (Vol. 3, pp. 1734-1743). IEEE.

Peng, B., & Li, L. (2015). An improved localization algorithm based on genetic algorithm in wireless sensor networks. *Cognitive Neurodynamics*, *9*(2), 249–256. doi:10.100711571-014-9324-y PMID:25852782

Rawat, P., Singh, K. D., Chaouchi, H., & Bonnin, J. M. (2014). Wireless sensor networks: A survey on recent developments and potential synergies. *The Journal of Supercomputing*, *68*(1), 1–48. doi:10.100711227-013-1021-9

Shang, Y., & Ruml, W. (2004, March). Improved MDS-based localization. In *IEEE INFOCOM 2004* (Vol. 4, pp. 2640–2651). IEEE. doi:10.1109/INFCOM.2004.1354683

Shi, Y. (2001, May). Particle swarm optimization: developments, applications and resources. In *Proceedings of the 2001 congress on evolutionary computation (IEEE Cat. No. 01TH8546)* (Vol. 1, pp. 81-86). IEEE. 10.1109/CEC.2001.934374

Talbi, E. G. (2009). *Metaheuristics: from design to implementation* (Vol. 74). John Wiley & Sons. doi:10.1002/9780470496916

Wang, F., Wang, C., Wang, Z., & Zhang, X. Y. (2015). A hybrid algorithm of GA+ simplex method in the WSN localization. *International Journal of Distributed Sensor Networks*, *11*(7), 731894. doi:10.1155/2015/731894

Yang, X. S. (2010). Firefly algorithm, Levy flights and global optimization. In *Research and development in intelligent systems XXVI* (pp. 209–218). London: Springer. doi:10.1007/978-1-84882-983-1_15

Yang, X. S., & Deb, S. (2009, December). Cuckoo search via Lévy flights. In *2009 World Congress on Nature & Biologically Inspired Computing (NaBIC)* (pp. 210-214). IEEE. 10.1109/NABIC.2009.5393690

Zhao, J., Xi, W., He, Y., Liu, Y., Li, X. Y., Mo, L., & Yang, Z. (2013). Localization of wireless sensor networks in the wild: Pursuit of ranging quality. *IEEE/ACM Transactions on Networking*, *21*(1), 311–323. doi:10.1109/TNET.2012.2200906

Chapter 2
Two–Sided Assembly Line Balancing Optimization With Spider Monkey Optimization

Ashish Yadav

(iD) https://orcid.org/0000-0002-8687-5398

Indian Institute of Information Technology Design and Manufacturing, Jabalpur, India

Sunil Agrawal

Indian Institute of Information Technology Design and Manufacturing, Jabalpur, India

ABSTRACT

Growing interests from customers in customized products and increasing competition among peers necessitate companies to configure and balance their manufacturing systems more effectively than ever before. Two-sided assembly lines are usually constructed to produce large-sized high-volume products such as buses, trucks, automobiles, and some domestic products. Since the problem is well known as NP-hard problem, a mathematical model is solved by an exact solution-based approach and spider monkey optimization (SMO) algorithm that is inspired by the intelligent foraging behavior of fission-fusion social structure-based animals. In this chapter, the proposed mathematical model is applied to solve benchmark problems of two-sided assembly line balancing problem to minimize the number of mated stations and idle time. The experimental results show that spider monkey optimizations provide better results.

DOI: 10.4018/978-1-7998-1626-3.ch002

INTRODUCTION

An assembly line is a production process where raw material transfer through conveyer, different workers and machine perform work on it and finally raw material converted into finished produced.

A two-sided assembly line is a type of production line in which different assembly tasks are performed in parallel at both sides of the line as shown in figure 1. In this situation, some of the assembly operations should be performed at strictly one side of the line (right or left side) and the others can be assigned to either side of the line. This type of lines is very important, especially in the assembly of large-sized, heavy products, like automobiles, trucks. There are several advantages of two sided assembly line balancing that is very helpful to increase the effectiveness and efficiency like shorter line length, reduced throughput time, lower cost of tools and fixtures, less material handling, saves some spaces on the assembly lines, increased line efficiency with reduced operator requirement., increased skill levels of operators, increased motivation of operators due to operation enrichment at combined workstations between two lines (Simaria et al, 2009; Wu et al, 2008).

The main difference in one-sided lines and two-sided lines is the sequence of the tasks within a workstation is not important on the other hand in two-sided assembly lines, this is a crucial factor for an efficient assignment of tasks. Tasks at opposite sides of the line can interfere with each other through precedence constraints which might cause idle time if a workstation needs to wait for a predecessor task to be completed at the opposite side of the line. This phenomenon is called interference (Yuan eta l, 2015; Taha et al, 2011).

LITERATURE REVIEW

Although researchers have focused on Two-sided ALB problems and, the literature review suggests that none of researchers focus on two-sided assembly line balancing problem (TALB) with spider monkey optimization the objective minimize idle time

Figure 1. Configuration of two sided assembly line

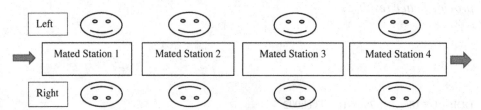

Table 1.: Literature review of two sided assembly line

Ref.N.	Authors	Optimization Methods	Minimize number of Workstations	Minimize Cycle time	Minimize number of mated stations	Minimize line length (space)	Workload/ task smoothness	Maximize work relatedness	Minimize production variance	Minimize idle time	Maximize slackness	Maximize production rate	Minimize cost (cost oriented)
							Objective Functions						
1	Simaria & Vilarinho 2009	Ant colony optimization	✓										
2	Hu, Wu et al. 2008	Other heuristic methods	✓							■			
3	Taha, et al. 2011	Genetic algorithm	✓		✓								
4	Yuan et al. 2015	Acceptance hill-climbing algorithm	✓		✓								
5	Kim, Song et al. 2009	Genetic algorithm		✓									
6	Kucukkoc & Zhang 2015	Genetic algorithm	✓			✓							
7	Delice et al. 2017	Particle swarm optimization	✓		✓								
8	Dashuang Li et al. 2016	Improved teaching–learning-based					✓						
9	Lee, Kim et al. 2001	Heuristic methods						✓			✓		
10	Ozcan & Gokcen et al. 2010	Tabu search	✓		✓								
11	Qiuhua Tang et al. 2016	Discrete artificial bee colony		✓						■			■
12	Yuan, Zhang et al. 2015	Honey bee mating optimization	✓		✓								
13	Rabbani et al. 2012	Genetic algorithm	✓	✓	■		■	■					
14	Ozcan, Gokcen et al. 2010	Tabu search	✓										

continued on the following page

Table 1. Continued

Ref.N.	Authors	Optimization Methods	Objective Functions										
			Minimize number of Workstations	Minimize Cycle time	Minimize number of mated stations	Minimize line length (space)	Workload/ task smoothness	Maximize work relatedness	Minimize production variance	Minimize idle time	Maximize slackness	Maximize production rate	Minimize cost (cost oriented)
15	Tang, et al. 2017	Hybrid teaching–learning-based		✓									
16	Ozcan 2010	Simulated annealing	✓		✓								
17	Chiang, et al. 2015	Particle swarm optimization	✓			✓							
18	Ozcan & Toklu 2010	Other heuristic methods	✓		✓								
19	Yilmaz Delice et al. 2016	Particle swarm optimization	✓			✓							
20	Ozbakir & Tapkan 2011	Bee algorithm	✓										
21	Roshani, & Fattahi et al. 2012	Simulated annealing	✓										✓
22	Li et al. 2017	Discrete cuckoo search	✓										
23	Ozcan & Toklu 2009	Simulated annealing	✓		✓	✓							
24	Kucukkoc & Zhang 2014	Agent-based Ant colony optimization	✓			✓							
25	Agpak & Zolfaghari 2015	Heuristic methods	✓			✓							
26	Purnomo & Wee 2014	Harmony search method	✓										
27	Chutima & Chimklai 2012	Particle swarm optimization			✓		✓	✓				✓	
28	Fattahi et al. 2016	Particle swarm optimization	✓	■	✓								✓

continued on the following page

Table 1. Continued

Ref.N.	Authors	Optimization Methods	Minimize number of Workstations	Minimize Cycle time	Minimize number of mated stations	Minimize line length (space)	Workload/ task smoothness	Maximize work relatedness	Minimize production variance	Minimize idle time	Maximize slackness	Maximize production rate	Minimize cost (cost oriented)
								Objective Functions					
29	Delice et al. 2016	Genetic algorithm	✓	■	✓	■							
30	Khorasanian et al. 2013	Simulated annealing	✓		✓		✓						
31	Sepahi et al. 2016	Heuristic methods	✓	✓									
32	Baykasoglu & Dereli 2008	Ant colony optimization	✓					✓					
33	Tuncel & Aydin 2014	Teaching learning based		✓									
34	Purnomo & Wee et al. 2013	Genetic algorithm		✓			✓						
35	Agpak & Yegul et al. 2012	Other heuristic methods	✓			✓							
36	Kucukkoc and Zhang 2015	Ant colony optimization	✓	✓									
37	Deming Lei et al. 2016	Variable neighborhood search		✓	✓								
38	Hu et al. 2018	Heuristic algorithm					✓						
39	Tapkan et al. 2016	Artificial Bee Colony algorithm	✓	■	■								
40	Gansterer et al. 2017	Differential evolution algorithm	✓		✓								
41	Kucukkoc 2016	Ant colony optimization	✓	✓		■							

and minimize the length of the line. Here spider monkey optimization applied for optimization that is first attempt in assembly line balancing optimization, this paper mainly presents following contributions to the research field:

1. A mathematical model of two-sided assembly line balancing problem is proposed with station oriented objective that is maximize the workload on each mated stations of assembly line.
2. The proposed mathematical model is tested on benchmark problem and is solved using exact solution approach Lingo -17 solver and met heuristic approximate solution approach solved by Matlab to obtain the optimal solutions.
3. The results of exact solution approach and approximate solution approach is compared which indicates that the spider monkey optimization provides better solutions in term of minimize number of workstations and reduces idle time.

The rest of the paper is organized as follows: TALB definition is given in section 3 with objectives, assumptions and constraints. Section 4 illustrates a solution approach that includes spider monkey optimization different phases. Section 5 indicates problem data and computational results. Conclusions and future work are presented in section 6.

MATHEMATICAL FORMULATION

Overview

The main objective of the proposed model is to assign the set of tasks in two-sided assembly line balancing problem in such a rearrange and systematic way so that mated station and single stations are reduced. Basically in this mathematical model objective function work on compactness in the beginning workstations which also helps to minimize the length of the line. Therefore, reduces the number of workstations and idle times on each workstation.

Assumptions

The TALB problem in this study includes the following assumptions:

*   A mass production of one homogeneous product on a serial line layout is considered
*   The precedence relationships and task times are known.
*   Task times are deterministic and independent of the assigned station.

- Cycle time is calculated according to demand over the planning horizon.
- The transportation time between the workstations is ignored.

Notations

Symbol Description
I Set of all assembly tasks
J Set of all mated-stations
K Set of all directions
i Index of assembly task; $i = 1, 2, ... I$
j Index of station; $j = 1, 2, ... J$
k Index of mated-station direction;

$$\begin{cases} 1\ indicates\ a\ left\ direction \\ 2\ indicates\ a\ right\ direction \end{cases}$$

(j,k) Index of station j and the associated mated-station direction k
$P(i)$ Set of immediate predecessors of task i
$S(i)$ Set of immediate successors of task i
T_i Completion time of task i
μ Large positive number
CT Cycle time

$$d_1 \begin{cases} 0\ if\ task\ i\ is\ a\ left-side \\ 1\ otherwise \end{cases}$$

$$d_2 \begin{cases} 0\ if\ task\ i\ is\ a\ right-side \\ 1\ otherwise \end{cases}$$

R^+ Positive real number

Decision Variables

Symbol Description
x_{ijk} Binary variable indicating if task i is assigned to mated-station (j,k)

$$\begin{cases} 1 \, if \, task \, i \, is \, assigned \, to \, station \left(j, k \right) \\ \quad 0, otherwise \end{cases}$$

st_i Start time of task i

t_i Task time of task i

Z_{ih} Binary variable indicating precedence relationships among the tasks in the same station

$$\begin{cases} 1 \, if \, task \, i \, is \, assigned \, before \, task \, h \, in \, the \, same \, station \\ 2, if \, task \, h \, is \, assigned \, before \, task \, i \, in \, the \, same \, station \end{cases}$$

$$ms_i \begin{cases} 1 \, if \, mated - station \, j \, is \, utilized \\ \quad 0, otherwise \end{cases}$$

$$ss_{jk} \begin{cases} 1 \, if \, station \left(j, k \right) is \, utilized \\ \quad 0, otherwise \end{cases}$$

$$Max \; Z = \sum_{j=1}^{J} \left(WL_j (J - j + 1) \right)^2 \tag{1}$$

$$WL_j = t_i * x_{ijk} \tag{2}$$

Non-linear objective function in equation (1) here $(J-j+1)$ is higher for initial stations and lower for ending stations which tends to increase the compactness in the beginning workstations which also helps to minimize the length of the line. Equation (2) represents sum of square of each workstation's workload to maximize the workload on each workstation. Therefore, reduces the number of workstations and idle times on each workstation.

$$\sum_{j=1}^{J}\sum_{k=1}^{2} x_{ijk} = 1$$

$$\forall i \in I$$

(3)

$$\sum_{j=1}^{J}(d_1 * x_{ij1} + d_2 * x_{ij2}) = 1$$

$$\forall i \in I$$

(4)

$$\sum_{k=1}^{2} x_{ijk} * (st_i + t_i) \le j * ct$$

$$\forall i \in I; j \in J$$

(5)

$$\sum_{k=1}^{2} \left(x_{ijk} * (j-1) * ct \right) \le st_i$$

$$\forall i \in I; j \in J$$

(6)

$$\sum_{j=1}^{J}\sum_{k=1}^{2} j * x_{hjk} - \sum_{j=1}^{J}\sum_{k=1}^{2} j * x_{ijk} \le 0$$

$$\forall i, h \in I; h \in p(i)$$

(7)

$$st_h - st_i + \mu * \left(1 - \sum_{k=1}^{2} x_{ijk}\right) + \mu * \left(1 - \sum_{k=1}^{2} x_{hjk}\right) \ge T_i$$

$$\forall i, h \in I; i \in P(h); j \in J$$

(8)

$$st_h - st_i + \mu * \left(1 - x_{ijk}\right) + \mu * \left(1 - x_{hjk}\right) + \mu(1 - \mu * (1 - z_{ih}) \ge T_i$$

$$\forall i, h \in I; i \notin p(h); h \notin p(i); \forall j \in J; k \in K$$

(9)

Figure 2. Spider Monkey Group
Source: Kucukkoc et al, 2016

$$st_i - st_h + \mu * \left(1 - x_{ijk}\right) + \mu * \left(1 - x_{hjk}\right) + \mu * \left(z_{ih}\right) \geq T_h$$
$$\forall i, h \in I; i \notin p(h); h \notin p(i); \forall j \in J; k \in K$$

(10)

$$x_{ijk} \in \{0,1\}$$

$$\forall i \in I; j \in J; \forall k \in K$$

(11)

$$ss_{jk} \in \{0,1\}$$
$$\forall j \in J; \forall k \in K$$

(12)

$$ms_j \in \{0,1\}$$
$$\forall j \in J$$

(13)

$$z_{ih} \in \{0,1\}$$
$$\forall i, h \in I; i \notin p(h); h \notin p(i) \tag{14}$$

$$st_i \in R^+$$
$$\forall i \in I \tag{15}$$

Constraints (2) and (3) ensure that all the tasks are assigned to the workstation and each task is assigned only once. Constraint (4) and (5) ensures capacity of workstation that's why it is a capacity constraint. Constraint (6) ensures that starting time of any task is equal to or greater than the completion time of immediate predecessor of that task in precedence diagram. Constraint (7) ensures precedence constraints. Constraint (8) to (10) are specially designed for two sided assembly line. Constraint (8) will be active when task h is a precedence of task i and are assigned at same mated station on opposite sides otherwise the constraint will not be active. When this holds, the constraint is applied to $st_{mi} - st_{mh} \geq t_{mh}$ which ensures that task h is assigned before task i. Constraints (9) and (10) become active when tasks h and i do not have any precedence relationship and are assigned on the same station (j, k). If i is assigned earlier than p, then constraint (9) become $st_{mh} - st_{mi} \geq t_{mi}$; if not, then constraint (10) becomes $st_{mi} - st_{mh} \geq t_{mh}$. Constraints (11) to (14) are the binary constraints and constraint (15) ensures that the starting time of any task is a positive integer.

SOLUTION APPROACH

Spider Monkey Optimization Overview

The spider monkeys follow a fission-fusion based social structure. The foraging behavior can be divided into four steps (Gansterer et al, 2018; Kucukkoc et al, 2016).

1. The monkeys search food generally in a group of 30-50 members lead by female monkey as a group leader.
2. Group leader is responsible to find sufficient food for all the group members, if not arranged on that case she divides the group into subgroups consisting of around 7 monkeys to reduce the competition.

3. Each subgroup leader is a female monkey that acts as a local group leader that female monkey is responsible for taking all the decisions for that particular subgroup.
4. Spider monkey subgroups communicate with each other to circulate information of food and boundaries.

Spider monkey optimization has six iterative phases .A brief description of each phase is given below (Bansal et al, 2014).

Local Leader Phase (LLP)

In the Local Leader phase, each Spider Monkey SM modifies its current position based on the information of the local leader experience as well as local group members' experience. The fitness value of so obtained new position is calculated. If the fitness value of the new position is higher than that of the old position, then the SM updates his position with the new one. The position update equation for i^{th} SM (which is a member of kth local group) in this phase is

$$SM_{ij}^{new} = SM_{ij} + U(0,1) \times (LL_{kj} - SM_{ij}) + U(-1,1) \times (SM_{rj} - SM_{ij})$$

Global Leader Phase (LLP)

In this phase, the positions of spider monkeys (SM_i) are updated based on a probabilities $prob_i$ which are calculated using their fitness. In this way a better candidate will have a higher chance to make itself better. The probability $prob_i$ may be calculated using following expression (there may be some other but it must be a function of fitness):

$$prob_i = 0.9 \times \frac{fitness}{max\ fitness} + 1$$

In GLP phase, all the SM's update their position using experience of global leader and local group member's experience. The position update equation for this phase is as follows:

$$SM_{ij}^{new} = SM_{ij} + U(0,1) \times (GL_j - SM_{ij}) + U(-1,1) \times (SM_{rj} - SM_{ij})$$

Local Leader Learning (LLL) Phase

The local leader updates its position in the group by applying the greedy selection.

If the fitness value of the new local leader position is worse than the current position then the local limit count is incremented by 1.

Global Leader Learning (GLL) Phase

In the global leader learning phase (GLL), the global leader is updated by applying the greedy selection in the population (the position of the SM with the best position is selected. The global limit count is incremented by 1 if the position of the global leader is not updated.

Local Leader Decision (LLD) Phase

If the local leader position is not updated for specific number of iterations which is called local leader limit (LLL), then all the spider monkeys (solutions) update their positions randomly or by combining information from global leader and local leader as follow

$$SM_{ij}^{new} = SM_{ij} + U(0,1) \times (GL_j - SM_{ij}) + U(0,1) \times (SM_{ij} - LL_{kj})$$

GLOBAL LEADER DECISION (GLD) PHASE

If the global leader is not updated for a specific number of iterations which is called global leader limit (GLL), then the global leader divides the (group) population into sub-populations (small groups).

Priority-based Encoding and Decoding

In this section we will introduce a priority-based spider monkey for solving the mathematical model. The priority-based spider monkey handle the problem of creating encoding while treating the precedence constraints efficiently. In this process chromosomes are defined as feasible precedence sequences of tasks. Here the length of the chromosome is defined by the number of tasks. Task-based representation is the most appropriate representation for assembly line balancing. To develop a priority-based spider monkey representation for the two sided assembly line model, there are two main steps:

Generate a Task Sequence

Step 1.1:   Generate a random priority to each task with task sided in the model using encoding procedure.

Step 1.2:   Decode a feasible task sequence T_S that satisfies the precedence constraints.

Assigning Tasks to Stations

Step 2.1:   Input the task sequence found in step 1.2.

Step 2.2:   Obtain a feasible solution set according to this task sequence.

Figure 3 indicate the flowchart of spider monkey optimization that indicate first initialize all parameter after that generate all population through encoding and evaluating all spider monkey using decoding procedure. Table 2 indicates parameter setting for spider monkey optimization algorithm.

Figure 3. Flowchart of SMO

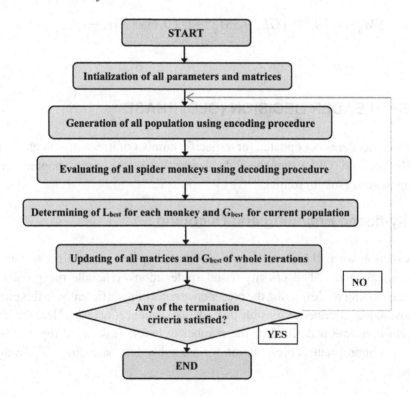

Table 2. Parameter settings for SMO algorithm

Parameter settings	SMO
Size of Group	80
Max number of subgroups	16
Global Leader Limit	50
Local Leader Limit	500

PROBLEM DATA AND COMPUTATIONAL RESULTS

Numerical Problem data

Table 3 indicate data of two sided assembly line balancing benchmark problem P(16),In this table task side and task processing time, immediate predecessors details are mentioned (Kucukkoc et la, 2015).

Table 3. Benchmark problem P(16) data

Task no	Side	Processing time	Immediate predecessors
1	E	6	-
2	E	5	-
3	L	2	1
4	E	9	1,2
5	R	8	2
6	L	4	3
7	E	7	4,5
8	E	4	6,7
9	R	5	7
10	R	4	7
11	E	6	8
12	L	5	9
13	E	6	9,10
14	E	4	11
15	E	3	11,12
16	E	4	13

Computational Results

Two-sided assembly line balancing problem (TALBP) is solved by Lingo 17 solver and SMO algorithm is programmed in MATLAB-14 programming language with Intel core i5, 3.20 GHz processor and 4GB of RAM. LINGO 17.0 mathematical programming software used branch and bound algorithm with mixed integer linear programming solver to solve the problem.

Figure 4 indicate that in problem (16) tasks 3,6 are assigned to left side mated station and task 1,2 are assigned to right side of mated-station. Similarly task 4 is assigned to left side mated station and task 5 is assigned right side of mated station. Here total number of mated stations are five. Results indicate green color shows the used time and orange color indicates the idle time and number inside the box depicts task.

Figure 5 shows the results of spider monkey optimization for two sided assembly line where number of individual produced on X line and mean represents on Y line.

Table 4 shows the results where spider monkey optimization is terminated when the number of produced individuals reaches 1000. The fourth and sixth columns present the optimal solutions found by Lingo -16 solver and the average of the spider monkey solutions, respectively. The fifth and seventh columns generally represent the CPU time required by each approach mixed integer programming based Lingo solver and Spider monkey optimization respectively. For the benchmark problem

Figure 4. Optimal task assignment of station oriented P (16) problem

LEFT	3	6	4		7	8	12	11	14	16
RIGHT	1	2	5			9	10	13	15	
Mated Stations	Mated Station 1		Mated Station 2		Mated Station 3		Mated Station 4		Mated Station 5	

Table 4. Solutions for SMO algorithm

Problem	Total No. of mated stations	Cycle time	MIP (Lingo Solver)		SMO	
			Optimal solution	CPU time	Mean	CPU time
P(16)	5	33.67	22	.90	22	.12

Figure 5. Plot between number of individual product and mean

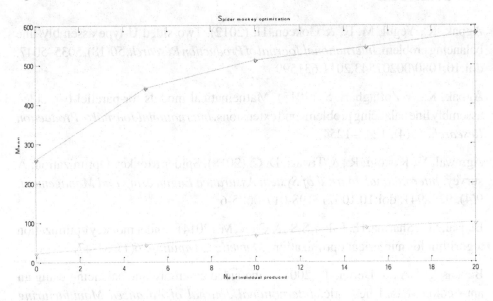

P(16), every SMO run finds the optimal solution. In this case SMO show smaller computational time as compare to the mixed integer programming based Lingo -16 solver.

CONCLUSION AND FUTURE RESEARCH

In this paper, we presented a mathematical model for solving the two-sided assembly line balancing with station oriented objective function that actually minimizing mated stations and reduce idle time for P(16) benchmark problem Spider monkey optimization is one of the swarm based nature inspired algorithm provide approximate results for NP hard problem and two sided assembly line balancing problem is one of them. The results of exact solution approach through Lingo -16 solver and approximate solution approach with Matlab software is compared which indicates that the spider monkey optimization provides better solutions in term of minimize number of workstations and reduces idle time

In future this mathematical model can be applied for two-sided assembly line balancing with stochastic approach and U type layout. Mixed-model or multi-objective combination of the TALB problem with latest meta-heuristic such as grey wolf, optimization and firefly optimization can be applied to solve TALB problem.

REFERENCES

Agpak, K., Yegul, M. F., & Gokcen, H. (2012). Two-sided U-type assembly line balancing problem. *International Journal of Production Research*, *50*(18), 5035–5047. doi:10.1080/00207543.2011.631599

Agpak, K., & Zolfaghari, S. (2015). Mathematical models for parallel two-sided assembly line balancing problems and extensions. *International Journal of Production Research*, *53*(4), 1242–1254.

Agrawal, V., Rastogi, R., & Tiwari, D. C. (2018). Spider Monkey Optimization: A survey. *International Journal of System Assurance Engineering and Management*, *9*(4), 929–941. doi:10.100713198-017-0685-6

Bansal, J.C., Sharma, H., Jadon, S.S., & Clerc, M. (2014). Spider monkey optimization algorithm for numerical optimization. *Memetic Computing, 6*(1), 31-47.

Baykasoglu, A., & Dereli, T. (2008). Two-sided assembly line balancing using an ant– colony-based heuristic. *International Journal of Advanced Manufacturing Technology*, *36*(5), 582–588. doi:10.100700170-006-0861-3

Chiang, W.-C., Urban, T. L., & Luo, C. (2015). Balancing stochastic two-sided assembly lines. *International Journal of Production Research*, *54*(20), 6232–6250. doi:10.1080/00207543.2015.1029084

Chutima, P., & Chimklai, P. (2012). Multi-objective two-sided mixed-model assembly line balancing using particle swarm optimisation with negative knowledge. *Computers & Industrial Engineering*, *62*(1), 39–55. doi:10.1016/j.cie.2011.08.015

(2016). Dashuang Li · Chaoyong Zhang · Xinyu Shao ·Wenwen Lin.,2016. A multi-objective TLBO algorithm for balancing two-sided assembly line with multiple constraints. *Journal of Intelligent Manufacturing*, *27*, 725–739.

Delice, Y., Aydogan, E.K., Ozcan, U., & Ilkay, M.S. (2017). Balancing two-sided U–type assembly lines using modified particle swarm optimization algorithm. *4 OR, 15*(1), 35–66.

Delice, Y., Kızılkaya Aydogan, E., & Ozcan, U. (2016). Stochastic two-sided U-type assembly line balancing: A genetic algorithm approach. *International Journal of Production Research*, *54*(11), 3429–3451. doi:10.1080/00207543.2016.1140918

Delice, Y., Kızılkaya Aydogan, E., Ozcan, U., & Ilkay, ˙. M. S. (2017). A modified particle swarm optimization algorithm to mixed-model two-sided assembly line balancing. *Journal of Intelligent Manufacturing*, *28*(1), 23–36. doi:10.100710845-014-0959-7

Dhar, J., & Arora, S. (2017). Designing fuzzy rule base using spider monkey optimization algorithm in cooperative framework. *Future Computing and Informatics Journal, 2*(1), 31–38. doi:10.1016/j.fcij.2017.04.004

Fattahia, P., Samoueib, P., & Zandiehc, M. (2016). *Simultaneous Multi-skilled Worker Assignment and Mixed-model Two-sided Assembly Line Balancing. International Journal of Engineering, 29*(2), 211–221.

Gansterer, M., & Hartl, R. F. (2018). One- and two-sided assembly line balancing problems with real-world constraints. *International Journal of Production Research, 56*(8), 3025–3042. doi:10.1080/00207543.2017.1394599

Gupta, K., Deep, K., & Bansal, J. C. (2017). Spider monkey optimization algorithm for constrained optimization problems. *Soft Computing, 21*(23), 6933–6962. doi:10.100700500-016-2419-0

Hu, X., & Wu, C. (2018). Workload smoothing in two-sided assembly lines. *Assembly Automation, 38*(1), 51–56. doi:10.1108/AA-09-2016-112

Khorasanian, D., Hejazi, S. R., & Moslehi, G. (2013). Two-sided assembly line balancing considering the relationships between tasks. *Computers & Industrial Engineering, 66*(4), 1096–1105. doi:10.1016/j.cie.2013.08.006

Kim, Y. K., Song, W. S., & Kim, J. H. (2009). A mathematical model and a genetic algorithm for two-sided assembly line balancing. *Computers & Operations Research, 36*(3), 853–865. doi:10.1016/j.cor.2007.11.003

Kucukkoc, I. (2016). Multi-objective Optimization of Mixed-model Two-sided Assembly Lines – A Case Study. *International Conference on Computer Science and Engineering*, 20-23.

Kucukkoc, I., & Zhang, D. Z. (2014). Mathematical model and agent based solution approach for the simultaneous balancing and sequencing of mixed-model parallel two-sided assembly lines. *International Journal of Production Economics, 158*, 314–333. doi:10.1016/j.ijpe.2014.08.010

Kucukkoc, I., & Zhang, D. Z. (2015, August 18). approach for parallel two-sided assembly line balancing problem. *Production Planning and Control, 26*(11), 874–894. doi:10.1080/09537287.2014.994685

Kucukkoc, I., & Zhang, D. Z. (2015). Type-E parallel two-sided assembly line balancing problem: Mathematical model and ant colony optimization based approach with optimised parameters. *Computers & Industrial Engineering, 84*, 56–69. doi:10.1016/j.cie.2014.12.037

Lee, T. O., Kim, Y., & Kim, Y. K. (2001). Two-sided assembly line balancing to maximize work relatedness and slackness. *Computers & Industrial Engineering, 40*(3), 273–292. doi:10.1016/S0360-8352(01)00029-8

Lei, D., & Guo, X. (2016). Variable neighborhood search for the second type of two-sided assembly line balancing problem. *Computers & Operations Research, 72*, 183–188. doi:10.1016/j.cor.2016.03.003

Li, Z., Dey, N., Ashour, A. S., & Tang, Q. (2017). Discrete cuckoo search algorithms for two-sided robotic assembly line balancing problem. *Neural Computing & Applications, 17*, 2855–2860.

Ozbakır, L., & Tapkan, P. (2011). Bee colony intelligence in zone constrained two-sided assembly line balancing problem. *Expert Systems with Applications, 38*(9), 11947–11957. doi:10.1016/j.eswa.2011.03.089

Ozcan, U. (2010). Balancing stochastic two-sided assembly lines: A chance-constrained, piecewise-linear, mixed integer program and a simulated annealing algorithm. *European Journal of Operational Research, 205*(1), 81–97. doi:10.1016/j.ejor.2009.11.033

Ozcan, U., Gokcen, H., & Toklu, B. (2010). Balancing parallel two-sided assembly lines. *International Journal of Production Research, 48*(16), 4767–4784. doi:10.1080/00207540903074991

Ozcan, U., & Toklu, B. (2008). A tabu search algorithm for two-sided assembly line balancing. *International Journal of Advanced Manufacturing Technology, 43*(7), 822–829.

Ozcan, U., & Toklu, B. (2009). Balancing of mixed-model two-sided assembly lines. *Computers & Industrial Engineering, 57*(1), 217–227. doi:10.1016/j.cie.2008.11.012

Ozcan, U., & Toklu, B. (2010). Balancing two-sided assembly lines with sequence-dependent setup times. *International Journal of Production Research, 48*(18), 5363–5383. doi:10.1080/00207540903140750

Purnomo, H. D., & Wee, H.-M. (2014). Maximizing production rate and workload balancing in a two-sided assembly line using Harmony search. *Computers & Industrial Engineering, 76*, 222–230. doi:10.1016/j.cie.2014.07.010

Purnomo, H. D., Wee, H.-M., & Rau, H. (2013). Two-sided assembly lines balancing with assignment restrictions. *Mathematical and Computer Modelling, 57*(2), 189–199. doi:10.1016/j.mcm.2011.06.010

Rabbani, M., Moghaddam, M., & Manavizadeh, N. (2012). Balancing of mixed-model two-sided assembly lines with multiple U-shaped layout. *International Journal of Advanced Manufacturing Technology*, *59*(9-12), 1191–1210. doi:10.100700170-011-3545-6

Roshani, A., Fattahi, P., Roshani, A., Salehi, M., & Roshani, A. (2012). Cost-oriented two-sided assembly line balancing problem: A simulated annealing approach. *International Journal of Computer Integrated Manufacturing*, *25*(8), 689–715. doi:10.1080/0951192X.2012.664786

Sepahi, A., & Naini, S. G. J. (2016). Two-sided assembly line balancing problem with parallel performance capacity. *Applied Mathematical Modelling*, *40*(14), 6280–6292. doi:10.1016/j.apm.2016.02.022

Simaria, A. S., & Vilarinho, P. M. (2009). 2-ANTBAL: An ant colony optimization algorithm for balancing two-sided assembly lines. *Computers & Industrial Engineering*, *56*(2), 489–506. doi:10.1016/j.cie.2007.10.007

Taha, R. B., El-Kharbotly, A. K., Sadek, Y. M., & Afia, N. H. (2011). A Genetic Algorithm for solving two-sided assembly line balancing problems. *AIN Shams Engineering Journal*, *3*(4), 227–240. doi:10.1016/j.asej.2011.10.003

Tang, Q., Li, Z., & Zhang, L. (2016). An effective discrete artificial bee colony algorithm with idle time reduction techniques for two-sided assembly line balancing problem of type-II. *Computers & Industrial Engineering*, *97*, 146–156. doi:10.1016/j.cie.2016.05.004

Tang, Q. H., Li, Z. X., Zhang, L. P., Floudas, C. A., & Cao, X. J. (2015). Effective hybrid teaching learning-based optimization algorithm for balancing two-sided assembly lines with multiple constraints. *Chinese Journal of Mechanical Engineering*, *28*(5), 1067–1079. doi:10.3901/CJME.2015.0630.084

Tapkan, P., Ozbakır, L., & Baykasoglu, A. (2016). Bee algorithms for parallel two-sided assembly line balancing problem with walking times. *Applied Soft Computing*, *39*, 275–291. doi:10.1016/j.asoc.2015.11.017

Tuncel, G., & Aydin, D. (2014). Two-sided assembly line balancing using teaching–learning based optimization algorithm. *Computers & Industrial Engineering*, *74*, 291–299. doi:10.1016/j.cie.2014.06.006

Wu, E.-F., Jin, Y., Bao, J.-S., & Hu, X.-F. (2008). A branch-and-bound algorithm for two-sided assembly line balancing. *International Journal of Advanced Manufacturing Technology*, *39*(9), 1009–1015. doi:10.100700170-007-1286-3

Yuan, B., Zhang, C., & Shao, X. (2015). A late acceptance hill-climbing algorithm for balancing two-sided assembly lines with multiple constraints. *Journal of Intelligent Manufacturing*, 26(1), 159–168. doi:10.100710845-013-0770-x

Yuan, B., Zhang, C., Shao, X., & Jiang, Z. (2015). An effective hybrid honey bee mating optimization algorithm for balancing mixed-model two-sided assembly lines. *Computers & Operations Research*, 53, 32–41. doi:10.1016/j.cor.2014.07.011

Chapter 3
Salp:
Metaheuristic–Based Clustering
for Wireless Sensor Networks

Vrajesh Kumar Chawra

(iD) https://orcid.org/0000-0002-5147-3065
National Institute of Technology, Raipur, India

Govind P. Gupta

(iD) https://orcid.org/0000-0002-0456-1572
National Institute of Technology, Raipur, India

ABSTRACT

The formation of the unequal clusters of the sensor nodes is a burning research issue in wireless sensor networks (WSN). Energy-hole and non-uniform load assignment are two major issues in most of the existing node clustering schemes. This affects the network lifetime of WSN. Salp optimization-based algorithm is used to solve these problems. The proposed algorithm is used for cluster head selection. The performance of the proposed scheme is compared with the two-node clustering scheme in the term of residual energy, energy consumption, and network lifetime. The results show the proposed scheme outperforms the existing protocols in term of network lifetime under different network configurations.

INTRODUCTION

Wireless Sensor Network (*WSN*) is the emerging area in the current age. A *WSN* is a collection of sensor nodes, where a sensor node is a small tiny device with limited energy and limited storage. The basic task for sensor nodes is to sense the physical

DOI: 10.4018/978-1-7998-1626-3.ch003

environment and transfer it to the nearest base station. The applications of wireless sensor network mainly include in health-care, military, environmental monitoring, home automation, & other commercial areas. There are many research challenges in WSN like path planning for data transfer sensor node to the base station, cluster formation and cluster-head selection, energy issues and network lifetime issues, etc.

After deployment of a sensor node in a particular area, nodes have to perform data-communication activities like sensing the data, transfer the sensed data to the base station, and some of them have to work as a relay node. Due to this activity highly energy consumption of a node. As we all know that a sensor node has limited energy resources. To overcome this type of issue Node clustering concept has been introduced. In node clustering, a group of sensor nodes is formed with similar size of sensor nodes. After deployment of nodes, n number of clusters are formed and each cluster has a Master cluster head(MCH). *MCH* collects the data from its cluster member. Node near to base station has to work as a sensing device as well as work as a relay node, due to this energy hole problem arises. To overcome this problem unequal clustering concept has been introduced. In this clustering, the distance between a node to the cluster head and distance between a node to the base station are the basic parameters to form a cluster. Node near the base station has less number of cluster members. As the distance increases the number of cluster member increases.

Cluster formation and cluster head selection are the major research issues. Many researchers adopt optimization techniques to solve real-time problems. These optimization techniques are based on animal or insects behavior. These algorithms are named as Nature-Inspired Optimization Algorithms. There are many nature-inspired algorithms is developed such as Genetic algorithm (GA) is based on Darwin evolution theory, Ant colony optimization(ACO) and Salp optimization (SO) inspired by the behavior of Ant and Salp insects to searching food and so on. A single real time problem can solve with many optimization techniques. In any optimization technique solution vector intialization is the first step, after some iteration operation are preformed and finally a resultant solution vector has been generated. To achieve the final result some algorithms are updating the solution vectors like in GA and some algorithms are updating the location of each solution vector-like PSO. The major disadvantage of these algorithms is the random selection method to generate a solution vector and the generated solution vector gives an approximate solution.

For clustering, many meta-heuristic based cluster formation and cluster-head section algorithm had proposed by many researchers. Among all, LEACH protocol (Heinzelman *et.al,* 2005) is the first clustering based protocol. It uses a probabilistic approach to select a CH. The setup phase and the steady-state phase are two basic steps that are involved in the LEACH protocol. An energy-efficient routing protocol that uses unequal clustering by Genetic algorithm (Hussain *et. al*, 2007) is used to select the cluster head. An energy-efficient particle swarm optimization (PSO) based cluster head selection (Rao *et al.*,2016) and cluster formation are introduced. Authors presented PSO based cluster head selection method by considering the fault-tolerance problem (Kaur *et al.,*2018). In this paper, the author selects a surrogate cluster head with the selection of a master cluster head. If master cluster head fails then surrogate node becomes cluster head. Moth Flame Optimization (MFO) is applied for the selection of the least number of CHs and routing (Mittal,2018). In this paper, the author considered multi-hop communication between CHs and the base station. Fuzzy logic approach and Ant Colony Optimization (ACO) meta-heuristic approach is proposed (Arjunan *et al.*, 2018) for the clustering problem. Fuzzy logic is used for unequal clustering and ACO is applied for routing. An uneven clustering and routing protocol based (Xiuwu *et al.*,2019) on glowworm swarm optimization (GSO). For cluster head selection author considers cluster head density, cluster head proximity distance, the energy of cluster head and compactness of the clusters. For unequal clustering and routing, the author adopted a chemical reaction based optimization technique (Rao *et al.2016).*

In this paper, we adopted the Salp metaheuristic technique based Cluster head selection technique for unequal clustering. For performance analysis, results of the proposed method are compared with hybrid dolphin echolocation and crow search optimization(DECSA) (Mahesh *et al.*, 2018) and Genetic algorithm based cluster head selection method (Yuan,2017).

The workflow of paper as follows section 2 explains the basic architecture of salp, section 3 network assumption for network design. section 4 detail description of salp metaheuristic based clustering scheme that consists of a fitness function used to selection of cluster head, flow work, and algorithm of salp optimization and cluster formation. Section 5 has a performance analysis of proposed method results are compared with well-known exiting algorithms Section 6 gives the conclusion of the paper.

OVERVIEW OF SALP SWARM OPTIMIZATION

In 2017, a new meta-heuristic approach named as Salp swarm optimization based on behaviour of Salp is introduced by Mirjalili. Salps belong to the family of Salpidae. The tissues of salp are highly similar to jellyfish with transparent barrel-shaped body and lives in the deep ocean (Mirjalili,2017). For movement in water salp pumped through the body as propulsion. Salp always forms a swarm called salp chain. Figure(1) shows basic salp architecture. For foraging process slap chain is very much useful. In this chain, there are two types of salp Leader salp and follower salp.

Figure 1. The basic architecture of a salp

NETWORK MODEL AND ASSUMPTION

For Network design, homogeneous nodes are considered. The term homogenous indicates that the communication range and energy resources of all node have equal capability. Initially, nodes are deployed randomly in a particular network area. All nodes are dynamic behavior. The first-order energy model is used (Heinzelman *et.al*, 2005) for the estimation energy consumption of the nodes.

SALP METAHEURISTIC-BASED CLUSTERING SCHEME

In this section, we present a detail explanation of the proposed scheme. This section consists of four subsections, the first section explains a basic overview of salp, section two the fitness function used, section three having novel meta-heuristic method for the selection of *CH* and after selection of the *CH*, Cluster formation of the process is explained in the last section.

Formulation of Fitness Function for Cluster-Head Selection

In section-1, After deployment of the sensor node, the base station broadcast its location. After receiving the message all sensor nodes sends their location and energy level information to the base station. For maximize the network lifetime, Base station elect a node as a *CH* that has a higher energy level, minimum node-degree, and less communication cost. This three-parameter are explained below

1. 1. **Residual Energy (f_{RE}):** Energy is one of the major factors for the selection of *CH*. A *CH* collect sensed data from its cluster member. Some selected *CH* nodes are not in the communication range of the base station. So these *CHs* have to use one or more intermediate *CH* nodes to transfer the data to the Base station. These intermediate nodes have to collect data and aggregate the collected data work as well as a relay node. A sensor node can become a *CH* if a node has higher residual energy. The residual energy can be defined below in eq.(1)

$$f_{RE} = \frac{m}{\sum_{i=1}^{m} E_{res}} \tag{1}$$

Where E_{res} indicates residual energy of mth node

2. 2. **Node Degree (f_{ND}):** A node that has a maximum number of cluster member can be select as *CH*. Node degree can define as follows as described in eq.(2).

$$f_{ND} = \frac{1}{\sum_{i=1}^{m} |Cm_i|} \tag{2}$$

Here CM_i is cluster member of the ith *cluster and m is a* number of cluster heads.

3. 3. **Inter-Cluster Communication Distance (f_{IC}):** A node can become a *CH* as the average distance between its cluster member and *CH* should be minimum. It means that the intra-cluster communication cost should be minimum.

$$f_{IC} = \frac{1}{m}\sum_{i=1}^{m}\frac{\sum_{j=1}^{cm_j}dist\left(Ch_i, Cm_j\right)}{\left(Cm_i\right)}$$ (3)

Here dist (CH_i, CM_j) is the distance between i^{th} *cluster head (CH_i)* and j^{th} *cluster member(CM_j)*.

These three basic parameters are used for the selection of *CHs*. To represent this parameter by using weighted sum as alpha(α) beta (β) and gamma (γ) Thus the Fitness function (F_{fit}) can be defined as follow.

$$F_{fit} = \pm \times f_{RE} + {}^2 \times f_{ND} + {}^3 \times f_{IC}$$ (4)

where alpha(α), beta (β) and gamma (γ) are weight factors used to calculate Fitness value of the solution vector and values of weight factor are in the range of [0,1].

Description of Proposed Salp-based Cluster Head Selection Algorithm

In this section, we present the detail working of the Salp-based *CHs* selection scheme. In Salp-Optimization there are two type of salps i.e. leader salp and follower salp. In the proposed method leader nodes are consider as Cluster head and follower salp as a cluster member. The leader salp is collecting the data from its follower salp and aggregate the data and transfer the information to base station. It may use single-hop or multi-hop communication channel as same as Cluster Head node work.

In Salp Swarm optimization is technique, the location of each salp is going to update for each iteration. After the deployment of a random number of sensor nodes in any network area. Selection of leader salp is based on the number of nodes deployed means 10% of the sensor node can be as leader salps. A population vector creation is the first step of the algorithm. A population vector consists of a set of leader salp node. There is n number of solution vector are randomly initialized. First, find the fitness value of each solution vector and find minimum fitness value among them. This minimum value store in Pbest or Global value and set of leader nodes as a Pvector. Now iteration starts, first find the c_1 as given formal and c_2 and c_3 are the randaom numbers. Update the location of each salp by eq.(5) and find the new position vector. Now calculate the fitness value and find cbest or local minima and compare with pbest and find minimum among them. Perform these steps until iteration ends. After completion of iteration, we will get an optimal set of leader salp with the new position.

For update the location of each leader salp or cluster head following equation 5 is used

$$x_j^i = \begin{cases} F_j + c_1\left(\left(ub_j - lb_j\right)c_2 + lb_j\right) & where \, c_3 \geq 0.5 \\ F_j + c_1\left(\left(ub_j - lb_j\right)c_2 + lb_j\right) & where \, c_3 < 0.5 \end{cases} \tag{5}$$

F_j. is position of salp node. Each salp node has communication range, based on communication range upper limit(ub) and lower limit(lb) is calculated as shown in eq.6 and eq.7. Suppose a leader salp coordinates are (x_{cordi} , y_{cordi}). So the upper limit will be communication range add with center coordinates and lower limit will be subtracted with center points. Let leader salp coordinates are (40,50) and Communication range is 20m so the upper limit will be ub_x is 60 and ub_y is 70 and the lower limit will be lb_x= 20 and lb_y=30.

$$ub_x = CR + x_{cordi}$$
$$ub_y = CR + y_{cordi} \tag{6}$$

$$lb_x = x_{cordi} - CR$$
$$lb_y = y_{cordi} - CR \tag{7}$$

In equation 5, the Update location of each salp is based on 3 three constants c_1, c_2 and c_3. Where c_1 depends on the number of iterations as shown in Eq. (8) and c_2 and c_3 are random numbers

$$c_1 = 2e^{-\left(\frac{4t}{T}\right)^2} \tag{8}$$

Where T is the total number of iteration, t is i^{th} number of iteration and c_2 and c_3 are generated uniformly in the interval of [0,1]. In all three constants, c_3 plays an important role in the update location for each leader salp node. Eq.(9) is used to find the new location of follower salp

$$x_i^t = \frac{1}{2}\left(x_i^t + x_i^{t-1}\right) \tag{9}$$

Algorithm 1.

Algorithm 1: The working of SO based CH selection algorithm
1. Input: T, N, m, t=1, Npop;
2. Initialization of population vectors
3. Calculate the fitness value as eq. (4) for each solution vector
4. Find Global best value i.e. Minimum fitness value
5. while t < T
6. calculate c_1 as in eq.(8)
7. find c_2 and c_3
8. for i=1:1:m
9. find ub and lb for each salp
10. calculate x_t^i eq.(5)
11. end
12. Calculate fitness value for each solution vector
13. Find local best solution vector
14. Compare with global value if minimum replaces with local value.
15. t=t+1;
16. end
17. The optimal set of cluster head with the new position

Algorithm 1 Explain the basic steps involved in the cluster head selection procedure and Figure1 explain the basic flow of cluster head selection process. In the first step, some basic parameter is initialized like the number of iteration indicates as T, the total number of solution vectors (Npop) and length of solution vector (m). Initialize population vector are randomly and calculate fitness function and find global.

For the current network scenario and problem statement eq.(9) is not applicable, means no update location for the follower salp. We are only updating the location of the leader salp. Applying the eq.(5) calculate the new location of each leader salp and find fitness value and local optima for the current iteration. After each iteration compares the result with global optima and finds the minimum fitness value. This procedure can follow until a number of iteration ends. After the final iteration, we will get the final position of leader salp or cluster head that covers the maximum node.

Formation of Load-Balanced Clusters

Salp-Optimization is used for the selection of cluster head as discussed in the last section, Now the cluster formation process starts. Where initially all selected salp node or leader salp broadcast their basic information like location coordinates, residual energy, node degree and distance between base station. After getting multiple messages, a follower node can join any leader salp. The proposed scheme uses a formula to join any leader salp known as Cluster$_{joincost}$ as expressed in eq.(10). The energy of leader salp, distance between base station with leader salp, node degree of

Figure 2. Flow-chart of the SO-based CH procedures

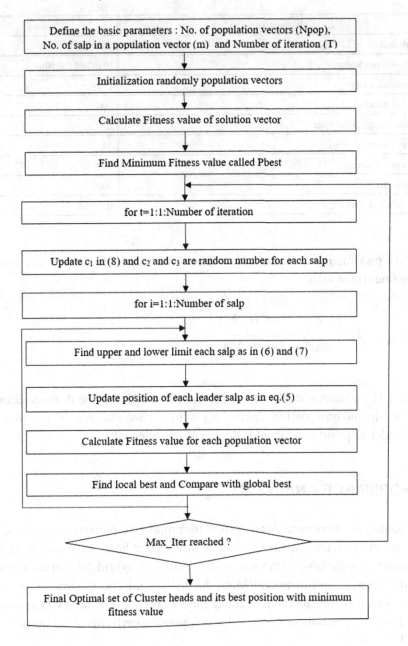

leader salp and distance between the leader and follower salp are the basic parameters to join any leader salp. Suppose an ith follower node wants to join a jth leader salp. So i^{th} salp node will calculate formula as given in eq.(10) for all leader salp nodes

Table 1. Parameter list

Parameter	Value
Network area	100 x 100
Location of Base Station	(0,0) and (50,50)
Communication range	20m
Number of iteration	500
The initial energy of the node	2J
Number of leader salp(m)	14
Number of population	100
Data bit length	4000
Weight factor (α, β and γ)	0.2,0.3,0.5

and find a maximizing cost value. Now i^{th} follower salp joins a leader salp that has the maximum cost value.

$$Cluster_{joincost}(i) = \frac{E_{ls_j} \times dist\left(ls_j, bs\right)}{dist\left(ls_j, fs_i\right) \times ND_{ls_j}} \tag{10}$$

Where E_{lsj} is energy level of jth leader salp, dist(ls_j, bs) is the distance between j^{th} leader salp and base station, dist(ls_j, fs_i) is the distance between i^{th} follower salp and j^{th} leader salp and ND_{lsj} is node degree of jth leader salp.

PERFORMANCE ANALYSIS

In this section, the performance analysis of the proposed scheme is presented results are compared with the existing meta-heuristic cluster head selection algorithms. Performance comparisons of the proposed scheme with hybrid dolphin echolocation and crow search optimization (Mahesh, 2019) and the GA-based approach (Yuan,2017). Network lifetime, residual energy and average energy consumption are the three basic parameters are used to compare the performance of the proposed method.

The simulation experiments are performed in MATLAB 2016b. To analysis the results, there is two network scenario, scenario-1 have base station location at (0,0), scenario-2 has a base station located at (50,50) and 100 x 100 network area is considered. The initial energy of all salp nodes is considered as 2J. Table 1 shows the basic parameter used in the proposed algorithm.

Performance Analysis in Term of Residual Energy

For performance analysis in term of the residual energy, we consider two network scenario. The results are compared with two existing algorithms for the selection of cluster head. Figure 3(a) illustrate the simulation experiment of the proposed scheme for scenario 1 and Figure 3(b) for scenario 2 in the term of residual energy. It has been found that as the number of rounds increases the residual energy of the proposed scheme decreases slower than the existing schemes. the proposed method behaves like that due to unequal clustering during the clustering process.

Performance Analysis in Term of Energy Consumption

The performance analysis in terms of average energy consumption shown Figure 4 (a), Figure 4 (b) for scenario1 and Figure 5(c) and Figure 5(d) for scenario 2. In Figure 6(a) and Figure 6(c) the number of rounds increases from 500 to 3000 in the interval of 500, it has been found that average energy consumption is slowly increasing compare to exiting scheme. The main reason for this performance where the cluster head or leader salp placed in the appropriate position so it covers a maximum number of member nodes. It has also found that average energy consumption is almost similar to the DECSA method. The performance analysis can be done by varying the number of nodes. In Figure 3(b) and Figure 3(d) nodes are vary from 100 to 500 in the interval of 50 nodes. In this analysis we found due to better placement of leader salp average energy consumption is minimum, compared to other schemes.

Performance Analysis in Term of Network lifetime

Figure 5 (a) shows the simulation experiments of the proposed scheme in terms of the network lifetime for scenario 1. In graph represents the first node dead for each scheme. It has been found that in LEACH protocol first node died in 976 rounds, in Genetic based approach first node died in 1500 rounds and DE based approach node died in 2000 rounds. Figure 4 (b) shows the simulation experiments of the proposed scheme in terms of the network lifetime for scenario 2. In graph represents the first node dead for each scheme. It has been found that in LEACH protocol first node died in 1076 rounds, in Genetic based approach first node died in 1675 rounds and DE based approach node died in 2200 rounds. It is also found that if the base station placed in the center of the network, network lifetime is also increased compared to scenario 1. These results show that the Salp - based approach has performed better

Figure 3. (a) Analysis in terms of residual energy for scenario-1, (b) Analysis in terms of residual energy for scenario-2

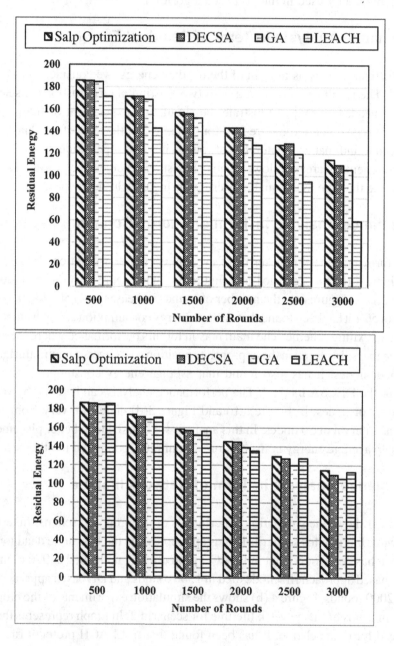

in terms of network life, due to all selected *CHs* gives better inter-cluster and intra-cluster communication.

Figure 4. (a, b) Analysis in terms of average energy consumption for scenario-1

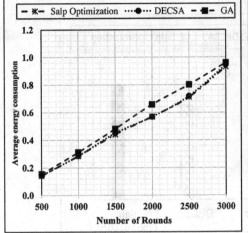 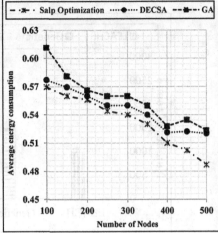

CONCLUSION

This paper discussed the unequal cluster head selection scheme by using the salp swarm optimization based meta-heuristic approach for *WSN*. The proposed Salp optimization-based meta-heuristic approach uses a novel fitness function with three variables: intra-cluster communication cost, residual energy, and node degree. Performance analysis of the proposed scheme and its comparisons with three existing schemes done by varying different network scenarios. A detail simulation experiments

Figure 5. (c, d) Analysis in terms of average energy consumption for scenario-2

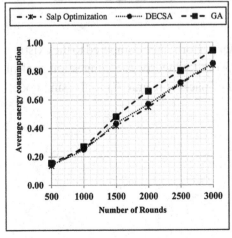 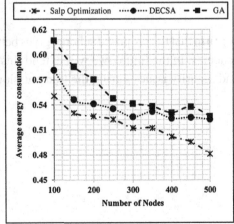

Figure 6. (a) Analysis in terms of Network lifetime for scenario-1, (b) Analysis in terms of Network lifetime for scenario-2

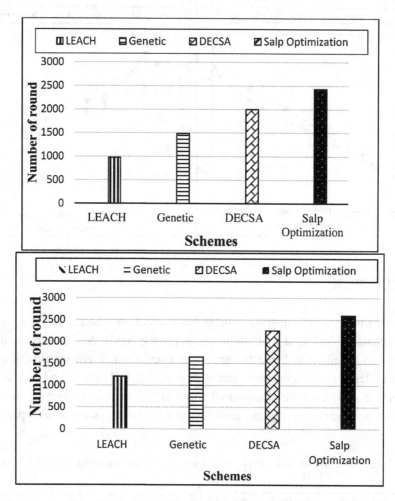

confirm that the proposed scheme gives better performance compared to the existing schemes. In the future, we will extend this work by incorporate congestion control and security issues during the transmission of packets from *CHs* to the sink node.

REFERENCES

Arjunan, S., & Sujatha, P. (2018). Lifetime maximization of the wireless sensor network using fuzzy-based unequal clustering and ACO based routing hybrid protocol. *Applied Intelligence, 48*(8), 2229–2246. doi:10.100710489-017-1077-y

Gupta, G. P. (2018). Improved Cuckoo Search-based Clustering Protocol for Wireless Sensor Networks. *Procedia Computer Science, 125*, 234–240. doi:10.1016/j.procs.2017.12.032

Gupta, G. P., & Jha, S. (2018). Integrated clustering and routing protocol for wireless sensor networks using Cuckoo and Harmony Search based metaheuristic techniques. *Engineering Applications of Artificial Intelligence, 68*, 101–109. doi:10.1016/j.engappai.2017.11.003

Heinzelman, W. R., Chandrakasan, A., & Balakrishnan, H. (2005). *Energy-efficient communication protocol for wireless microsensor networks.* doi:10.1109/hicss.2000.926982

Kaur, T., & Kumar, D. (2018). Particle Swarm Optimization-Based Unequal and Fault Tolerant Clustering Protocol for Wireless Sensor Networks. *IEEE Sensors Journal, 18*(11), 4614–4622. doi:10.1109/JSEN.2018.2828099

Mahesh, N., & Vijayachitra, S. (2019). DECSA: Hybrid dolphin echolocation and crow search optimization for cluster-based energy-aware routing in WSN. *Neural Computing & Applications, 31*(S1s1), 47–62. doi:10.100700521-018-3637-4

Mirjalili, S., Gandomi, A. H., Mirjalili, S. Z., Saremi, S., Faris, H., & Mirjalili, S. M. (2017). Salp Swarm Algorithm: A bio-inspired optimizer for engineering design problems. *Advances in Engineering Software, 114*, 163–191. doi:10.1016/j.advengsoft.2017.07.002

Mittal, N. (2019). Moth Flame Optimization Based Energy Efficient Stable Clustered Routing Approach for Wireless Sensor Networks. *Wireless Personal Communications, 104*(2), 677–694. doi:10.100711277-018-6043-4

Pooranian, Z., Barati, A., & Movaghar, A. (2011). Queen-bee Algorithm for Energy Efficient Clusters in Wireless Sensor Networks. *Engineering and Technology, 5*(1), 1080–1083.

Rao, P. C. S., Jana, P. K., & Banka, H. (2017). A particle swarm optimization based energy efficient cluster head selection algorithm for wireless sensor networks. *Wireless Networks, 23*(7), 2005–2020. doi:10.100711276-016-1270-7

Srinivasa Rao, P. C., & Banka, H. (2017). Novel chemical reaction optimization based unequal clustering and routing algorithms for wireless sensor networks. *Wireless Networks, 23*(3), 759–778. doi:10.100711276-015-1148-0

Xiuwu, Y., Qin, L., Yong, L., Mufang, H., Ke, Z., & Renrong, X. (2019). Uneven clustering routing algorithm based on glowworm swarm optimization. *Ad Hoc Networks, 93*, 101923. doi:10.1016/j.adhoc.2019.101923

Yuan, X., Elhoseny, M., El-Minir, H. K., & Riad, A. M. (2017). A Genetic Algorithm-Based, Dynamic Clustering Method Towards Improved WSN Longevity. *Journal of Network and Systems Management, 25*(1), 21–46. doi:10.100710922-016-9379-7

Chapter 4
Nature–Inspired–Based PTS for PAPR Reduction in OFDM Systems

Mohamed Mounir

ⓘ https://orcid.org/0000-0002-9929-7224

El-Gazeera High Institute (EGI) for Engineering and Technology, Egypt

Mohamed Bakry El Mashade

ⓘ https://orcid.org/0000-0002-1852-3286

Al Azhar University, Egypt

Gurjot Singh Gaba

Lovely Professional University, India

ABSTRACT

OFDM is widely used in high data rate applications due to its ability to mitigate frequency selectivity. However, OFDM suffers from high PAPR problem. This degrades the system performance. PTS is a promising PAPR reduction technique. However, its computational complexity is large; to reduce it, different suboptimal solution (heuristics) were presented in literature. Heuristics PTS algorithms can be categorized into descent-heuristics and metaheuristics. In this chapter, descent-heuristics-based PTS and metaheuristics-based PTS are compared. Results showed that RS-PTS is the best one among descent-heuristics algorithms. Metaheuristics algorithms can also be classified into single solution-based methods and nature-inspired methods. Among metaheuristics algorithms, two natural inspired algorithms and one single solution-based methods, namely PSO, ABC, and SA, were selected to be compared with descent-heuristics algorithms. Results showed that PTS based on nature-inspired methods is better than PTS based on descent heuristics and PTS based on single-solution metaheuristics method.

DOI: 10.4018/978-1-7998-1626-3.ch004

INTRODUCTION

In recent high data rate application such as Wireless Wide Area Network (WWAN), Wireless Local Area Network (WLAN), Long-Term Evolution (LTE) the 3GPP 4G, and Asymmetrical Digital Subscriber Loop (ADSL), Orthogonal Frequency Division Multiplexing (OFDM) is used due to the ability of OFDM to mitigate Frequency selectivity in communication channels. Thanks to simple equalization process of OFDM (i.e. one tap frequency equalizer). However, OFDM suffer from disadvantage, namely high Peak-to-Average Power Ratio (PAPR). High PAPR signal reduce Power Amplifiers (PA) efficiency. As the PAs have to work with large Input-back-off (IBO) to preserve the signal from nonlinear distortion. Reducing IBO will cause the signal to be nonlinearly amplified. Nonlinearly amplified signal will suffer from Bit Error Rate (BER) degradation and Out-of-Band (OOB) radiation. In order to increase HPA efficiency without BER degradation or OOB emission, different PAPR reduction techniques were introduced in literature (Mounir et al., 2017). Among them, Partial Transmit Sequence (PTS) got a large attraction in literature, due to its high PAPR reduction gain with a small number of side information bits, in addition to small computational complexity in the receiver side. However, PTS requires large computational complexity in the transmitter side. Finding the optimum solution for PTS is combinatorial (Discrete) optimization problem (Youssef, Tarrad, & Mounir, 2016). In literature, different suboptimal solutions were proposed to reduce PTS computational complexity in the transmitter side.

Heuristics methods of PTS can be categorized into metaheuristics and descent heuristics. In descent heuristics, only downhill moves are accepted. In contrary, uphill moves may be accepted to prevent fast stuck to local minimum. Metaheuristics methods may be classified into single solution based methods (such as, simulated annealing (SA)) and population based methods, also called Nature Inspired methods (e.g. Grey Wolf Optimization (GWO) algorithm, Cuckoo Search (SC), BAT algorithm (BA), Firefly algorithm (FA), Artificial Bee Colony (ABC), Particle Swarm Optimization (PSO), and Genetic Algorithm (GA)) (Yang, 2010).

In literature, there are number of descent heuristics algorithms used with PTS, such as, iterative flipping algorithm (IPTS) (Cimini, & Sollenberger, 2000) random search based PTS (RS-PTS) (Cimini, & Sollenberger, 2000), and gradient descent based PTS (GD-PTS) (Han, & Lee, 2004). Similarly, metaheuristics base PTS are found in literature, such as, SA based PTS (Jiang, Xiang, Richardson, Guo, & Zhu, 2007), PSO based PTS (Wen, Lee, Huang, & Hung, 2008), ABC based PTS (Wang, Chen, & Tellambura, 2010), FA based PTS (Singh, & Patra, 2018), CS based PTS

(Zhou, & Yao, 2017), and GWO based PTS (Rao, & Malathi, 2019). In this chapter, descent heuristics based PTS and metaheuristics based PTS are compared, among metaheuristics based PTS techniques SA was selected as single solution method and PSO and ABC was selected as a nature inspired methods. In this chapter different heuristics based PTS algorithms are compared according to the required number of searches to get the same PAPR reduction gain/performance.

This chapter is organized as follows. In section 2 OFDM system model and high PAPR problem are presented. PTS technique is introduced in section 3. Reduction of PTS computational complexity is discussed in section 4. PTS optimization problem was formulated as a discrete optimization problem in section 4.1. In section 4.2, algorithms of PTS based descent heuristics such as IPTS, RS-PTS, and GD-PTS are described, there PAPR reduction performance and computational complexity are compared. In section 4.3, algorithms of PTS based metaheuristics i.e. SA-PTS, PSO-PTS, and ABC-PTS are described and the influence of their controlling parameters on the PAPR reduction gain is discussed. Also, a comparison between PTS based descent heuristics and PTS based metaheuristics is introduced in this section. Future research directions are described in section 5. Section 6 concludes the results.

OFDM SYSTEM MODEL

OFDM is the inverse Fourier transform of orthogonal subcarriers modulated by complex symbols mapping coded bits. Practically, frequency domain vector S is converted to time-domain vector X, by aid of Inverse Fast Fourier Transform (IFFT). Let N be the number of subcarriers and then $S = \begin{bmatrix} S_{[0]} & \cdots & \cdots & S_{[k]} & \cdots & S_{[N-1]} \end{bmatrix}$ denotes the information vector in the frequency domain, where k_{th} subcarrier is carrying the complex symbol $S_{[k]}$. Samples of discrete time baseband OFDM symbol have the following values;

$$X_{[n]} = \frac{1}{\sqrt{N}} \sum_{k=0}^{N-1} S_{[k]} e^{j \frac{2\pi nk}{N}}, 0 \leq n \leq N-1 \tag{1}$$

where, $X_{[n]}$ is n_{th} sample in the time-domain vector $X = \begin{bmatrix} X_{[0]} & \cdots & \cdots & X_{[n]} & \cdots & X_{[N-1]} \end{bmatrix}$, which is the modulated OFDM symbol. Based on theorem of central limit (CLT), samples of time-domain OFDM signal $X_{[n]}$ follows Gaussian distribution, with the assumption that, frequency-domain symbols $S_{[k]}$ are statistically independent and number of subcarriers N is sufficiently large. For discrete time version of OFDM signal, PAPR is given by;

$$PAPR = \frac{Max_{n \in [0,N]} |X_{[n]}|^2}{E\{|X_{[n]}|^2\}} \qquad (2)$$

where, $E\{\cdot\}$ is the statistical average. Complementary Cumulative Distribution Function (CCDF) of PAPR is the probability that the PAPR exceeds a threshold $PAPR_o$ (*i.e.* $CCDF = prob\{PAPR > PAPR_o\}$)

Commonly, CCDF is used to measure PAPR reduction gain of the different techniques. Practically, PAPR of analog OFDM signal in time domain is estimated by means of oversampling (Mounir et al., 2017). An analytical approach of the $CCDF_c$ of the oversampled OFDM signal was presented in (Wei, Goeckel, & Kelly, 2002);

$$CCDF_c = Pr\{PAPR > \xi_0\} = 1 - exp\left(-Ne^{-\xi_0}\sqrt{\frac{\pi}{3}}\log N\right) \qquad (3)$$

ξ_0 is a predefined threshold (i.e. $PAPR_o$).

PARTIAL TRANSMIT SEQUENCE (PTS)

PTS technique presented in (Muller, & Huber, 1997a; Muller, & Huber, 1997b) by Muller and Huber. PTS partitions OFDM symbol to V disjoint subblocks. So that, each subcarrier can be only used in one subblock and set to zero in all other subblocks. This can be written mathematically as $S = \sum_{v=1}^{V} S^{(v)}$. Thus, all sub-Blocks have the same size equal to the original block size (Müller, & Huber, 1997c). In PTS phase rotation is applied to all subblocks independently, while in SLM phase rotation was applied to all subcarriers block (Cho, Kim, Yang, & Kang, 2010). PTS-OFDM transmitter is shown in Figure 1.

PTS partitions the OFDM block S to V subblocks, as the follows;

Figure 1. PTS-Transmitter

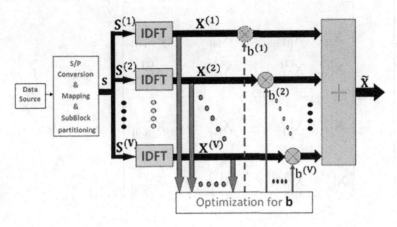

$$
\begin{bmatrix}
\mathbf{S}^{(1)} \\
\mathbf{S}^{(2)} \\
\vdots \\
\mathbf{S}^{(v)} \\
\vdots \\
\mathbf{S}^{(V)}
\end{bmatrix}_{(V \times 1)}
=
\begin{bmatrix}
s_{[0]}^{(1)} & s_{[1]}^{(1)} & \cdots & s_{[k]}^{(1)} & \cdots & s_{[N-1]}^{(1)} \\
s_{[0]}^{(2)} & s_{[1]}^{(2)} & & s_{[k]}^{(2)} & & s_{[N-1]}^{(2)} \\
\vdots & & \ddots & \vdots & & \\
s_{[0]}^{(v)} & s_{[1]}^{(v)} & & s_{[k]}^{(v)} & \cdots & s_{[N-1]}^{(v)} \\
\vdots & & \cdots & \vdots & & \\
s_{[0]}^{(V)} & s_{[1]}^{(V)} & & s_{[k]}^{(V)} & \cdots & s_{[N-1]}^{(V)}
\end{bmatrix}_{(V \times N)}
\tag{4}
$$

Where $\mathbf{S}^{(v)}$ is the subblock number v^{th} among V sub-blocks all one of them has a length N equal to the length of the original OFDM block. Then the time-domain version of each subblock can be obtained by tacking the IFFT of each one of the subblocks in the previous set of sub-blocks. (*i.e.* Equation (5) will be the time-domain version of equation (4)).

$$
\begin{bmatrix} \mathbf{X}^{(1)} \\ \mathbf{X}^{(2)} \\ \vdots \\ \mathbf{X}^{(v)} \\ \vdots \\ \mathbf{X}^{(V)} \end{bmatrix}_{(V \times 1)}
=
\begin{bmatrix}
X^{(1)}_{[0]} & X^{(1)}_{[1]} & \cdots & X^{(1)}_{[n]} & \cdots & X^{(1)}_{[N-1]} \\
X^{(2)}_{[0]} & X^{(2)}_{[1]} & & X^{(2)}_{[n]} & & X^{(2)}_{[N-1]} \\
\vdots & & \ddots & \vdots & & \\
X^{(v)}_{[0]} & X^{(v)}_{[1]} & & X^{(v)}_{[n]} & \cdots & X^{(v)}_{[N-1]} \\
\vdots & & \cdots & \vdots & & \\
X^{(V)}_{[0]} & X^{(V)}_{[1]} & & X^{(V)}_{[n]} & \cdots & X^{(V)}_{[N-1]}
\end{bmatrix}_{(V \times N)}
\tag{5}
$$

Then by exploiting the linearity property of IFFT, the time-domain version of the original OFDM symbol can be obtained by combining the above set of sub-Blocks vertically across rows. Where the linearity property of IFFT ensure the following

$$
\mathbf{X} = \sum_{v=1}^{V} \mathbf{X}^{(v)} = \mathrm{IFFT}\{\mathbf{S}\} = \mathrm{IFFT}\left\{\sum_{v=1}^{V} \mathbf{S}^{(v)}\right\} = \sum_{v=1}^{V} \mathrm{IFFT}\left\{\mathbf{S}^{(v)}\right\}
\tag{6}
$$

But till now there are no changes happened for PAPR reduction. Reduction of the PAPR will be done by multiplying each sub-Block $\mathbf{X}^{(v)}$ by the its optimum phase factor $\hat{b}^{(v)} = e^{j\not{\phi}^{(v)}}$ before combining these subblocks or PTS$_s$ where the optimum phase vector $\hat{\mathbf{b}}$ is selected from a set of phase vectors $\mathbf{b}$ as per (7). So that the PAPR of $\mathbf{S}$ can be minimized.

$$
\hat{\mathbf{b}} = \begin{bmatrix} \hat{b}^{(1)} & \cdots & \cdots & \hat{b}^{(v)} & \cdots & \hat{b}^{(V)} \end{bmatrix} = \min_{\left[b^{(1)} \; \cdots \; b^{(V)} \right]} \left(\max_{0 \leq n < N} \left| \sum_{v=1}^{V} \left(b^{(v)} * X^{(v)}_{[n]} \right) \right| \right)
\tag{7}
$$

The OFDM signal in time domain after optimization and combination of PTS$_s$ is as follows;

$$
\tilde{\mathbf{X}} = \sum_{v=1}^{V} \left(\mathbf{X}^{(v)} * b^{(v)} \right) = \sum_{v=1}^{V} \left(\mathrm{IFFT}\left\{\mathbf{S}^{(v)}\right\} * b^{(v)} \right)
\tag{8}
$$

Which has the lowest PAPR among the all other alternative transmit sequences.

Figure 2.

$$[\hat{b}^{(1)} \quad \hat{b}^{(2)} \quad \hat{b}^{(3)} \quad \hat{b}^{(4)}] = \begin{bmatrix} 1 & 1 & 1 & 1 \\ 1 & 1 & 1 & -1 \\ 1 & 1 & -1 & 1 \\ 1 & 1 & -1 & -1 \\ 1 & -1 & 1 & 1 \\ 1 & -1 & 1 & -1 \\ 1 & -1 & -1 & 1 \\ 1 & -1 & -1 & -1 \end{bmatrix}$$

In practical, finding the optimum phase rotational factor per subblock is an exhaustive search process. In order to reduce required number of searches, possible values of rotational factor is restricted to small set of phases (W). Then, p the set of possible rotational factors is given by $p = \left\{ e^{j2\mathring{A}/W} \Big|_{l=0,1,\cdots,W-1} \right\}$. Moreover, computational complexity of PTS can be more reduced without performance loss by setting the phase factor of the first subblock to unity (*i.e.* $b^{(1)} = 1$). Thus, number of possible phase rotational vectors (solution) will be reduced to $W^{(V-1)}$ (Han, & Lee, 2005). As example if we partition an OFDM block into 4 sub-Blocks, and set the number of allowed phase factors to $2, (i.e. V = 4, W = 2)$ then the number of possible vectors of phase factors (solutions) that will be searched is $W^{(V-1)} = 2^{(4-1)} = 8$ as the follows;

Usually number of allowed phase factor W is set to 2 or 4 i.e. $p = \{\pm 1\}$ or $p = \{\pm 1, \pm j\}$ respectively, to get an implementational advantage, as no actual multiplications are needed to combine the PTS$_s$ in Eq. 8. (Müller, & Huber, 1997a; Müller, & Huber, 1997c).

PAPR reduction performance of PTS depends on three factors: **1)** Subblock partitioning method (in literature there are three schemes namely Pseudo-Random, Adjacent, and interleaved) **2)** The set of possible rotational factors (p) **3)** Subblocks number (V). (Han, & Lee, 2005)

Subblocks partitioning methods are illustrated in Figure 3. Among the three partitioning schemes pseudo-random provides the highest PAPR reduction gain (Müller, & Huber, 1997b). In other hand, Adjacent sub-Blocks Partitioning not require any change in the already found standards (such as 802.16) if it used in their transmitters, only it require at least one pilot in each sub-Block to allow the receiver to equalize the phase rotation of each sub-Block (as if it was a channel effect) rather than side information. Generally, PTS uses $\log_2 W^{(V-1)}$ side information bits.

Figure 3. Methods of sub-Blocks partitioning in PTS

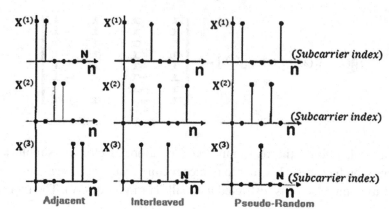

PTS computational complexity has three components. First one (c_{FFT}), is the V IFFT$_s$. Second component (c_{sp}), is the $W^{(V-1)}$ superpositioning of all PTS$_s$. Thirdly, the calculation of the PAPRs (metric) for selection (c_{met}). The computational complexity of PTS is then given by;

$$c_{PTS} = V \cdot c_{FFT} + W^{(V-1)} \cdot \left(c_{sp} + c_{met} \right) \tag{9}$$

The three components of the computational effort of PTS (*i.e.* c_{FFT}, c_{sp}, and c_{met}) are given in Table 1 in terms of real additions and multiplications (Youssef et al., 2016).

It can be shown that, c_{FFT} is the major component that influence the computational complexity of PTS.

Table 1. Components of the computational complexity of PTS.

Real Multiplication			Real Addition		
c_{FFT}	c_{sp}	c_{met}	c_{FFT}	c_{sp}	c_{met}
$2LNV \log_2 LN$	0	$W^{(V-1)}2LN$	$3LNV \log_2 LN$	$2LN(V-1)W^{(V-1)}$	$W^{(V-1)}LN$

PTS COMPUTATIONAL COMPLEXITY REDUCTION

From preceding section we know that one of the drawbacks of PTS is its high computational complexity. Also we know that the PTS computational effort consists of the IFFT of the V subblocks, the $W^{(V-1)}$ superpositions of all partial sequences, and the calculation of the PAPR_s (metric) for the selection. In literature several researches were done to reduce the computational complexity of one or more of the three basic components of the computational complexity of PTS. Reduction of the IFFT computational complexity is done in (Kang, Kim, & Joo, 1999) by using efficient special constructed IFFT that exploiting the majority of zeros in subblocks. Other approaches reduce the computational complexity by modifying the PTS objective function (metric of the selection) which reduces the required number of multiplications (Nguyen, & Lampe, 2008). In literature, there are large number of researches try to reduce the computational complexity by using suboptimal search methods rather than the optimal search method (Cimini, & Sollenberger, 2000; Han, & Lee, 2004; Jiang et al., 2007; Rao, & Malathi, 2019; Singh, & Patra, 2018; Wen et al., 2008; Wang et al., 2010; Zhou, & Yao, 2017), which reduce the complexity of both number of superpositions that needed to be combined and number of PAPR_s calculations (metric) needed for the selection. These methods will be discussed, classified and compared in the following subsections.

Suboptimal Searching Methods

Finding the optimum phase vector $\hat{b}$ for PTS is a discrete optimization problem which is also called combinatorial optimization problem (CO);

$$\underset{b}{\text{minimize}}\left(f\left(b \right) \right) \tag{10}$$

$$\text{subject to}: b_v \in \left\{ e^{j\phi^{(v)}} \right\} \tag{11}$$

$$f\left(b \right) = \frac{\underset{0 \leq n < N}{\max}\left| \sum_{v=1}^{V}\left(b_v * X_{[n]}^{(v)} \right) \right|^2}{E\left[\left| \sum_{v=1}^{V}\left(b_v * X_{[n]}^{(v)} \right) \right|^2 \right]} \tag{12}$$

Where $Æ^{(v)} \in \left\{ \dfrac{2Àl}{W} \right|_{l=0.1\cdots,W-1} \right\}$

Equation (10) is the objective function of the problem which is nothing rather than PAPR minimization of an OFDM symbol. Constrained ensure that rotational phase factors are selected from the set of possible values. Optimum solution of (10) means that a set of $W^{(V-1)}$ candidate solutions have to be searched. Practical solution of this problem becomes impossible at high number of subblocks ($e.g. V \geq 16$) (Jiang et al., 2007). Thus, suboptimal PTS techniques which provide non-ideal solutions regard (10). Suboptimal algorithms (also called heuristics) reduce the computational complexity of PTS by shrinking required number of searches. In literature, different heuristics algorithms were used to reduce the computational complexity of PTS. A heuristics algorithm is said to be better than the other, if it reduces required complexity (number of searches) to achieve the same PAPR reduction performance or better than the other. Heuristics algorithms of PTS can be classified into **metaheuristics** and **descent Heuristics** (Nguyen, & Lampe, 2008). The two categories and some of the methods which fall under them will be discussed in the following subsections.

Descent Heuristics based PTS

In descent heuristics algorithms there is a trial solution b' generated per iteration if it is better than the current solution b it will be accepted (i.e. downhill moves are only accepted). At the end of iterations current solution b will be the best solution $\hat{b}$ (Nguyen, & Lampe, 2008). In literature there are numbers of descent heuristics algorithms were used to reduce PTS computational complexity, such as, iterative flipping PTS algorithm (IPTS) (Cimini, & Sollenberger, 2000) random search based PTS (RS-PTS) (Cimini, & Sollenberger, 2000), and gradient descent based PTS (GD-PTS) (Han, & Lee, 2004).

Iterative flipping PTS Algorithm (IPTS)

A suboptimal combining technique introduce by Cimini and Sollenberger in (Cimini, & Sollenberger, 2000), this can be applied to binary case $\left(W = 2, i.e. P = \{\pm 1\} \right)$ and also can be generalized for any number of allowed phases.

In IPTS, OFDM symbol is portioned to V subblocks. Find the PAPR of the original OFDM symbol. Set $b = [1,1,\ldots 1 \ldots,1]$ the all one phase vector as an initial solution. Then, flip the second subblock phase rotation factor (*i.e.* $b_2' = -1$). Find the new $PAPR'$. If $PAPR' \leq PAPR$, then $b_2 = -1$ will be kept in the final vector of phase factors $\hat{b}$, else b_2 will be return back to its initial value ($b_2 = 1$). The process of flipping and exploring the phase factors of the others subblocks will be continued, so the final vector of phase factors $\hat{b}$ will be produced (Cimini, & Sollenberger, 2000; Han, & Lee, 2004).IPTS algorithm is summarized as follows;

Algorithm 1. Iterative flipping-PTS (IPTS) Algorithm

```
1. Firstly, OFDM system is partitioned into V subblocks
2. Use b = [1,1,...,1,......,1] as a current solution. Compute PAPR
of the OFDM symbol
3. For v=2 to V
3.1 Change b'ᵥ among all possible values of P. Compute PAPR'
of the new solution
3.2 For each possible value of b'ᵥ:
If PAPR' ≤ PAPR
bᵥ = b'ᵥ
Else
bᵥ = bᵥ Keep bᵥ unchanged
End if
4. End for
5. Output: b̂ = b
```

The search complexity of IPTS technique is proportional to $((W-1)(V-1))+1$. Fig. 4 compares between IPTS and OPTS, in OFDM system uses 16-QAM, N= 256 subcarrier and 16 subblocks with contiguous partitioning scheme where number of allowed phases for PTS is 2 $(W = 2)$. OFDM signal is oversampled by L=4. It can be shown that, at $CCDF_c = 10^{-3}$ IPTS has PAPR reduction gain of $3dB$ in comparison with $4.4dB$ for OPTS.

However, IPTS greatly reduces the computational complexity of PTS, it worse degrade the PAPR reduction performance of PTS. So, other efficient heuristics methods are needed to decrease the gap between conventional PTS and suboptimal PTS techniques (Han, & Lee, 2004).

Figure 4. comparison between IPTS and OPTS

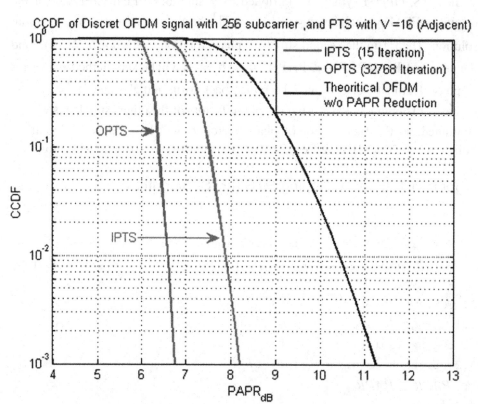

Random Search based PTS (RS-PTS)

Random search (RS) is the simplest heuristics algorithm introduced in (Cimini, & Sollenberger, 2000) to be used with PTS. In RS a trial solution b' is selected randomly, if $f(b') \leq f(b)$ the trial solution is accepted. RS is done by multiplying the transmitted sequence (data sub blocks) by a number I of phase sequences selected randomly from the search space of the phase sequences $\left(W^{(V-1)}\right)$, then the best one –that gives the lowest PAPR– is chosen to be transmitted. RS-PTS search complexity proportional to I. Although RS-PTS technique have no order in changing the phase factors, just random, but it can explore any arbitrary number of phase sequences. Performance of RS-PTS for $I = \{5, 16, 64, 256, \text{and } 900\}$ is shown in

Figure 4, parameters of simulation is the same as that of Figure 3. It can be noted that, when the number of randomly selected phase sequences (I) is increased, performance of RS-PTS get closer to OPTS in the expense of increasing complexity. However, excessive increase in I, is lead to small enhancement in PAPR Reduction performance. Also, Figure 5 compares between the performance of RS-PTS and IPTS for the same amount of complexity (i.e. same number of Iterations), we can note that RS-PTS and IPTS have the same performance especially for PAPR values that have a probability of occurrence less than 1%, except that there is a very little enhancement (within $0.1dB$) in the performance of IPTS for PAPR values that have a probability of occurrence greater than 1%. That is because IPTS has a better order in changing the phase factors than RS-PTS which choose the vectors of phase factors randomly.

Figure 5. Comparison between OPTS and RS for different number of iteration (I=5, 16, 64,256,900)

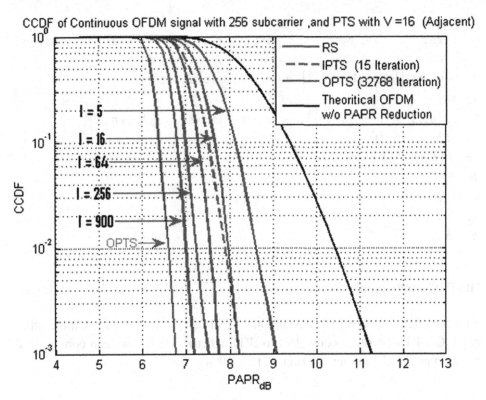

Gradient Descent based PTS (GD-PTS)

This technique presented in (Han, & Lee, 2004) by Han and Lee. Firstly, assume current solution is given by all one vector $b = [1,1,1,\dots\dots,1]$. Any other solution can be assumed, as the performance of this technique doesn't depend on the initial solution. Then, all trial solution b' (neighborhood) within a circle of radius r is searched. where r a predefined hamming distance from the current solution b. The best solution $\hat{b}$ of this algorithm is given by;

$$\hat{b} = arg\left\{ \max_{b'-b_H \leq r} \left(f(b) - f(b') \right) \right\} \tag{13}$$

Where $._H$ is the hamming distance between two vectors. Value of r varies from 1 to V. GD-PTS algorithm is summarized as follows;

Algorithm 2. GD-PTS Algorithm

1. Firstly, OFDM symbol is partitioned into V subblocks. Define I as a maximum number of iterations.
2. Use $b = [1,1,\dots,1,\dots\dots,1]$ as a current solution.
3. For i=1 to I
2.1 Search all neighborhood of b within a radius r.
2.2 For each b' :
If $f(b') \leq f(b)$
$b = b'$
End if
4. End for
$\hat{b} = b$

GD-PTS search complexity proportional to $\left[I \times \left(\sum_{i=1}^{r} \left((W-1)^i \times C_i^{(V-1)} \right) \right) \right] + 1$. GD-PTS becomes equivalent to conventional PTS (OPTS) when $r = V$. On the other hand, GD-PTS becomes equivalent to IPTS when $r = 1$. So, we can compromise between gain and complexity (Han, & Lee, 2004).

Figure 6 compares PAPR reduction performance of GD-PTS at different number of iterations I and different radius values r by using the same parameters as that in Figure 3, except that PTS partitioning method is Pseudo-Random rather than adjacent. It can be noted that, increasing r or increasing I for the same r will enhance PAPR reduction performance of GD-PTS. However, increasing r is more efficient than increasing I. Moreover, excessive increase in number of iterations $(I > 3)$ has no influence on the PAPR reduction gain.

Figure 7 compares between the three Descent Heuristic methods (i.e. GD, RS, IPTS) for the same amounts of complexity-same number of searches. At small number of searches (e.g.16 searches) IPTS overcome RS-PTS especially for PAPR values that have a probability of occurrence greater than 0.1%, that is expected as IPTS has a better order in changing the phase factors than RS-PTS which update the vector of phase factors randomly. But although GD-PTS seems to have a well-designed method in changing the phase factors better than IPTS and RS-PTS, it has a performance worse than both IPTS and RS-PTS, and this can be owing to that at small number of searches $\left(\text{e.g.16 searches}\right)$

Figure 6. Effect of increasing r and I on GD-PTS

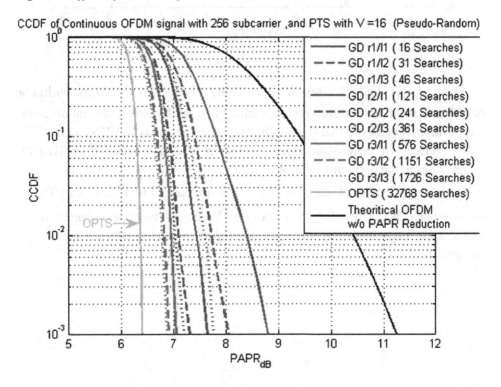

CCDF of Continuous OFDM signal with 256 subcarrier ,and PTS with V =16 (Pseudo-Random)

Legend:
- GD r1/I1 (16 Searches)
- GD r1/I2 (31 Searches)
- GD r1/I3 (46 Searches)
- GD r2/I1 (121 Searches)
- GD r2/I2 (241 Searches)
- GD r2/I3 (361 Searches)
- GD r3/I1 (576 Searches)
- GD r3/I2 (1151 Searches)
- GD r3/I3 (1726 Searches)
- OPTS (32768 Searches)
- Theoritical OFDM w/o PAPR Reduction

Figure 7. Comparison of PAPR reduction performance of the three descent heuristic methods (GD, RS, and IPTS) for the same number of searches (i.e. computational complexity)

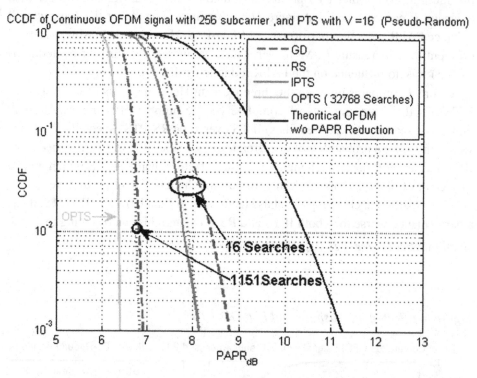

$(r = 1/I = 1)$ GD-PTS restricts searching process to solutions within a neighborhood circle of radius 1 (i.e. searching only within solutions that differ by one position from the original seed). While the other two methods IPTS and RS-PTS can stroll freely in the all search space, so they have a more chance than GD-PTS to get closer to the optimum solution.

But at large number of searches $(e.g. 1151\, searches)$ GD-PTS and RS-PTS get nearly coincidence. Thus RS-PTS can be considered as the best one among the other Descent Heuristic searching methods developed to reduce PTS computational complexity.

Metaheuristics Based PTS

However descent heuristics methods reduce the search complexity, they don't perform well. They fast stuck to local minima, as they only accept downhill moves. In contrary, metaheuristics accept both downhill and uphill moves to overcome stuck to local minima (Nguyen, & Lampe, 2008). In literature, there are several metaheuristics algorithms used with PTS such as SA, PSO, and ABC.

Simulated Annealing Based PTS (SA-PTS)

Simulated Annealing (SA) mimics the metallurgical annealing process, in which the material will be heated and cooled in controllable manner to enhance purification of the crystal. Simulated Annealing concept can be used in optimization. SA-PTS algorithm can be summarized as follows;

Algorithm 3. SA-PTS Algorithm

```
1. Define initial T and Choose initial vector b
2. Loop i =1 to I
2.1 Choose new trial solution b' using cyclic bit-flipping
2.2 Generate r, where r is a uniformly distributed random
number in (0,1)
2.3 Switch case
```

2.4 Case1: $\left(f\left(b'\right) < f\left(b\right)\right)$ and $\left(f\left(b\right) < f\left(\hat{b}\right)\right)$

$b = b'$

$\hat{b} = b$

```
2.5 Case2:
```

2.6 Case3: $\left(f\left(b'\right) > f\left(b\right)\right)$ and $\left(r < e^{\frac{-\left(f\left(b'\right) < f\left(b\right)\right)}{T}}\right)$

$b = b'$

```
2.7 End switch case
2.8 Update T in accordance with the cooling schedule
3. End loop
4. Output b̂
```

Temperature scheduling in annealing process could be Constant Temperature T, Geometric, or Gaussian cooling. Here we use the Constant Temperature 0.5 as the three annealing schedules perform the same. Value of T must be chosen carefully. If T is large, SA will be similar to RS. On the other hand, SA will be similar to iterative flipping, if T is small.

The following simulation is done on OFDM system use 16-QAM, N= 256 subcarrier, and oversampled by factor L=4. PTS with 16 sub block Pseudo-random partitioning is used, number of allowed phases for PTS are W=2.

Figure 8 Compares SA-PTS performance with RS-PTS for the same amount of computational complexities (I=16, 64, and 256) it can be noted that SA overcome RS in the high probability PAPR values i.e. Lower PAPR Values. But it fast stuck to local optima and become worse than RS that is because SA is one of metaheuristics methods that fall under the category of local search methods.

Figure 8. Comparison between SA-PTS, RS-PTS for the same computational complexities (16, 64,256 search)

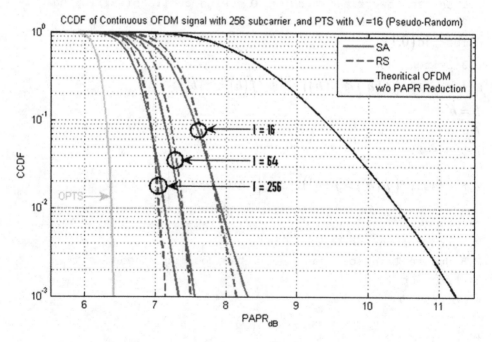

Particle Swarm Optimization based PTS (PSO-PTS)

PSO was introduced in 1995 Dr. Eberhart and Kennedy. PSO mimics the intelligence of a bird swarm. Particles are moved in guidance of their own best known position (Local optimum), in addition to, global best position of the swarm. The movements of the swarm are guided by discovering new local optimum positions. The global optimum solution is the best among the local optimum solutions. The process is repeated for certain number of iterations (Dorigo, Montes de Oca, & Engelbrecht, 2008; Gao, 2011; Khademi, 2010). The algorithm of PSO-PTS is given below;

Algorithm 4. PSO-PTS Algorithm

1. Define I, S , C_1, C_2, ω_{max} and ω_{min} .
2. Generate positions X_i and velocities V_i of the initial population $i \in [1 : S]$.
3. Calculate the PAPR (fitness) of each particle X_i.
4. Set the initial best local position per particle $P_i = X_i$.
5. Find the best global position P_g
6. For $t = 1$ to G
6.1 For $i = 1$ to S
For $v = 1$ to V
Update velocity and position by (14) and (15), respectively.
End for
Calculate PAPR (fitness) of each particle X_i.
Update P_i
6.2 End for
6.3 Update P_g and $\omega(t)$.
7. End for
8. Output $\hat{b} = P_g$

Equation that used to update position and velocity for all dimensions of each particle in the swarm per generation is as follows (Khademi, 2010; Wen et al., 2008);

$$V_{iv}^{(t+1)} = \omega(t) V_{iv}^{(t)} + C_1 r_1 \left(P_{iv}^{(t)} - X_{iv}^{(t)} \right) + C_2 r_2 \left(P_{gv}^{(t)} - X_{iv}^{(t)} \right) \qquad (14)$$

$$X_{iv}^{(t+1)} = X_{iv}^{(t)} + V_{iv}^{(t+1)} \tag{15}$$

$$\omega(t) = \omega_{max} - \left(\frac{\omega_{max} - \omega_{min}}{G-1}\right)(t-1) \tag{16}$$

Where

i : is the ith particle from the swarm of S particles

t : is the tth Generation from the maximum number of Generations G

d : denote the dth Dimension from V Dimensions of the objective Function

V_i : is the ith particles velocity vector, represented as $V_i^{(t)} = \begin{pmatrix} V_{i1}^{(t)} & V_{iv}^{(t)} & \cdots & V_{iV}^{(t)} \end{pmatrix}$

X_i : is the ith particles position vector, represented as $X_i^{(t)} = \begin{pmatrix} X_{i1}^{(t)} & X_{iv}^{(t)} & \cdots & X_{iV}^{(t)} \end{pmatrix}$

$X_{iv}^{(t)} \in U$ and U denotes the domain of objective function.

P_i : is the local best position, which is the previous best position this i^{th} Particle has achieved so far, and represented as $P_i = \begin{pmatrix} P_{i1} & P_{iv} & \cdots & P_{iV} \end{pmatrix}$.

P_g : is the Global best position, which is the previous best position obtained so far by any particle in the whole swarm, and represented as $P_g = \begin{pmatrix} P_{g1} & P_{gv} & \cdots & P_{gV} \end{pmatrix}$

C_1 & C_2 : they control the individual and public cooperative behavior of particles, respectively. Increasing C_1 causes particles to be more attracted to their local best positions $P_{id}^{(t)}$. On the other hand, increasing C_2 causes particles to be attracted to the global best position $P_{gd}^{(t)}$.

r_1 & r_2 : two randomly generated numbers uniformly distributed in range r_1 & $r_2 \in [0:1]$.

$\omega(t)$: is the inertia weight, ω_{max} is the Maximum inertia weight, and ω_{min} is the Minimum inertia weight

If the velocity of a particle is fast it may overlap a promising zone on the solution space without searching it adequately. So that, maximum velocity factor $Vmax$ is necessary to control exploration process (Gao, 2011). The need for $Vmax$ may be disregard by using inertia weight $\omega(t)$. Inertia weight controls the process of exploration and exploitation. Thus, high initial value of inertia weight is necessary for exploration process. Then decaying the inertia weight linearly will be suitable for exploitation. Experimental results suggest inertia weight $\omega_{max} = 0.9$ and $\omega_{min} = 0.4$ to compromise between the exploitation and exploration processes (Khademi, 2010; Wen et al., 2008).

Original PSO algorithm updates the global best position P_g after updating positions and best local positions P_i of all particles, this is called synchronous update mode. Synchronous update delays the propagation of global best solution P_g. Asynchronous update mode is used to speed up propagation of global best solution P_g. Asynchronous updates the global best solution P_g after each best local position P_i update (Dorigo et al., 2008).

Figure 9 compares between OPTS and PSO-PTS, in case of PTS with 16 Pseudo-random partitioned subblocks and number of allowed phases is W=2, in an OFDM system with 16-QAM, 256 subcarrier, and oversampled by factor L=4.

Figure 9. Comparison between PSO and RS for the same computational complexity (900 searches)

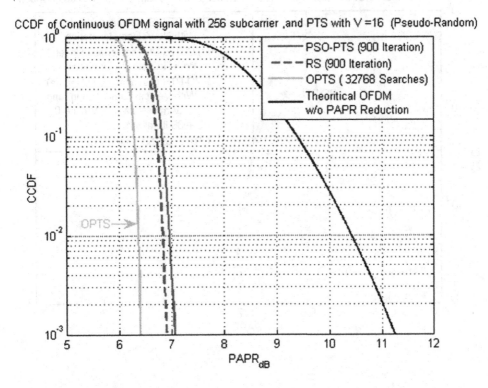

It can be noted that, when $P_r\left(PAPR > PAPR_o\right) = 10^{-3}$ the PSO-PTS reduce the PAPR to approximately 7.1dB, that is nearly $4\,\text{dB}$ less than the original OFDM signal and greater than the optimum (OPTS) by $0.65\,\text{dB}$. But unfortunately RS-PTS is better than PSO-PTS by nearly 0.2dB

Figure 10 shows how we can enhance the performance of PSO-PTS to outperform RS-PTS by changing the update mechanism of P_g and P_i to be asynchronous rather than synchronous, but it still worse than the RS-PTS. So we add another enhancement to the asynchronous PSO-PTS by limiting the velocity to the search space i.e. from 0 to 2π, it can be noted that PSO-PTS becomes better than RS-PTS by 0.03dB.

Artificial Bee Colony based PTS (ABC-PTS)

ABC algorithm was introduced in 2005 by Karaboga. It simulates honey bees swarm behavior. In ABC there are three components of the swarm namely; employed bees,

Figure 10. Comparison of PAPR reduction performance of Synchronous, Asynchronous and Asynchronous PSO with limitation on velocity along with RS and OPTS.

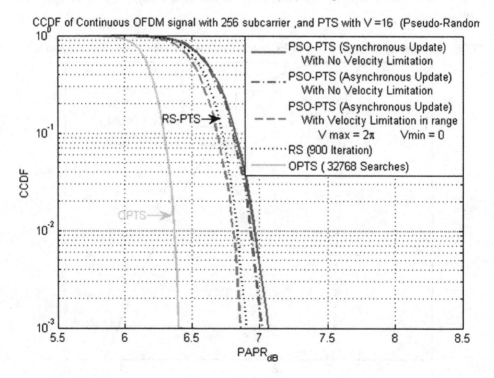

unemployed bees (onlooker or scout bees), and food sources' positions. Employed bees collect nectar amount and position of food sources. Then, employed bees share this information with onlooker bees. Based on this information onlooker bees try to find more worthy sources, while scout bees search solution space randomly. In ABC algorithm process of exploitation is controlled by employed and onlooker bees, while scout bees responsible for exploration process (Ercin, & Coban, 2012). The ABC algorithm is shown below (Ercin, & Coban, 2012; Taşpinar, Karaboğa, Yildirim, & Akay, 2011; Wang et al., 2010)

Algorithm 5. ABC-PTS Algorithm for PAPR Reduction

1. Setup: Set maximum cycles number (*MCN*). Determine population size (*SN*) which equal to number of food sources, employed bees, and onlooker bees. Define *Limit* value, which is the number of visits - determined by the trial counter - after which the food source is considered as exhausted position.

2. Initialization: Generate *SN* random food source positions $\mathbf{b}_i = \begin{bmatrix} b_{i1} & b_{i2} & \cdots & b_{iV} \end{bmatrix}$ where, $i \in [1 : SN]$ and V is the number of PTS subblocks. Determine the amount of nectar (fitness) for each food source position (solution) as follows;

$$\text{Fitness}(b_i) = \frac{1}{1 + f(b_i)} \quad (17)$$

3. For Cycle=1 to *MCN*.

a. For each employed bee find a new food source position $\mathbf{b}'_i$ using;

$$b'_{il} = b_{il} + \varnothing_{il}(b_{il} - b_{kl}) \quad (18)$$

In condition that $i \neq k$. where $k \in [1 : SN]$, $l \in [1 : V]$ and $\varnothing_{il}$ is randomly generated number in the range $\varnothing_{il} \in [-1 : 1]$.

b. Quantize b'_{il} values using for an onlooker using (19) or (20) to be suitable to PTS as ABC not originally designed for CO problems.

$$if\, w = 2: b'_{il} = \begin{cases} 1 & if\, \pi\big/4 \leq b'_{il} < 5\pi\big/4 \\ -1 & else \end{cases} \qquad (19)$$

$$if\ w = 4: b'_{il} = \begin{cases} j & if\ \pi/4 \le b'_{il} < 3\pi/4 \\ -1 & if\ 3\pi/4 \le b'_{il} < 5\pi/4 \\ -j & if\ 5\pi/4 \le b'_{il} < 7\pi/4 \\ 1 & else \end{cases} \quad (20)$$

c. Evaluate the fitness of the new solutions $\mathbf{b'_i}$ using (17).

d. For all employed bees $i \in [1:SN]$

If $f(\mathbf{b'_i}) \le f(\mathbf{b_i})$

$\mathbf{b_i} = \mathbf{b'_i}$

Else

$counter_i = counter_i + 1$

End if

e. Employed bees transfer food sources' positions and their nectar amount to onlooker bees in the colony. Onlooker bees chose food sources based on selection probability $\mathbf{P_i}$ of each food source, as follows;

$$\mathbf{P_i} = \frac{Fitness(\mathbf{b_i})}{\sum_{i=1}^{SN} Fitness(\mathbf{b_i})} \quad (21)$$

Thus, solutions with high probability will be selected by most onlooker bees.

f. Each onlooker bee finds a new food position according to (18), discretize it according to (19) or (20), and evaluate it using (17).

g. Repeat step 3.4 for each onlooker bee $i \in [1:SN]$.

h. For each food source position $i \in [1:SN]$

If $counter_i \ge Limit$

Scout bee will replace this abandoned position by a new one using (22);

$$b_{il} = b_l^{min} + (b_l^{max} - b_l^{min}) * Rand \quad (22)$$

where b_l^{max} and b_l^{min} are the upper and lower bounds for each dimension, respectively.

End if

i. Find the best solution for this cycle $\hat{b}_{Cycle}$.

4. End For.

5. Output the best solution $\hat{b}$ and $f(\hat{b})$ where $\hat{b} = \hat{b}_{MCN}$.

Performance of ABC algorithm is controlled by a three parameters; maximum number of cycles (MCN), population size (SN), and Limit value (Ercin, & Coban, 2012). In the following we will show the influence of these parameters on the performance of ABC-PTS.

The following simulations is done on OFDM system uses 16-QAM, N= 256, and oversampled by factor $L = 4$. PTS with V=16, $W = 2$ and Pseudo-random partitioning is used.

Figure 11 compares the performance of OPTS and the suboptimal search method ABC-PTS, for different number of searches – proportional to computational complexity – (*I= SN * MCN* =30*30=900). The limit value is chosen as 5. We can

Figure 11. Comparison between ABC-PTS and OPTS with search complexity (900 and 1200 searches)

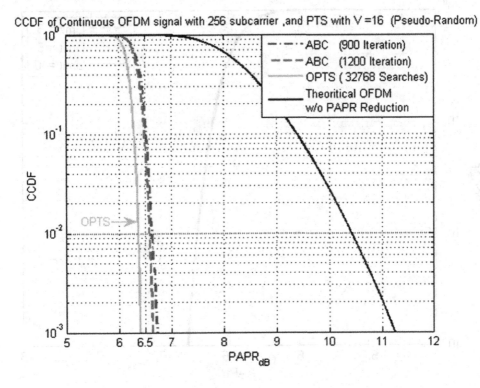

note that at $P_r(PAPR > PAPR_o) = 10^{-3}$ the ABC-PTS reduce the PAPR to approximately $6.8dB$, that is nearly $4.5\,dB$ less than the original OFDM signal and greater than the optimum (OPTS) by $0.35\,dB$.

The effect of increasing the *Limit* value on PAPR reduction gain is studied in Figure 12. As shown the value of *Limit* doesn't affect the PAPR reduction performance.

In ABC algorithm there are $(I = MCN \times SN)$ solutions to be tested to find the near optimum solution (Taşpinar et al., 2011). Thus, increasing *MCN* or *SN* will enhance the PAPR reduction performance of ABC-PTS. But increasing which of them will give the best performance.

Figure 13 Compares PAPR reduction performance for different $(MCN \times SN)$ combinations in two cases. In the first case, number of searches $I = MCN \times SN = 64$ this number can be generated by one of the following combinations

Figure 12. Effect of Limit value on the PAPR reduction performance of ABC-PTS

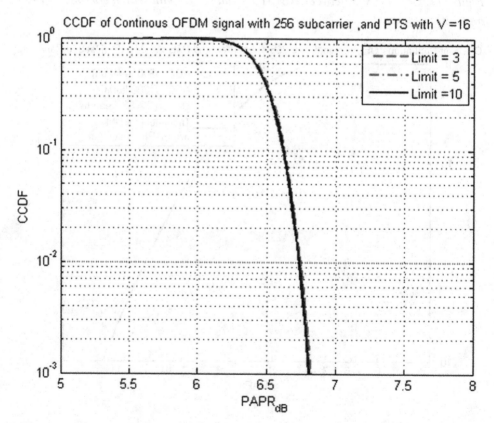

Figure 13. Comparison of PAPR reduction performance of ABC-PTS for different combinations of MCN* SN at two cases (1) 64 searches and (2) 256 searches

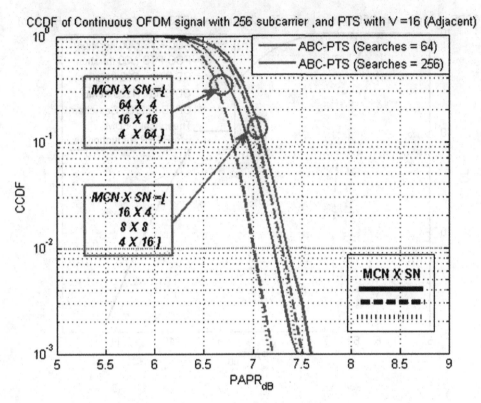

$[4 \times 16, \ 8 \times 8, \ or 16 \times 4]$. Second case MCN $\times$ SN $= 256$ can be generated by one of the following $[4 \times 64, \ 16 \times 16, \ or 64 \times 4]$. It can be noted that, increasing population size (SN) is better than increasing maximum number of cycles (MCN) from PAPR reduction point of view.

Figure 14 compares the performance of ABC-PTS and the other suboptimal search methods for the same computational complexity, with respect to the OPTS. It is clear that ABC-PTS overcomes the others for the same computational complexity.

Finally, it is obvious that for the same search complexity (number of searched solutions) PAPR reduction gain of PTS based on nature inspired metaheuristics methods is better than that of descent heuristics methods and single solution metaheuristics methods (such as SA).

Figure 14. PAPR reduction performance of different heuristics algorithms (ABC, PSO, RS, and GD) along with Optimum PTS.

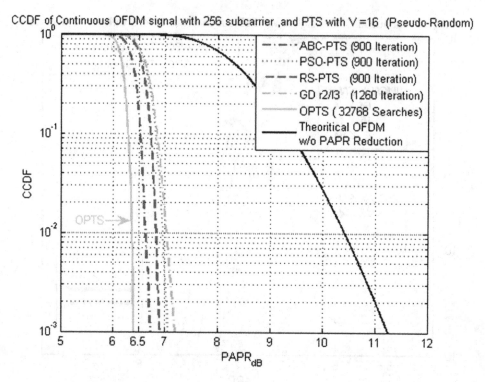

CCDF of Continuous OFDM signal with 256 subcarrier ,and PTS with V =16 (Pseudo-Random)

FUTURE RESEARCH DIRECTIONS

OFDM was used in the 4th generation of mobile while a new wave forms based on multicarrier principles is expected to be used in the 5th generation of mobile such as, Universal Filtered Multi-Carrier (UFMC), Filter Bank Multicarrier (FBMC), and Generalized Frequency Division Multiplexing (GFDM. This new wave forms will also suffer from the high PAPR problem. So, there will be a need for PAPR reduction techniques such as PTS. 5th generation and IoT devices will require high speed processing. Hence, PTS based nature inspired heuristics algorithms will be a candidate solution for PAPR reduction. The other nature inspired heuristics algorithms may be also compared with ABC to find if there is any heuristics algorithm better than it for PTS.

CONCLUSION

In high data rate communication systems, OFDM is usually used to overcome frequency selectivity problem. But, OFDM itself suffer from another problem called high PAPR, which degrades its performance from different aspects. PTS is a powerful PAPR reduction technique. However, it requires high computational complexity. Heuristics optimization is used to find the suboptimal solution for PTS. Heuristics algorithms for PTS can be categorized into metaheuristics and descent heuristics. In this chapter, descent heuristics, such as, IPTS, RS-PTS, and GD-PTS were compared with metaheuristics based PTS techniques. SA was selected as single solution metaheuristics method and PSO and ABC was selected as a nature inspired metaheuristics methods. Results showed that, RS-PTS is the best one among descent-heuristics algorithms. Results also showed that, PTS based on single solution metaheuristics method (*i.e.* SA-PTS) is better than RS-PTS in Low PAPR values which are more frequent. But, RS-PTS outperforms SA-PTS in high PAPR values which are rarely occur. Also, asynchronous PSO-PTS with limitation on velocity outperforms RS-PTS. Results also showed that, ABC-PTS is better than PSO-PTS. Finally it can be said that, PTS based on nature inspired metaheuristics methods is better than PTS that based on descent heuristics and PTS based on single solution metaheuristics methods.

REFERENCES

Cho, Y. S., Kim, J., Yang, W. Y., & Kang, C. G. (2010). *MIMO-OFDM wireless communications with MATLAB*. John Wiley & Sons. doi:10.1002/9780470825631

Cimini, L. J., & Sollenberger, N. R. (2000). Peak-to-Average Power Ratio reduction of an OFDM signal using partial transmit sequences. *IEEE Communications Letters, 4*(3), 86–88. doi:10.1109/4234.831033

Dorigo, M., Montes de Oca, M. A., & Engelbrecht, A. (2008). Particle swarm optimization. *Scholarpedia, 3*(11), 1486. doi:10.4249cholarpedia.1486

Ercin, Ö., & Coban, R. (2012). Identification of linear dynamic systems using the artificial bee colony algorithm. *Turkish Journal of Electrical Engineering & Computer Sciences, 20*(Sup. 1), 1175-1188. doi:10.3906/elk-1012-956

Gao, W. (2011). *Intelligent processing in wireless communications using particle Swarm based methods* (PhD. Dissertation). Syracuse University.

Han, S. H., & Lee, J. H. (2004). PAPR reduction of OFDM signals using a reduced complexity PTS technique. *IEEE Signal Processing Letters, 11*(11), 887–890. doi:10.1109/LSP.2004.833490

Han, S. H., & Lee, J. H. (2005). An overview of peak-to-average power ratio reduction techniques for multicarrier transmission. *IEEE Wireless Communications, 12*(2), 56–65. doi:10.1109/MWC.2005.1421929

Jiang, T., Xiang, W., Richardson, P. C., Guo, J., & Zhu, G. (2007). PAPR Reduction of OFDM Signals Using Partial Transmit Sequences with Low Computational Complexity. *IEEE Transactions on Broadcasting, 53*(3), 719–724. doi:10.1109/TBC.2007.899345

Kang, S. G., Kim, J. G., & Joo, E. K. (1999). A Novel Subblock Partition Scheme for Partial Transmit Sequence OFDM. *IEEE Transactions on Broadcasting, 45*(3), 333–338. doi:10.1109/11.796276

Khademi, S. (2010). *OFDM Peak-to-Average-Power-Ratio Reduction in WiMAX Systems* (MSc. Thesis). Chalmers University of Technology, Goteborg, Sweden.

Mounir, M., Youssef, M. I., & Tarrad, I. F. (2017, December). On the effectiveness of deliberate clipping PAPR reduction technique in OFDM systems. In *2017 Japan-Africa Conference on Electronics, Communications and Computers (JAC-ECC)* (pp. 21-24). IEEE. 10.1109/JEC-ECC.2017.8305769

Müller, S. H., & Huber, J. B. (1997a). OFDM with Reduced Peak–to–Average Power Ratio by Optimum Combination of Partial Transmit Sequences. *Electronics Letters*, *33*(5), 368–369. doi:10.1049/el:19970266

Müller, S. H., & Huber, J. B. (1997b, September). A Novel Peak Power Reduction Scheme for OFDM. In *IEEE Conference Proceedings PIMRC 1997* (pp. 1090-1094). IEEE. 10.1109/PIMRC.1997.627054

Müller, S. H., & Huber, J. B. (1997c, Nov.). A Comparison of Peak Power Reduction Schemes for OFDM. In IEEE GLOBECOM '97 (pp. 1-5). IEEE. doi:10.1109/GLOCOM.1997.632501

Nguyen, T. T., & Lampe, L. (2008). On Partial Transmit Sequences for PAR Reduction in OFDM Systems. *IEEE Transactions on Wireless Communications*, *7*(2), 746–755. doi:10.1109/TWC.2008.060664

Rao, R. S., & Malathi, P. (2019). A novel PTS: Grey wolf optimizer-based PAPR reduction technique in OFDM scheme for high-speed wireless applications. *Soft Computing*, *23*(8), 2701–2712. doi:10.100700500-018-3665-0

Singh, M., & Patra, S. K. (2018). On the PTS Optimization Using the Firefly Algorithm for PAPR Reduction in OFDM Systems. *IETE Technical Review*, *35*(5), 441–455. doi:10.1080/02564602.2018.1505563

Taşpinar, N., Karaboğa, D., Yildirim, M., & Akay, B. (2011). PAPR reduction using artificial bee colony algorithm in OFDM systems. *Turkish Journal of Electrical Engineering and Computer Sciences*, *19*(1), 47–58. doi:10.3906/elk-1003-399

Wang, Y., Chen, W., & Tellambura, C. (2010). A PAPR reduction method based on artificial bee colony algorithm for OFDM signals. *IEEE Transactions on Wireless Communications*, *9*(10), 2994–2999. doi:10.1109/TWC.2010.081610.100047

Wei, S., Goeckel, D. L., & Kelly, P. E. (2002). A modern extreme value theory approach to calculating the distribution of the peak-to-average power ratio in OFDM systems. In *2002 IEEE International Conference on Communications. Conference Proceedings. ICC 2002 (Cat. No. 02CH37333)* (Vol. 3, pp. 1686-1690). IEEE. doi:10.1109/ICC.2002.997136

Wen, J. H., Lee, S. H., Huang, Y. F., & Hung, H. L. (2008). A suboptimal PTS algorithm based on particle swarm optimization technique for PAPR reduction in OFDM systems. *EURASIP Journal on Wireless Communications and Networking*, *2008*(14). doi:10.1155/2008/601346

Yang, X. S. (2010). *Nature Inspired Metaheuristics Algorithms*. Luniver Press.

Youssef, M. I., Tarrad, I. F., & Mounir, M. (2016, December). Performance evaluation of hybrid ACE-PTS PAPR reduction techniques. In *2016 11th International Conference on Computer Engineering & Systems (ICCES)* (pp. 407-413). IEEE. 10.1109/ICCES.2016.7822039

Zhou, J., & Yao, X. (2017). A hybrid approach combining modified artificial bee colony and cuckoo search algorithms for multi-objective cloud manufacturing service composition. *International Journal of Production Research*, 55(16), 4765–4784. doi:10.1080/00207543.2017.1292064

Chapter 5

Optimization of Energy Efficiency in Wireless Sensor Networks and Internet of Things:
A Review of Related Works

Hassan El Alami
National Institute of Posts and Telecommunications (INPT), Rabat, Morocco

Abdellah Najid
National Institute of Posts and Telecommunications (INPT), Rabat, Morocco

ABSTRACT

Energy consumption is a constraint in the design architecture of wireless sensor networks (WSNs) and internet of things (IoT). In order to overcome this constraint, many techniques have been proposed to enhance energy efficiency in WSNs. In existing works, several innovative techniques for the physical, the link, and the network layer of OSI model are implemented. Energy consumption in the WSNs is to find the best compromise of energy consumption between the various tasks performed by the objects, the detection, the processing, and the data communication tasks. It is this last task that consumes more energy. As a result, the main objective for the WSNs and the IoT is to minimize the energy consumed during this task. One of the most used solutions is to propose efficient routing techniques in terms of energy consumption. In this chapter, the authors present a review of related works on energy efficiency in WSNs and IoT. The network layer routing protocols are the main concerns in this chapter. The interest is focused on the issue of designing data routing techniques in WSNs and IoT.

DOI: 10.4018/978-1-7998-1626-3.ch005

INTRODUCTION

In recent years, covering a wide field of application, Wireless Sensor Networks (WSNs) play an important role in collecting data from an environmental context, monitoring, monitoring or other applications. The fact that the network is wireless allows more flexibility for deployment compared to a wired deployment that requires cabling. On the other hand, the WSNs are a very important technology in the Internet of Things (IoT). These networks allow presenting the characteristics and the state of the objects (or environments) in which are implanted (or deployed) like Web services on Internet. Sensors are therefore invited to play the role of hosts of the Internet (often client/server) and communicate with each other and with hosts already connected to the Internet. In addition, the WSNs and IoT are being solicited and must respond to new constraints of WSN and IoT applications. Among these constraints, we can cite:

- **Autonomy:** Sensors and connected objects are usually able to operate autonomously in terms of energy source. The consideration of all the elements contributes to the energy consumption in the electronic circuits of the sensor or object, since the data communication consumes more energy, and again the communication power in terms of transmission to a big effect on the amount of energy used.
- **Mobility:** Sensors or moving objects in the network can move freely and independently. At any time, new equipment can join or leave the network. The change of the topology of a network during the time results from the failures of the sensors or the breaks of the links between them.

In this chapter, we first present a general overview of the WSNs, their architectures, their characteristics, their principal applications, their protocol architecture, their characterized models and their factors, their routing protocols and their constraints. Then we present the IoT, its architecture, its different application domains, its communication paradigms, its life cycle, its constraints related to the deployment and its data routing. Finally, we present the different wireless communication technologies used by the WSNS and the IoT.

WIRELESS SENSOR NETWORKS

WSNs generally consist of a large number of sensors, stationary or mobile, communicating with each other by radio, often randomly deployed in an area of interest (refer Figure 1). The latter is usually a hostile environment, isolated or difficult

Figure 1. Architecture of a WSN

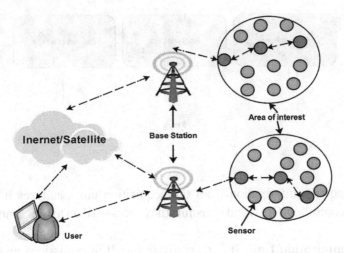

to control, where the mission of a sensor is each time to collect, in an autonomous way, accurate data from the deployment area. Depending on the type of sensor, the information detected may be temperature, humidity or movement or other physical quantity. The data collected by these sensors are routed directly or by other sensors step by step to a base station (BS). The BS can be connected to a data processing server, called a task manager, usually via the Internet or satellite. In addition, the user can address his requests to the sensors by specifying the information of interest and by targeting the sensors that should be interested.

TYPICAL ARCHITECTURE OF A SENSOR

The typical hardware architecture of a sensor consists of four-unit units, an acquisition unit, a processing unit, a communication unit, and a battery, which are shown in figure 2.

The operation of each unit is defined as follows:

- **Acquisition Unit:** It consists of a sensor that obtains measurements on environmental parameters and an analog/digital converter that converts the information collected and transmits it to the processing unit.
- **Processing Unit:** It consists of a processor and a memory integrating a specific operating system. This unit has two interfaces: an interface with the acquisition unit and another with the communication unit. The processing

Figure 2. Sensor architecture

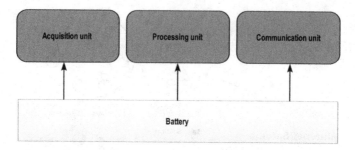

unit acquires information from the acquisition unit, analyzes it through a microcontroller (CPU) and transmits the processed data to the communication unit.

- **Communication Unit:** It is responsible for all transmissions and reception of data via a radio link.
- **Battery:** The sensor has a battery to power all electronic components and units. Generally, in most cases, changing the battery is impossible. For this, energy is the most valuable resource since it has a direct impact on battery life.

In addition, In the technology market, there are several types of commercially available sensors, such as Tmote Sky, MicaZ and TelosB (refer figure 3). Each of the sensors has different properties from the other; table 1 describes the technical characteristics of the three sensors mentioned.

Characteristics of the WSNs

The integration of WSNs with the physical world has made the mode of operation different from that of traditional wireless networks. The WSNs have special features that make the development of applications trivial. Indeed, the WSNs have distinguished characteristics such as:

- **Dynamic Topology:** In mobile WSNs, the sensors move in an arbitrary manner, thus making the topology of the network frequently changing.
- **Constraints of energy, storage and computing:** The most critical feature in the WSNs is the modesty of its energy resources as each sensor in the network is limited by the battery capacity. The challenge in this case is to optimize the energy consumption in WSNs by proposing techniques for maximizing the

Figure 3. Different types of sensors

Tmote Sky   MicaZ   TelosB

network lifetime such as routing protocols. In addition, because of its small size, the sensors are limited in storage capacity.

- **Scaling:** WSNs are characterized by the number of very important sensors. It can even reach thousands or more. The challenge in such a case is that the network is able to maintain its performance with this large number of sensors.
- **Random deployment:** sensors are often randomly distributed, in the case of monitoring natural sites as an example, which requires routing protocols be efficient.
- **Data redundancy:** in the case where the sensors are randomly deployed in the area of interest, the data detected and communicated by multiple or multiple sensors near the same target captured are redundant. This leads to a waste of resources such as energy, bandwidth and memory.

WSNS APPLICATIONS

WSNs are currently used in a number of diverse and continuously expanding application areas (Taruna, S., Jain, K., & Purohit, G. N., 2011). The miniaturization

Table 1. Technical characteristics of the sensors

Sensor	Microcontroller	Horloge (MHz)	RAM (Ko)	Radio	Battery
Tmote Sky	MSP430	7.37	10	CC2420	2 x AA
MicaZ	ATmega 128I	7.37	4	CC2420	2 x AA
TelosB	MSP430	8	10	CC2420	2 x AA

of micro-sensors, the reduction in their cost, the widening of the range of available sensor types (thermal, optical, speed, etc.) and the evolution of wireless communication technologies have diversified the fields of applications of WSNs. In this context, the WSNs can be used in different areas, such as military, environmental, medical and home automation. Figure 4 shows examples of applications of WSNs.

Military Applications

The military field has been a fundamental axis for the development of the WSNs. The latter can be quickly deployed into a battlefield or hostile region without any infrastructure. Because of their ease of deployment, self-organization and fault tolerance, the WSNs will play greater role in future military systems and make future wars more intelligent with less human involvement. The Distributed Sensor Network (DSN) project (Aceto, G., Botta, A., De Donato, W., & Pescapè, A., 2013) at the Defense Advanced Research Projects Agency (DARPA) was one of the first projects in the 1980s that used the WSNs to collect distributed data. Researchers at the Lawrence Livermore National Laboratory at the University of California applied the Wide Area Tracking System (WATS) (ranjal, J., Monteiro, E., & Silva, J. S., 2015). This network is composed of gamma-ray detectors and neutrons to

Figure 4. WSNs applications

Military applications

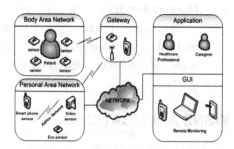

Medical applications

Environmental applications

Home Automation applications

detect and detect nuclear devices. It is able to perform constant monitoring of an area of interest. It uses data aggregation methods to report them to a smart center. The researchers then set up another network called Joint Biological Remote Early Warning System (JBREWS) (Fleisch, E., 2010) to warn troops in the battlefield of possible biological attacks.

Medical Applications

In the field of medicine, the WSN can be used to permanently monitor the vital organs of the human being through micro-sensors that can be swallowed or implanted under the skin (blood glucose monitoring, cancer detection, etc.). This network can also facilitate the diagnosis of some diseases by performing physiological measurements such as blood pressure and heartbeat using sensors each having a specific task. The physiological data collected by the sensors can be stored for a long time for tracking a patient (Koch, S., 2006). On the other hand, these networks can detect abnormal behaviors (falling of a bed, shock, cry, etc.) in dependent persons (disabled or elderly). Recently, the Wireless Body Area Network (WBAN) (Jovanov, E., Milenkovic, A., Otto, C., & De Groen, P. C., 2005) technology has attracted the attention of many researchers and industry. WBAN is a radio-frequency based wireless network technology that involves interconnecting micro-sensors on, around or in the human body. These sensors can act as actuators.

Environmental Applications

Environmental monitoring is one of the first WSNs applications (Jang, W. S., & Healy, W. M., 2009). In environmental monitoring, sensors are used to monitor a variety of parameters or environmental conditions. For example, the distribution of thermo-sensors in a forest can help detect a possible start of fire and subsequently facilitate the fight against wildfires before their spread. The distribution of chemical sensors in urban settings can help detect pollution and analyze air quality and water quality. Similarly, their deployment in industrial sites prevents industrial risks such as leakage of toxic products.

PROTOCOL ARCHITECTURE OF WSNs

In WSNs, the protocol stack is a particular application of a set of protocols where each stack layer relies on those below to provide additional communication functionality. In this type of network, no protocol stack has been standardized. However, the protocol stack proposed by article (Akyildiz, I. F., Su, W., Sankarasubramaniam, Y., & Cayirci, E., 2002) is taken up by the majority of the works dealing with the theme of the WSNs. figure 5 shows the protocol stack used by the WSNs. This protocol stack includes the application layer, the transport layer, the network layer, the data link layer, the physical layer, the energy management plan, the mobility management plan, and the task management plan. Depending on the type of sensors, different applications can be used and built on the application layer (Schott, W., Gluhak, A., Presser, M., Hunkeler, U., & Tafazolli, R., 2007).

Roles of Layers

- **Physical Layer:** It deals with the specification of wireless support, carrier frequencies, etc. This layer meets the needs of simple but robust modulation, and transmission and reception techniques. At the physical layer level, the power dissipation may be affected by the application environment, the choice of the type of modulation, or the frequency band used. It is beneficial in terms of energy that researchers in the physical layer choose a multi-hop transmission rather than a direct transmission that requires significant transmission power (Akyildiz, I. F., Su, W., Sankarasubramaniam, Y., & Cayirci, E., 2002).

Figure 5. Protocol stack of WSNs

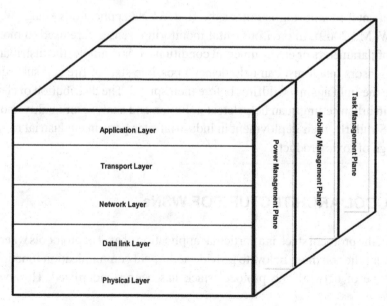

- **Link Layer:** Specifies how data is sent between two sensors in a distance of one hop. It consists of two sub-layers: the Logical Link Control (LLC) sub-layer and the Media Access Control (MAC) sub-layer.

- **Network Layer:** This layer is used to manage the addressing and routing of data in the network. The routing of data in this type of network often uses the multi-jumps of the emitter sensor to the receiver sensor considering the specificities of WSNs. In addition, traditional Ad hoc network routing protocols are incompatible with WSNs due to energy and scalability constraints (Akkaya, K., & Younis, M., 2005). In the WSNs, the metrics considered in path cost optimization are: the residual energy of each network sensor (Akyildiz, I. F., Su, W., Sankarasubramaniam, Y., & Cayirci, E., 2002), the energy level required to transmit the data and the data routing time. The most used addressing in WSNs is geographic addressing.

- **Transport Layer:** This layer is responsible for data transport, flow control, order conservation of data, and management of any transmission errors. The User Datagram Protocol (UDP) remains the most common protocol between a sending sensor and the receiving sensor. Among other things, the use of the Transmission Control Protocol (TCP) is avoided due to the small size of sensor memory that does not allow it to store large amounts of information for the management of the task communication.

- **Application Layer:** it interfaces with the applications. This is the level closest to the users. Many configuration profiles can be used in this layer. In addition, several protocols have been proposed in the literature such as the Sensor Query and Data Dissemination Protocol (SQDDP) that allows the user to query the network based on the geographical position of the sensors (Akyildiz, I. F., Su, W., Sankarasubramaniam, Y., & Cayirci, E., 2002) and the Sensor Management Protocol (SMP) allows the user to implement administrative tasks related to network configuration, sensor operation, synchronization between sensors and sensor movement.

Management Plans

- **Power Management Plane:** The functions integrated at this level consist in controlling and managing the energy consumption in the sensors. Therefore, a sensor can for example turn off its reception interface as soon as it receives information from a neighboring sensor to avoid receiving duplicate information. In addition, when a sensor has a low energy level, it can send an alert to other sensors informing them that they cannot participate in routing tasks, and keep the remaining energy in the detection capabilities.

- **Mobility Management Plane:** This plan is responsible for detecting and recording the movements of the sensors, so as to enable them to keep a continuous path towards the end user, and to maintain a recent view of neighboring sensors. This vision is necessary to be able to balance the execution of the tasks and the energy consumption.

- **Task Management Plane:** During a target detection operation in a specific region, it is not necessary for all sensors in that region to perform the detection task in synchronized mode. Some sensors do the task of detection more than others and this depending on whether their remaining energy is sufficient or not. It basically depends on the nature of the sensor, its energy level and the region in which it was distributed.

CHARACTERISTIC MODELS OF WSNS

Detection Model

The binary disc model (Kone, C. T., 2011) is one of the simplest detection models. This model assumes that a sensor is able to detect only events and targets within its detection range. In this model, the detection range of each sensor is equivalent to the detection radius (or range) Rd in a circular disk.

The binary disc model extension has been proposed in the work (Zou, Y., & Chakrabarty, K., 2003) under the name "probabilistic sensing model" illustrated in figure 6. This probabilistic model reflects the uncertain action of sensor detection such as infrared or ultrasonic sensors.

In this model, if R_u is an uncertain detection zone radius of a sensor C such as $R_u < R_d$ then a sensor could detect with probability p an event or target located in an area between $R_d - R_u$ and $R_d + R_u$. The probability of coverage of a point Z by a sensor C is expressed by equation (1).

$$P(C) = \begin{cases} 0, & R_d + R_u \leq dist(C,Z) \\ e^{-w\alpha^\beta}, & R_d - R_u \prec dist(C,Z) \prec R_d + R_u \\ 1, & R_d + R_u \geq dist(C,Z) \end{cases} \tag{1}$$

Where,

Figure 6. Probabilistic sensing model

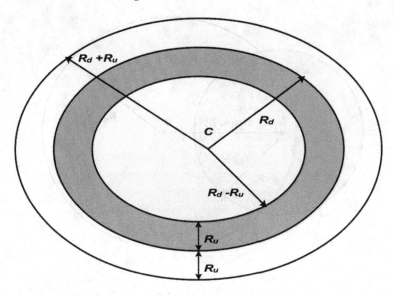

$$\alpha = dist(C, Z) - (R_d - R_u) \tag{2}$$

Where and are parameters that are used to measure the probabilities of detecting an event at a certain sensing range of a sensor and *dist (C, Z)* is a distance between the C sensor and the Z point. will be able to say that all the points are covered by a given sensor if they are at a distance below $(R_d + R_u)$ of this sensor, and all the points being in the interval $[R_d - R_u, R_d + R_u]$ have a coverage (<1) that decreases exponentially with distance. However, the points are covered or not covered, beyond a distance $(R_d + R_u)$.

Communication Model

The performance of a wireless network is determined by the wireless communication channel in which it operates. In WSNs, the sensors communicate at low power and therefore the radio links are very unreliable. Therefore the modeling of the communication proves very difficult. Figure 7 shows a unidirectional wireless link between two A and B sensors based on the "binary disc" model (Kone, C. T., 2011). In this model, we assume each A sensor is able to transmit its data to any sensor within its communication range noted Ra. The range of communication of each sensor varies according to the level of its transmission power.

Figure 7. Binary disc model

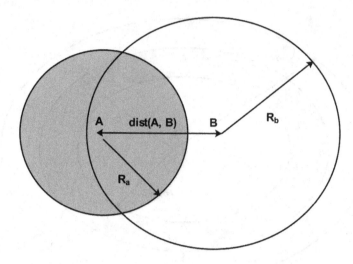

Thus, authors assume that two sensors A and B can communicate symmetrically if and only if the Euclidean distance between them is as small as at least their communication ranges (i.e, *dist (A, B) <min (R_a, R_b)*). The communication between the sensors, in the "binary disc" model, is therefore purely based on geometrical considerations. According to this model, the power loss of the signal noted *PL (d)* (including antenna gains) is a deterministic function PL_o *(d)* of the distance d between the sensors. The function PL_o *(d)* is expressed in decibel as indicated by equation (3).

$$PL_o(d) = PL(d_o) + 10.\eta.\log_{10}(\frac{d}{d_o})$$ (3)

Where d_o is the reference distance, is the propagation loss coefficient, $PL(d_o)$ is the attenuation due to the attenuation at the reference distance d_o. The received single power (P_r), at a distance d, is the output power of the transmitter (P_t) minus propagation attenuation $PL(d)$, could be obtained as indicated by the following equation:

$$P_r = P_t - PL(d_o)$$ (4)

In some types of WSNs applications such as mobility, environment and obstacles; certain physical phenomena have been generated, such as interference, diffusion, diffraction and reflection which degrade the quality of the signal. Thus, in scientific literature, some studies have presented statistical models of radio propagation taking into account these different physical phenomena. As an example, the "log normal shadowing path loss" model considers "shadowing" and multipath effects, the Signal-to-Noise Ratio model (SNR) considers the background noise on the signal, or the Signal-to-Interference-plus-Noise Ratio model (SINR) considers the effects of interference and noise on the signal.

In the log-normal shadowing path loss model (Rappaport, T. S., 1996), the propagation attenuation at a distance of *PL(d)* is presented as shown in equation (5).

$$PL(d) = PL_o(d) + X_\sigma = PL(d_o) + 10.\eta.\log_{10}(\frac{d}{d_o}) + X_\sigma \tag{5}$$

With the parameters $d_o, d,$ and $PL(d_o)$ defined previously, is a Gaussian distribution of zero mean (in *dB*) with a standard deviation to model the effect of shadowing. Another element that has been considered for determining the behavior of wireless communication is the background noise. Indeed, the temperature of the environment influences the thermal noise generated by the antennas of the receiver and the transmitter. According to (El Alami, H., & Najid, A., 2018), when the transmitter and receiver antennas have the same ambient temperature, then the background noise could be expressed as follows:

$$P_n = (F + 1).k.T_o.B \tag{6}$$

Where *F* is the noise factor, *k* is the Boltzmann constant, to the ambient temperature, and *B* is the noise bandwidth. In the *SNR* model (Zuniga, M., & Krishnamachari, B., 2004) for a P_t output power of the transmitter, the *SNR*, in *dB*, at a distance *d* is given as equation (7).

$$SNR(d) = P_t - PL(d) - P_n \tag{7}$$

Where the expression of *PL(d)* is the same as that of the log normal shadowing path loss model defined in equation (8).

In (Moscibroda, T., & Wattenhofer, R., 2006), the SINR model assumes that a sensor cannot correctly receive a signal even if it is close to the transmitter due to the effects of interference and noise. Therefore, if $P_r(A)$ designates the power of the signal received by a node B from a node A, and N denotes the density of the noise, then the sensor B correctly receives the signal if the ratio of the power of the received signal and the sum of the powers of the noise and interference is greater than a certain threshold which is expressed as follows:

$$\frac{P_r(A)}{N + \sum_{n_k \in \psi / n_i} P_r(n_k)} \geq SINR_\theta \tag{8}$$

Where ψ denotes to all sensors.

Model of Energy Consumption

The energy consumption in a sensor is usually done during detection, data processing and communication. Thus, the expression of this energy could be given by the following formula (Akkaya, K., & Younis, M., 2005):

$$E_{Total} = E_{Detection} + E_{Acquisition} + E_{Communication} \tag{9}$$

- **Detection Energy:** This is the energy consumed by a sensor during the activation and data collection state. The cost of this energy depends on the type of sensor (image, sound, temperature, etc.) and tasks (data collection, sampling and conversion of physical signals into electrical signals, etc.) assigned to it.
- **Communication Energy:** This is the energy consumed by a sensor when activating its communication units (transmitter/receiver). This energy is much more consumed than that of detection. This energy is available in transmission energy and reception energy. It is determined by the amount of data to be communicated and the transmission distance, as well as by the physical properties of the radio module. The emission of a signal is characterized by its power. Indeed, when the power of emission is high, the signal will have a great range and the consumed energy will be important. The transmission of a bit of information can consume as much as the execution of a few thousand instructions has been presented in (Pottie, G. J., & Kaiser, W. J. 2000). The most used model to estimate only the energy consumed by a sensor to transmit an information bit to another sensor located at a distance d is expressed as follows (Heinzelman, W. R., Chandrakasan, A., & Balakrishnan, H., 2000):

$$E(d) = d^{\alpha} + c \qquad\qquad (10)$$

Where $\alpha \geq 2$ is the propagation attenuation exponent according to environment and $c \geq 0$ is constant which illustrates the energy required to transmit a quantity of detected data. This model simplifies the energy dissipation in transmission while a sensor also consumes energy in reception and even when it is at rest or listening without reception. In the energy consumption model for communication energy, we distinguish four modes of sensor operation (Emission T_x, Reception R_x, Idle listening, and Sleep) and a state of transition between operating modes called Switch. For a given sensor, the energy cost for each of its operating modes is denoted $E_{T_x}(k,d)$, $E_{R_x}(k)$, E_{idle}, E_{sleep}, and E_{sw}, respectively; where k is the number of cocks in a message. Figure 8 shows antenna and power consumption models by a sensor for communication (Heinzelman, W. R., Chandrakasan, A., & Balakrishnan, H., 2000).

To send a message of k bits over a distance d, the energy consumed is given by the following formula:

$$E_{T_x}(k,d) = E_{T_x}(k) + E_{T_x-amp}(k,d) \qquad\qquad (11)$$

Where E_{T_x-amp} is amplification energy during the burst phase.

The energy consumed to receive a message of k bits is given by the formula below:

$$E_{R_x}(k) = E_{elec}.k \qquad\qquad (12)$$

Figure 8. Power consumption model for communication

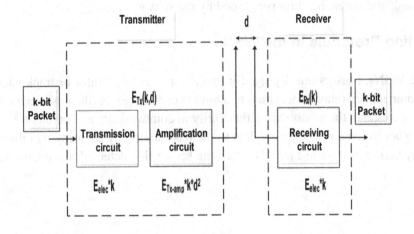

Where E_{elec} is the transmission energy / electronic reception.

The energies dissipated by the sensor given in Idle listening, Sleep, and Switch mode are given by the following formulas:

$$E_{idle} = I_{idle}.V_b.T_{idle} \tag{13}$$

$$E_{sleep} = I_{sleep}.V_b.T_{sleep} \tag{14}$$

$$E_{sw} = I_{sw}.V_b.T_{sw} \tag{15}$$

Where, I_{idle}, I_{sleep}, and I_{sw}, respectively are the current intensity for the Idle listening, Sleep, and Switch modes. T_{idle}, T_{sleep}, and T_{sw} are the switching time for Idle listening, Sleep, and Switch modes, respectively. V_b represents the voltage supplied by the energy source (i.e., the battery).

- **Data Acquisition Energy: This is the energy consumed by a sensor when activating its data processing unit (CPU). The data processed by the sensors are scalar types such as temperature, humidity, pressure, etc. So the energy consumed for data acquisition is lower than the communication energy.**

In addition, the energy required to emit *1 kb* over a distance of 100 m is almost equivalent to the energy required to execute 3 million instructions with a speed of 100 million instructions per second. Figure 9 illustrates the energy consumed for each task and for each action performed by the sensor.

Routing Protocols in the WSNs

In the WSNs, sensors are deployed in large numbers to monitor or track such an environment and relay information to a remote control center (the base station). To achieve this end, the sensors have the ability to communicate and collaborate with each other to route the collected data to the base station by ensuring its reliability and by taking the shortest path between the sensor that detected this phenomenon

Figure 9. Energy consumption by a sensor

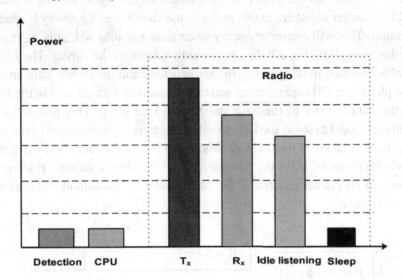

and the base station. This operation allows the routing of information between the sensors and the base station then and it consists of finding the shortest routes. In this context, several routing protocols have been proposed in literatures such as flat routing protocols, geographic routing protocols and hierarchical routing protocols (Al-Karaki, J. N., & Kamal, A. E., 2004). In addition, the constraints presented in the WSNs have given rise to different routing protocols than those of the Ad-hoc networks since the energy constraint arises strongly in the WSNs. As a result, the routing protocols designed for the RCSFs must ensure the routing of data between any network sensor and the base station at a lower cost in terms of energy. The deployment of sensors depends on the application of RCSFs. It can be completely random as in the case of surveillance (monitoring of natural sites for example) where the number of sensors is important. In this case, hierarchical routing protocols can be used.

LEACH Protocol

Low Energy Adaptive Clustering Hierarchy (LEACH) (Heinzelman, W. B., Chandrakasan, A. P., & Balakrishnan, H., 2002) is one of the first hierarchical and proactive protocols based on the clustering algorithm for homogeneous WSNs.

Clustering is based on the power of the announcement signal sent by the cluster head (CH). Cluster members in this protocol use the CHs as a gateway to reach the base station. This will conserve energy since transmissions will only be made by CHs rather than all nodes. All data processing is local to the cluster. The LEACH protocol is executed in two phases: the set-up phase and the steady state phase. In the first phase, the CHs are selected and the clusters are formed, and in the second phase, the data transfer to the base station will take place. This protocol uses a probabilistic model to select the CHs to balance the energy dissipation of the nodes. This decision is taken by the node by choosing a random number between 0 and 1. The node becomes a CH for the current round if the chosen number is lower than the threshold $T(n)$ (refer equation (16)), otherwise the node should join the nearest CH in its vicinity.

$$T(n) = \begin{cases} \dfrac{p}{1 - p.(r \bmod (\frac{1}{p}))} & \text{si } n \in G \\ 0 & \text{sinon} \end{cases} \tag{16}$$

Where p is the desired percentage of the CHs, r is the current round and G is the set of nodes that have not been CHs in the last $1/p$ rounds.

TEEN Protocol

The Threshold-sensitive Energy Efficient Sensor Network (TEEN) protocol (Manjeshwar, A., & Agrawal, D. P., 2001) is a hierarchical and reactive clustering protocol that has been designed for critical applications where the change of some parameters may be abrupt. The network structure is based on a multilevel hierarchical grouping where the closest sensors form clusters. Then this clustering process goes to the second level until the base station is reached. After clustering, each CH sends two thresholds to cluster members; a Hard Threshold (HT) representing the threshold value of the parameter monitored and a soft threshold is a small variation of the value of the monitored parameter. The occurrence of this small Soft Threshold (ST) variation allows the sensor that detects it to signal it to the base station by transmitting an alert message. Therefore, the soft threshold will minimize the number of transmissions since it does not allow transmission if there is little or no change in the value of the monitored parameter. At the beginning, the sensors listen to the medium continuously and when the sensed value of the monitored parameter exceeds the HT, the sensor transmits the data. The captured value is stored in an internal variable called the detected value. Then, the sensors will send data only if the current value of the monitored parameter is greater than the HT value or differs from the detected value by an amount equal to or greater than the ST value. Since the sending of data consumes more energy than the detection of the data, then the energy dissipation in the TEEN protocol is less important than in proactive protocols or those that transmit data periodically

SEP Protocol

Stable Election Protocol (SEP) (Smaragdakis, G., Matta, I., & Bestavros, A., 2004) uses the clustering and assume that all nodes were equipped with the same initial energy. In order to take full advantage of the heterogeneity of the nodes, SEP is a hierarchical and proactive protocol based on the clustering algorithm for heterogeneous WSNs. It defines two levels of energy. Based on these energy levels, the nodes are classified into two types, normal nodes and advanced nodes. Nodes having more energy times than normal nodes are called advanced nodes. Therefore, advanced nodes are more preferred for selection of CHs because of their assigned probability weights. The probability of the normal nodes p_n differs from the advanced nodes p_a as follows:

$$P_n = \frac{p}{1+a.m} \tag{17}$$

$$P_a = \frac{p.(1+a)}{1+a.m} \tag{18}$$

Where m is the fraction of advanced nodes. From equations (17) and (18), it is clear that advanced nodes are more likely to select CHs than normal ones.

DEEC Protocol

Design of Distributed Energy Efficient Clustering Protocol (DEEC) (Qing, L., Zhu, Q., & Wang, M., 2006). It is protocol proactive and has been proposed for heterogeneous WSNs. In this protocol, the nodes are equipped with different energy levels at the start of the network operation. The selection of CHs is based on the ratio of the residual energy of a node to the average energy of the network. Nodes with higher residual energy are more likely to be CH. This makes the energy distribution even among the nodes. The DEEC protocol extends the period of network stability because nodes with more residual energy frequently become CHs. Cluster formation in the DEEC is similar to that of LEACH. However, the probability that the nodes become CHs is different. This probability is given by the equation (19).

$$P(i) = \frac{p_{opt}.N.(1+a).E_i(r)}{(N + \sum_{i=1}^{i_{max}} a_i).\overline{E(r)}} \tag{19}$$

Where p_{opt} is the desired probability of CHs, N is the number of nodes, $E_i(r)$ is the residual energy of a node, and $\overline{E(r)}$ is the average energy of the network.

WSNS CONSTRAINTS

The design and realization of the RCSFs depend on several constraints influencing the performance of WSNs. The main constraints are summarized in the following points:

- **Material Constraints:** Generally, the sizes of the sensors are rather reduced, as well as the resistance of the sensor to the likely breaks and accidents. On the other hand, the sensors also have a limited processing capacity. Indeed, manufacturers want to make simple, small and inexpensive sensors that can be mass marketed.
- **Security:** The WSNs are more affected by the security factor than traditional networks. This is justified by the physical challenges and constraints that make the control of the information transmitted must be reduced. Military and medical applications require a very high level of security. Cryptography techniques designed for this type of network must take into account the limited resources that they present.
- **Data Redundancy:** In most cases, the WSNs being quite large, this means that sensors that are fairly close in terms of distance can detect the same events or the same information. These last ones are very correlated spatially

and temporally. This can generate redundant information transmitted to the base station and also to the user. The reduction of the redundancy of data transmitted by the sensors makes it possible to minimize the energy consumption in the network and thus to optimize its lifetime (El Alami, H., & Najid, A., 2019).

- **Energy Consumption:** Typically, changing the sensor battery is almost impossible in most WSNs applications. Thus, it is difficult to replace the batteries after unloading. As a result, the energy consumption at the sensor level has a large impact on the lifetime of the network. Several techniques are proposed to optimize the energy consumption in these networks. These techniques are applied either at the physical layer, at the link layer or at the network layer.

INTERNET OF THINGS

According to the International Telecommunication Union (ITU), the IoT is a global network for the information society, providing advanced services by interconnecting objects through existing evolution in interoperable information and communication technologies (ITU, 2018).

The IoT is a combination of a number of advanced technologies, which will radically change our societies in a few years (Cui, X., 2016). In (Bandyopadhyay, D., & Sen, J., 2011), the main technology pilots, potential applications and challenges related to IoT were presented. The fundamental problems identified are interoperability and interconnected objects. They allow adaptation and autonomous behaviors with confidence, security and privacy of users. A research group called *IPSo Alliance* has been promoting the use of IP for intelligent miniature object networks. Numerous research works followed one another and all focused on achieving, in the best conditions, the design of the WSNs, the vision of the IoT and leading it to maturity despite all the challenges raised.

IoT Architecture

According to (Atzori, L., Iera, A., & Morabito, G., 2010), the IoT architecture is organized into three main layers: the data perception layer, the network layer, and the application layer. Figure 10 represents such architecture.

Figure 10. Architecture of IoT

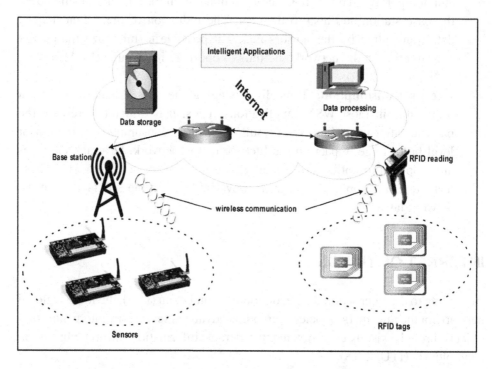

Perception Layer

The perception layer, at the lower level in the hierarchy, is responsible for collecting data in their environment. This layer thus comprises the device necessary to achieve the collection of contextual data of the connected objects, namely the sensors, the RFID tags, cameras, etc.

Network Layer

The network layer is responsible for the reliable communication of the data produced in the perception layer as well as the assurance of connected inter-object connection and between smart objects and the other devices of the Internet. Sometimes the data from the perception layer is huge because the number of objects connected to the Internet is increasing rapidly. For this, it is necessary to offer data storage techniques and data processing on the Internet. This is ensured by Cloud Computing services which provide elastic management of storage and processing resources on data centers residing on the Internet and which are able to effectively absorb the data load generated by the IoT.

Application Layer

The application layer defines service profiles and data management techniques of different types, from different objects (sensors, RFID tags, etc.). In addition, according to (Granjal, J., Monteiro, E., & Silva, J. S., 2015), the IoT architecture can be extended to a fourth layer called the middleware layer between the application layer and the other two layers. The middleware layer serves as an interface between the hardware layer and the applications. This layer includes quite complicated functionalities allowing the management of the objects, and also the aggregation, the analysis of data and the control of access to the services.

IOT APPLICATIONS

IoT is the subject of many development applications. Some of them are the improved version of the CWHN applications and some are completely new and have already been implemented. Most areas of application translate into a high level of quality of life. Industrial automation and environmental monitoring applications have found new opportunities and new service areas using IoT. Figure 11 shows some areas of IoT applications (Leblium, 2018).

Smart Cities

Smart Cities refers to cities that use information and communication technologies to improve the quality of urban services and the standard of living of people. Smart cities include the following services:

- **Smart Parking:** Monitoring the availability of parking spaces in the city.
- **Structural Health:** Monitoring of vibrations and physical conditions in buildings, bridges and historic monuments.
- **Smartphone Detection:** Detect phone devices and in general any device that operates with WiFi or Bluetooth interfaces.
- **Intelligent Lighting:** Intelligent lighting adapted to the weather conditions in the street lamps.
- **Smart Roads:** Smart highways with warning and diversion messages depending on weather conditions and unexpected events such as accidents or traffic jams.

Figure 11. Applications of IoT

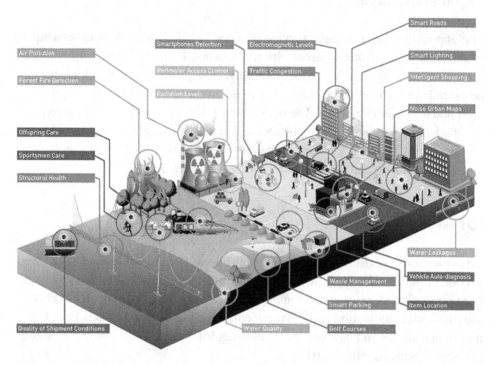

Smart Environment

Smart Environments are spaces in which WSNs and the Internet have been integrated, to react to events and monitor them. They gave rise to the following applications:

- **Forest Fire Detection:** Flue gas monitoring and pre-emptive fire conditions to define warning zones.
- **Air Pollution:** Control of CO_2 emissions from factories, pollution emitted by cars and toxic gases generated on farms.
- **Landslide and Avalanche Prevention:** Monitoring of soil moisture, vibration, and density to detect hazardous patterns in field conditions.
- **Early Detection of Earthquake:** Distributed control in specific locations of tremors.

Smart Metering

The Smart Metering is a meter that has a technology called Automated Meter Reading (AMR) (Kelley, R. H., Carpenter, R. C., Lunney, R. H., & Martinez, M., 2000). For example, it measures the amount of electricity consumption, gas water in a precise and detailed way in real time. The data is transmitted by radio waves or Power-Line Communication (PLC) to the metering network manager. Smart meters are used in different areas:

- **Smart Grid:** Monitoring and management of energy consumption in power grids.
- **Photovoltaic Installations:** Monitoring and optimization of performance in solar power plants.
- **Water Flow:** Measurement of water pressure in water transport systems.

COMMUNICATION PARADIGMS FOR IOT

As IoT is communicating objects across the unified Internet, objects can be humans and intelligent machines of all kinds. These objects can connect as shown in figure 12 which illustrates three connectivity paradigms in the IoT: (i) Machine-to-Machine (M2M), (ii) Machine-to-Human (M2H) and (iii) Human-to-Human (H2H).

Figure 12. Paradigms of communication in the IoT

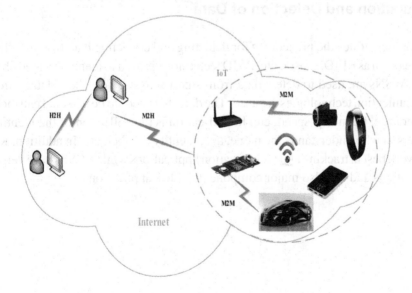

- **Machine-to-Machine (M2M) Connectivity:** This type of connectivity occurs when a machine (object) wants to share its collected data with another machine. For example, the temperature controller in the car asks its buzzer to turn on or off when the timer is triggered. This type of connectivity is the soul of the IoT environment. It achieves the main goal of the IoT to modernize an individual's life to make it better. This broader connectivity can be developed in the following categories that actually imply this M2M communication.
- **Machine-to-Human Connectivity (M2H):** This connectivity is used when a machine must provide important information in response to all requests to humans or when humans need to connect with the machine to control it. For example, when the owner enters the house, the garage door confirms his entry by sending a message to the owner.
- **Human-to-Human Connectivity (H2H):** This type of connection is used when a human connects with other humans to build and enjoy social relationships. They share pictures and every moment of their life with other humans. To do this, they must connect to the Internet.

LIFE CYCLE OF IOT

In IoT, smart objects go through four phases: (i) Data Acquisition and Detection, (ii) Data Communication, (iii) Data Processing and Information Management, and (iv) Actions and use of data in applications. These four phases are briefly described in the following subsections.

Acquisition and Detection of Data

This phase defines the procedures for detecting and collecting data from intelligent devices such as RFID, sensor, etc. RFID technology is used to identify tagged objects while WSNs are used to detect data from smart sensors. To collect data, wireless communication technologies are used. The data that needs to be detected can include temperature, humidity, speed, etc. Identification is the collection of the identity of the person who understands the name, age, identity number, etc. In addition, RFID tags work best in tracking and identification applications while RCSFs have versatile applications and are also major components in IoT applications.

Data Transmission

The transmission of collected data to applications of user is done by wireless communication technologies. So, techniques are needed to deal with heterogeneity (different types of sensors, tags, etc.), address the large number of devices and use IPv6 addressing to ensure device scalability.

Data Processing and Information Management

This phase consists of the compute units and methods that process and analyze the collected data that is generated by the IoT objects, so effective axes are needed like Cloud Computing, Big Data and Data Analytics to manage and store this data.

Data analysis

In this last phase, mechanisms are proposed to use the processed data by transmitting them to actuation applications. These applications are different services such as activity recognition of patients with Alzheimer's disease, fire detection and triggering by an actuator, detection of a suspicious person, etc. This can be achieved through artificial intelligence.

IOT ARCHITECTURE REQUIREMENTS

The IoT is a concept that is both advantageous and promising, and that will be able to propose effective solutions to the problems of monitoring and surveillance in different fields of application. However, the IoT raises some requirements and challenges. In literatures (Al-Fuqaha, A., Guizani, M., Mohammadi, M., Aledhari, M., & Ayyash, M., 2015), specific requirements and challenges are introduced in the following subsections.

Scalability

As the IoT plans to connect thousands of low power devices through the Internet, it imposes new challenges on the underlying architecture in scalability. That is, the architecture of the IoT must support thousands of devices efficiently. Current solutions such as IPv6 have a large address space that can be used for IoT devices. Addressing IoT devices is not the only problem; one of the other challenges in IoT is the large amount of data used by IoT devices that requires better scalability management.

Mobility

The number of mobile devices connected to the Internet exceeds fixed devices. Mobile devices like tablets, smart phones have a limited life. Some IoT applications involve and require anytime, anywhere users want to check their email and/or make calls anywhere, anytime. To provide fast and reliable connectivity and make data available everywhere, the network architecture should support mobility and roaming.

Security and Confidentiality

In some scenarios of IoT such as smart health and smart hospital, the data that needs to be transmitted is very sensitive. If a hacker tries to change them, this can lead to an alarming situation. To enable the IoT to be more effective in terms of security, it should ensure authorization, confidentiality and integrity.

Data Availability

In the TCP/IP model, whenever a node moves from one place to another, the data it supposed to provide becomes unavailable. The same case also occurs when a device whose battery is exhausted is not able to transmit data. Additionally, Internet users can not receive data at this time due to the occurrence of a Denial of Service (DoS) attack. The DoS attack occurs because the current architecture of the Internet cannot control the data according to demand while transmitting this data.

Energetic Efficiency

Obviously, thousands of devices, especially sensors, need a huge amount of energy to perform IoT tasks. In addition, most objects have a low autonomy as the sensors. Energy efficiency mechanisms are therefore needed to make this universal connectivity possible in the form of IoT.

ROUTING IN IOT

Routing in IoT is the vital feature that ensures the smooth routing of data between objects in the same network. In addition, the routing protocol is a key element to ensure optimum communication between these objects, because it allows for each object to decide how to join another object. Constraints on objects (low power, unstable communications) must be taken into account for the development of appropriate routing protocols. In this section, authors present the Routing Protocol for Low Power and Lossy Networks (RPL), specially designed for IoT.

RPL Protocol

RPL protocol (Winter, T., Thubert, P., Brandt, A., Hui, J., Kelsey, R., Levis, P., & Alexander, R. 2012) is an IPv6 routing protocol for low-power, high-loss IoT networks. It forms a dynamic, optimized topology with loop avoidance and consideration of QoS parameters for IPv6 datagram between source and destination. Each gateway sensor behaves like an IP router, it first reassembles all the fragments to rebuild the initial IPv6 datagram, and then it analyzes the destination IPv6 address to decide whether the packet will be delivered to the transport layer or whether it must be routed to another sensor until it arrives at the correct end destination.

RPL Operation

The RPL routing protocol describes a method of constructing a logical graph called Destination Oriented Directed Acyclic Graph (DODAG). The first goal of RPL is to optimize the sensor paths compared to the root DODAG in order to favor sensor collection at the root DODAG. For example, we will try to get routes with the lowest number of hops to join the root sensor. The metric can be the energy level remaining in the sensors of a low power network and high loss rate, the number of transmissions needed to reach the root sensor, the average time of communications, the loss rate, etc. During the construction of the graph, the sensors use the objective function which determines the method of calculation of the routing metric, and exchange four types of messages: DIO (DODAG Information Object), DIS (DODAG Information Solicitation), DAO (DODAG Destination Advertisement Object) and DAO-ACK (DAO Acknowledgment) Mohamed, B., & Mohamed, F., 2015).

- The DIO message is broadcast first by the root sensor to trigger the graph construction process. The neighboring sensors of the root sensor receive the message and decide whether they can join the graph or not (the decision depends on several metrics such as the objective function and the cost of the advertised path). Once the sensor has joined the graph, it automatically has a route to the root sensor. If the sensor is configured to be like a router, it in turn broadcasts its local knowledge on the graph (its links) to its neighbors.
- The DIS message is used by the sensors to request information about the graph from neighboring sensors that will respond by sending a DIO message.

- DAO messages are used to announce the presence of the sensor to its parent in the graph. The latter updates its routing table by adding a corresponding input to the child sensor. The process recursively recurs and ascends until we reach the root sensor.
- The DAO-ACK message is sent by the parent sensor to the child sensor, in response to its DAO message (to acknowledge receipt).

The RPL protocol supports two types of routing: data source routing (stateless) and local path decision routing (with state). In data source routing, the entire route to be taken is signaled in the packet, and the gateway sensors pass it to its final destination based on this information. On the other hand, in the second type, the packet carries only the address of the final destination, and the routing is decided at the level of each gateway according to the information contained in the local routing table. The routing table includes information for distinguishing the upstream flows (directed to the root sensor) from the downstream flows (directed to the sensors). The root sensor therefore maintains a complete list of all sensors in the tree. To avoid routing loops, each sensor must calculate its position (or rank) in the hierarchy relative to the root. The value of the rank becomes more important than the distance between the root and the sensor. Routing metrics considerations may impact the position calculation procedure. So, the local communications between sensors having a parent in common do not need to go through the root. However, sensors that do not have a common secondary root must pass through the root, as shown in figure 13, where the blue arrows represent local calls, and numbers 0 to 3 represent the ranks of the sensors in the graph.

Figure 13. Construction of a DODAG by RPL

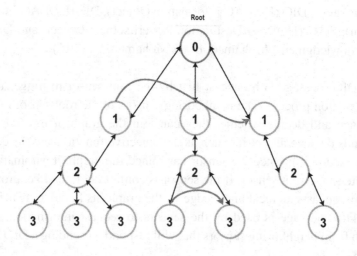

COMMUNICATIONS SYSTEMS FOR THE WSNs AND IOT

There are several standards for high-speed data transport in the WSNs and IoT networks. Some objects such as sensors do not need a very high bandwidth, but rather a low latency time and very low energy consumption hence the need to design other standards capable of to meet these requirements. Figure 14 represents some examples of communications systems used for the WSNs and the IoT (i-scope, 2018).

6LOWPAN

6LoWPAN (IPv6 Low Power Wireless Personal Area Networks) (Parnian, A. R., Parsaei, M. R., Javidan, R., & Mohammadi, R., 2017) is a communication system for IoT devices. It is proposed to provide IPv6 compatibility over IEEE 802.15.4. Although there are challenges in IEEE 802.15.4 networks: the minimum IP packet size is 1280 bytes while the maximum transmission unit (MTU) for IEEE802.15.4 is only 127 bytes so that fragmentation and reassembly are necessary tasks to do by the data link layer. Significant header overhead created by the upper layers

Figure 14. Communications Systems for the WSNs and IoT

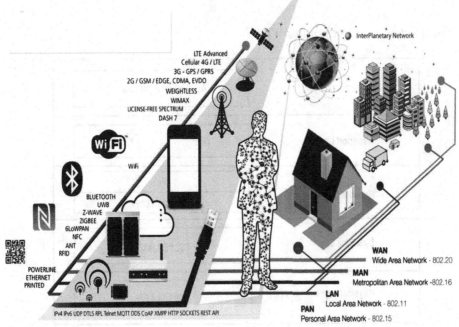

leaving almost no payload size available for application layer data and sending the IPv6 40-byte packet header over the IEEE 802.15.4 link is completely a waste of bandwidth. It is therefore essential to facilitate the transmission of IP packets on the IEEE 802.15.4 link layer. The adaptation layer (refer figure 15) is required to address the specified challenges and provide a solution for sending long IP packets on the link layer supporting a packet length of 127 bytes.

The 6LoWPAN communication system performs header compression, routing overload reduction, and other necessary steps as an adaptation layer. It defines other standards to simplify the discovery of neighbors and facilitate other routing requirements. This is the main step towards the realization of the IoT and is a basic work for other research in the IoT.

ZIGBEE

ZigBee technology (Baronti, P., Pillai, P., Chook, V. W., Chessa, S., Gotta, A., & Hu, Y. F., 2007) is one of the emerging technologies for wireless communication with low power consumption and low cost. It is defined by the IEEE 802.15.4 standard which defines the protocol stack (refer figure 16) for the wireless personal network with very low data rates.

ZigBee technology offers features that better meet the needs of the RCSFs and IoT:

Figure 15. Protocol stack of 6LoWPAN

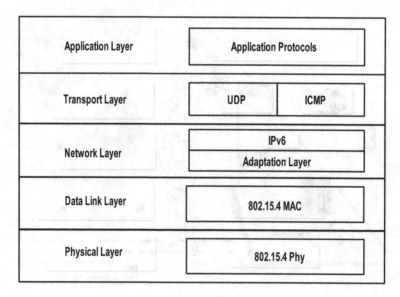

Figure 16. Protocol stack of ZigBee

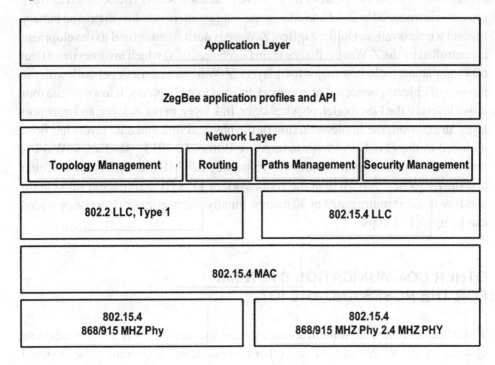

- Frequency bands: 868, 915 and 2.4 GHz,
- Transfer rate up to 250 Kbps,
- Range of signal transmission from 10 to 75 m, depending on the sensors used,
- Encryption AES (Advanced Encryption Standard) data,
- Low energy consumption.

   Due to its attractive features, ZigBee technology has become the most adopted technology in most applications of WSNs and IoT (El Alami, H., & Najid, A., 2017) where the need for flow is dropped for proper energy efficiency, as in the case of applications in smart home.

Z-WAVE

The Z-Wave communication system (Marksteiner, S., Jimenez, V. J. E., Valiant, H., & Zeiner, H., 2017) was developed in 2001 and uses low-power radio technology in the 868 MHz frequency band. It is designed specifically for home automation applications. The latest update of the Z-Wave communication system, called Z-Wave Plus, was introduced in 2013 and adds some improvements such as improved battery life and wireless range. Unlike ZigBee, Z-Wave is not a standard and its development is controlled by the Z-Wave Alliance team (Z-Wave, 2018) which involves more than 600 companies, including major IoT players. Z-Wave uses a mesh network with the number of objects connected in a network limited to 232 objects. It involves the four lower layers of the OSI model, physical layer, link layer, network layer, and transport layer. In addition, the implementation of the physical link and data layers has been included in the ITU G.9959 (Brandt, A., & Buron, J., 2015) standard. Z-Wave is able to work on the common industrial frequency 828 MHz in the European Union and the frequency 908 MHz in the framework of IMS (IP multimedia subsystem) bands with a maximum range of 30 meters. Finally, the maximum data rate provided can be up to 100 kbps.

OTHER COMMUNICATION SYSTEMS FOR THE RCSFS AND THE IOT

The aforementioned communications systems are not the only communications systems for the WSNs and IoT and other communications systems to be explored such as LoRAWAN and SigFox. LoRaWAN (Wixted, A. J., Kinnaird, P., Larijani, H., Tait, A., Ahmadinia, A., & Strachan, N., 2016) is a wireless communications system that enables low-speed communication of low-power objects communicating with LoRa modulation technology (LoRa Alliance, 2017) and connected to the Internet via gateways, thereby contributing IoT. LoRaWAN has a maximum data rate of 27 Kbps and consists of at least one network server, a gateway and a terminal that can collect data from thousands of sensor nodes deployed miles away. The SigFox (Sigfox, 2018) communication system is an ultra narrowband system with low overhead and low data rates. Like LoRaWAN, SigFox is also capable of transmitting over long distances. It uses a frequency band of 868 MHz, dividing the spectrum into 400 channels of 100 Hz. Its coverage is about 30 to 50 km in rural areas and about 3 to 10 km in urban environments. These communications systems are used in the context of smart cities, smart homes, and so on.

CONCLUSION

The WSNs offer an interesting perspective: that of networks able to self-configure and manage their topologies autonomously. In addition, the performance criteria for WSNs different from those of conventional networks and therefore the solutions to be provided are new. Indeed, the WSNs are destined to become objects and thus must be able to be used easily, while keeping a transparency of the network vis-à-vis the user.

We list many applications of the WSNs, especially in those that do not require high bandwidth. The realization of such types of networks requires the implementation of techniques developed for conventional wireless networks. However, most of the techniques developed for these are not transferable to the WSNs.

Since the WSNs play a vital and important role in the IoT and enable the representation of dynamic real-world characteristics in the virtual world of the Internet, the WSNs and the IoT are a fertile line of research and we find them varied applications and in many areas of modern life. However, there are still several constraints to solve in order to be able to use them in real cases. As future work is to design and develop hierarchical routing protocols that extend the network life as much as possible. On the other hand, a worrying vision at the moment is the integration of the WSNs into Internet (i.e., IoT) in terms of energy efficiency and scalability. This vision involves the implementation of new concepts and models: large scale WSNs modeling, energy management and routing technique in ecological and evolutionary IoT.

REFERENCES

Aceto, G., Botta, A., De Donato, W., & Pescapè, A. (2013). Cloud monitoring: A survey. *Computer Networks, 57*(9), 2093–2115. doi:10.1016/j.comnet.2013.04.001

Akkaya, K., & Younis, M. (2005). A survey on routing protocols for wireless sensor networks. *Ad Hoc Networks, 3*(3), 325–349. doi:10.1016/j.adhoc.2003.09.010

Akyildiz, I. F., Su, W., Sankarasubramaniam, Y., & Cayirci, E. (2002). Wireless sensor networks: A survey. *Computer Networks, 38*(4), 393–422. doi:10.1016/S1389-1286(01)00302-4

Al-Fuqaha, A., Guizani, M., Mohammadi, M., Aledhari, M., & Ayyash, M. (2015). Internet of things: A survey on enabling technologies, protocols, and applications. *IEEE Communications Surveys and Tutorials, 17*(4), 2347–2376. doi:10.1109/COMST.2015.2444095

Al-Karaki, J. N., & Kamal, A. E. (2004). Routing techniques in wireless sensor networks: A survey. *IEEE Wireless Communications, 11*(6), 6–28. doi:10.1109/MWC.2004.1368893

Alliance, Z.-W. (n.d.). *Z-Wave*. Available: https://www.z-wave.com

Atzori, L., Iera, A., & Morabito, G. (2010). The internet of things: A survey. *Computer Networks, 54*(15), 2787–2805. doi:10.1016/j.comnet.2010.05.010

Bandyopadhyay, D., & Sen, J. (2011). Internet of things: Applications and challenges in technology and standardization. *Wireless Personal Communications, 58*(1), 49–69. doi:10.100711277-011-0288-5

Baronti, P., Pillai, P., Chook, V. W., Chessa, S., Gotta, A., & Hu, Y. F. (2007). Wireless sensor networks: A survey on the state of the art and the 802.15. 4 and ZigBee standards. *Computer Communications, 30*(7), 1655–1695. doi:10.1016/j.comcom.2006.12.020

Bazan, O., & Jaseemuddin, M. (2011). A survey on MAC protocols for wireless adhoc networks with beamforming antennas. *IEEE Communications Surveys and Tutorials, 14*(2), 216–239. doi:10.1109/SURV.2011.041311.00099

Brandt, A., & Buron, J. (2015). *Transmission of IPv6 packets over ITU-T G. 9959 Networks* (No. RFC 7428).

Cui, X. (2016). The internet of things. In *Ethical Ripples of Creativity and Innovation* (pp. 61–68). London: Palgrave Macmillan.

El Alami, H., & Najid, A. (2017). Gateways Selection for Integrating Wireless Sensor Networks into Internet of Things. In *Europe and MENA Cooperation Advances in Information and Communication Technologies* (pp. 423–430). Cham: Springer. doi:10.1007/978-3-319-46568-5_43

El Alami, H., & Najid, A. (2018). MS-routing-G i: Routing technique to minimise energy consumption and packet loss in WSNs with mobile sink. *IET Networks*, *7*(6), 422–428. doi:10.1049/iet-net.2017.0258

El Alami, H., & Najid, A. (2019). ECH: An Enhanced Clustering Hierarchy Approach to Maximize Lifetime of Wireless Sensor Networks. *IEEE Access: Practical Innovations, Open Solutions*, *7*, 107142–107153. doi:10.1109/ACCESS.2019.2933052

Fleisch, E. (2010). What is the internet of things? An economic perspective. *Economics, Management & Financial Markets*, *5*(2).

Granjal, J., Monteiro, E., & Silva, J. S. (2015). Security in the integration of low-power Wireless Sensor Networks with the Internet: A survey. *Ad Hoc Networks*, *24*, 264–287. doi:10.1016/j.adhoc.2014.08.001

Heinzelman, W. B., Chandrakasan, A. P., & Balakrishnan, H. (2002). An application-specific protocol architecture for wireless microsensor networks. *IEEE Transactions on Wireless Communications*, *1*(4), 660–670. doi:10.1109/TWC.2002.804190

Heinzelman, W. R., Chandrakasan, A., & Balakrishnan, H. (2000). Energy-efficient communication protocol for wireless microsensor networks. In *System sciences, 2000. Proceedings of the 33rd annual Hawaii international conference on*. IEEE. 10.1109/HICSS.2000.926982

Jang, W. S., & Healy, W. M. (2009, September). Assessment of Performance Metrics for Use of Wireless Sensor Networks in Buildings. *The International Symposium on Automation and Robotics in Construction (ISARC 2009)*.

Jovanov, E., Milenkovic, A., Otto, C., & De Groen, P. C. (2005). A wireless body area network of intelligent motion sensors for computer assisted physical rehabilitation. *Journal of Neuroengineering and Rehabilitation*, *2*(1), 6. doi:10.1186/1743-0003-2-6 PMID:15740621

Kelley, R. H., Carpenter, R. C., Lunney, R. H., & Martinez, M. (2000). *U.S. Patent No. 6,088,659*. Washington, DC: U.S. Patent and Trademark Office.

Koch, S. (2006). Home telehealth—Current state and future trends. *International Journal of Medical Informatics*, *75*(8), 565–576. doi:10.1016/j.ijmedinf.2005.09.002 PMID:16298545

Kone, C. T. (2011). *Architectural design of a large wireless sensor network* (Doctoral dissertation). Henri Poincaré-Nancy I University, France.

LoRa Alliance™ Technology. (n.d.). Available: https://www.lora-alliance.org/What-Is-LoRa/Technology

Manjeshwar, A., & Agrawal, D. P. (2001). TEEN: a routing protocol for enhanced efficiency in wireless sensor networks. In *Null* (p. 30189a). IEEE.

Marksteiner, S., Jimenez, V. J. E., Valiant, H., & Zeiner, H. (November, 2017). An overview of wireless IoT protocol security in the smart home domain. In Internet of Things Business Models, Users, and Networks, 2017 (pp. 1-8). IEEE. doi:10.1109/CTTE.2017.8260940

Mohamed, B., & Mohamed, F. (2015). Qos routing rpl for low power and lossy networks. *International Journal of Distributed Sensor Networks*, *11*(11), 971545. doi:10.1155/2015/971545

Moscibroda, T., & Wattenhofer, R. (2006). The Complexity of Connectivity in Wireless Networks. In Infocom (pp. 1-13). Academic Press. doi:10.1109/INFOCOM.2006.23

Parnian, A. R., Parsaei, M. R., Javidan, R., & Mohammadi, R. (2017). Smart Objects Presence Facilitation in the Internet of Things. *International Journal of Computers and Applications*, *168*(4).

Pottie, G. J., & Kaiser, W. J. (2000). Wireless integrated network sensors. *Communications of the ACM*, *43*(5), 51–58. doi:10.1145/332833.332838

Qing, L., Zhu, Q., & Wang, M. (2006). Design of a distributed energy-efficient clustering algorithm for heterogeneous wireless sensor networks. *Computer Communications*, *29*(12), 2230–2237. doi:10.1016/j.comcom.2006.02.017

Rappaport, T. S. (1996). *Wireless communications: principles and practice* (Vol. 2). Prentice Hall PTR.

Rodoplu, V., & Meng, T. H. (1999). Minimum energy mobile wireless networks. *IEEE Journal on Selected Areas in Communications*, *17*(8), 1333–1344. doi:10.1109/49.779917

Schott, W., Gluhak, A., Presser, M., Hunkeler, U., & Tafazolli, R. (2007). e-SENSE protocol stack architecture for wireless sensor networks. In Mobile and Wireless Communications Summit, 2007. 16th IST (pp. 1-5). IEEE.

Sigfox. (n.d.). Available: http://www.sigfox.com

Smaragdakis, G., Matta, I., & Bestavros, A. (2004). *SEP: A stable election protocol for clustered heterogeneous wireless sensor networks*. Boston University Computer Science Department.

Taruna, S., Jain, K., & Purohit, G. N. (2011). Application domain of wireless sensor network:-a paradigm in developed and developing countries. *International Journal of Computer Science Issues*, 8(4), 611.

The Internet of Things (IoT) - essential IoT business guide. (n.d.). Available: https://www.i-scoop.eu/internet-of-things guide/ #The_growing_role_of_fog_and_edge_computing_in_IoT

The Internet of Tings. (n.d.). Available: https://www.itu.int/itunews/manager/display.asp?lang=fr&year=2005&issue=09&ipage=things&ext=html

Top 50 Internet of Things Applications. (n.d.). Available: http://www.libelium.com/resources/top_50_iot_sensor_applications_ranking/

Winter, T., Thubert, P., Brandt, A., Hui, J., Kelsey, R., Levis, P., & Alexander, R. (2012). *RPL: IPv6 routing protocol for low-power and lossy networks* (No. RFC 6550).

Wixted, A. J., Kinnaird, P., Larijani, H., Tait, A., Ahmadinia, A., & Strachan, N. (2016). Evaluation of LoRa and LoRaWAN for wireless sensor networks. In SENSORS, 2016 IEEE (pp. 1-3). IEEE. doi:10.1109/ICSENS.2016.7808712

Zou, Y., & Chakrabarty, K. (2003). Sensor deployment and target localization based on virtual forces. In *INFOCOM 2003. Twenty-Second Annual Joint Conference of the IEEE Computer and Communications. IEEE Societies* (Vol. 2, pp. 1293-1303). IEEE. 10.1109/INFCOM.2003.1208965

Zuniga, M., & Krishnamachari, B. (2004). Analyzing the transitional region in low power wireless links. In *Sensor and Ad Hoc Communications and Networks, 2004. IEEE SECON 2004. 2004 First Annual IEEE Communications Society Conference on* (pp. 517-526). IEEE. 10.1109/SAHCN.2004.1381954

Chapter 6
Energy–Efficient Routing for WSNs

Padmapriya N.
IFET College of Engineering, India

N. Kumaratharan
Sri Venkateswara College of Engineering, India

Aswini R.
IFET College of Engineering, India

ABSTRACT

A wireless sensor network (WSN) is a gathering of sensor hubs that powerfully self-sort themselves into a wireless system without the use of any previous framework. One of the serious issues in WSNs is the energy consumption, whereby the system lifetime is subject to this factor. Energy-efficient routing is viewed as the most testing errand. Sensor organizes for the most part work in perplexing and dynamic situations and directing winds up repetitive assignment to keep up as the system measure increments. This chapter portrays the structure of wireless sensor network the analysis and study of different research works identified with energy-efficient routing in wireless sensor networks. Along these lines, to beat all the routing issues, the pattern has moved to biological-based algorithms like swarm intelligence-based strategies. Ant colony optimization-based routing protocols have shown outstanding outcomes as far as execution when connected to WSN routing.

DOI: 10.4018/978-1-7998-1626-3.ch006

INTRODUCTION TO WIRELESS SENSOR NETWORKS

A Wireless sensor system can be characterized as a system of gadgets that can communicate the data accumulated from a checked field through wireless connections. The information is sent through different nodes, and with a gateway, the information is associated with different systems like wireless Ethernet. Wireless sensor systems involve a major amount of self-governing nodes that are outfitted with sensing capacities, wireless interfaces, and restricted memory and energy sources. Sensor networks are helpful in scattered and steady detecting of various kinds of mortal occasions and happenings of interesting incidence. For the most part, the sensors are statically organized over tremendous zones. However, they can be versatile additionally and capable in working with the atmosphere. The sensor networks can be used in a comprehensive continuum of uses in both military and civilian situations, environmental checking, examination for security, modernized healthcare insurance, scholarly structure robotization, programmed traffic instrument and item tracking.

In the sensor networks distinctive sensors pass on their information towards a observing data collecting node generally known as a sink that achieves total data aggregation and analysis. Nodes can likewise transmit information to the intermediate nodes that can autonomously or mutually deal with the information before transmitting it to the global sink or towards a global sink, and perform inadequate incomplete data aggregation on the route. This is known as in-network data aggregation that is utilized for energy optimization. Sensors have short correspondence range and these structure a framework less system over a typical remote channel. The two information and control parcels are coordinated through single hop or through multi-hop. Sensors communicate with one another in the system to finish distinctive activities. Sensors expend a ton of during communication and other activities.

WSN is a collection of wireless nodes with restricted vitality abilities that might be mobile or stationary and are found haphazardly on a dynamically evolving condition. The routing strategies choice is an imperative issue for the productive conveyance of the packets to their goal. Additionally, in such systems, the connected routing strategy ought to guarantee the base of the vitality utilization and consequently augmentation of the lifetime of the system. One of the first WSNs was structured and created amidst the 70s by the military and defense industries. WSNs were additionally utilized during the Vietnam War so as to help the recognition of foes in remote wilderness territories. In any case, their usage had a few downsides including that the expansive size of the sensors, the energy they expend and the limited network capability. From that point forward, a great deal of work on the WSNs field has been done bringing about the improvement of the WSNs on a wide assortment of uses and frameworks with tremendously changing necessities an attributes. In the meantime, different energy-efficient routing protocols have been structured and produced for WSNs so as to help proficient data delivery to their goal. Along these lines, every energy-efficient routing protocol may have explicit attributes relying upon the application and network architecture. (Nikolaos A. Pantazis, Stefanos A. Nikolidakis & Dimitrios D. Vergados, 2013) The WSNs might be utilized in an assortment of regular day to day life activities or services.

In WSNs all sensor nodes endeavor to gather information and send detecting information to the base station (BS). The wireless communication utilizes a fixed node in the focal point of condition that is utilized to gather data from other sensor nodes called BS. In some cases, source and goal are not in the area and they have multihop distance with one another where this distance prompts more energy utilization. The node energy consumption is the measure of energy each node expends for sending/accepting information to/from different nodes. The summation of energy consumption by system nodes demonstrates the system energy consumption. Since these energy sources are key and have a straight impact towards the system lifetime, new protocols establishment or improvement in current protocols appears to be vital for better energy saving in the system. (Ehsan Amiri, Hassan Keshavarz, Mojtaba Alizadeh, Mazdak Zamani &Touraj Khodadadi, 2014)

Wireless sensor systems (WSNs) are self- healing mesh networks used to screen physical procedures utilizing sensors and report sensor readings to intrigued nodes with regards to the system. WSNs have different applications spreading over from farming and natural to military uses. For instance,

WSNs have been utilized to screen soil dampness and saltiness in a land district to decide appropriate systems for water system (Cardell-Oliver, 2005). WSNs normally comprise of minimal effort nodes that are battery powered. Accordingly, there are imperatives forced by finite energy resources (Camilo et al, 2006) and exposure to environmental conditions.

These should be tended such that the system can work for whatever length of time that conceivable and can overcome singular node disappointments (when a node comes up short on energy or is harmed). One territory where these issues are tended to is in the structure of routing algorithms specific for use in WSNs. These algorithms endeavor to tackle the briefest way issue, while limiting energy necessities and amplifying the lifetime of nodes in the system. They additionally consider the likelihood ofnode failures and the requirement for some dimension of dynamic routing of packets when making routing decisions at each node.

The present engaging field of research is Wireless Sensor Networks (WSN), due to its wide scope of uses in various fields, WSN comprises of countless randomly deployed sensor motes and perform the essential elements of detecting, computations and communications. In most recent couple of years WSNs has turned into an explorative Research zone and WSN is a prime essential to give, robust service in threatening situations. As of now observed power utilization is a dispute in sensor systems, which rotate around the constrained power assets. Contingent upon the extent of the sensor bits the structure of the battery size limits the life time of the network. (Rajesh SL & Dr.Somashekhar C Desai, 2014)

Routing in Wireless Sensor Networks

The way toward building up ways from a source to a sink crosswise over at least one transfers is called routing. Routing Protocols are in charge of distinguishing or finding courses from source to sink (W. Dargie and C. Poellabauer,2010) . As for Network Organization most routing protocols fit into one of three classes in particular flat based, hierarchical-based and location based. Regarding Route Discovery there falsehoods two sorts of protocols to be specific Reactive Protocol and Proactive Protocol. In view of Protocol Operation there are different protocols specifically Negotiation Based, Multipath Based, Query Based, QoS Based and Coherent Based.

Routing is a standout amongst the most imperative protocols that expend energy in the system. Routing has been characterized as a dynamic improvement task going for giving ways that are ideal as far as certain criteria, for example, least separation, maximum bandwidth, and most brief deferral and fulfilling a few imperatives, for example, constrained intensity of nodes and restricted limit of remote connections. Routing is one of the serious issues in theWSN and is a standout amongst the most intriguing examination fields in the correspondence network.The routing of the data is therefore done locally and hop-by-hop. (P. M. Fernandez,2003)

Routing as a rule coordinates dependent on the routing records that exist in every node routing table (RT) to different goals in the system. The RT is an information table that is put away in node memory records defeats to exceptional nodes. These days, algorithms act contrastingly to discover the route among sender and destination; more algorithms just discover a path and some routing algorithms discover a multipath.The multiroute algorithm squander more system assets due to more message transmission rather than the single-way algorithm. E. Amiri, H. Keshavarz, H. Heidari, E. Mohamadi, and H. Moradzadeh, 2013). Proactive, reactive, and hybrid (H. Keshavarz, R. M. Noor, and E. Mostajeran,2013) are three principle classifications of routing algorithms. Proactive or, on the other hand, the table-driven calculations dependably display a new list of routes. Proactive calculations have a slowreaction in the system with more disappointment and rebuilding. Examples of proactive algorithms are FSR (A.Iwata,C.-C.Chiang,G.Pei, M.Gerla, &T.-W.Chen, 1999) and DSDV (E. Perkins & P. Bhagwat, 1994). The reactive or ondemand routing algorithm apply flooding technique for discovering only one path between the source and destination. If the route exists previously, the new route solicitation won't acknowledge them.

High latency time in path finding is one of these algorithms' impediment and another is forced overhead on the system because of the flooding method; by the by it has less overhead contrasted with that for the proactive gathering. The most acclaimed routing protocols of this gathering are DFS (D.B.Johnson & D.A.Maltz, 1996) and AODV. The third category is known as the hybrid. They are a blend of the reactive routing protocols and proactive routing protocols.ant colonu is a standard answer for finding ideal way (from source to goal) that is proposed by Dorigo et al. in 1992 for finding answers to optimization problems, for example, travelling salesman problem (TSP) with multiagents. By focusing on built-in properties of routing, it will be appropriate to be resolved by the ant colony algorithm.

Sensor nodes are described by severe memory, CPU, and energy restrictions. In addition, the topology of a WSN is timevariant because of versatility or incitation planning. Thus, the plan of a routing protocol for WSNs ought to dependably give a smooth tradeoff among lifetime and proficiency. From one hand, the packet forwarding and handing-off procedure ought to be energy- aware so as to expand the lifetime. From the other hand, because of the touchy idea of a large portion of the WSN-based applications, packet transmission from sensor nodes to the investigation focus ought to be dependable despite the fact that the topology of the system changes. In the accompanying, we list the most essential contemplations identified with the improvement of WSN routing protocols. (Mohamed Hamdi, Nejla Essaddi, & Noureddine Boudriga, 2008)

1. **Process Distribution:** Due to the constrained transmission scope of the basic sensor nodes, only multi-hop routing methodologies can apply to WSNs. Methodologies including a focal node playing out all routing computations can not be considered. Henceforth, source and middle nodes ought to execute explicit procedures so as to decide to which neighboring node an incoming packet ought to be passed on.

2. **Overhead Reduction**: Since the topology of the sensor arrange oftentimes changes, new routing tables ought to be fabricated adaptively. The exchange of routing information over the system ought not include an imperative overhead to the transmitted messages. Routing protocols ought to along these lines decrease the measure of exchanged information

3. **Energy Conservation:** As it has been expressed above, energy productivity is the most vital angle that one should think on while tending to WSN-based applications. The central thing to ask is whether it is smarter to contribute the energy resources in sending information or in performing calculations? The majority of the references talking about this issue concur that correspondence is impressively more costly endeavor than calculation. Accordingly, the routing algorithm ought to envelop calculation forms at whatever point conceivable to spare energy resources.

4. **Memory Conservation:** Due to the memory constraints of the sensor nodes, enormous routing tables would be difficult to deal with. This implies suitable components ought to be created to control the measure of the stored routing data. It ought to likewise be seen that versatility and energy searching protocols intensify the vital requirement for such size control systems.

5. **Resiliency:** When nodes are versatile or depend on action booking for their activity, they may vanish at unforeseeable purposes of time until it comes back to the same area or it gets an activation message. This might influence the conveyance of the forwarded packets to the investigation focus. A potential arrangement is to utilize more than a solitary way between the sender node and the investigation focus. Multi-path routing gives not just route redundancy yet additionally the chance to actualize load adjusting systems.

Challenges Connected to Routing in Wireless Sensor Networks

Routing in WSNs is trying because of the inalienable attributes that recognize these systems from different remote systems, for example, mobile ad hoc systems or cellular systems. Because of the special qualities and eccentricities of a WSN, the current routing protocols produced for wireless ad hoc networks systems cannot be legitimately connected to WSNs. The structure of a routing protocol for WSNs needs to consider the lack of quality of the remote channel, the potential powerful changes in the system topology, just as the limited processing, storage, bandwidth, and energy capacities of the WSN nodes. Hence, unique methodologies are required to guarantee effective routing among the nodes of a WSN. The plan of routing protocols in WSNs is affected by numerous elements. These variables represents a few difficulties that must be defeated before proficient correspondence can be accomplished in WSNs. In the accompanying, we condense a portion of the routing challenges and design issues that influence routing in WSNs.

- **Energy Consumption:** Energy consumption is viewed as one of the significant concerns in the improvement routing protocols for WSNs. Sensor nodes can deplete their constrained supply of energy while performing calculations and transmitting data in a remote situation. While building their routing tables, nodes consume energy by exchanging information with their neighbors. Moreover, as a result of the restricted energy resources of WSN nodes, messages should be conveyed in the most energy-efficient way without compromising the exactness of the data content. Shortest path algorithms need to embrace measurements, such as energy-efficiency.
- **Scalability:** As the extent of the system increments, or the quantity of nodes builds, the routing protocol ought to have the capacity to adjust to the progressions and give sufficient execution. WSNs may comprise of an expansive number of nodes, and in this way, the data every node acquires about the system topology is restricted. Henceforth, fully distributed protocols, which work with constrained information of the topology, should be created to give versatility. Moreover, when the density might be high in the system, nearby data exchange ought to likewise be constrained to improve the energy efficiency.
- **Node Mobility:** Now and again, nodes are not stationary. Node mobility presents changes in the neighborhood relations; nodes move out of scope of their neighbors and consequently are never again ready to communicate with the old neighboring nodes while they come extremely close to new nodes. A perfect routing protocol for WSN ought to have the capacity to convey information messages from source to destination notwithstanding when a portion of the intermediate nodes move far from their neighbors range. This muddles the plan of the routing protocol as it presents extra routing overhead. Route stability is an essential issue, notwithstanding energy and different perspectives. Henceforth, the routing protocol ought to be versatile to dynamic changes in the system topology
- **Node Deployment:** Node deployment in WSNs can be either deterministic or haphazardly performed, which is subject to the required application. In the deterministic way to deal with arrangement, every one of the nodes are

set in predefined positions and messages are directed through ways that are pre-decided. Be that as it may, in the arbitrarily deployed nodes, nodes might be set haphazardly in subjective positions. The system topology can change progressively amid the lifetime of the system. At first, sensor nodes might be ignorant of the system topology. The relative locations of the neighbors of a node and the overall area of the nodes in the system fundamentally influence the routing performance. This is actually an errand of a routing protocol which ought to give topology data with the end goal that the neighbors of every node are found and routing choices are made in like manner.

- **Robustness:** Routing in WSNs depends on the sensor nodes to deliver information in a multi-hop way. Consequently, routing protocols work on these nodes rather than devoted switches, such as in the Internet. These nodes comprise of minimal effort equipment which may result in startling disappointments to such a degree, that a node might be non-operational. Accordingly, routing protocols ought to give robustness to sensor node failures.

- **Application:** The sort of utilization is additionally vital for the structure of routing protocols. If there should be an occurrence of checking applications, static courses can be reused to keep up productive conveyance of the perceptions all through the lifetime of the system. Then again, in occasion based applications, since the nodes are usually in sleep mode, at whatever point an occasion happens, courses ought to be created to deliver the event data in a convenient way.

Routing Techniques for WSN Classification

1. Network Structure
2. Communication Model
   a. Query-Based Protocols
   b. Coherent and Non-Coherent-Based Protocols:
   c. Negotiation-Based Protocols

Topology Based Protocols

1. Location-based Protocols
2. Mobile Agent-based Protocols

Reliable Routing Protocols

1.   Multipath-Based Protocols
2.   QoS-Based Protocols

Routing in WSNs might be more requesting than different remote systems, similar mobile ad-hoc networks or cellular networks for the accompanying reasons:

- Sensor nodes request cautious asset the executives in view of their extreme requirements in energy, handling and capacity limits.
- Almost all utilizations of WSNs require the stream of sensed information from numerous sources to a specific base station.
- Design prerequisites of a WSN rely upon the application, in light of the fact that WSNs are application-explicit.
- The nodes in WSNs are generally stationary after their sending which results in unsurprising and non-visit topological changes.
- Data gathering is, under ordinary conditions, in view of the area, in this way, position familiarity with sensor nodes is imperative. The situation of the sensor nodes is identified by utilizing techniques dependent on triangulation for example radio strength from a couple of known focuses. Until further notice, it is conceivable to utilize Global Positioning System (GPS) equipment for this reason. Also, it is positive to have arrangements free of GPS for the location issue in WSNs
- In WSNs, there is a high likelihood that gathered information may show some unwanted repetition which is important to be utilized by the routing protocols to improve energy and data transfer capacity use. Due to every one of these inconsistencies, a few new routing systems have been created and proposed to take care of the routing issue in WSNs. These routing systems have considered the inalienable highlights of WSNs alongside the application and design prerequisites.

A high efficient routing scheme will offer critical power cost decreases what's more, will improve arrange network's life span. Finding and maintaining routes in WSNs is a noteworthy issue since energy requirements and sudden changes in node status (e.g., inefficiency or failure) offer ascent to visit and unanticipated topological adjustments. Routing methods for WSNs utilize some outstanding Routing strategies, appropriate for WSNs, to limit energy utilization. Al-Karaki extend the classification initially, the routing protocols can be ordered into four principle plans: Network Structure Scheme, Communication Model Scheme, Topology Based Scheme and Reliable Routing Scheme,

- **Network Structure:** The structure of a system can be characterized by node consistency. The nodes in certain systems are considered to be conveyed consistently and be equivalent to one another, or different systems make distinctions between various nodes. All the more explicitly, the principle characteristic of the routing protocols having a place with this class is how the nodes are associated also, they course the data dependent on the systems. This addresses two types of node deployments, nodes with the same level of connection and nodes with different hierarchies. Therefore, the schemes on this category can be further classified as follows:

- **Flat Protocols:** All the nodes in the system assume a similar job. Flat system architecture presents a few points of interest, including negligible overhead to keep up the framework between conveying nodes.

- **Hierarchical Protocols**: The routing protocols on this plan force a structure on the system to accomplish energy efficiency, security, and versatility. In this class of protocols, arrange nodes are sorted out in groups in which a node with higher residual energy, for instance, assumes the role of a cluster head. The cluster head is in charge of organizing exercises inside the group and sending data between clusters. Clustering can possibly decrease energy utilization and expand the lifetime of the system. They have high conveyance proportion and versatility and can adjust the energy utilization. The nodes around the base station or cluster head will exhaust their energy sources quicker than different nodes. System disconnectivity is where sure areas of the system can wind up inaccessible. On the off chance that there is just a single node interfacing a piece of the system to the rest and flops, at that point this segment would cut off from the remainder of the system.

- **Communication Model:** The Communication Model customized in a routing protocol is identified with the way that the fundamental task of the protocol is followed so as to route packets in the system. The protocols of this classification can convey more information for guaranteed measure of energy. Additionally as far as dispersal rate and energy use the conventions of this class can perform close the hypothetical ideal in point-to-point and broadcast networks. The issue with Communication Model protocol is that they don't have high conveyance proportion for the information that are sent to a goal. In this way, they don't ensure the conveyance of information.

The protocols on this plan can be delegated pursues:

- **Query-Based Protocols:** The destination nodes proliferate a question for information (detecting task) from a node through the system and a node having this information sends the information, which coordinates the inquiry, back to the node, which in turn starts the question.
- **Coherent and Non-Coherent-Based Protocols:** In coherent routing, the information is sent to aggregators after a base preparing. In non-lucid information preparing routing, nodes locally process the raw data before it is sent to different nodes for further handling.
- **Negotiation-Based Protocols:** They use meta-data dealings to diminish excess transmissions in the system
- **Topology Based Protocols:** Topology-based protocols utilize the rule that each node in a system keeps up topology data and that the primary procedure of the protocol task depends on the topology of the system. The protocol on this plan can be additionally delegated pursues:
- **Location-based Protocols:** They exploit the position data so as to hand-off the got information to just certain regions and not to the entire WSN. The protocol of this class can discover a way from a source to a goal and limit the energy utilization of the sensor nodes. They have restricted adaptability on the off chance that that the nodes are mobile. Additionally a node must know or find out about the areas of different nodes.
- **Mobile Agent-based Protocols:** The mobile agent protocols are utilized in WSNs to course information from the detected zone to the goal and this is a fascinating division. The mobile agent frameworks have as a primary segment a portable specialist, which moves among the nodes of a system to play out an errand self-rulingly and wisely, based on the environment conditions. Mobile agent protocols may give to the system additional adaptability, just as new capacities as opposed to the traditional WSN tasks that depend on the client-server computing model.
- **Reliable Routing Protocols:** The protocols on this plan are stronger to course disappointments either by accomplishing load adjusting courses or by fulfilling certain QoS measurements, as delay, energy, and bandwidth. The nodes of the system may experience the ill effects of the overhead of keeping up directing tables and the QoS measurements at every sensor node. The protocols are delegated pursues:
- **Multipath-Based Protocols:** They accomplish load adjusting and are resilient to route failures.

- **QoS-Based Protocols:** The system needs to adjust between energy utilization and information quality. At whatever point a sink demands for information from the detected nodes in the system, the transmission needs to meet explicit dimension of quality.

The most vital elements that impact the choice of a routing protocol are:

- **Network Dynamics:** The fundamental parts in a sensor network are the sensor nodes, sink and monitored events. In the majority of the system designs sensor nodes are thought to be stationary. Then again, supporting the portability of sinks or cluster heads is some of the time important. Routing messages sent or got from nodes are all the more testing since course stability turns into an essential improvement factor, notwithstanding vitality, transfer speed and so forth. The detected occasion can be dynamic or static and this relies upon the application. Along these lines, in an objective recognition application, the occasion is dynamic, however forest monitoring for early fire prevention is a static event.
- **Node Deployment:** This influences the execution of the Routing protocol. The arrangement might be deterministic or self-sorting out. In deterministic circumstances, the sensors are set physically and every one of the information are directed through pre-characterized ways. In self-sorting out frameworks, the sensor nodes are dissipated arbitrarily and create an infrastructure in an ad hoc manner.
- **Energy Considerations:** The set up of a course is extraordinarily affected by energy contemplations. Since the transmission intensity of a remote radio relies upon separation squared or order in the presence of obstacles, multi-hop routing will expend less vitality than direct correspondence. In any case, multi-hop directing may include critical overhead for topology the board and medium access control. In Contrast, direct Routing performs well enough in the event that every one of the nodes are extremely near the sink.
- **Data Delivery Models:** The data delivery model to the sink, depending upon the utilization of the sensor network, can be continuous, event-driven, query-driven and hybrid. In the continuous delivery model, every sensor sends information intermittently. In event-driven and query-drivenmodels, the transmission of information is activated when an occasion happens or an inquiry is produced by the sink. In addition, there are a few systems that apply a crossover demonstrate utilizing a blend continuous, event-driven and querydriven data delivery. The Routing protocol depends on the data delivery model, particularly with respect to the minimization of energy consumption and route stability.

- **Node Capabilities:** In a sensor network, various functionalities can be related with the sensor nodes. In many systems, a nodecan be committed to a specific unique capacity, for example, relaying, sensing and aggregation, as connecting with the three functionalities at the equivalent time on a node may rapidly deplete the energy of that node.

- **Data Aggregation/Fusion**: The sensor nodes may create comparative parcels from various nodes that can be accumulated so the quantity of transmissions would be decreased. Data aggregation is the mix of information from various sources. This can be satisfied by utilizing capacities, for example, suppression, min, max and average. These capacities can be performed either mostly or completely in every sensor node. The calculation can be less energy consuming than correspondence and substantial energy savings can be gotten through information collection. This method can accomplish energy effectiveness and traffic optimization in various Routing protocols. In many system designs all collection capacities are appointed to all the more dominant and specific nodes.

- **Energy Balanced Network:** When building up a energy efficient routing protocol the load balancing of the energy that the sensors expend ought to be one of the primary focuses of the protocol. This implies the Routing protocols need to limit the energy consumption of the system by choosing the shortest routes as well as the courses that will prompt the expansion of the network lifetime.

- **Network Security**: An imperative factor, aside from energy consumption, is the security that the protocols can offer to ensure against listening in and malevolent conduct and further developed plans to be created.

- **Nodes Mobility**: The nodes in the WSN were thought to be static. In the most recent years there is an expanded enthusiasm for applications that help the portability of the clients. A case of this is the medical care applications where the mobile sensors are connected to the patients and need to send proceeds with information from the patient to the specialist. There are a few protocols that spread this, yet at the same time there is a great deal of degree for future research around there.

- **Performance Evaluation on Real Environment**: The vast majority of the protocols for the WSNs have been assessed through simulations. Notwithstanding, it is essential to assess the execution of these protocols in genuine conditions with a great deal of clients

- **Real-Time Application and QoS**: It is a continuous need to grow ongoing application that will offer high level of QoS to the end clients. In this manner, it is critical for the researchers to try a great deal of endeavors to create

Routing protocls that will offer QoS to real-time applications Incorporation of Fixed with Mobile Networks. The majority of the applications, for instance in medicinal services checking, require the information gathered from the sensor nodes to be transmitted to a server with the goal that the specialist may access and make an analysis or send prescription to the patients. In this case the Routing prerequisites of every condition are unique, further research is important for dealing with this sort of circumstances.

- **QoS routing protocols**: The QoS is imperative in the conveyance of the information in basic applications, for example, medicinal services. In this way, the advancement of Routing protocols that consider both energy efficiency and precise conveyance of information will help on this direction.

Energy Efficient Routing Protocols in WSN

Energy efficiency of a system is a huge worry in wireless sensor organize (WSN). Nowadays systems are ending up huge, so data accumulated is ending up significantly bigger, which all devour a lot of energy bringing about an early passing of a node. Along these lines, numerous energy efficient protocols are created to diminish the power utilized in information examining and accumulation to broaden the lifetime of a system. Following are some energy efficient routing protocols:

LEACH "Low-Energy Adaptive Clustering Hierarchy"

(Kazem Sohraby, Daniel Minoli & Taieb Znati, 2007) In this sort of various hierarchical protocol, a large portion of the nodes impart to cluster heads (C.H). It comprises of two stages:

- **The Setup Phase**: in this stage, the clusters are requested and afterward Cluster Head(CH) has been chosen. The undertaking of CH is to cumulate, wrapping, and forward the data to the base station (Sink). (N. A. Pantazis, S. A. Nikolidakis, & D. D. Vergados, 2013)
- **The Study State Phase**: In the previous state, the nodes and the CH have been composed, however in the second province of "LEACH", the information is conveyed to the base station (Sink). Term of this stage is longer than the previous state. To limit the overhead, the term of this stage has been expanded. Every node in the system, contact with the group head, and move the information to it and after that CH will build up the timetable to move the information of every node to base station. (J. N. Al-Karaki, and A. E. Kama, 2004)

- **PEGASIS "PEGASIS "Power-Efficient Gathering in Sensor Information Systems":** It is a "chain-bases protocol" and an overhauling of the "Filter". (Jayashri Deb Sinha and Subhabrata BarmanIn, 2012). "PEGASIS" each node moves just with a nearby neighbor to coordinate and acquire data. It receipts goes imparting to the BS, in this way diminishing the amount of energy expended per round. The nodes are thusly that a chain ought to be created, which can be finished by the sensor nodes alongside utilizing an algorithm.Then again, the BS can register this chain and transmission of it to all the sensor nodes. To build up the chain, it is normal that all nodes have all inclusive data of the framework and that a ravenous calculation is locked in. Therefore, the structure of the chain will start from the remote node to the closer node. In the event that a node terminates, the chain is modified in the comparable technique to dodge the dormant node.

- **TEEN " Threshold Sensitive Energy Efficient Sensor Network Protocol ":**The TEEN is a various leveled protocol intended for the conditions like unexpected changes in the detected properties, for example, temperature. For a responsive system, the primary created protocol was TEEN (Roseline, R.A. & Sumathi, P,2012) . The decrease of the quantity of transmissions is the motivation behind a hard edge, which is finished by enabling the nodes to transmit just when the detected quality is in the scope of intrigue. The quantity of transmissions is decreased by delicate edge by keeping away from every one of the transmissions which may happen when the detected quality is changed marginally or not changed. TEEN is well pertinent for time significant issues and is moreover very effective as far as sparing energy and reaction time. It additionally enables the client to deal with the power usage and exactness to suit the application.

- **APTEEN " Adaptive Threshold sensitive Energy Efficient Sensor Network ":** The "APTEEN" is a development of "TEEN" and objectives at both taking episodic data gatherings and answering to time-basic occasions. When the BS details the cluster, the C.H transmits the highlights, the estimations of edge and schedula of transmission to all nodes. After that, the C.H performs data amassing, which has as a result to protect power. The primary bit of leeway of "APTEEN" rather than "TEEN", is that node use a littler sum control. then again, the essential hindrances of APTEEN are the inconvenience and that it brings about lengthier delay times. A. Manjeshwar & D. Agrawal, 2014)

- **Directed Diffusion**: Directed diffusion is information driven routing protocol for gathering and distributing the data in WSNs. It has been created to address the prerequisite of information spilling out of the sink toward the sensors, for example at the point when the sink demands specific data from these sensors. Its principle target is expanding the system lifetime by acknowledging fundamental energy saving. So as to satisfy this goal, it needs to keep the collaborations among the nodes inside a constrained situation by message trade. A limited collaboration that gives multipath conveyance is a one of a kind element of this protocol. This exceptional component with the capacity of the nodes to react to the questions of the sink brings about impressive energy savings. (Sohraby, D.Minoli, T.Znat, 2007)

- **Energy-Efficient Sensor Routing (EESR):** EESR is a flat routing algorithm proposed especially to diminish the power use and information dormancy, and to give adaptability in the WSN. Mostly, it comprises of Gateway, Base Station, Manager Nodes, and Sensor Nodes. Their obligations are: Gateway Delivers messages from Manager Nodes or structures different systems to the Base Station, which has additional detail than typical sensor nodes. It sends and gets messages to/from Gateway. Additionally, it sends inquiries and gathers information to/from sensor nodes. Manager Nodes and Sensor Nodes gather information from the environment and send it to one another in 1-Hop separation till the Base Station. (H. Oh and K. Chae, 2007)

ENERGY EFFICIENT ROUTING

Energy efficiency is a key factor in WSNs since the gadgets utilized in WSNs are asset compelled. Since the accessible energy assets limit the general task of sensors, energy consumption should be limited for the system to be worked for a more drawn out period. Despite the fact that principle point of WSN is to transmit information proficiently, the significant structure objective is to improve the system lifetime. The most ideal approach to accomplish this objective is to consolidate energy efficient routing protocols. Execution of routing protocols are assessed utilizing a few measurements, for example, Energy per bundle, Energy and Reliability, Network Lifetime, Average Energy Dissipated, Low Energy Consumption, Total Number of Nodes Alive, and so forth. At present, look into is being accomplished for creating routing protocols that will devour less energy for expanding the network lifetime. (Rault, Tifenn, Abdelmadjid Bouabdallah, & Yacine Challal, 2014)

Energy Saving Approaches

There are certain ways to deal with handle the energy consumption issue, for example, radio enhancement, information decrease, rest/wakeup plans, battery repletion and energy efficient routing. We are keen on the energy efficient routing systems and are sorted as pursues:

- **Cluster Architectures:** Network is composed as clusters where each cluster is has a cluster head (CH) that assumes the liability of organizing the correspondence exercises of individuals. CHs speaks with another CHs or to the base station. Clustering procedures improve energy efficiency by restricting vitality utilization of the nodes. Network scalability is additionally improved by the various leveled structures in the system.
- **Energy as a Routing Metric:** The setup path phase considers energy as a measurement. Thusly, routing algorithms can choose the following bounce by centering the most brief ways as well as on its lingering energy.
- **Multipath Routing:** Single way routing quickly depletes energy of nodes on a chose way and when the node depletes out of power, another path should be remade. Multipath directing interestingly, substitutes sending nodes in this way adjusting energy among the nodes. It empowers the system to recuperate quicker from disappointment and improves the system dependability.
- **Relay Node Placement:** The beginning time exhaustion of nodes can be kept away from by the even appropriation of nodes by placing a few relay nodes. This improves the energy balance between nodes, inclusion, and limit and maintains a strategic distance from sensor problem areas.
- **Sink Mobility:** An enormous outstanding task at hand is focused on the nodes closer to the sink (base station) since all the traffic is coordinated towards the sink through them. Subsequently their battery gets drained quicker than other sensor nodes. The load can be adjusted by permitting a portable base station which gathers node data by moving in the system. Sink portability improves network, dependability and diminishes crash, conflict and message misfortune.

ENERGY EFFICIENT HIERARCHICAL BASED ROUTING

Information transmission is the noticeable energy consumer in WSNs. This requests a requirement for a design where the transmission to a Base Station (BS) is kept as little as could be expected under the circumstances and that all controls are made at node level. Likewise adaptability demonstrates to be notable as number of nodes develops and the size of system gets expanded. A reasonable methodology is the various leveled design. Here, the whole system is sorted out into some virtual layers (groups) and nodes in a similar layer are doled out with a similar job. A portion of the nodes are chosen as head (CH) of each bunch so as to adequately oversee assignments among the nodes. Grouping lessens the load on system by using the connection among the information. At that point this data is totaled, bringing about increasingly proficient energy utilization. CHs are in charge of social affair and aggregating the information from nodes lastly transmit it to the BS.

The primary objective of hierarchical based routing protocol is to effectively keep up the energy consumption of sensor nodes by including them in multi-bounce correspondence inside a group and by performing information total and combination so as to diminish the quantity of transmitted messages to the sink and transmission separation of sensor nodes. Each clustered system is said to have three attributes: group properties, CH properties and grouping process properties. Bunch properties incorporate number of groups, group size, inter-cluster and intra- cluster correspondence. The CHs can be either stationary or mobile, the system can be homogenous or heterogeneous and the chosen CHs have extensive impact on the clustering algorithm performance. The clustering algorithms can be either dispersed or concentrated and every algorithm has a one of a kind CH decision component. There are a few various hierarchical protocols, for example, LEACH, LEACH-C, PEGASIS, TEEN, APTEEN, BCDCP, HEED, and so on.

Swarm Intelligence Inspired Energy Efficient Routing Protocols

The Swarm intelligence (SI) (E. Bonabeau, M. Dorigo, G. Theraulaz, 1999) is a nearly crisp subject that was in the past communicated as ''Each exertion which plan new techniques or scattered issue-comprehending systems animated by the agreeable activities of bugs and other creature societies''. The SI framework shapes a self-governing dispersed framework that can display adaptable, enthusiastic, and versatile behaviors. The SI systems join other standard structures, for example, Ant Colony Optimization (ACO) (M. Dorigo, T. Stützle (Eds.), 2004) (M. Dorigo, T. Stützle (Eds.) R. Sharma, D.K. Lobiyal, 2015), Particle Swarm Optimization (PSO) (F.V.D. Bergh, A. Engelbrecht, 2006), Bee Colony organization (C. Ozturk, D. Karaboga, and B. Gorkemli, 2011), intelligent water drop method, cuckoo search method (M. Dhivya and M. Sundarambal, 2011), the glow-worm (GSO), Bat algorithm and schools of fishes (S. Sendra, L. Parra, J. Lloret, and S. Khan, 2015).

The fundamental procedures of these natural associations have been changed to plan novel dispersed optimization algorithms for the elaboration of the SI-motivated directing methods for the sensor systems. The creepy crawly social orders function as an agreeable unit and basically resolve routing issues. Creepy crawlies decide and make ways that can be trailed by different bugs to effectively move in reverse and advances from their province to wellsprings of nourishment. The comparability among the SI frameworks and routing in sensor systems is exceptionally high. These organic frameworks can be acknowledged as a scattered adaptable arrangement of discourteous control bundles that utilization the energy and computational sources to find the ways in the system or in the environment. Attributable to these similarities between looking through practices of SI colonies and network routing, a relatively incredible number of SI-inspired routing protocols have been anticipated for wireless sensor systems, in recent years.

Swarm Intelligence Nature in Routing Protocols

Maximum of the SI inspired routing protocols that are created for sensor systems are enlivened by exercises apparent in ant and, bee colonies. Furthermore, the looking through examples of the insect colonies have helped a central wellspring of inspiration to structure an assortment of new routing techniques. The expectation rests in the point that, all through of looking, the substances of the province commonly explore the surroundings to decide sources of food of nourishment and, when found them, they set up courses among the perch and the sources of food. The bugs pursue a similar course to go and to return, as to effectively move the nourishment back to the perch (home). Subsequently, the helpful looking through movement contains scattering investigation, location, setting up, and routine with regards to optimized routing paths in lively atmospheres. This technique is much like the course setting up procedure by sensor nodes in the sensor systems. Here, sensor nodes all in all build up multi-hop routes towards the sink node. The sensors trade the control bundles, build up courses and after that select an ideal way towards the sink for information transmission.

The swarm intelligence can be outlined as pursues:

- (an) It is de-centralized together; control is totally appropriated among various substances.
- (b) The communication procedure is totally confined among the elements.
- (c) Every one of the substances display comparative conduct without counseling one another

Ant Colony Optimization

Ant Colony Optimization based approaches It has been seen that ants store a synthetic like material (pheromone) while moving over a way. The correspondence between the ants depends on the measure of pheromones, delivered by the ants. More is the amount of the pheromone on a way, more it will be trailed by different ants

Bee Colony Optimization

The Bee Colony Optimization (BCO) is another Swarm Intelligence (SI) optimization method and it depends on wellorganized work business and power exhaustion. It is a multi-agent spread worldview. In the BCO paradigm, there are three kinds of honey bees; Queen, drones and Workers. There are three kinds of honey bees in the workers' gathering, The nourishment is gathered by the gathering of laborers. Some are the utilized honey bees that chase for the nourishment and pass on its data (fitness value) to the onlooker honey bees that select the best quality food. The scout honey bee look for a crisp nourishment food source. Dancing bees attract the onlookers bees towards the food source. A fitness value is evaluated for each new food source and the utilized honey bee recalls the one which has higher fitness value that is transmitted to the onlooker honey bees.

Particle Swarm Optimization

It is a renowned SI-inspired technique which is animated by the social deeds of the species, for example swarm of flying creatures, fish school .The populace based optimizes a fitness function. It practices the swarm of particles (search point) and pursue the fitness of each point. Each molecule is connected with some speed that encourages a molecule to make a trip to a superior position. Singh et al. anticipated a power mindful PSO enlivened clustering technique. It finds the ideal position (at focus of mass) for the cluster head. This optimization of the cluster head position decreases the normal separation of all group individuals to the group head. The decreased separation helps with lessening the power expended during the transmission. It considers N particles around the centre of mass and the speed of the particles is relied upon the lingering power and the amount of sensor nodes close it

ENERGY EFFICIENT ROUTING PROTOCOLS BASED ON ANT COLONY OPTIMIZATION FOR WIRELESS SENSOR NETWORKS

Energy Efficient Ant Based Routing (EEABR)

EEABR algorithm proposed by T. Camilo et al, 2006 is an extemporized routing protocol dependent on Ant Colony Optimization (ACO) metaheuristic. The protocol was planned with a goal to improve sensor nodes energy by decreasing correspondence overhead in finding the ways from source to goal. The protocol includes new functionalities in pheromone tables updation of sensor nodes.

Algorithm

1.   In EEABR routing protocol, at normal interim timeframe, from each organize node, a forward ant is propelled to decide a way from nest to food source. The identifier of each visited node is spared in memory and conveyed forward by ant. Each system node has routing table with N passages, one for every conceivable arrangement, and goal is one of the passage in nodes routing table.
2.   At each node, the ant chooses the following jump utilizing the equivalent ACO metaheuristic probabilistic principle.
3.   When the forward ant achieves the food goal, it is transmitted back to continuing ant, whose principle assignment is to refresh the pheromone trail of the way utilized by forward ant to reach from home to source and furthermore put away in memory.
4.   The goal node registers the measure of pheromone trail that the ant will drop during the adventure, before backward ant begins the voyage.
5.   When the node, gets the retrogressive ant originating from neighboring node, it refreshes the routing table.
6.   When the backward ant achieves the home, the genuine way is controlled by other ants to pursue.

Simulation of EEABR with BABR (Basic Ant Based routing algorithm) and IABR (Improvised Ant-Based Routing Algorithm) is done on NS-2 test system on changed parameters like Average Energy, Minimum Energy, Standard Deviation and Energy

Efficiency and overall EEABR performs much better when contrasted with other two routing protocols. The main downside of EEABR is absence of QoS and to some degree delay in bundle conveyance

Ant Chain Protocol

Ant-Chain, a hierarchical protocol is an energy efficient algorithm for Wireless Sensor Networks was being created by Ding and Liu in 2005 with essential core interest towards energy efficiency, maximizing the lifetime of the sensor node and data integrity. It is fundamentally a centralized algorithm where the obligations of sensor nodes and the sink nodes are divided relying upon their equipment assets and relative separations so as to optimize the energy and decrease transmission delays. Ant-Chain algorithm is helpful in those applications where the sensor nodes area is realized well ahead of time. Ant Chain has an edge over different algorithms like LEACH and PEGASIS on the ground of energy efficiency. The downside of this algorithm is that it is incorporated in nature which thus wipes out the capacity of strength in it

Ant Aggregation

The advancement of Ant Aggregation was done by Misra and Mandal in 2006 on the grounds of contention that a multi hop communication model combined with in-organize accumulation can prompt the decrease in utilization of energy by sensor nodes and which thusly prompts the system lifetime upgrade. The protocol being created focuses on the issue of ideal total in multicast tree which is essentially a NP-difficult issue. It is a hierarchical protocol. The principle goal of this algorithm was to construct least cost accumulation trees, under which forward ants either search for way which is most brief to the sink note or for a near to total focuses. In each node, a forward ant is unicast to the following hop with a specific likelihood characterized in the protocol. In this way, we can say that Ant Aggregation performs better as far as energy efficiency when connected to the sensor syatem.

Pheromone Based Energy Aware Directed Diffusion (PEADD)

Pheromone Based Energy Aware Directed Diffusion (PEADD) protocol is an information driven protocol and is viewed as another variation of Directed Diffusion and is based on Ant Colony Optimization heuristic. The protocol was created by Zhu in 2007 to improve the lifetime of sensor organizes by just including high energy nodes during the time spent information gathering. In this algorithm ants increment the pheromone on a way relatively to the rest of the energy levels of the node. Therefore, the ways with bigger remaining energy are expanded and others are decreased. The degree of pheromone is refreshed remembering the measure of transmitting information. PEADD uses the general ant based routing as far as determination and updation of course

Ant Colony Multicast Trees (ACMT)

Ant Colony Multicast Tress (ACMT) algorithm was proposed by De-min et al in 2008 with the reason to improve the lifetime of sensor arrange by taking energy consumption into thought. In ACMT calculation, ants find the trees with all goal nodes. Each node on the tree which has been found is present node. Each step made by every ant has no other importance of any way than to empower the present tree to become further. This algorithms returns positive input instrument of basic ant colony algorithm. The designers of this algorithms have contrasted this and YANG model and Flooding and have watched critical enhancements as to performance via simulation

Improvised Ant Colony Routing (IACR)

Improvised Ant Colony Routing (IACR), a progressive convention, was proposed by Peng et al in 2008 which is basically an improvement over ant colony routing. The fundamental preferred position of this protocol that it thinks about the usage of energy by sensor nodes alongside QoS (Quality of Service) parameter.

The algorithm being proposed comprises of two sections:

1. Routing Discovery It is done similarly as in basic ant colony routing protocol..
2. Route Maintenance The routing table is refreshed with the progressions at the equivalent time when the topology changes.

Adaptive Clustering for Energy Efficient WSN based on ACO (ACO-C)

ACO-C is an area based, another adaptive clustering energy efficient routing protocol was actualized by Ziyadi et al in 2009. The routing fundamentally works on two parameters: Distance minimization between the source node and sink node; Data Aggregation among all the sensor nodes. The specialist has recreated the proposed algorithms in MATLAB and has additionally contrasted the outcomes with LEACH. It was being seen after recreation that ACO-C performs better as far as energy efficiency yet results are not noteworthy when contrasted with LEACH-C and PSO-C protocols.

Energy Efficient ACO Based QoS Routing (EAQR)

This is a Hierarchical protocol and was formed by taking into consideration the arrangement of sensors in the sensor systems where there is non-consistency in traffic, thusly different issues like clog which hampers the performance of the system. In this way, Jietai et al. in year 2009 proposed Energy Efficient ACO based QoS rputing protocol dependent on Ant Colony Optimization. The principle parameters on which this algorithm proposed is concentrated is QoS and adjusting energy consumption in sensor network. By presenting measurements like least way energy and way jump check what's more, by methods for propelling pheromone trail model of the ant colony system, the algorithm gives different approaches to improve execution of continuous and normal traffic. The algorithm being proposed by specialists was effectively reenacted in NS-2 test system and has demonstrated execution upgrades as far as Average ETE delay, Average ETE delay jitter, Packet delivery ratio.

CONCLUSION

Notwithstanding numerous uses of wireless sensor networks, it is important to transmit data properly with respect to control usage and system life expectancy just as restricted assets of such systems. WSNs are intended for explicit applications. Since radio transmission and gathering devours enormous measure of energy, power is a significant factor to be examined upon. The restricted energy resources of sensors makes energy efficiency one of the significant difficulties in the structure of WSNs. Protocols structured should point in keeping sensors alive for extensive stretch in order to satisfy the application necessities. The most huge trouble in such systems is directing and moving information to the goal node in consistence with the energy issue. Thusly, energy-efficient routing protocols have critical and compelling jobs in wireless sensor systems. They are isolated into three noteworthy groups dependent on information, network structure and reliability. In this examination, energy-efficient routing protocols were researched in WSN. At that point the basic arrangements were presented and related parameters of relating protocols were contrasted with one another. In spite of the way that these protocols are performing admirably as far as energy protection however issues like quality of service (QoS) would be relied upon to deliver to guarantee use of most energy capable path for information move and moreover guaranteeing ensured information move rate or deferral. Hierarchical architecture approach is the best to give adaptability alongside an all-inclusive system lifetime. Sensors without energy can never again achieve its job except if source of energy is renewed. Wireless sensors that are powered by ambient energy harvesting is a promising innovation for some detecting applications. Another intriguing issue with regards to routing is that most of the present routing shows acknowledge that the sensor center points and the sink is stationary. In conditions, for instance, on the combat zone where the sink and possibly the sensors ought to be flexible. In such cases, new routing systems are required remembering the ultimate objective to manage the overhead of movability and topology changes in such power compelled conditions.

REFERENCES

Al-Karaki, J. N., & Kamal, A. E. (2004). Routing techniques in wireless sensor networks: A Survey. *IEEE Wireless Communications*, *11*(6), 6–28. doi:10.1109/MWC.2004.1368893

Amiri, E., Keshavarz, H., Heidari, H., Mohamadi, E., & Moradzadeh, H. (2013). Intrusion detection systems in MANET:a review. *Proceedings of the International Conference onInnovation, Management and Technology Research*, 1–6.

Amiri, Keshavarz, & Alizadeh, Zamani, & Khodadadi. (2014). Energy Efficient Routing in Wireless Sensor Networks Based onFuzzy Ant Colony Optimization. *International Journal of Distributed Sensor Networks*.

Bergh, F. V. D., & Engelbrecht, A. (2006). A study of particle swarm optimization particle trajectories. *Information Sciences*, *176*(8), 937–971. doi:10.1016/j.ins.2005.02.003

Bonabeau, E., Dorigo, M., & Theraulaz, G. (1999). *Swarm Intelligence: From Natural to Artificial Systems*. New York: Oxford University Press.

Camilo, T., Carreto, C., Silva, J., & Boavida, F. (2006). An Energy-Efi cient Ant Base Routing Algorithm for Wireless Sensor Networks. *ANTS 2006 – Fifth International Workshop on Ant Colony Optimization and Swarm Intelligence*, 49-59.

Cardell-Oliver, R. (2005). *Soil Moisture Monitoring with Wireless Sensor Networks*. University of Western Australia. Retrieved from www.csse.uwa.edu.au/adhocnets/WSNgroup/soilwater-proj

Dargie & Poellabauer. (2010). *Fundamental of Wireless Sensor Networks: Theory and Practice*. John Wiley & Sons.

Dhivya, M., & Sundarambal, M. (2011). Cuckoo Search for data gathering in Wireless Sensor Networks. *International Journal of Mobile Communications*, *9*(6), 642–656. doi:10.1504/IJMC.2011.042781

Dhivya, M., Sundarambal, M., & Anand, L. N. (2011). Energy efficient computation of data fusion in wireless sensor networks using cuckoo based particle approach (CBPA), International Journal of Communications. *Network and System Sciences*, *4*(4), 249–255. doi:10.4236/ijcns.2011.44030

Ding, N., & Liu, P. X. (2005). A centralized approach to energy-efficient protocols for wireless sensor networks. In *Mechatronics and Automation, 2005 IEEE International Conference* (*Vol. 3*, pp. 1636-1641). IEEE.

Dorigo, M. (1992). *Optimization, learning and natural algorithms* (Ph.D. thesis). Politecnico di Milano, Milan, Italy.

Dorigo, M., & Di Caro, G. A. (1999). The ant colony optimization metaheuristic. In D. Corne & M. Dorigo (Eds.), *New Ideas in Optimization* (pp. 11–32). McGraw-Hill.

Dorigo, M., & Stützle, T. (Eds.). (2004). Ant Colony Optimization. MIT Press.

Fernandez, P. M. (2003). *Circuit switching in the Internet* (Ph.D. thesis). Stanford University.

Frey, H., R¨uhrup, S., & Stojmenovi'c, I. (2009). *Routing in wirelesssensornetworks. In Guide to Wireless Sensor Networks* (pp. 81–111). Berlin, Germany: Springer. doi:10.1007/978-1-84882-218-4_4

Haidar, Ghassempour, & Braun. (2012, Mar.). Nature-inspired routing algorithm for wireless sensor networks. *Australian Journal of Electrical and Electronics Engineering*.

Hamdi, Essaddi, & Boudriga. (2008). *Energy-Efficient Routing in Wireless Sensor Networks Using Probabilistic Strategies*. IEEE Communications Society.

Holger Karl and Andreas Willig. (2005). *Protocols and Architectures for Wireless Sensor Networks*. John Wiley & Sons, Ltd.

Iwata, A., Chiang, C.-C., Pei, G., & Gerla, M. (1999, August). Scalable routing strategies for ad hoc wireless networks. *IEEE Journal on Selected Areas in Communications*, *17*(8), 1369–1379. doi:10.1109/49.779920

Jietai, W., Jiadong, X. U., & Mantian, X. (2009). EAQR: An energy-efficient ACO basedQoS routing algorithm in wireless sensor networks. *Chinese Journal of Electronics*, *18*, 113–116.

Johnson & Maltz. (1996). *Dynamic source routing in ad hoc wireless networks. In Mobile Computing* (pp. 153–181). NewYork, NY: Springer.

Katkar & Ghorpade. (2015). A Survey on Energy Efficient Routing Protocol forWireless Sensor Networks. *International Journal of Computer Science and Information Technologies, 6*.

Kennedy, J., Eberhart, R. C., & Shi, Y. (2001). *Swarm Intelligence*. San Francisco, CA: Morgan Kaufman.

Keshavarz, H., Noor, R. M., & Mostajeran, E. (2013). Using routing table lag to improve performance of AODV routing protocol for VANETs environment. *Proceedings of the 9th Interna-tional Conference on Computing and Information Technology (IC2IT '13)*, 73–82.

Manjeshwar & Agrawal. (2001). TEEN: A routing protocol for Enhanced Efficiency in Wireless Sensor Networks. *Proceedings of 15th International Parallel and Distributed Processing Symposium* (IPDPS'01) Workshops, 2009-2015.

Manjeshwar, A., & Agrawal, D. (2002). APTEEN: A Hybrid Protocol for Efficiency Routing and Comprehensive Information Retrieval in Wireless Sensor Networks. *Proceedings of International Parallel and Distributed Processing Symposium*, 195-202.

Misra, R., & Mandal, C. (2006). Ant-aggregation: ant colony algorithm for optimal data aggregation in wireless sensor networks. In *Wireless and Optical Communications Networks, 2006 IFIP International Conference on*. IEEE. 10.1109/WOCN.2006.1666600

Oh, H., Bahn, H., & Chae, K. (2005, August). An Energy-Efficient Sensor Routing Scheme for Home Automation Networks. *IEEE Transactions on Consumer Electronics, 51*(3), 836–839. doi:10.1109/TCE.2005.1510492

Oh, H., & Chae, K. (2007). An Energy-Efficient Sensor Routing with low latency. *Scalability in Wireless Sensor Networks IEEE 2007 International Conference on Multimedia and Ubiquitous Engineering*, 147-152. 10.1109/MUE.2007.75

Ozturk, Karaboga, & Gorkemli. (n.d.). Artificial bee colony algorithm for dynamic deployment of wireless sensor networks. *Turkish Journal of Electrical Engineering & Computer*.

Pantazis, N. A., Nikolidakis, S. A., Vergados, D. D., & Member, S. (2013). Energy-efficient routing protocols in wireless sensor networks: A survey. *IEEE Communications Surveys and Tutorials, 15*(2), 551–591. doi:10.1109/SURV.2012.062612.00084

Pantazis, Nikolidakis, & Vergados. (2013). Senior Member, Energy-Efficient Routing Protocols in Wireless Sensor Networks: A Survey. IEEE Communications Surveys & Tutorials, 15(2).

Peng, S., Yang, S. X., Gregori, S., & Tian, F. (2008, June). An adaptive QoSand energy-aware routing algorithm for wireless sensor networks.In *Information and Automation, 2008. ICIA 2008. International Conference on* (pp. 578-583). IEEE

Perkins, C. E., & Bhagwat, P. (1994). Highly dynamic destination-sequenced distance-vector routing (DSDV) for mobile comput-ers. *Computer Communication Review, 24*(4), 234–244. doi:10.1145/190809.190336

Rabiner, W., Chandrakasan, A., & Balakrishnan, H. (2000). Energy-Efficient Communication Protocol for Wireless Microsensor Networks. *Hawaii International Conference on System Sciences*, 10-19.

Rajesh, S. L. (2014, December). Nature Inspired Energy Efficient Wireless Sensor Networks Using Dynamic Sleep-Active Algorithm. *International Journal for Research in Applied Science and Engineering Technology, 2.*

Rault, T., Bouabdallah, A., & Challal, Y. (2014). Energy Efficiency in wireless sensor networks: A top-down survey. *Computer Networks, 67*, 104–122. doi:10.1016/j.comnet.2014.03.027

Roseline, R. A., & Sumathi, P. (2012). Local clustering and threshold sensitive routing algorithm for Wireless Sensor Networks. In *Devices, Circuits and Systems (ICDCS), 2012 International Conference*. IEEE.

Sen, J., & Ukil, A. (2009, May). An adaptable and QoS-aware routing protocol for Wireless Sensor Networks. In *Wireless Communication, Vehicular Technology, Information Theory and Aerospace & Electronic Systems Technology, 2009. Wireless VITAE 2009. 1st International Conference on* (pp. 767-771). IEEE. 10.1109/WIRELESSVITAE.2009.5172546

Sendra, S., Parra, L., Lloret, J., & Khan, S. (2015). Systems and Algorithms for Wireless Sensor Networks Based on Animal and Natural Behavior. International Journal of Distributed Sensor Networks.

Sharawi, M., Emary, E., Saroit, I. A., & El-Mahdy, H. (2014). Bat Swarm Algorithm for Wireless Sensor Networks Lifetime Optimization. *International Journal of Science and Research, 3*(5), 654–664.

Sharma, R., & Lobiyal, D. K. (2015). Dual Transmission Power and Ant Colony Optimization Based Lifespan Maximization Protocol for Sensor Networks *International Journal of Business Data Communications and Networking, 11*(1), 1–14. doi:10.4018/IJBDCN.2015010101

Sinha & Barman. (2012). Energy Efficient Routing Mechanism in Wireless Sensor Network. *IEEE Conference on Recent Advances in Information Technology.*

Sohraby, K. (2007). *Wireless Sensor Networks.* Elsevier Inc. doi:10.1002/047011276X

Sohraby, K., Minoli, D., & Znati, T. (2007). *Wireless Sensor Networks, Technology, Protocols, and Applications*. Hoboken, NJ: John Wiley & Sons, Inc. doi:10.1002/047011276X

Zhu, X. (2007). Pheromone based energy aware directed diffusion algorithm for wireless sensor network. In Advanced Intelligent Computing Theories and Applications. With Aspects of Theoretical and Methodological Issues (pp. 283-291). Springer Berlin Heidelberg. doi:10.1007/978-3-540-74171-8_28

Ziyadi, M., Yasami, K., & Abolhassani, B. (2009, May). Adaptive clusteringfor energy efficient wireless sensor networks based on ant colonyoptimization. In *Communication Networks and Services Research Conference, 2009. CNSR'09. Seventh Annual* (pp. 330-334). IEEE

Chapter 7
A Study on Energy–Efficient Wireless Sensor Network Protocols

Devika G.

(iD) https://orcid.org/0000-0002-2509-2867
Government Engineering College, KR Pet, India

Ramesh D.
Sri Siddhartha Institute of Technology, India

Asha Gowda Karegowda
Siddaganga Institute of Technology, India

ABSTRACT

Many original ideologies are being applied as solutions to the problems of wireless sensor networks with the rigorous experimentation and advancement in technology and research. This chapter reviews various energy-efficient routing algorithms, classifying them based on methodology applied. The classification is based on design approach used to solve the basic problem arising in construction of transmission path between source and base station (BS) with minimum energy consumption. The pros and cons of routing algorithms for WSN are analyzed. The parameters to be considered in evaluation of all routing protocols are summarized.

DOI: 10.4018/978-1-7998-1626-3.ch007

INTRODUCTION

Wireless sensor networks have potential to monitor environments for both military and civil applications (Iyengar et.al.(1995), Pottie et. Al(2000),Khan et. Al.(1999), Akyildiz et.al.(2005)). WSN are also known as motes which has got sensing ability. Normally they exist in group for communicating sensor nodes which works in a co-operative and coordinating manner to collect data from physical world as of their respective communication protocols (Fazlic et.al(2019)). Every node present in WSN has processing capability, RF transceiver, power source apart from sensing and actuating units (Khan et. Al.,1999). The processed data will be forwarded to sink (destination node) using single or multiple routes (Mao et.al, (2013), Ramson et.al.,(2017)).

There are several constraints in WSN among which the major concern of interest factor in WSN is energy efficient routing since sensor life time is limited as they dependent on batteries. In sensor network, a wireless media is used to link nodes for communication purpose. The commonly used transmission media are briefed in table 1.

In this paper, a broad categorization of energy-aware routing algorithms is done. Design issues and routing protocol objectives are discussed in section 2 followed by broad categorization of routing protocols in section 3. Section 4 covers detailed study of heuristic approach for energy efficient routing algorithms. Section 5 covers detailed study of meta heuristic approach for energy efficient routing algorithms. The rest of this paper included as follows. In section 2 a brief review of energy efficient algorithm is considered. The classification of routing algorithm is described in section 3. Evaluation parameters are described in section 4. In section 5, a brief review of various simulators is presented. Lastly, in section 6 a brief conclusion and enhancement is described.

Energy-Efficient WSN Routing

Routing is a process of discovering an effective and efficient transmission path between nodes. The routing table may be built to store routing information for route maintenance or for future communications. Because the major concern is limited energy there is a demand for energy efficient routing algorithms. The various design issues of routing algorithms are briefed below.

Table 1. Transmission media for sensors

Name	Standard	Bandwidth	Transmission range as (m)	Data rates (Mbps)	Network size	Advantages	Devices	Application
Wi-Fi	IEEE802.11	2.4GHz	100	11	32	Flexibility speed	Laptops, consoles	Internet access, web, email
WiMax	IEEE802.29	220MHz	50	30-40	54Mbps	Long range	PC peripherals	Broadcast connections
WiMedia	IEEE802.15.3	300GHz	10	11-15	245	High data rates	Speaker, printers	Real time multimedia streaming
Bluetooth	IEEE802.15.1	915MHz	100-50	3-4	7	Low cost	Mobile phones, mouse, keyboards	Cable replacement
Zigbee	IEEE802.15.4	2.4GHz	100	100	65000	Reliability	Embedded sensors	Low power devices communication
Bluetooth low energy	BLE	2.4GHZ	50	10	15	Low cost and power, more reliable	mouse, keyboards	Low power devices communication
Z-wave	IEEE802.11, 802.15, 802.16	900GHz	10-30	Upto 100	232	Lower power	Home devices	Low cost
Insteon	X-10	915MHz	Upto 25	1.2-180	Not limited	Network will be made up of independent devices	Motion Embedded devices	Low cost and power requirements
Cellular	IMT-2000	1900MHz	35Km	35-118gbs	Not limited	More coverage, high data rates	Mobile phones	Mover coverage area with more data rates

Design Issues of Routing Protocol

1. **Energy Resource:** The limited available in sensors has to be judiciously used in an efficient manner without compromising on accurate and timely transmission of data using appropriate routing algorithms.
2. **Dynamic Network Topology:** Network topology can be designed either predefined or on using random strategy.
3. **Network Size:** Number of nodes defines the network size which may vary on time basis.
4. **Data heterogeneity:** Based on the type of data to be sensed, data sensors can be either Homogeneous or heterogeneous.
5. **Node Failure:** There may be failure of one or more nodes either because of limited energy or harsh environment. The consequences of node failure are reflected in the form of packet loss and overall reduction in network energy to reconstruct new path for sending the lost packet.

6. **Node Mobility:** The node in the WSN can be either mobile or fixed.
7. **Communication Overhead:** In WSN, communication happens among the nodes as well as between the nodes and the Base station (BS).
8. **Node Density:** The high-density featured sensor nodes deployment is required to observe physical phenomena in detail. The routing protocol should support in-network combination of the information from a large number of nodes consuming less amount of energy.
9. **Life Time:** Sensors will normally be deployed in areas unreachable to humans and cannot be monitored physically or replaced frequently hence energy of sensors to be utilized in an intelligent manner to prolong network lifetime. So, it is very much required to prolong the life time of sensors while carrying out its necessary operations.
10. **Addressing:** Since IP based addressing cannot be used in sensors, local nodes identification can be included with in network.
11. **Application:** It is very important to know type of application for which routing protocol is being designed. Moreover, event location is not fixed since it is directly related to the event and so new routes should be generated for each event.

Routing Protocols Objectives

Some of objectives of routing protocols are:

- **Data Assurance:** The message delivery ratio is one of the measures for data assurance.
- **Quality of Service:** It demands accurate and in time delivery of data.
- **Optimality:** The routing algorithms have to optimise in terms of throughput and minimizing mean packet delay. Here there is a tradeoff and one has to choose depending on his suitability.
- **Load Balancing and Network Lifetime:** To conserve energy as well as for accurate data delivery(avoiding flooding) data fusion can be adopted.
- **Differentiated Services:** Sensors can be heterogeneous based on applications

Classification of Routing Protocols

A routing process is needed to select the best path(s) from the source node to the destination node. Routing may also be designed and optimized to support some specific requirements of applications and networks. These requirements include energy and bandwidth efficiency, quality of service, scalability, ad hoc support, throughput, mobility and reliability. This will cause wide variation in requirements, which cannot be fulfilled by a single routing protocol. Correspondingly, many different protocols are found, which have been designed to fit some specific requirements. A broad classification of energy efficient algorithm is presented in figure 1.

In general, routing in WSNs can be divided into heuristic and meta-heuristic algorithms based on routing procedures applied on WSN. Further heuristic algorithms are classified according to design consideration for routing as follows architecture, communication model, data delivery, path establishment, network operation, network structure and performance. Routing path will be designed applying fuzzy logic, swarm intelligence, immune system, genetic algorithm techniques, and neural networks in meta-heuristic algorithms.

Figure 1. Broad classification of routing algorithm

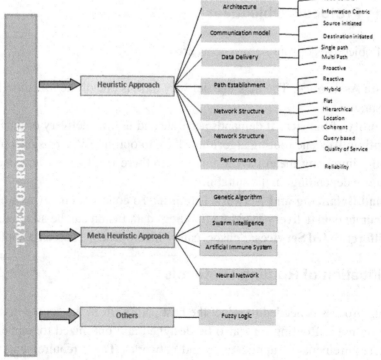

WSN HEURISTIC ROUTING ALGORITHMS

Architecture Based Routing

Architecture based routing can be categorized under two categories: node-centric and information –centric approach. The major difference between the two approaches is that, node based approach provides node's identity in addition to data transmission whereas; information centric mainly concentrates on data transmission.

Node-Centric Approach: The major design concern of this routing communication is totally based on IP address of nodes. The routing process will be initiated or continued until the source and destination will know their corresponding address else they will not be able set any type communication links. Once the addresses are set there is a normal transmission of messages between them (Suhonen et.al,2007).

Message queue telemetry transport (MQTT) (Ephremides et.al, 1987) uses TCP for communicating messages by considering QOS parameters. Publish-subscribe architecture is applied in MQTT controlled by the broker which maintains routes between them even when they are not active. Publishers are initiator of information and then forwards to subscriber. Comparatively, Constrained Application Protocol (CoAP)(Lin et.al, 1987) has less overhead as it is designed applying UDP protocol and hence, it is widely accepted for WSN applications. Its architecture is based on representational state transfer, which has capability to operate on HTTP. The information can be retrieved as URIs. To operative modes are supported: request response and resource observe. In first method client will forward request to server and in turn server response to it. In later type, request is made to observed objects in URIs'. The chance of interference is more and network reliability is less. A variant of CoAP is implemented in (XU et.al, 2002) applying multicast technique to transmit messages. But it still does not guarantee message is transmitted to intended node. The algorithms still suffers from reliability and scalability problem. The cost of maintaining message using multicast technique is more and demands adoption of improved technique (Locke et.al, 2018). The energy efficiency for WSN provided is not sufficient and can be improved by applying better strategies other than traditional techniques. The method can be improved by applying decentralized method rather than centralized method depending on server (Bormann et.al, 2018).

Information-Centric Approach

This approach of architecture is based on information and it does not keep track of nodes address. The node which needs information post request in network. When the information is found then node will connect and accept information through transmission. Nodes which encounter the information will maintain a copy in its cache hence, in future if any nearest nodes request for same information then, it will be forwarded to the requested node in minimum time without creating traffic imbalance (Rahaman et.al, 2018).

The Direct Diffusion [DD](Bormann et.al,2018) protocol is a traditional routing algorithm for sensor network. The sensor nodes broadcast the interest messages (demand for particular kind of data) to whole network. If a node has interest message it will forwards message to the requested node via neighbor node using multiple paths. The data can reach by multiple paths to sink in reverse direct of interest. DD use reinforcement to ensure optimal route between source and sink. Then, sink according to its local rules will set one node as neighbor based on higher data rate. Sink nodes guaranteed route reliability by monitoring multiple paths. The protocol can be improved by reducing data flooding in both the directions.

The protocol for PCs' are designed for content centric network (Rahaman et.al, 2018). Since, this proposed protocol is not suitable for WSN, it is redefined to cope with standards of Zigbee (Ishaq et.al, 2016). Further to eliminate data flooding problem a new information centric routing protocol (Hui et.al, 2018) was proposed with data aggregation to minimize energy with in network. The routing is based on objective function consisting of data messages of different types in different paths. The nodes execute objective function to select relay nodes for every traffic contents. Initially node will broadcasts message informing outgoing traffic content types, corresponding traffic volume and candidate selection criteria. The indented candidate nodes respond with message containing node ID and estimated life time if they are chosen to forward the data. The nodes will rank candidates applying objective function and then assign a relay node to corresponding traffic. Further nodes maintain a different routing entry for each piece of content. Aggregation of information avoids' transmission of redundant data and hence prolong network life span.

Communication Model

Communication based routing algorithms are classified as source-initiated and destination-initiated protocols.

Source-Initiated Protocols: Route discovery from source to destination is initiated by source. Dynamic Source Routing (DSR) is an Ad Hoc routing protocol which is based on the theory of source-based routing rather than table-based. This protocol is source-initiated rather than hop-by-hop. Basically, DSR protocol does not need any existing network infrastructure or administration and this allows the

Network to be completely self-organizing and self-configuring. This Protocol is composed of two essential parts of route discovery and route maintenance. Every node maintains a cache to store recently discovered paths. When a node desires to send a packet to some node, it first checks its entry in the cache. If it is there, then it uses that path to transmit the packet and also attach its source address on the packet. If it is not there in the cache or the entry in cache is expired (because of long time idle), the sender broadcasts a route request packet to all of its neighbors asking for a path to the destination. The sender will be waiting till the route is discovered. During waiting time, the sender can perform other tasks such as sending/forwarding other packets. As the route request packet arrives to any of the nodes, they check from their neighbor or from their caches whether the destination asked is known or unknown. If route information is known, they send back a route reply packet to the destination otherwise they broadcast the same route request packet. When the route is discovered, the required packets will be transmitted by the sender on the discovered route. One of the main benefit of DSR protocol is that there is no need to keep routing table so as to route a given data packet as the entire route is contained in the packet header. The limitations of DSR protocol is that this is not scalable to large networks and even requires significantly more processing resources than most other protocols. In order to obtain the routing information the time consumption is more (Ren et.al, 2013).

Destination-Initiated Protocols: Route discovery from destination to source is initiated by destination. During setup phase, BS being a destination initiates process of route. The BS will discover the best route keeping track of various parameters like reliability, energy usage, bandwidth and others. The cost decreases, the node redirects its gradient and transmits the route advertisement (RADV) with updated costs to its neighbors. If the route advertisement contains a sink/interest pair that is previously unknown, the node sends an interest request (IREQ). The IREQ is replied to with an interest advertisement (IADV), which contains the application-specific description of interests, such as the type of data and collection interval. Each node in the network broadcasts its RADV periodically or when a route cost changes significantly in order to maintain routing and interest information (Locke et.al, 2012).

Data Delivery Based Routing Algorithms

This can be broadly classified under two types: single v/s multiple paths.

Single Path: The BS will communicate to each sensor directly on static or dynamically formed routes, if it needs to get any information likewise sensor nodes will communicate directly with BS. It improves the performance (better throughput, faster routing, enhanced load distribution, support for QoS, and reliability)(Jin et.al, 2016).

Shortest-Path Distance Algorithm: This technique is based on finding the shortest path having shortest distance between source node and sink node in WSN in a single direct communication link. Dijkstra's algorithm is used to find the shortest single path between sink and source node (cali et.al, 2015).

Shortest-Path Hop Algorithm

Destination sourced distance vector (DSDV) finds the path with minimum hop-count between a given source node and the sink node in WSN (clause et.al, 2001, Perkins et.al,2002). The authors in DSDV Routing Protocol in Ad-Hoc Wireless Sensor DRPAWSN] (Dijkstra,1959) consider DSDV algorithms for end-to-end communication transmission construction, avoiding multiple path or multi hop with in network. An application of DSDV in energy efficient WSN is presented for application areas like MANETS, small scale wireless applications based on zigbee and tracking applications (Ouafaa, 2005). The DSDV [23] algorithm is designed using table driven routing scheme for WSN using Bellman-Ford algorithm where each node will act as a router to forward data and as well maintain route information in table even when the network is idle. The breadth-first search (BFS) algorithm is applied to implement the routing protocol (Perkins et.al,1999, Ghawy et.al,2005) to determine energy efficient path between nodes for communication.

Multi Path: In contrast to single path, multi path is established between nodes to communicate among nodes more than one route and hence helps in reliability and guaranteed delivery of message. Bee-sensor (Ouafaa et.al, 2005) works with design principles of multi path algorithm. It imitates the behavior of swarm of bees. The routing process works in three phases. Clusters are formed in first phase: it involves connecting surrounding nodes to form a group. Followed by identification of multi-path routes using residual energy of nodes in the second phase and data is transmitted in the third phase once the path is set.

Highly-resilient Energy-Efficient Multipath Routing in Wireless Sensor Networks (HEMR) constructs multiple partially disjoint paths and also provides fault tolerance. Two path reinforcement messages are used for path construction. The first path identified is considered as primary path and next identified path as alternate path reinforcement. If primary path goes down then, messages are forwarded on alternate path to reach source node. The same computation is done on all nodes until sink node is reached. The routing algorithm is reliable at the cost of energy and space (Shi et.al,2012).

An Energy-Efficient Multipath Routing Protocol for Wireless Sensor Networks (EEMR) designed for WSN for efficient routing protocol. It is a distributed, localized and expandable multi path routing algorithm to distribute traffic over multiple paths by load balancing algorithm is applied. The route setup initiation will be done when any node identifies events. The sink can send multiple route requests at a time for its neighbor identification and adopts the one which consumes minimum time within the paths identified in the set time and the rest identified paths are discarded. Data transmission is guaranteed at the cost of time and energy (Prasan et.al, 2012).

Maximally Radio-Disjoint Multipath Routing for Wireless Multimedia Sensor Networks (MRMRW) is architectural based routing protocol for WSN. This (Eslaminejad et.al, 2011) protocol constructs multiple paths and applied to multimedia based applications. Adaptive incremental method is used to construct minimum interfering paths of shortest path. The protocol avoids the situation of congestion or bandwidth shortage by identifying additional routes in such situations. The avoiding of interference of messages is avoided by sending some nodes to sleep mode where nodes activities are completely stopped.

Interference-Aware Multipath Routing Protocol for QoS Improvement in Event-Driven Wireless Sensor Networks (IMRQI) is designed to minimize energy consumption and overlapping. All sensors location information is considered for construction of two collision free paths between source and sink. Based on concept of overhearing routes are constructed for each communication link (LU et.al, 2007).

Low Interference Energy-efficient Multipath Routing (LIEMRO)(Ganeshan et.al,2001): LIEMRO concentrates on QOS parameters in construction of multiple communication paths within a network. The node disjoint mechanism is applied in identifying route and load balancing is operated with in network to distribute traffic. Cost is assigned for each link based on Expected transmission count metric. It broadcast's the control packets to its neighbors; during path identification to sink using residual energy metric. The route formation initiation will be done when event occur. The route setup phase will be started by source node to sink. Data with lower energy rates will be preferably transmitted over link having low residual energy to save energy of nodes. The major identifiable problems are it will not consider service rate and storage capacity of nodes to adjust or to predict traffic rates.

Multipath Routing with Novel Packet Scheduling Approach (MRNPS) designed for Wireless Sensor Networks to route packets in ordered way. This routing technique is based on constructing multiple paths between nodes to increase reliability and use scheduling policy to transmit data. Each node maintains five queues; two for incoming and three for outgoing transmission of data. Each node in a network will actively participate in transmission of packet by assigning priority to packet, scheduling it in appropriate queue and forwarding them when they need to be based on scheduling policy based on priority rule to next nodes. The load with in network can be regulated by tuning queue length. The algorithm is complex in maintaining queues which may lead to transmission delay and failure detection is not employed (Lu et.al,2007, Mimour, 2009).

Greedy Perimeter Stateless Routing (GPSR): The GPSR routing uses positions of node and destination to make forwarding decisions. It uses greedy forwarding technique to route packets. The nodes which receives packet will simply forward it to its next nearer neighbors. The algorithm does not require any storage. The major shortfall is that nodes path are create only when any neighbor goes down (Wang et.al, 2009).

Two-Phase geographical Greedy Forwarding (TPGF) is a routing protocol which constructs route based on multiple node disjoint paths. The identification of path for transmission is done by applying greedy techniques. The links are static for communication and forward packets to nodes under consent. The protocol does not support dynamic routing (Radi et.al, 2013).

On-demand geographic routing: The routing algorithm constructs path for communication between source node and sink. The source enables route establishment by identifying two paths without designing any routing message only based on location of nodes. The rectangular zones are constructed between source and sink which is fixed until few nodes are dead. The length of transmission range is twice the distance between nodes and builds multiple communication path between them. The identified routes will be non–interfering from one to another (Couto et.al, 2003).

Non-Interfering Multipath Geographic Routing (NIMGR): The protocol generates two deviation angles from source node to sink. The paths are identified in such a way that they are non-interfering and non proximal to one another. It considers lines which are twice radial from source to sink pairs. In this technique transmission delay is less. But it does not consider all nodes energy for identification of paths (Cherian et.al, 2007).

Node-disjoint multipath routing with zoning [NDMR]: The author has concentrated to improve routing algorithm with path efficiency. The two-hop neighbor information is stored in every node and network area is divided into zones between sources to sink. Multiple disjoint paths are identified between every node to sink. Likewise, two routes are maintained in network one within zone communication considered as local and another across as global communication. The algorithm works well in uniform distributed network. Protocol requires more memory and more chances of interference among communicating nodes (Karp et.al, 2000).

Ad hoc on-demand multipath distance vector [AOMDV]: The routing protocol builds multiple paths for transmission of packets from source to sink through guarantee loop free and disjointness of alternateness. Routes identification do not demand location of nodes and neglects coupling problem (Shu et.al, 2008).

The comparison of data delivery(*single and multi path*) based heuristic WSN routing is summarized in Table 2.

Table 2. *Comparison of data delivery (single and multi path) based WSN.*

Routing technique	Distribution of nodes	Control message overhead	Uniform energy distribution	Energy efficiency	Scalability	Transmission delay	Algorithm complexity	Data aggregation	Simulation Tool
HEMR	Random	Very high	Low	Moderate	High	High	Minimum	N	Qualnet
EEMR	Random	Low	Very low	Minimum	High	High	Minimum	N	NS2
MRMRW	Random	High	Good	Minimum	Low	More	Moderate	N	NS2
IMRQI	Random	Low	Moderate	Moderate	Low	High	More	N	Ns2
LIEMRO	Random	Moderate	Good	High	Low	More	More	N	NS2
MRNPS	Random	Good	Good	Moderate	Low	More	More	N	NS2
GPRS	Random	Very low	Low	Moderate	Moderate	High	More	N	JAVASIM
TPGF2	Random	Very high	High	High	Low	Low	Low	N	JAVASIM
OGR	Uniform	Very low	Low	Moderate	Low	High	Low	N	Sim
NIMGR	Uniform	High	Low	Low	More	Low	More	N	NS2
NMDR	Uniform	Low	High	Moderate	More	High	Low	N	Sim
AODR	random	Low	Good	High	Good	High	More	N	Sim

Path Establishment Based Routing Algorithms

Path establishment mainly deals with route formation either on-demand or on regular or both.

Proactive Model: The design of this model mainly concentrates on forming path in a proactive manner or when need reactively. Routing information is collected database in routing tables; the information is used to build a routing path. It works efficiently if network is best suitable for flooding. Here all the nodes present in networks will forward Hello message initially and get know the neighbors of them in network. Each node maintains information in table structure for future use. The existing nodes can make use of the next node transmit (Yi et.al, 2009). Few architectural models uses cross layer solution to delay the replay to route request based on energy levels, which balances the nodes energy with in network [42]. This protocol optimizes present status of the link by classical mechanisms and use concept of multipoint relays if required. It is favorable for traffic patterns with more number of communicating sub nodes. AODV algorithm is best example for it.

Optimized Link State Routing (OLSR): It is a proactive routing protocol where the routes are always available when needed. OLSR is an optimized version of a pure link state protocol. The topological changes cause the flooding of the topological information to all available hosts in the network. To reduce the possible overhead in the network protocol multipoint relays (MPR) are used. Reducing the time interval for the control messages transmission brings more reactivity to the topological changes (Voigt et.al, 2010). OLSR uses two kinds of the control messages namely hello and topology control. Hello messages are used for finding the information about the link status and the host's neighbours. Topology control messages are used for broadcasting information about its own advertised neighbours, which includes at least the MPR selector list (Fu et.al, 2009).

Reactive Model: This design technique mainly concentrates on path establishment in on-demand when required as it node need to communicate on a real time based. It starts discovering a new link establishment when it is required by a source node for transmitting data packets. Normally, model involves two operations: route discovery and route maintenance. The first operation is used when route needed to be discovered, it uses 3 message route requests, route replay or route error. Depending on the requirement node can sent a request to setup a route to any specific node or can replay for a request sent or if any node identifies link error or some other catastrophic errors it uses route error message to inform to other nodes.

Adhoc On-demand Distance Vector (AODV): This protocol performs route discovery using control messages route request (RREQ) and route reply (RREP) whenever a node wishes to send packets to destination. When source node receives the route error (RERR) message, it can reinitiate route. Neighbourhood information is obtained from broadcasted hello packets. It is a flat routing protocol which does not need any central administrative system to handle the routing process. AODV tends to reduce the control traffic messages overhead at the cost of increased latency in finding new routes. The AODV protocol is a loop free and uses sequence numbers to avoid the infinity counting problem which is typical to the classical distance vector routing protocols (Xue et.al, 2006).

Location Aided Routing (LAR): Location aided routing (Hanke, 2007), is an enhancement to flooding algorithms to reduce flooding overhead. Most on-demand methods, including DSR and AODV use flooding to obtain a route to the destination. LAR aims to reduce the overhead to send the route requests only into a specific area, which is likely to contain the destination. For this purpose the notions of expected zone and request zone are introduced. The expected zone covers the area in which the destination is expected. Since the expected zone need not contain the source node, a larger area must be covered by flooding. This expanded expected zone is called request zone and is used to restrict the flooding; i.e. only nodes that are part of the request zone can forward a route request. On unsuccessful route discoveries, the request zone may need to be expanded further, possibly covering the whole network. Such subsequent route requests increase the initial latency for connections. This results in a tradeoff between reduced overhead and increased latency which needs to be balanced carefully.

Dynamic Source Routing (DSR): In dynamic source routing, source node floods a route request to all nodes which are in the wireless transmission range. Source routing protocol is composed of two main mechanisms to allow the discovery and maintenance of source routes in the ad hoc networks. In route discovery mechanism wireless node floods a route request to all nodes which are in the wireless transmission range. The initiator (source) and target (destination) of the route discovery is identified by each route request packet. The source node also provides a unique request identification number in its route request packet. For responding to the route request, the target node generally scans its own route cache for a route before sending the route reply toward the initiator node. However, if no suitable route is found, target will execute its own route discovery mechanism in order to reach toward the initiator (Heinzelman et.al 2000). The route maintenance mechanism is used when the source node is unable to use its current route to the destination due to changes in the network topology. In such case, the source has to use any other route to the destination. In order to discover new route can identified by calling request once again. A routing entry in DSR contains all the intermediate nodes of the route rather than just the next hop information. A source puts the entire routing path in the data packet and the packet is sent through the intermediate nodes specified in the path. If the source does not have a routing path to the destination, then it performs a route discovery by flooding the network with a route request (RREQ) packet. Any node that has a path to the destination in question can reply to the RREQ packet by sending a route reply (RREP) packet. The reply is sent using the route recorded in the RREQ packet. The advantages of this routing are to provide multiple routes and avoid loop formation where as disadvantages are large end-to-end delay, scalability problems caused by flooding and source routing mechanisms.

Hybrid Model: This design technique combines merits of above mentioned methods. It involves reactive and proactive routing models in the existing network. It is suited when size of network is large and of heterogeneous so, that network can be grouped as inter and intra clusters. In such structures depending on requirement can go on either proactive or reactive. Intra clusters do not require frequent changes in communication can use proactive mean while inter communication can be designed using reactive form communication with the active node in communicating cluster. It may also use border-cast resolution protocol to identify itself between on cluster to another (Intanagonwiwat et.al, 2000).

Zone Routing Protocol (ZRP): Proactive routing uses excess bandwidth to maintain routing information, while reactive routing involves long route request delays. Reactive routing also inefficiently floods the entire network for route determination. The zone routing protocol (ZRP) (Intanagonwiwat et.al, 2000) aims to address the problems by combining the best properties of both the proactive and reactive approaches. In ad-hoc network, it can be assumed that the largest part of the traffic is directed to nearby nodes. Therefore, ZRP reduces the proactive scope to a zone centered on each node. In a limited zone, the maintenance of routing information is easier. Further, the amount of routing information never used is minimized. In ZRP each node is assumed to maintain routing information only for those nodes that are within its routing zone. Because the updates are only propagated locally, the amount of update traffic required to maintain a routing zone does not depend on the total number of network nodes. A node learns its zone through a proactive scheme Intra zone Routing Protocol (IARP). For nodes outside the routing zone, Inter zone Routing Protocol (IERP) is responsible for reactively discovering routes to destinations located beyond a node's routing zone. The IERP is distinguished from standard flooding-based query/response protocols by exploiting the structure of the routing zone. The routing zones increase the probability that a node can respond positively to a route query. This is beneficial for traffic that is destined for geographically close nodes (Kumar et.al, 2014).

Network Structure Based Algorithms

Network structure based algorithms can be grouped into Flat, Hierarchical and location based algorithms. In flat network structure data from source to destination is forwarded by establishing a path, where in each node in the path finds the next neighbor nodes to reach sink. Hierarchical network structure works in two phases: (i) cluster formation and cluster–head selection (ii) data transmission from CH's to sink or chain of CH's to sink. Location based architecture uses position and location information of the nodes to provide higher scalability and efficiency.

Flat Network

In flat networks architecture routes are formed through broadcasting of information by nodes to get it updates. The techniques used for data transfer are: flooding, forwarding and data centric based routing. All nodes in network are considered equal and have equal opportunity in gathering information. The sensor nodes have same capacity in terms of energy and computing and they have same tasks to play in sensing. The broadcasting becomes inefficient if the size of network grows. Considering network dimensions normally flat architecture is suitable for small sized network. Few examples protocols designed with SEER uses this architecture, where initially network information are built and stored in routing tables. It includes the all basic information of network maintenance including energy level of near nodes, hop count and other parameters (Devika et.al, 2015).

Flooding: In flooding (Miao et.al, 2010) nodes which receives packet will broadcast it to their neighbors. The same operations will be carried by received nodes until maximum hops count is reached or packet reaches its destination. In flooding routing design [figure 2] packets are forwarded to the neighbors without checking if it has received the same packet from other neighbors which leads to uncontrolled flooding. The major problems in flooding are raise in packet overhead, delay in transmission and cross hearing. Improvement of uncontrolled flooding is gossiping where packet is transmitted to choose one neighbor at random.

Sensor Protocols for Information via Negotiation [SPIN]: SPIN which is another best example for controlled flooding. It is information-centric, source-initiated protocol. The communication is based on negotiation between communication nodes. The advertisement message will be sent when new nodes joins a network. The nodes which require any message will sent a request through broadcast, the

Figure 2. Flooding protocol scenario

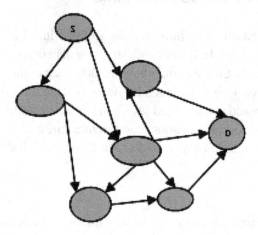

nodes which are nearby to the requested nodes will send the required information. Flooding throughout the network will be avoided as most of the time information is send from the neighbor (Devika et.al, 2015)as in figure 3. The problem with this routing technique is that data delivery is not guaranteed and it is not suitable for reliable data transmission applications.

Direct diffusion is also an information-centric with information storage in network. The complete information of network structure will be known to each node. The node with interest connects to another node if it finds required information storage in it. Normally information will be set from the initiator. The messages are reduced in the network as only packets related to interest will be send which reduce size and number leading in energy efficiency (Devika et.al, 2015). This algorithm includes elements: interest, data, gradient and reinforcement. The packet of interest will be broadcasted by sink; the nodes will set a gradient of interest for its neighbor and

Figure 3. SPIN scenario

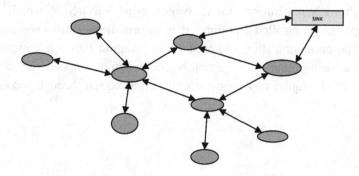

Figure 4. (a) Broadcasting interest (b) Establishment of gradients (c) Data propagation (d) Selecting and reinforcing path e- Transmitting data

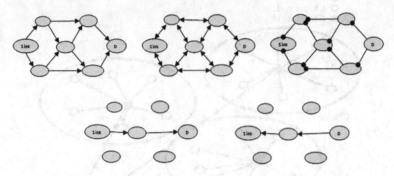

store the same in its cache. Then based on event packet will be sent to sink. This process is repeated by each node receiving data packet. The sink will reinforces path to received exploratory packets. The main demerits of DD routing algorithm are more overhead in matching queries, need for memory and applications which requires continuous data. The DD operations are shown in figure 4.

Rumor Routing (RR) (KO et.al, 1998): Once the sink identifies the occurrence of event in a network it will add the event to the corresponding nodes local table as well as create an agent which acts as an intermediate between sink and node with an event. The source node will make a decision to forward data based on signal strength of the queries received from its neighbors. The major problems occurs when information from event sensed node [source] cannot reach sink when if any link goes down in particular the agent.

Gradient-Based Routing (GBR): This routing algorithm is an enhancement applied to DD. The hops are not limited in networks that are diffused. The objective of GBR is to determine shortest path to reach sink node. The node will determine a parameter height, which is difference between nodes height and its neighbor. A traffic

Figure 5. Rumor routing scenario

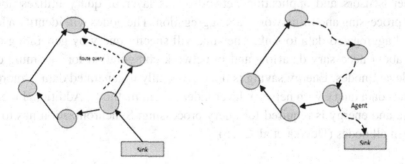

Figure 6. Cluster formations in Leach

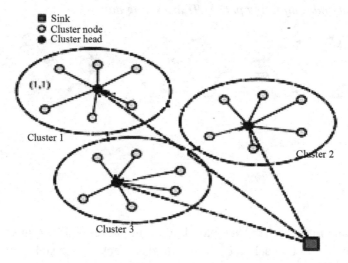

spreading techniques is introduced to maintain traffic inside network. This routing is suitable to deliver messages in point to point and not for broadcasting. The route cannot be decided if paths are overused. The nodes which are nearer to sink will lose energy more compared to others as they are overused (Abramson et.al, 1970).

Constrained Anisotropic Diffusion routing protocol (CADR): It is an extended form of DD. The main aim is to reduce latency and bandwidth. The information communication is considered to route query to neighbor. The routing is based on greedy search to make local decision. The decision can be in 3 modes: highest objective function, steepest gradient and local gradient. This routing technique minimizes energy usage in determining routes and maximizes data gain by having irregular walk with some steps. The data and queries (in terms of size and format) are not specifically defined between nodes and sink which is the major problem (Ehsan et.al, 2012).

Cougar: This routing technique is suitable for distributed system as it considers network as a distributed database system. The query system is introduced in between sensors and application network. This layer of query utilizes abstract query processing and in-network data aggregation. The nodes will identify a leader to send aggregated data to sink. The sink will specify query by generating query plans about necessary dataflow and in-network computation for incoming query for relevant nodes. Energy saving is done especially if generated data is more and provides data query with network layer independent methods. Additional memory storage and energy is required for query processing. Synchronization has to exist between all nodes (Devika et.al, 2015)

Figure 7. Cluster formations in HEED

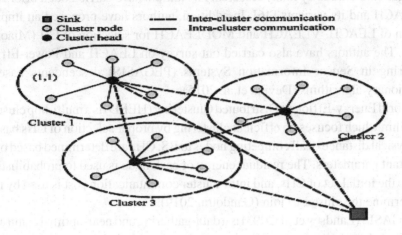

Active Query Forwarding in Sensor Networks (ACQUIRE): The routing technique is similar to COUGAR in querying sensor for distributed network. The queries are considered as an active entity. They are forwarded through network to find solution. Look – ahead parameter are considered to resolve query. The energy efficiency can be controlled by varying parameter by limiting number of hops in querying process. Identification of shortest path is done at the cost of energy consumption (Devika et.al, 2016).

Hierarchical Approach

In this model nodes communication can be established as cluster or chain or tree structure for larger sensor networks. The network is divided into several groups or clusters which are organizational component of network. This is efficient way of transferring data packets in the network. The clusters designated as group leader namely cluster head; it will be responsible for co ordination between nodes under its responsibility. Normally it includes data aggregation and /or compression of data collected to communicate further to sink. This process will allow reduction of data to be transmitted and hence are considered as energy efficient algorithms when compared to flat approach.

LEACH (Low-Energy Adaptive Clustering Hierarchy) is a hierarchical, cluster based protocol that utilises randomised rotation of local CHs to evenly distribute the energy load among sensor nodes in the network (Devika et.al, 2015). It involves two phase operation; data aggregation at cluster level followed by transmission of aggregated data from each CH to sink. Variants of LEACH have been proposed which varies based on cluster formation, cluster head selection process and data aggregation methods by many researchers. Authors have carried out a brief survey of LEACH and its variants [46]. In addition, authors have proposed an improved version of LEACH, VLEACH and MODLEACH for selection of CH (Miao et.al, 2010). The authors have also carried out survey on LEACH and Power-Efficient Gathering in Sensor Information Systems (PEGASIS) descendents based on evolutionary algorithms (Devika et.al, 2015).

Hybrid Energy-Efficient Distributed Clustering (HEED) is a multi-hop clustering algorithm which focuses on efficient clustering by proper selection of CHs based on the physical distance of all competing nodes to BS. CHs are determined based on two important parameters. The residual energy of each node is used to probabilistically choose the initial set of CHs, and intra-cluster communication cost is used by nodes to determine the cluster to join (Gandotra, 2019).

PEGASIS (Landsey et.al, 2003) is a data-gathering and near-optimal chain-based algorithm. The concept of energy conservation is included with nodes by creation of a chain structure comprising all nodes and continually data aggregation across the chain, but not directly by forming clusters. In this protocol, only one node in any given transmission time-frame allotted by BS will send the data to BS by forming a chain from source to BS. Data-fusion occurs at every node in the sensor network allowing for all relevant information to permeate across the network. In order to increase network lifetime, nodes need only to communicate with their closest neighbours, and they take turns in communicating with the BS. The chain formation of nodes is shown in Figure 8.

Threshold Sensitive Energy-Efficient Sensor Network (TEEN) (Manjeshwar et.al, 2001, Li et.al, 2012)a routing protocol for enhanced energy efficiency for WSN, is proposed. It is implemented for reactive network. In protocol, the overall performance depends on a simple temperature sensing applications. Each node within a cluster takes turns to become a CH for a time interval called cluster period. APTEEN scheme is proposed to handle both proactive and reactive kind of application as an improvement over TEEN [63]. The cluster-formation phase is the same as in LEACH. The changes are made in steady phase. In A hybrid Protocol for Threshold Sensitive Energy-Efficient Sensor Network(APTEEN), after deciding CH in each period the CH first broadcasts parameters like attributes, threshold, and schedule

Figure 8. Chain based data transmission approach in PEGASIS

$$c0 \longrightarrow c1 \longrightarrow c2 \longleftarrow c3 \longleftarrow c4$$
$$\downarrow$$
$$\text{BS}$$

and count time. Literally, both TEEN and APTEEN have the same drawbacks of additional burdens and complexity of cluster construction and tracking at different levels using time control. The communication slots for APTEEN between CH to BS are shown in figure 9.

EECS is a clustering algorithm developed by extending LEACH known as Energy-Efficient Clustering Scheme (EECS) (Ding et.al, 2015), in which the candidates compete among themselves to be getting selected as a CH. If a given node does not find a node with more residual energy, then it becomes a CH. EECS extends LEACH algorithm by dynamic sizing of clusters based on cluster distance from the BS.

The authors in DWEHC (Neamatollahi et.al, 2011) have designed distributed weight based energy- efficient hierarchical clustering to attain better cluster sized minimum energy consumable network. The weight of an element in sensor is computed on energy reserved and proximity of neighbors. The node consisting of largest weight will be chosen as CH and other near nodes as members of clusters. Depending on size of network either singe hop or multi hop clustering transmission routes are built. The algorithm is energy efficient is network size is less but complexity and energy consumption be higher with larger sized network.

Another distributed clustering hybrid algorithm proposed is hybrid clustering approach (HCA) (Wang et.al, 2007). The clusters are formed on dynamic basics when energy level of sensors goes below predefined in CH. The base station will inform all nodes to form clusters in next beginning round. It also sends a particular synchronization pulse to all nodes. At wake of, pulse nodes will set for re-clustering. The delay between the request for re-clustering time and the actual start of the process is more.

With an objective to prolong WSN distributed election clustering protocol (DECP) (Gong et.al, 2007) was proposed. The communication cost and residual energy of nodes are considered for forming clusters and it's CHs'. Heterogeneous nodes are used for construction of two-level network. The clusters are formed at regular intervals. DECP will balance energy of all nodes is considered and energy with higher rate are considered for CH election. The protocol will consume more energy for inter cluster communication.

Figure 9. Slot of TDMA allotted to transmit from CH to BS (APTEEN)

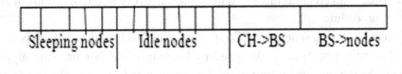

In MRPWSN (Kumar et.al,2009) distributed, multi-hop routing protocol consisting of unequal clustering for WSNs is proposed to prolong network lifetime. The sink node positioned in the middle of the sensing area to bring about energy utilization and Once again selection of CH is based on residual energy. The sensor node requires additional memory storage for table with distance value of each node so to deciding center sink node.

In energy efficient heterogeneous clustered scheme (EEHC) (Zhou et.al,2007) is proposed. The design is cluster based and selection of cluster head is based on weights decided on residual energy of each node. The nodes positioned in WSN are heterogeneous in terms of energy levels and are grouped in 3 groups: super, advanced and normal nodes. The network is aimed at prolonging lifetime of network with minimized energy utilization. Super nodes are furnished with *n* times and advanced nodes are n-1 times more energy than the normal nodes, where n and n-1 are fixed constants. The two operative phases are same as LEACH. Even though the algorithm is improved form LEACH it requires extra computation time and storage hence storage of three groups of node.

Energy dissipation forecast and clustering management (EDFCM) distributed, clustering protocol is proposed in (Li et.al, 2005). On-stage energy consumption is estimated and applied for selection of cluster-head in EDFCM. The management nodes are considered for selection of CH in each round results in energy efficient network.

Energy-efficient unequal clustering (EEUC) (Quai et.al,2006) protocol for periodical data gathering application in WSNs is proposed. The energy within sensor is managed evenly by concentrating on hot spot issue which normally arises in multi-hop scenario. When the CHs nearer to the base station dies at a faster rate because of more transmissions, this problem is considered as hot spot issue which troubles substantial relay traffic. As a solution to this problem, protocol forms more clusters of smaller size near to base station. Even intra cluster correspondence will consume less energy. It resolves hot-spot issue at the cost of energy for computing and fro formation of clusters.

A distributed multilevel clustering algorithm for heterogeneous wireless sensor networks [MLCH] (Ye et.al, 2005) where CH selection is based on energy level of each node and average energy of each node of network. The overall lifetime of CH is decided by initial energy and residual energy ratios. This algorithm suffers in fixing cluster-head election threshold to be used in every iterative rounds of cluster formation procedure.

Efficient clustering scheme (EECS) (Ehasn et.al, 2011) which helps in periodical data gathering applications is designed by keeping LEACH clustering algorithm as a base. During cluster formation the BS broadcasts a `hello' message to all the nodes at energy level fixed by sink node. In the wake of getting 'hello' message, the sink node will form clusters based on signal strength followed by CH selection based on residual energy. The major drawback is the excess time required for the sink to monitor the energy levels of cluster head and clusters.

Fast Local Clustering service (FLOC) is a distributed clustering WSN protocol (Zohre et.al, 2010)concentrates on minimizing energy consumption by focusing on designing even sized messages for communication between node and sink. It tries to construct even sized clusters to reduce overlapping and interferences in addition avoids frequent cluster formation. Every sensor nodes are within unit separation from the cluster-head by applying this concept messages interferences will be minimized. Frequent cluster formation is avoided. Initial time of deployment is high to have unit distance sensor nodes to build even sized network.

Distributed clustering algorithm for self-configuring and self-healing multi-hop [DCSSM](Prasad et.al, 2007) protocol wherein overlapping between nodes within radial distance is less, as a result of the cellular hexagonal structure of the nodes. The author as tried to attain to geographical clustering in expansive scale networks by enforcing bound on the network with some predefined span of the cells. Further network utilizes far-reaching range for the hexagons to minimize energy utilization and unwavering quality for intra-cell correspondence. Self-healing property keep track all nodes operations of node join, node leave, node movement and node crash in the network. Even though with, minor modifications algorithm suffers from collecting local information continuously during the operative period of clusters.

Multi-hop Overlapping Clustering Algorithm (MOCA) for wireless sensor network with design strategy of cluster (Yu et.al., 2007). Here the author is contended to nullify interference and assure to make the clusters overlapped to encourage numerous applications. The algorithm designed with inter-cluster routing, topology revelation, node localization and recovery from cluster-head failure. In this algorithm every node within the radial distance of k –hop is considered and selected every node to become CH or member of any cluster based on visibility region within the range where k is a predefined estimation of cluster radius. After cluster formation, each node is either a CH or at a distance of k-hop from at least one CH. The gateway nodes or routing node within network are prone to failure because cluster nodes overlap during inter cluster communications.

Power-Efficient and Adaptive Clustering Hierarchy (PEACH) protocol for wireless sensor networks based on design principles of tree and cluster (XU et.al, 2001). The protocols design and working procedure is versatile, hierarchical, scalable and power efficient clustering protocol. Clusters are framed with minimum overhead and CH will also get selected consuming less energy. The nodes are unaware of location in the WSN deployed region. In this protocol the overhead for promoting about CH and to join cluster-heads are minimized to a greater extent. This algorithm operates on probabilistic energy-aware routing protocols like EAR, EAR-DPS, and GEAR in identification of CH. The algorithm has to keep track of all nodes identity.

The comparison of network structure - hierarchical based heuristic WSN routing is summarized in Table 3.

Location Based Approach

The performance of WSN is directly influenced by placement of sensors within network. Location based architecture uses the positional location of nodes information to provide efficiency and scalability at higher rate. In location based protocols, each node should know its location information or should be able to collect through GPS. Initiation node for communication must know location of collecting node which is being the destination for it. The nodes must also its neighbours each others. The two types of location based are GPS and non-GPS location based. Location aided routing (LAR) (Yu et.al, 2001), uses location information through locating information obtained from GPS to identify nodes new paths. So by identifying positions of nodes it limits search to be in smaller regions called "request zone". The search will significantly minimize messages transacting within the networks. The area is being identified by earlier information of the nodes. Same smaller process can be extended to whole network areas. Sensor localization information is normally utilized for self organizing and configuring network which is purely deciding based on event locations (Yang et.al,2005, Zhang et.al, 2006). Several localization schemes are developed which actively and diversely support location based services and applications. The existing localization schemes can be categories as into three categories: 1.Range-based 2.Range-free and 3.Mobile beacon-assisted scheme.

In Greedy Perimeter Stateless Routing (GPAR) (Yang et.al,2003) authors have innovated a routing protocol for wireless datagram networks, which keeps track of the positions of routers and a packet's destination to make packet forwarding decisions. The nodes will get information about all its neighbors sing GPSR. The routing decision is made based on local information of nodes. The algorithm consists of two methods for forwarding packets: greedy forwarding, which is used wherever possible, and perimeter forwarding, which is used in the regions greedy forwarding cannot be.

Energy Aware Greedy Routing (EAGR) system a greedy routing protocol is defined in GPSR (Zhanget.al, 2004). The cost is assigned for each transmission path between nodes and sink. EAGR builds cost metric of a node in a network depend

Table 3. Comparison of Hierarchical based WSN routing algorithms.

Routing Technique	Distribution Of Nodes	Control Message Overhead	Uniform Energy Distribution	Energy Efficiency	Scalability	Transmission Delay	Algorithm Complexity	Data Aggregation	Simulation Tool
LEACH	Very Low	Good	Very Low	Moderate	Moderate	No	High	Yes	Matlab
HEED	Moderate	Very Good	Moderate	Moderate	High	No	High	Yes	Matlab
PEGASIS	Very High	Very Good	Low	Moderate	Low	No	Low	Yes	Matlab
TEEN	Moderate	Very Good	Low	Good	Very Low	Yes	High	Yes	Sim
APTEEN	Low	Very Good	Low	Moderate	Low	Yes	High	Yes	Sim
EECS	Very High	Very Good	Moderate	Good	Very Good	Yes	High	Yes	Matlab
DWEHC	Uniform	Low	Moderate	Moderate	Low	Yes	More	Yes	Matlab
HCA	Random	Moderate	Low	Good	Minimum	No	More	No	NS2
DECP	Uniform	Low	Moderate	Average	Very Low	Yes	Low	No	Sim
MRPWSN	Random	High	Moderate	Good	More	No	More	No	NS2
EEHU	Random	Low	High	Good	More	No	Moderate	Yes	NS2
EECU	Uniform	Moderate	Low	Good	More	More	Moderate	No	OMNET
EDFCM	Uniform	Moderate	Very Low	Low	Less	Moderate	More	No	NS2
MLCH	Random	Low	Moderate	Low	Low	Moderate	Moderate	No	MatLab
EECS	Uniform	Low	Moderate	Good	Low	Low	Moderate	No	NS2
FLOC	Uniform	High	Moderate	Good	Very Low	Low	Moderate	No	NS2
DCMMS	Random	Moderate	Low	Good	Minimum	No	More	Yes	OMNET
MOCA	Uniform	Low	Moderate	Average	Very Low	Yes	Low	Yes	SIM
PEACH	Random	High	Moderate	Good	More	No	More	Yes	MatLab

on the following constraints of a neighboring node: Distance from the destination, Fraction of energy consumed, and Rate of energy consumption. In this protocol the node are required for each other node i to advertise its location as (iX, iY, iZ), fraction of energy consumption and rate of energy consumption. All the information is packed in 'HELLO' packet with the node id. Each node broadcasts HELLO packets to all its neighbors. Each HELLO packet on receiving node maintains a neighbor table containing following the information about its neighbor: Identification number (ID), Geographical location, Faction of energy consumption and Rate of energy consumption. Each time the node receives the HELLO packet it updates its neighbor table. When there is a request for route finding each node selects the hop which is energy efficient. The routes are considered as which have maximum remaining energy, which has minimum energy consumption rate and which is nearer to the destination node.

In Minimum energy communication network (MECN) (Liu et.al, 2003) aims to construct a network which is energy efficient by considering all mobile nodes. It guarantees to maintain a minimum energy network for wireless networks by utilizing low power GPS to locate all nodes. Although, the protocol assumes a mobile network, it is best applicable to sensor networks, which are not mobile. The topology for stationary nodes is also built which consumes less energy. MECN considers a master site as the information sink, which is always the case for sensor networks. Every node identifies is relay node in its vicinity to transmit data to next nearest relay node which is nearer to it are finally to reach sink. Transmitting through those nodes is more energy efficient than direct transmission. The main goal of this protocol is to discover a sub- system which will have less number of nodes and can reach out consuming minimum amount of energy between two particular nodes. In this way following from smaller communication step by step overall global transmission path is built for every pair of nodes. The identification is achieved by localized search for each node considering its relay region. The algorithm is being processed in 2 operative phases: in initial phase a sparse matrix is built considering two-dimensional plane of all nodes through local computation in nodes and communication. By considering all nodes placement has graph. The graph enclosed consists with optimal links in terms of energy consumption. In next phase based on information regarding distance collected in phase one, determines a optimal links on enclosed graph. The Bellmann-Ford shortest path algorithm is applied considering minimum power cost for all routes. In case mobility GPS is used for positioning coordinates or nodes in network or not. Self-reconfiguring nature of MECN can dynamically adapt to node's failure as well as it can dynamically deploy new sensors.

The extension of MECN is small minimum energy communication network (SMECN) proposed in (KO et.al, 1998). In MECN, it is assumed that every node can transmit to every other node in a network but which is not possible every time. SMECN considers possible obstacles between any pair of nodes which is an improvement to its ancestor protocol. Similar to MECN the network is assumed to be fully connected. The number of hops and edges are considered in building small sub-network in SMECN. The energy required to in maintaining and transmitting is minimum when compared with MECN has it is built utilizing broadcast messages which is not required for SMECN. If broadcasts are able to reach to all nodes in a circular region around the broadcaster then further replications are avoided. As a result, the number of hops for transmissions will decrease. Cost to build and maintain is less in SMECN is comparatively less to that of MECN. Finding a sub-network with minimum and smaller number of edges will introduce more overhead in this protocol.

Geographic adaptive fidelity (GAF)(Mavue et.al, 2001) is allocation based energy aware routing algorithm designed initially for mobile ad-hoc networks. Then it was also applied for sensor networks. GAF saves energy by turning off unnecessary nodes in the network without affecting the routing quality. The location of every nodes is identifies itself using GPS. The energy usage is minimized by turning of nodes when they are not in use. The nodes are assumed to be placed in virtual grid. The nodes are associated to each other by its actual locations; the nodes which belong to same grid are considered to be associated to each other and are equivalent and allocated with same cost. Applying GAF node transmission cast can be reduced.

Localized Energy-Aware Restricted Neighborhood routing (LEARN) ()Gupta et.al, 2004) protocol is a location aware routing algorithm designed to minimize energy usage within network. Thus, algorithm guarantees the energy efficiency of the route. The transmission route is built dynamically by identifying the next node to be communicated for transmission of message through it based on highest energy to travel long distance i.e. to next neighboring node with one single hop. If any node is not identified with these particular characteristics then minimum residual energy neighborhood is identified to reach with single hop or else the algorithm fails. The algorithm is designed for three- dimensional networks it derive its critical transmission radius in 3D in random network is considered.

A localized power-aware routing algorithm designed to route nodes in energy efficient manner by knowing location of all nodes (Zohre et.al, 2007). The algorithm minimizes energy consumption keeping look on power and cost of localized routing. The transmission power is made linear by placing node between any nodes based on optimal power needed for communication. The distance between source and destination are considered with attempts to build efficient route between nodes. The identification of routes for transmission is longer.

SPAN proposed in (Jin et.al,2012) is a position based algorithm selects some nodes as coordinating nodes based on their locations. The coordinator nodes are considered for maintaining network to forward and backward messages. The coordinators are selected by sink node based on location, to suite to monitor, collect and send messages at regular basics. The new coordinator nominated for next round may not be always nearer to previous coordinator. The architecture is more centralized hence local coordination is less among nodes and saves energy for longer time.

Geographic and Energy-Aware Routing (GEAR)(Bandyopadhyay et.al, 2003) utilizes nodes location information and each node will know location and will be able to collect positional information and existing level of energy to heuristically construct routes in a network. The node will be able to communicate in single hop between every neighbor nodes dissipating minimum energy as well all nodes are aware of its location information. The nodes will be assigned with two costs: estimated and learned to route request packet and to forward it to destination. The estimated cost is required to transmit messages to destination in terms of amount of energy. The cost of estimation is estimated energy levels of nodes in a network and estimated at every source nodes using objective function built on energy and distance to the destination. The learning cost is an updated estimated cost with reference to dynamically measured at each node. When route request is received learned cost value is updated according to the length of last traversed link and residual energy level at the node. The packet is forwarded to node which is of minimum cost with single hop neighbor node to destination. The same actions are performed until message reached to its target. The same operation of sensing and forwarding message is done in a greedy manner until all nodes die.

Recursive geographically forwarding routing technique (RGF) is location based routing technique (Rathi et.al, 2015). The packets are forwarded or restricted on flooding technique. In this case, the packet is forwarded through the destination to intended region using RGF or flooding technique. In this protocol, the geographical network is divided into four parts. Information regarding to it will be sent all nodes in network. The packet that is being sent during communication will consist of information of four copies and fifth packet are separately created and forwarded to each other. The same functioning is repeated until the message reach out to target node. Although restricted flooding is simpler to implement it is not necessarily consumes more amount of energy based on deployment of nodes. The routing delay will be less if size of network is small. Similarly number of messages will increase at a greater level when number of nodes increase to the target node when destination region is large.

Greedy perimeter stateless routing (GPSR) proposed in (Godebole et.al, 2012). The data packets are forwarded based on decisions using nodes location information made in nodes. It uses greedy forwarding and perimeter forwarding techniques to transmit data packets to the nodes. They forward nodes to node that are always closer to the target node. In regions of the network where such a greedy path does not exist, the protocol recovers by forwarding in perimeter mode. The position of a packet's destination and positions of the next hop neighbor are sufficient to make correct forwarding decisions, without any other topological information.

Energy-efficient geographic routing (EEGF) (Chen et.al, 2009) is a location based routing protocol. The characteristics of network considered for making routing decision are: nodes location information and energy consumption. The nodes are not forwarded with decision based on energy level of neighbor or distance to it rather decision is based made on to transmit packet to nodes which are closer to optimal relay position. The optimal relay node is computer by broadcasting a message consisting of location and residual energy. For this very reason not information regarding to neighbors are maintained. A protocol is localized and energy efficient. The working of algorithm will be condition it nodes are deployed in a uniform manner.

Location-based energy aware and reliable (LER) is a location based sensor network routing algorithm (Winter et.al, 2011). The location information of all nodes will be retrieved through GPS. Each node sends location information to its neighbors and constructs routing table. The routing table consists of neighbor node id and distance from the destination node. The routing decision is based on distance. The node with shortest distance will get selected as the candidate relay node to send information.

A reactive geographic routing protocol has been proposed in (Chou et.al, 2008). It is a combination of reactive routing mechanism and geographic routing. It is calculating the shortest distance between destination node and neighbor node. The protocol uses two new measures to improve the performance of routing protocol. First, to reduce the consumption, it uses reactive routing mechanism to mitigate the routing overhead. Second, to improve reliability, it finds the optimal path from the many available paths.

Energy-efficient geographic routing algorithm has been proposed in (EEGP) (Soliman et.al, 2011). For making routing decision protocol considers three factors: routing distance, signal interference, and computation cost. In the protocol, two methods for the routing decision have been proposed. In the first method, it takes the decision based on the distance and signal interference. It finds the Euclidean distance from the transmitter node to the destination node and interference power. In the second method, it takes the decision based on the maximum power consumption and interference power. The first method is considered when network is less busy and later on is used when network is busy in transmitting more umber of messages.

The comparison of network structure - location based heuristic WSN routing is summarized in Table 4.

Performance

This architecture mainly concern with performance issues like real time, robust, throughput, latency, scalability, reliability, energy conservation, and other QoS parameters. As design is self organizing and infrastructure less design semantics need be understood and examined at minutiae level. Numerous routing protocols are designed with an aim with subset of parameters but most of or none of them comprehended with all performance issues. The protocols can be further classified on route design as proactive, reactive and hybrid algorithms (Yang et.al, 2013,). If in creating applications they are more restricted on issues like delay, latency, error in bits, throughput, data loss, jitter, reliability then in such situation QoS get its importance. The mainly occurring challenges in design and requirements for designing multimedia's wireless network is dealt and surveyed in Ramson et.al, (2013). The same issues will also need to be concerned in WSN. In addition they have to look up on issues of guaranteed throughput, classification of data patterns, traffic pattern, prioritization and different delays.

Reliable routing algorithm (RRA) finds the most reliable path between each sensor node and the sink node (at the beginning of simulation). This protocol does not consider other factors such as the number of hops or the length of end-to-end path. Existing protocols such as TADR (Akkaya et.al, 2005) and CBF (Shafiullah et.al, 2008) consider reliability as one of the factors for achieving a reliable data transmission in WSN but involving the tradeoff with other factors.

Sequential Assignment Routing (SAR) (Shobraoi et.al, 2009) is a routing protocol which concentrates on the energy efficiency and QOS factors in constructing WSN. The nodes to the sink communication is tried to achieve a more energy efficient structure and also made reliable by creating multiple paths from nodes to sink and also maximizes fault tolerance of the network. The SAR protocol builds tree structure rooted at one-hop neighbors of the sink. The protocol actions are built considering QoS metric, energy resource on each path and priority level of each packet. The node to forward to next node will decide which route to be selected among the multiple paths constructed as tree structure. For identification of multiple paths, energy resources and QoS on the path will be considered. Any nodes failure will be communicated among local nodes and routing table will be updated accordingly, further occurring problems will be resolved automatically. The protocol offers less power consumption, focuses only on energy consumption of each packet without considering its priority, ensures fault-tolerance, and easy recovery. The protocol suffers from the overhead of maintaining routing tables and status of all nodes.

Table 4. Comparison of location based WSN

Routing technique	Distribution of nodes	Control message overhead	Uniform energy distribution	Energy efficiency	Scalability	Transmission delay	Algorithm complexity	Data aggregation	Simulation Tool
EAGR	Uniform	Good	Very low	Moderate	Moderate	No	High	Yes	Sim
GPER	Random	Very good	Moderate	Moderate	High	No	High	Yes	NS2
MECN	Random	Very good	Low	Moderate	Low	No	Low	Yes	NS2
SMEN	Random	Very good	Low	Good	Very low	Yes	High	Yes	Opnet
GAF	Uniform	Very good	Low	Moderate	Low	Yes	High	Yes	Opnet
LEARN	Uniform	Very good	Moderate	Good	Very good	Yes	High	Yes	NS2
LRP	random	Low	Moderate	Moderate	Low	Yes	More	Y	Qualnet
SPAN	Random	Moderate	Low	Good	Minimum	No	More	N	NS2
GEAR	Uniform	Low	Moderate	Average	Very low	Yes	Low	N	NS2
RGF	Random	High	Moderate	Good	More	No	More	N	NS2
EEGF	Uniform	Very good	Moderate	Moderate	Low	No	Low	Yes	Matlab
LER	Uniform	Moderate	Low	Good	More	More	moderate	N	NS2
EEGP	Uniform	Moderate	Very low	Low	Less	moderate	More	N	NS2

SPEED routing protocol (He, et.al, 2003) is a real time application based on guaranteed end-to-end delay. The communication link is wireless and transmits data packets with certain speed. The link is proactively labeled by communication speed and link length. The packets estimation delay will be calculated on links before reaching target node. Each node discovers its single-hop neighbourhood and then establishes the local links using a geographic forwarding technique. The protocols design is complex and time consuming in estimating nodes liveness.

Stateless Non-deterministic Geographic Forwarding (SNGF) (Feelmban et.al, 2006) is an improvement designed for SPEED. The SNGF is designed in four steps: identified nodes exchange to collect local neighbor information at each node. The single-hop neighbors are built in identifying multiple paths. Delay estimation is calculated knowing packets and transmitted until an acknowledgement message is received through the same link. It is used to measure packet speed at each node to select the links which meets the speed requirements. Neighbourhood feedback ratio will discard links which cannot provide desired packet delivery delay and/or speed. Source nodes send single-hop neighbours which are not able to establish communication links according to the QoS requirements. Further nodes will be discarded for unsuitable links and forward data packets only through the links which are able to guarantee QoS requirements. Finally, Back-pressure re-routing is used to detect network congestion when packet is not delivered. Nodes are able to meet QoS requirement to communicate with next available links that should meet when node fails. The probability of packet failures/lose is decreased as QoS links are reliable enough to forward data packets. The energy consumption is more in this algorithm in densely deployed networks.

Energy-aware QoS routing protocol (Liu et.al, 2012) will forward data packets through links in an energy efficient way. The cost value is assigned to each link to provide reliability and energy efficient. The cost is assigned based on residual energy of nodes, required energy for forwarding a packet and link message creates error rate. The end-to-end delay requirement is based on smallest cost of paths selected applying Dijkstra algorithm amongst all available links. The packets are classified into real-time and non-real-time categories to guarantee end-to-end delay. The bandwidth is assigned to each class based on amount of available bandwidth on all links. The algorithm will assign bandwidth to every node before it gets deployed. According to network consumer priority requirements a packets will be transmitted through reserved bandwidth among queuing classes. The deployment with in network is done before to initial bandwidth allocation prior to deployment. The bandwidth is not properly managed between classes of real and non-real time class of transmissions for longer period with more number of nodes. The priority of bandwidth, network topology, available nodes may change over period of time.

In Multi-tier Grid Routing Protocol (MGRP) (sinhg et.al, 2013) is a special hybrid multi- tier structure is introduced for data distribution. The nodes are divided into square grids of different size or of same size among all observations. The optimized clusters are formed within each grid, which sends reliable data packets to its next higher CH. The uppermost CH from the neighbor grids further negotiates to construct the data d-tree from which the mobile sink can be reached and transmit queries.

An energy efficient and QoS aware multi-path routing protocol for WSN (QSR) (Maksimovic et.al, 2014) was designed to satisfy the reliability and delay requirements of real time applications. The protocol is constructed by concentrating on QOS parameters to prolong its lifetime by balancing energy in a network. During the setup phase delay for every pair communication is computed and link with minimum delay will be is given more packets to transmit on compared to other nodes. The end to end delay is reduced by spreading out the traffic across other chosen multiple paths. The throughput will be increased by introducing data redundancy. The initial packet is split into several sub-packets, error correction codes are added and then the sub-packets are transmitted over the available multiple paths considering end to end delay into account.

The Multi-path and Multi-Speed routing protocol (MMSPEED)(Shyan et.al, 2012) is designed using cross layer approach between network and MAC layer to provide QoS differentiation in terms of reliability and timeliness. For reliability, protocol uses probabilistic multi-path forwarding to control the number of packet delivery paths depending on the required end-to-end reaching probability. The timeliness is provided with multiple network-wide speed options so that various traffic types can dynamically choose the proper speed options for their packets depending on their end-to-end deadlines. These two methods are desirable for scalability and adaptability in a large scale networks.

The comparison of performance based heuristic WSN routing is summarized in Table 5.

META- HEURISTIC WSN ROUTING ALGORITHMS

Fuzzy Logic Algorithms

This architectural design is based not only any two set of values like true or false which normally used for logical computing, but it considers many variables valued between 0-1. From there itself its fuzzy logics' flexibility and allowance for members

Table 5. Comparison of Performance based WSN

Routing technique	Distribution of nodes	Control message overhead	Uniform energy distribution	Energy efficiency	Scalability	Transmission delay	Algorithm complexity	Data aggregation	Simulation Tool
RRA	Very low	Good	Very low	Moderate	Moderate	No	High	Yes	Qualnet
SAR	Moderate	Very good	Moderate	Moderate	High	No	High	Yes	Omnet
SPEED	Very high	Very good	Low	Moderate	Low	No	Low	Yes	NS2
EQRP	Moderate	Very good	Low	Good	Very low	Yes	High	Yes	Matlab
MGRP	Low	Very good	Low	Moderate	Low	Yes	High	Yes	NS2
QSR	Very high	Very good	Moderate	Good	Very good	Yes	High	Yes	MatLab
MMSPEED	Uniform	Low	Moderate	Moderate	Low	Yes	More	Yes	Matlab

with set of membership comes. As many other techniques have demerit of proper datasets. As shown in Figure it involves the process from applying a input or sets of input through obtaining output. In between includes three major operations: fuzzification, fuzzy interference engine and defuzzification. The interference engine will apply fuzzy rules designed for the application. In first step each parameter which are input are going to be associated with membership function and forwarded for next step computing. The next operation will be carried on according to rules, the output produced will be defuzzified to get a snappy value and presented. They can be used for variant of applications like MAC protocol, queries, redundancy reduction, event forecasting, deployment, clustering, and others (Bandopadhya et.al, 2003).

In Energy-Efficient Fuzzy-Logic-Based Clustering Technique for Hierarchical Routing Protocols(EFCT) (Rathi et.al, 2013) fuzzy logic (Mamdani et.al, 2001) has been adopted for cluster head selection using five descriptors': remaining energy of the given sensor node i.e. residual energy, distance of sensor nodes from the BS, density of other surrounding sensor nodes around the candidate CH, compaction of nodes around the sensor node, and the Location suitability (a more suitable location for a CH node is a location with lower total communication energy). Each of the linguistic variables is divided into overlapping fuzzy sets, called membership functions. Linguistic terms for input variables are defined as {low, medium and high} for residual energy; {close, medium, far} for distance from BS; {Low, high} for average energy i.e. location suitability, ' {low. high} for density and {low, high} for compaction. Linguistic terms for output variable chance of node has CH as: VVlow, Vlow, low, LLmid, Lmid, mid, Hmid, HHmid, high, Vhigh, VVhigh} . The Fuzzy Logic-based Energy-Efficient Clustering for WSN FL-EEC/D technique uses the fuzzy model for CH election. It manages the distribution of CHs based on determining and enforcing a specific minimum separation distance say d between CHs ensure their fair distribution. Minimum distance d is adaptive conditional to dimensions of the WSN, the network size i.e. number of nodes, and the preferred CHs percentage. The clustering algorithms energy efficiency in terms of capability of balancing of energy distribution is evaluated using Gini index. Results of Fuzzy based CH selection is compared with LEACH and k-means.

In cluster based routing algorithms, in addition to CH work load, the neighbour nodes of CH also play a vital role in data transmission during intra-cluster multi-hop communication. These neighbour nodes of CH consume extra energy than the farther nodes. The neighbour nodes of CH may die prematurely due to low residual energy and which leads to re-establish new routing link and hence consume network energy. Energy Efficient Distributed clustering algorithm using Fuzzy approach (EEDCF)

(Godbole et.al, 2012) for wireless sensor networks with non-uniform distribution has been proposed to solve the problem of premature death of neighbour node of CH. Each node uses the TSK fuzzy inference system to study whether it fits to be the CH compared with its neighbour nodes. The input parameters for TSK FIS are node residual energy, node degree and neighbour nodes' residual energies. The linguistic terms for input variables are as follows: Node residual energy{low, medium, high}, node degree { less, average, enormous}, neighbour node residual energy { weak, normal, strong} The neighbour nodes' residual energies parameter is important to optimize the load balance of relay nodes and in turn elude the hotspots problem and helps in extending the lifetime of the network system by consuming less network energy. The linguistic terms for the output variable CH selection are {low, medium, high, average, and weak, normal, strong}. Results of EEDCF algorithm are compared with DFLC (Distributed Fuzzy Logic-based Clustering algorithm)) and ADEEG (Energy-Aware Data Energy-Efficient Gathering protocol) for wireless sensor networks algorithm and prove to improve average life time and data transmission efficiency and reduce number of dead nodes.

In cluster based WSN, the energy of nodes can be saved when the nodes of a cluster transmit data by participating in cooperative Multiple Input Multiple Output (MIMO)(Myoung et.al, 2008). A cooperative MIMO clustering protocol is proposed using Type-2 fuzzy logic (T2FL) for CH and cooperative node (CN) selection. The proposed T2FL has three fuzzy descriptors: concentration, distance to base station and residual energy and the confidence factor (output variable with fuzzy linguistic terms as Very poor, Poor, Below Average, Average, Above Average, Strong, and Very Strong) is evaluated for the node to become non cluster head, or CH or CN. A node with high confidence factor is elected as cluster head node for each round for data transmission. The proposed method is evaluated using three measures: Network life time, average energy dissipation, and throughput and fist node death.

Fuzzy-logic-based energy optimized routing (FLEOR) (Jalaleddin et.al, 2011) algorithm is proposed not only to minimize energy consumption but also to balance data traffic among nodes. Degree of Closeness of Node to the Shortest Path{ far, medium, close), degree of Closeness of Node to Sink { far, medium, close}, and { poor, medium, good} are the three input parameters for the Mamdani FIS with 27 inference rules to identify the output fuzzy variable which determines the chance for one forwarding neighbor which has been selected as next hop. Degree of Closeness of Node to the Shortest Path and degree of Closeness of Node to Sink reflect the measure of energy efficiency for selecting one node as next hop, and Degree of Energy Balance shows the measure of energy balance for routing decision. The output fuzzy variable is divided into seven levels, very small, small, rather small, medium, rather large, large, and very large. The algorithm has proved in extension of network lifetime, achieved energy efficiency and energy balance together when compared to predicting based distributed energy-balancing routing (PDEBR), minimum transmission energy (MTE) routing, greedy perimeter stateless routing (GPSR), and energy accounted minimum hop routing (EAMHR).

The comparison of fuzzy logic based meta - heuristic WSN routing is summarized in Table 6.

Swarm Intelligence [SI] Algorithms

The SI was firstly given an expression by Beni and Wang with the framework of cellular robotic system. SI is much restricted version of computational intelligence studies on collective behaviour of elements in natures in a multi-agent self-organized and decentralized behaviour. The basic design consists of locally interacting simple agents, global behaviours of intelligence, search and optimization problem. The design structure involves population interacting locally and locally to globally with one to another. There is fixed or federal controlling in SI. The SI simulated behaviour can be viewed and idealized in nature natural collection of behaviours like, ant colony, honey combing, bacteria moulding, animals herding, bird flocks, fish schools, and other collection. The maximum expertise algorithm in various research and practical areas are optimisation algorithm of ant colony and practical swarm. So in future there is much scope to experiment with parameters like throughput, delay, path establishment, formation of clusters, packet transmission other optimization behavioural principles of other nature inspired collection of animals or birds(Guru et.al, 2013).

Energy-aware clustering for WSNs using particle swarm optimization [ECWPSO] (Hussain et.al, 2007) is a routing protocol have defined a new cost function for particle swarm optimization(PSO), with the objective of simultaneously minimizing the intra-cluster distance and optimizing the energy consumption of the network. In this protocol the operation completely is based on a centralized control algorithm that is implemented at the BS. The proposed protocol operates in rounds, where each round begins with a setup phase in which clusters are formed. This is followed by a steady state phase which works in similar approach as in LEACH. At the starting of each setup phase, all nodes send information about their current energy status and locations to the BS. Based on this information, the BS computes the average energy level of all nodes. Nodes with a sufficient energy are selected as CHs; the

Table 6. Comparison of fuzzy logic based WSN

Routing technique	Distribution of nodes	Control message overhead	Uniform energy distribution	Energy efficiency	Scalability	Transmission delay	Algorithm complexity	Data aggregation	Simulation Tool
Fuzzy-Clusters	Random	Medium	Medium	Very good	Low	Medium	Low	Y	NS-2
EFCT	Random	Medium	Medium	Very good	Low	Medium	Low	N	MATLAB
EEDCF	Random	Low	Very low	Good	Medium	Low	Medium	N	NS2
MIMO	Random	Low	Medium	Good	Low	More	Medium	N	NS2
AFED	Uniform	Low	Medium	Medium	Low	More	Low	N	NS3
FLEOR	Random	Medium	Low	Good	Medium	More	Low	N	NS2

nodes with an energy level above the average are eligible to be a CH candidate for this round. Next, the BS runs the PSO algorithm to determine the best K CHs that can minimize the cost function based on distance between nodes in a cluster to CH. The cost function forms compact clusters with the optimum set of nodes that have sufficient energy to perform the CH tasks. For a sensor network with N nodes and K predetermined number of clusters. The clusters are formed by initializing S particles to contain K randomly selected CHs among the eligible CH candidates. For each node cost function is applied and later on distance between a particle and CH is computer for all the particles in the network. The personal and global best for each particle is found. Regularly particles are updated based on particle velocity and distance from the CH. The same steps are repeated until the maximum number of iterations reached. The selection of CH and their member's information will be sent to BS; it in turns transfers a cluster id to CHs. Once the CH finishes receiving data from its entire members at the end of each frame, the CH performs data fusion and sends the fused data to the BS.

WSN clustering using particles swarm optimization for reducing energy consumption [WCPSO] (Xue et.al, 2006) have introduced an approach for clustering sensor networks based on Particle Swarm Optimization (PSO) algorithm using the optimal fitness function with an aim to extend network lifetime. The parameters used in this algorithm are residual energy density, the distance from the BS, intra-cluster distance from the CH. In clustering phase, the particles are generated randomly. Then the best points are selected as the CHs and other nodes which are located near each CH becomes the member of the cluster and then fitness function is calculated for every CH. If the fitness function is better than global best it is substituted. Then each node prepares a control message that contains identity and value of its residual energy and sends it directly to the BS. The BS which receives the information performs clustering operation. Assigns the nodes into cluster based on the distances according to the validity index. Once the clusters are formed then further operations are performed similar to LEACH.

Inter-cluster ant colony optimization algorithm for WSN in dense environment based on ant-colony optimization [IACOW] is a routing protocol. In this paper (Guru et.al, 2005), Inter cluster Ant Colony Optimization algorithm (IC-ACO) has been proposed that relies upon ACO algorithm for routing of data packets in the network with an aim to minimize the efforts wasted in transferring the redundant data sent by the sensors which lie in the close proximity of each other in a densely deployed network. In this approach, LEACH algorithm is used as the basis for the randomized selection of CHs. The protocol works in two phases. In the first phase, the CHs have been selected and nodes classify themselves into clusters. In the second phase, minimization of redundant data transmission and routing of data based on ant colony optimization are performed with in the cluster. Selection of CHs, minimization of redundancy and IC-ACO to route the data packets within the cluster are applied until all the nodes are dead in the sensor network. Improvement can be done in selection of the CH.

An Energy-Efficient Ant-Based Routing Algorithm for WSNs (AEARW) (Arabshahi et.al, 2001) aims to minimize communication load and maximize energy savings. The authors concentrate on two problems. Firstly, the older method of storing the route details in a routing table. Secondly, on quality of the path established from source node to BS node. The memory Mk of each ant is reduced to just two records, the last two visited nodes. Since the path followed by the ants is no more in their memories, a memory must be created at each node that keeps record of each ant that has received and sent a packet. If no record is found, the node saves the required information, restarts a timer, and forwards the ant to the next node. If a record containing the ant identification is found, the ant is eliminated and backward ant searches its memory to find the next node to where the ant must be sent. The vector E_k was erased from the forward ant's k then only carry the average energy till the current node (E_{Avgk}), and the minimum energy level registered (E_{Mink}). These values are updated by each node that receives the forward ants. When the forward ant reaches the BS-node these values are used to calculate the amount of pheromone trail used by the corresponding backward ant. To lose part of the pheromone strength during its way to the source node. So, those nodes near the BS-node will have more pheromone levels than remote nodes to find better paths. Maintenance of two BSs is a problem in this protocol.

Improved low energy adaptive hierarchy protocol based on local centroid bat algorithm [ILEHP] for designing bat algorithm. In this paper (Sim et.al, 2003) authors have applied a bat algorithm technique to solve some disadvantage in LEACH like random selection of CH, taking no account of the remaining energy and position of nodes, along with an aim to improve the poor local search capability of the algorithm. The improved protocol divides the CH selection process into optimization of temporary CH and formal CH selection. In this protocol, they will generate temporary CHs by following traditional LEACH protocol at the first round. Later on, optimizes these CHs based on LCBA and select formal CHs based on residual energy.

A New BBC based LEACH Algorithm for Energy Efficient Routing in WSN [ANBLE] (Iyengar et.al, 2007) is a based on big bang crunch. The protocol consider traditional LEACH algorithm's cluster formation using big bang crunch based meta-heuristic algorithm with an objective to optimize battery utilization. The proposed protocol applies the fitness function on nodes and selects the CH where all the nodes are considered as particles are arranges into an order by way of a convergence operator center of mass then, cluster member are joined around the center mass of CH by adding or subtracting a normal random number whose value decreases as the iterations elapse. The simulation carried in MatLab tool in comparison with LEACH.

Hybrid Approach for Energy Optimization in WSNs [HAEOW] routing protocol based on firefly and ABC. In this paper (Basyal et.al, 2007) a hybrid clustering approach is proposed to minimize the energy of the network so as to increase the life time of WSN. The cluster based firefly and artificial bee colony (ABC) algorithm are implemented. Two problems are concentrated like selection of CH and cluster formation. Initially the selection of CH and CH formation of cluster remains same as LEACH for first round. From the existing CH are checked for residual energy if CH is eligible to continue as CH for next round, if it as with firefly technique, it will continue as CH for next round, else the selection of next CH is done with highest residual energy in the cluster. This process is repeated for all clusters in the network. Then, selection of CH done based on optimization of ABC using residual energy of the current CH; then top required n nodes with highest residual energy are set as CHs. The steady phase remains same as LEACH.

Clustering approach for WSNs based on Cuckoo Search Strategy (CWCSS) (Muraleedharan et.al, 2004) a clustering protocol based on the breed parasitism of few cuckoo bird spices with an aim to increase the lifetime of the network. The CHs are computed randomly as in LEACH. Once the CHs are selected, they will broadcast the message. Non-CH nodes in the network treat CHs as the nest, then, tries to choose a best CH based on residual energy of CH, distance between CH and BS, and distance between CH and non-CH. The non-CH will send JOIN_REQ for the chosen CH. JOIN_REQ is treated as the cuckoo egg. CHs on the reception of the request generates a random probability of whether to accept or reject the request based on the threshold value, which changes from round to round and whether the rejection probability cross the threshold or not. This phenomenon is mapped to the rejection or acceptance of cuckoo eggs by the host bird with some probability. In this proposed work, a JOIN_REQ is considered only if non-CH nodes threshold probability is more than threshold probability in CH; else a node is rejected by CH. The entire nodes in the plot, splits itself into formation of clusters and enter the steady-phase communication, where actually the transmission of sensed information happens between the nodes and the BS.

Flower Pollination Optimization Algorithm for WSN Lifetime Global Optimization [FPOAW] (Forster et.al, 2009) is an energy aware clustering mode designed in an objective to achieve the global optimization for WSN lifetime. A candidate CH is to be selected for every cluster from the flower pollination clustering. The CH is selected as the node inside the cluster with the most remaining energy. It searches for optimal distribution of nodes on clusters. The objective; fitness function are employed to minimize the intra-cluster compactness with minimum distance between nodes in same cluster. In flower pollination optimization the number of cluster are formed based on distance between CH and nodes in a cluster with a goal to find the number of cluster centers that minimize the intra-cluster distance. The steady phase of the protocol remains unchanged.

Cluster Formation of Wireless Sensor Nodes using Adaptive Particle Swarm Optimization [CFWAPSO] (Zhang et.al, 2006) applies selection of the CH with an aim to increase energy efficiency. The selection of the CH using fitness function based on particle velocity and position of PSO is applied in BS. BS will then broadcast selection of CHs' to all nodes. Once the CH are selected the process of cluster forming is similar to the LEACH protocol.

Fire-LEACH: A Novel Clustering Protocol for WSNs based on Firefly Algorithm[FL]()Wang et.al, 2006) approach used for improving the LEACH protocol for reducing in steady state energy consumption. The BS broadcasts the percentage of CHs requirements for the entire network. Based on this randomly CHs are selected as in LEACH. All the CHs learn about the ordinary nodes and other CHs in the plot. Then they broadcast the packet of interest by introducing the intensity value that is calculated based on, intensity value of all nodes in network for that round. The firefly algorithm is applied to compute this value using distance of CH and non-CH nodes, which serves to be an objective function for all sensor nodes. All the CHs store the maximum of the intensity values calculated with all the other non-CH nodes in the network belonging to a particular round. The non-CH nodes now compare their intensity values with all the other CHs intensity values and attach to a CH that is having more intensity value than their values, by sending a join request packet. This process leads to a cluster formation. After the formation of the clusters, the network enters to the steady state phase; further steps are same as in LEACH.

Achieving energy efficiency in WSN using Gravitational Search algorithm (GSA) (AEEWG) (Yu et.al, 2006) is applied for CH selection based on Newtonion law of gravity and the law of motion. Here agents are considered as objects and their performance based on its masses. All objects are attached to one another by a gravitational force which causes the movement of objects globally. While forming clusters GSA clustering method is used. CH for each cluster is selected based on the nodes distance from BS in the cluster, node being in central position in cluster and remaining energy.

An energy-aware clustering for WSNs using PSO algorithm (PSO-C) is a centralized clustering protocol implemented at the BS (Shaoqiang et.al, 2007). It considers' both energy available to nodes and physical distances between the nodes and their CHs. This protocol defines a cost function which tries to minimize both the maximum average Euclidean distance of nodes to their associated CHs and the ratio of total initial energy of all nodes to the total energy of the CH candidates. It also ensures that only nodes with sufficient energy are selected as CHs. PSO-C outperforms both LEACH and LEACH-C in terms of the network lifetime and the throughput.

A centralized PSO protocol for Hierarchical Clustering (PSO-HC) for WSN is proposed in (Islam et.al, 2006). They tried to maximize the network lifetime by minimizing the number of active CHs and to maximize the network scalability by using two-hop communication between the sensor nodes and their respective CHs. The elect of using a realistic network and energy consumption model in cluster-based communication for WSN was investigated. Extensive simulations show that PSO-HC outperforms the well-known cluster-based sensor network protocols in terms of average consumed energy and throughput.

The comparison of swarm intelligence based meta - heuristic WSN routing is summarized in Table 7.

Artificial Immune System [AIS] Based Algorithms

The design strategy concerns on principles extracted and inspired by immune system of animal, birds, humans, plants for learning and memory. AI applies adaptive and combated pathogens mechanisms in living bodies for problem solving. It uses once again population agents similar to SI, to learn and identify patterns of antigens that intrude a system. The enhancement can be made in this study by adding stimulated selection, colonial reproduction and adaptation in identification of pathogens. The greater part of research of this area is currently can be viewed in pattern recognition (Arabshahi et.al, 2001, Sim et.al, 2003).

The Distributed Node and Rate Selection (DNRS) (Iyengar et.al, 2007) routing method designed on the principles of natural immune system. Based on the B-cell stimulation in immune system, DNRS selects the most appropriate sensor nodes that send samples of the observed event, are referred to as *designated nodes*. The aim of the designated node selection is to meet the event estimation distortion constraint at the sink node with the minimum number of sensor nodes. DNRS enables each sensor node to distributively decide whether it is a designated node or not. In addition, to exploit the temporal correlation in the event data DNRS regulates the reporting frequency rate of each sensor node while meeting the application-specific delay bound at the sink. Based on the immune network principles, DNRS distributive selects the

Table 7. Comparison of swarm intelligence based WSN

Routing Technique	Distribution of nodes	Control message overhead	Uniform energy distribution	Energy efficiency	Scalability	Transmission delay	Algorithm complexity	Data aggregation	Simulation Tool
PSO with time varying inertia weight	Uniform	Very low	Medium	Good	Low	Low	Medium	N	Omnet
PSO with time varying acceleration constants	Random	Low	Low	Average	Low	Low	Medium	N	Sim
Hierarchical PSO with time varying acceleration constants	Uniform	Low	Low	Average	Medium	Medium	High	N	Sim
PSO with supervisor student mode	Random	Very low	Medium	Very Good	Medium	High	Medium	N	sim
Ant-based	Random	Very low	Medium	Average	Low	Low	Medium	Y	Sim
Collaborative Clustering	Uniform	Low	Medium	Good	Low	Medium	High	Y	Sim
Ant-Building	Random	Low	Medium	Good	Medium	Low	Medium	N	Prowler
ECWPSO	Uniform	low	Medium	Good	Low	low	Low	Y	MATLAB
WCPSO	Uniform	low	Low	Good	Low	Medium	Medium	N	MATLAB
IACOW	Random	low	Medium	Good	Low	Medium	High	Y	Omnet
ARW	Uniform	low	Medium	Medium	Low	Medium	High	Y	Omnet
ILEHP	Random	Very low	Low	Medium	High	Medium	Low	N	MATLAB
ANBLE	Random	Very low	Medium	Good	Low	Medium	Low	N	MATLAB
HAEOW	Random	low	Medium	Good	Low	Low	Medium	Y	NS2
CWCSS	Grid	low	Low	Good	High	Medium	Medium	Y	Sim
FPOAW	Uniform	low	Medium	Average	Low	Low	High	Y	MATLAB

continued on the following page

Table 7. Continued

Routing Technique	Distribution of nodes	Control message overhead	Uniform energy distribution	Energy efficiency	Scalability	Transmission delay	Algorithm complexity	Data aggregation	Simulation Tool
CFWAPSO	Uniform	low	Medium	Average	Low	Low	Low	Y	NS2
FL	Grid	low	Medium	Average	Low	Medium	Medium	N	Sim
AEEWG	Random	low	Medium	Medium	Low	Medium	High	Y	NS2
EDGWACO	Random	low	Medium	Medium	Low	Medium	High	Y	MATLAB
CERW	Uniform	low	Medium	Good	High	Medium	Low	N	Omnet
AKERWH	Grid	Low	Medium	Medium	Low	Low	Low	N	MATLAB
AIEBBO	Random	Low	Low	Medium	Low	Medium	Medium	Y	Sim
BEDGACO	Random	Low	Low	Good	high	Low	Medium	Y	Sim
RCCHBO	Random	Low	Low	Average	High	Medium	High	Y	NS2
PIWRH	Random	Low	Medium	Average	High	Medium	Medium	N	MATLAB
MOIAR	Uniform	Low	Low	Low	High	Medium	medium	N	MATLAB

appropriate reporting frequencies of sensor nodes according to the congestion in the forward path and the event estimation distortion periodically calculated at the sink by Adaptive LMS Filter. DNRS provides the minimum number of designated nodes to reliability and also exploit the temporal correlation in the event data whereby it provides the significant energy saving.

Genetic Algorithm [GA] Based Algorithms

GA design methodology, involves representation of chromosome initialized randomly as population. The chromosome undergoes the process of selection, crossover, mutation to find optimal chromosome with fitness function as evaluation parameter. GA works on the principle of survival of the fittest. GA has been explored in WSN field mainly for Cluster formation.

In this paper (Tiago et.al, 2003), a genetic algorithm based method (GABEEC) is proposed to optimize the lifetime of wireless sensor networks. The proposed method is a cluster based approach like LEACH. The method has 2 phases which are Set-up and Steady-state phase. In the set-up phase, static clusters are created which do not change throughout the network except for dynamically selected CH. The fitness function employed is based on distance between node to CH and from CH to BS. Selection is based on Roulette-Wheel selection method. Then crossover and mutation function is employed to choose the best in local optimum. The steady phase and selection of CH remains same as LEACH protocol.

In this paper an Improved LEACH Multi-hop Routing Protocol Based on Genetic Algorithms for Heterogeneous Wireless Sensor Networks [ILMGHW] (Cao et.al, 2004) a multi-hop routing algorithm LEACH-Genetic Algorithm is proposed to improve single-hop system in the LEACH. GA uses mechanisms similar to biological evolution, such as reproduction, mutation, recombination, and selection. The distance between CHs and BS is tried to be shortest path. The CHs which lies far away from BS communicates with it through the transit CHs and nodes which are nearer to BS can communicate with it directly. During set-up phase the clusters are formed as in LEACH then, BS-centered multi-hop path between CH's to BS is obtained by applying GA method. Selection is done by applying Roulette selection method and fitness function is based on length of the links in the network. The steady phase remains same as LEACH.

New Clustering Protocol for Wireless Sensor Networks Using Genetic Algorithm Approach [NCWG] (Archana et.al, 2014) is used to optimize lifetime and energy consumption of network. The algorithm improves by considering coverage metric.

Figure 10. Two successive clustering

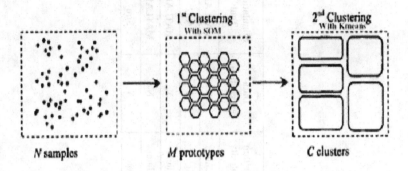

The designed algorithm is centralized and runs in BS. The fitness value will be assigned for each node during the set-up phase. The value depends on total energy of the network and distance of each node to BS. Further selection of the CH will be based on assigned fitness value itself. Cluster formation and steady phase remains same as LEACH. A novel genetic algorithm in LEACH-C routing protocol for sensor networks [NLRS] (Leela et.al, 2014) works on centralized protocol. The nodes with residual energy above the average energy are chosen randomly for initial generation. In next rounds the selection of nodes is based on two fitness values, first value depends on distance between node to CH and second value depends on distance between CH and BS.

GA based energy efficient routing (GAEER) (Tiago et.al, 2006) for data gathering of relay nodes is presented to enhance the life time of a network. BS will identify relay nodes and then all the nodes will choose one hop neighbors to relay nodes. Protocols supports inter and intra communication applying GA technique. Initial population and fitness function is based on greedy technique. The protocol applies relay node reselection mechanism, which will reselect on the basis of sensor nodes residual energy in a balance way and relay node searches their closest neighbor relay nodes for inter-cluster communication. The intra cluster communication is required to communicate its sensed data relay node, they will aggregate and forward to next relay node towards BS.

The comparison of genetic algorithm based meta -heuristic WSN routing is summarized in Table 8.

Neural Network [NN] Based Algorithms

NN intended to architecture of WSN with natural cognition principles, which imitates the brains of animals or humans beings. The graph topology with artificial neurons with large system is interconnected either in parallel or distributed components.

Table 8. Comparison of genetic algorithm based WSN

Routing technique	Distribution of nodes	Control message overhead	Uniform energy distribution	Energy efficiency	Scalability	Transmission delay	Algorithm complexity	Data aggregation	Simulation Tool
GABEEC	Uniform	low	Medium	Good	Low	Low	Medium	N	MATLAB
ILMGHW	Random	Very low	Average	Medium	Very low	Low	High	Y	NS2
NCWG	Random	Very low	Medium	Medium	Low	Low	Medium	Y	MATLAB
NLRS	Grid	Very low	Medium	Good	Low	Low	Medium	N	MATLAB
GAEER	Random	Low	Medium	Medium	Low	Medium	More	Y	Sim

Figure 11. Comparison of different simulators

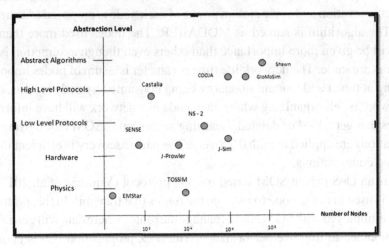

Synapses are a special weighed interconnection of neurons mechanism. The packets or data needed to be processed are forwarded on sensors which are connected by artificial neurons for processing. NN includes input and output complex inter connection which can be supervised or unsupervised, which are process viewed most. The internal process of interconnection of them in finding patterns and relationship construction is the main internal logic of interconnection of neurons to be done to obtain effective result. It includes algorithms: Perceptron neural networks, and self- organizing maps.

NN do not directly and independently help in energy conservation but, they help in working as intelligent tools in an easier, efficient, and desirable manner (Kumar et.al, 2014). Another difficulty with NN is in appropriate selection of topology. Further, neural network classification based on energy efficiency done as follows:

Energy Efficient Path Discovery

NN are appropriate in some special scenarios to develop complex tools including path discovery. An unsupervised NN structure self-organizing map [SOM] consisting of neurons arranged in a regular grid manner. Weight vectors (or synapses) connect the input layer to output layer which is called map or competitive layer. Each neuron vector will activate a neuron in output layer based on similarity rule which is decided based on Euclidian distance of two vectors the same learning process will be carried on considering two neurons until stabilization of weight vectors. In this manner energy efficient path is discovered for network based on learning process applying Euclidian distance

An intelligent method based SOM NN which optimizes the routing in terms of energy conservation and computation power of each node is proposed (Aksher et.al, 2019). The algorithm is named as MODABER. The nodes used more than other nodes will be given more importance than others even though assumption is made all sensors are same. The network life time parameter is a sum of nodes importance in routing at time t and amount of energy being consumed by node are considered. The network is self organizing where each node in a network will have information on nodes that get added or deleted. Learning algorithm is SOM based using linear computations are applied to path discovery. The path discovery is efficient in terms of limited computations.

SIR is an QoS driven SOM based routing protocol (Vinithan et.al, 2017). The SOM N is used in every node to manage the routes that transmit. In this protocol all nodes are employed with SOM NN to manage the routes where data will get transmit. AI is combined to improve performance. The back propagation NN is applied to predict the final power level of the node in this protocol to resolve hotspot problem. The prediction of hot spot is made by defining a 3-layered back propagation NN with parameters: distance from sink, number of neighbors, and agent's accessibility by finally identifying power level of node at the end of WSN lifetime.

Energy Efficient Clustering and Cluster Head Selection

LEACH based centralized proposal Low Energy Adaptive Connectionist Clustering (LAC) (Garg et.al, 2014) using SOM based clustering protocol is designed. The cluster formation is designed by sink nodes in first level using SOM; construction is done in two phases cluster setup and cluster formation. Second level clustering is done by applying k-means. After cluster formation steady phase will work similar to LEACH until nodes dead level falls below threshold.

Energy Based Clustering Self Organizing Map [EBCSOM] applies Kohonen SOM NN for clustering with a study of analysis on unpredictable behaviors of network parameters and applications is proposed (Bayrakal et.al, 2012). The SOM by applying Kohonen considering for nodes are applied by taking different parameters of sensors such as direction, position, number of hops, energy levels, sensitivity, latency and others. By applying SOM preliminary phase is pre-treated forming clusters and then SOM is clustered by K means. The BS has to select m nodes with highest energy in network for determining weight matrix. The weight vectors for SOM: x and Y coordinated and nodes energy level. The input samples are first normalized with min-max normalization method. The balanced clusters are formed by moving the nodes with energy towards max energy nodes.

Energy Based Clustering Self organizing map (EBCS)(Long et.al, 2014) protocol cluster sensor nodes based on multiple parameters energy level and coordinates, through using Self Organizing Map neural network capability in multi dimensional data clustering to from clusters which balance clusters in order to better energy consumption ensured more network coverage by random and dispersed dying of sensors. The input for SOM are every nodes x and y coordinates for cluster formation. The selection of CH for each cluster is based on maximum energy sensor, nearest sensor to BS and nearest sensor to gravity center of the cluster.

Neural Network based reliable routing(NNRR)(Norouzi et.al, 2011) enhances the reliability in packet transmission by predicting energy robust and near-by nodes in data forwarding towards the destination applying back propagation NN algorithm for data transmission. To determine shortest path data transmission use neighbor node distance and its energy, distance or range difference is estimated based on Euclidian distance. The algorithm considers routing nodes energy robustness in order to predict energy loss due to insufficient battery energy required for data forwarding which avoids retransmission. The protocol is evaluated for reduced power consumption, improved packet delivery ratio, increased throughput, and better delay with reduced sampling rate.

Energy Efficient Data Fusion and Association

Normally filters such as Kalman filter or Bayesian theorem with predefined numbers are used in NN. In few cases non specified statistical model are used with intelligent methods such as rule based fuzzy logic or NN (Rahmanian et.al, 2011). NN eliminate environmental or intentional jamming on sensory data according to training. Multi sensor data fusions are support easily in NN.

A distributed system is considered for creating multiple sensors and associate them or classify related to target. It works on hop based to find optimal solution (Seetaram et.al, 2009). The algorithm will not consider for more than two targets designed then it is resolved with NP-hard algorithm.

The identification and classification of objects in a network is done similar to human brains applying associative nature of NN. The network can be unstable but stability is supported with forcing weight matrix to symmetric main diagonal and recurrent network contain associative memory. Hop field NN consisting of feedback from output to input is included (Bhatti et.al, 2014).

Hop field NN is used in (Vinithan et.al, 2017) to store average correlations between components of all patterns in every single sensor. The corrupted or lost packets can be recreated in an efficient manner by applying association technique of NN. Also correlated patters can be generated from data.

The comparison of neural network based meta heuristic WSN routing is summarized in Table 9.

7 Evaluation of Algorithm of WSN

Evaluation of WSN should has to be done with respect to some performance matrices in order to know and prove improvement in performance of novel designed algorithms when compared to primitive once. The following are few lists of parameters which will evaluate the algorithms and their importance.

- **Lifetime and Energy-Efficiency Definitions:** It means the time from where the network starts its operation till the phase network has completed its operation
- **Numbers of Clusters with Robustness:** The number of clusters heads decides number of clusters with the network based on placement of sensors, transmission path length and range, type of sensors, size of data to me sensed and received.
- **Number of Data Packets Transmitted:** The maximum numbers of data packets being transmitted in network also known as throughput.
- **Energy Consumption:** Energy consumption evaluates the total energy dissipated in the network for all its activities conducted in network lifetime.
- **Efficiency with Respect to Lifetime:** The productivity and utilization of WSN will be decided by critical parameter lifetime of network. If lifetime is more elongated then expense is required will be less.

Implementation Tools for WSN

WSN can be designed and analyzed using three methods: i) analytical methods ii) Computer simulations iii) Practical implementations. Among the three simulation of WSN is the most common adopted method. WSN basic structure will hinder from complete or accurate analysis. Accordingly simulation is widely included method for analyses.

The commonly used WSN simulators are briefed in table 11.

The comparisons of various simulators are shown in

The biggest strength of WSN is its ability to apply in field and under any environment unlike standalone networks. WSN consist of very interesting and multidisciplinary field of research with huge number with varying application applications. In future sensors play a key role in shaping and making smarter in fields like health, smart home, environment monitoring, security, IoT and others.

Table 9. Comparison of neural network WSN routing algorithms

Routing technique	Distribution of nodes	Control message overhead	Uniform energy distribution	Energy efficiency	Scalability	Transmission delay	Algorithm complexity	Data aggregation	Simulation Tool
LAC	Random	low	Medium	Good	Low	Low	Medium	N	MATLAB
EBCSOM	Uniform	Very low	Average	Medium	Very low	Low	High	Y	MATLAB
EBCS	Grid	Low	Medium	Medium	Low	Low	Medium	Y	MATLAB
NNRR	Grid	Low	Medium	Good	Low	Low	Medium	N	MATLAB

Table 10. Comparison of routing techniques for WSN

Type of routing	Merits	Demerits
Information- centric	Improves network efficiency and content distribution performance by satisfying user request	More complex and time consuming
Node-centric	Scalable, and balance load among all nodes	Consumes more energy in large size
Source initiated	Dynamically route will be created	Not suitable for large network as metadata size increase
Destination- initiated	Route maintenance is easier. Works well for multiple sink nodes also	Complex to build route.
Single path	Easy to build and maintain	Data loss or inaccurate data may happen in network
Multi path	Fast, accurate data delivery will be done	Maintenance cost is more.
Proactive	Identification of routes is faster. Suited for large and dense networks predominantly.	When the instability increases, the need for route updates and control traffic increases which leads to inefficiency.
Reactive	Route can be discovered when required efficiency is more	Network construction will be slow. The reconstruction will be time longer and failure more
Hybrid	The Routing Protocol will able be customize simple and flexible	With the added cost of increased complexity due to increased functionality and source code.
Flat	Avoids the flooding of data Transmit data is minimal	Scalability is minimum suitable only for small networks. Overhead of maintaining resources
Query based	Node identification easier and storage is not required	Complex to maintain if multiple queries
Coherent	Easier to construct	Depends on protocol operations
Hierarchical	Energy efficient, scalability and extends lifetime	Data aggregation is required too
Location	As location aware route set up is easy	Not suitable few applications
Fuzzy	Less computational complexity Construction of route is easier through rules	They are not robust, they give same importance to all factors
Swarm Intelligence	Highly scalable, self organising	Few techniques are very expensive
Artificial immune system	Self learning, high robust	Cannot detect synergetic effects
Neural networks	Storing information on entire network, work with incomplete knowledge, fault network	Unexplained behavior of the network, difficulty in showing problem

Table 11. Commonly used WSN simulators

Simulator	Programming language	Characteristics	Advantages	Downloadable website
NS-3	C++ Python	Object oriented discrete. Easy to add new protocols A large number of protocols available publicly Availability of a visual tool	Graphics support is less, more time required to run protocol	http://www.nsnam.org
NS-2	C++	Discrete event network simulator packet-level, link layer and up, wired and wireless	Supports only two wireless MAC protocols, 802.11, single hop TDMA protocol, more time requirement, poor graphical tool	http://www.isi.edu/ nsnam/ns/
TOSIM	Nesc	It can be used as simulator and an emulator for WSNs; Provides obvious advantages for projects deal with MICA nodes, High degree of accuracy or running the application source code unchanged. Availability of a visualization tool.	Compilation steps lose the finegrained timing and interrupt properties of the code, All nodes in the network must run identical code; The network environment is not modeled	http://www.Tinyos. stanford.edu/
GLOMOSIM	pesc	Parallel simulation capability. It is tailored specifically for wireless networks. Availability of a visualization tool.	Effectively limited to IP networks because of low level design assumptions. Unavailability of new protocols	http://pcl.cs.ucla.edu/ projects/glomosim
OMNeT++	C++	Discrete-event; Structured around simple modules; Has a versatile GUI	Model building may require special training; Needs long time for learning how to use the simulation packages; Results may be difficult to interpret	http://omnetpp.org
UWSIM	C++	Publicly available and designed solely for UWSN.	Supports only a limited number of functionalities and calls for extension	http://irs.uji.es/uwsim
Avrora	JAVA	Can handle networks having up to 10,000 nodes. Enables validation of time-dependent properties of large-scale networks	Fails to model clock drift. 50% slower than TOSSIM. Cannot model mobility	http://www.cs.ucla. edu/avrora
SENSE	C++	Platform-independent Users can assemble application-specific environments Defines an environment as a grid of interchangeable tiles. Designed around a component structure; Overcome the scalability issues inherent in object-orientated structures, Balanced consideration of modeling methodology and simulation efficiency. Memory-efficient, fast, extensible, and reusable.	Not accurately simulate a MAC protocol. Provides support for sensors, actuators, and physical phenomena only for sound Lacks of developed extensibility; Does not include functionality such as sensing Not accurate evaluation of WSN research. Lacks a comprehensive set of models Absence of a visualization tool	http://www.ita.cs.rpi. edu
COOJA	JAVA	Concerning both simulated hardware and software. Larger-scale behavior protocols and algorithms can be observed.	Not extremely efficient. Supports a limited number of simultaneous node types. Making extensive and timedependent simulations difficult	http://www.contiki-os.org
Castalia	C++	Physical process modeling, sensing device bias and noise, node clock drift, and several MAC and routing protocols implemented.	Highly tunable MAC protocol and a flexible parametric physical process model. Not a sensor specific platform. Not useful if one would like to test code compiled for a specific sensor node platform.	https://castalia.npc. nicta.com.au/
Emstar	Linux	May be run on a diverse set of execution platforms. Combination of simulator and emulator. EmStar's use of the component-based model allows for fair scalability	Only run code for the types of nodes Does not support parallel simulations. Not as efficient and fast as other frameworks	http://www.usenix.org
OPNET	C/C++	Object-orientated, developed for military applications; Suitable for heterogeneous networks with various protocols; Uses a hierarchical strategy to organize the models	Quite expensive for commercial usage; Limited in scalability and extensibility	http://www.riverbed. com

continued on the following page

Table 11. Continued

Simulator	Programming language	Characteristics	Advantages	Downloadable website
J-SIM	JAVA	Provides support for energy modeling, with the exception of radio energy consumption, Support mobile WSNs. Component-oriented architecture. Improving on the inter-communication efficiency It is application development environment based on the component-based software architecture, Autonomous Component Architecture	Low efficiency of simulation. The only MAC protocol provided for wireless networks is 802.11. Unnecessary run-time overhead, slower than other simulators Relatively complicated to use; No real established user base; Not widely adopted	http://www.physiome.org
Visual sense	Ptolemy II	Provides an accurate and extensible radio model as well as a sound model that is accurate enough to use for localization.	Does not provide any protocols above the wireless medium, or any sensor or physical phenomena other than sound.	http://ptolemy.berkeley.edu
Prowler	Matlab/JAVA	Easy debugging, provide visualization, event driven nature Probabilistic WSN simulators. (J)Prowler provides an accurate radio model.	Provides only one MAC protocol, the default MAC protocol of TinyOS.	http://www.isis.vanderbilt.edu
Sensorsim	JAVA	Not limited to the implementation of distributed protocols Can simulate vast networks Object oriented discrete event; Provides advanced models for network hardware	Detailed simulations of issues such as radio propagation properties or low-layer issues are not well considered. Hard to develop extensions; Limited in Scalability	http://www.dl.acm.org
GTSNetS	C++	Scalable, highly extensible and customizable; Enables the simulation of sensor control networks; Supports a large variety of TCP-based applications; Provides a robust interface for creating network graphs	Requires extensive centralized computational power; Requires huge memory as the Network scale increased	https://www.computer.org/csdl/GTSNets
SenSim	JAVA	Modules are present to represent each protocol layer	Requires a reasonably high learning; There are not many developed protocols available for it	https://m.apkpure.com
Jist	JAVA	JiST is a high-performance discrete event simulation engine that runs over a standard Java virtual machine. It converts an existing virtual machine into a simulation platform, by embedding simulation time semantics at the byte-code level.	Runs only on JVM,	http://jist.ece.cornell.edu
Qualnet	C++	Scalable, model fidelity, portable, extensibility. Optimize new and existing models. Analyse performance of network.	It is commercial tool, it hides code for certain projects,	http://scalable-networks.com

Sensors can be found in all technologies, environment and infrastructure in near future according to researchers and industrialist by its inherent characteristic. Scope of WSN can be seen in IOT, security, data integrity, accountability, detection, tracking, analysis. The applications of WSN can be extended further by integrating with other technologies like big data, neural network, bio-inspired computing, fog computing, edge computing, machine learning, deep learning.

CONCLUSION

WSN is playing an important role in wireless networking domain. One of the major challenges of WSN is to prolong the network life using energy efficient routing. This paper presents a comprehensive review of energy efficient routing algorithms categorized as heuristic and meta-heuristic algorithms. The following routing algorithms under heuristic are covered namely: architecture based, communication model, data delivery, path establishment, network operation, network structure and performance. The literature survey reveals that hierarchical routing algorithms under network structure category are explored at a higher rate compared to other categories. The following routing algorithms under meta-heuristic are covered namely: Fuzzy logic, swarm intelligence, immune system, genetic algorithm and neural network. Under meta- heuristic approach immune system for network routing is still an emerging field where as lot of work is being carried out using others (FL, SI, GA, NN) which mainly attempt to optimise routing parameters. The chapter also covers a brief comparison of various simulators used for simulating WSN.

REFERENCES

Abramson, N. (1970). The Aloha System: another alternative for computer Communications. *Proceedings of November 17-19, 1970, Fall Joint computer conference*, 281-285. 10.1145/1478462.1478502

Akkaya, M. Y., & Younis, M. (2005). Energy and QoS Routing for Wireless Sensor Networks. *Cluster Computing*, 8(2), 179–188. doi:10.100710586-005-6183-7

Aksher. (2019). *A new neural network based energy efficient clustering protocol for WSN*. Academic Press.

Akyildiz, F., Weilian, S., Sankarasubramania, Y., & Cayirci, E. (2002). A survey on sensor networks. *IEEE Communications Magazine*, 40(8), 102–114. doi:10.1109/MCOM.2002.1024422

Rostami & Mottar. (2014). Wireless sensor network clustering using particles swarm optimization for reducing Energy Consumption. *International Journal of Managing Information Technology*, 6(4).

Seetharam, Acharya, Bhattacharyya, & Naska. (2009). Energy Efficient Data Gathering Schemes in Wireless Sensor Networks Using Ant Colony Optimization. *Journal of Applied Computer Science & Mathematics*, 5(6), 1-13.

Anjali, S., & Garg, A. (2013). Location aided destination initiated data tranfe in WSN. *4th International Conference on Reliability*.

Arabshahi, P., Gray, A., Kassabalidis, I., El-Sharkawi, M. A., Marks, R. J., Das, A., & Narayanan, S. (2001). Adaptive routing in wireless communication networks using swarm intelligence. *Proc. the 9th AIAA Int. Communications Satellite Systems Conf.*

Archana. (2014). A New BBC based LEACH Algorithm for Energy Efficient Routing in WSN. *International Journal of Engineering and Computer Science*, 3(2), 3914-3918.

Bandyopadhyay, S., & Coyle, E. (2003). An energy efficient hierarchical clustering algorithm for wireless sensor networks. *Proceedings of the 22nd Annual Joint Conference of the IEEE Computer and Communications Societies (INFOCOM 2003)*. 10.1109/INFCOM.2003.1209194

Bashyal, S., & Venayagamoorthy, G. K. (2007). Collaborative routing algorithm for wireless sensor network longevity. *Proc. 3rd Int. Conf on Intelligent Sensors, Sensor Networks and Information Processing*. 10.1109/ISSNIP.2007.4496896

Bormann, C., Castellani, A. P., & Shelby, Z. (2012). CoAP: An Application Protocol for Billions of Tiny Internet Nodes. *IEEE Internet Computing, 16*(2), 62–67. doi:10.1109/MIC.2012.29

Vinutha, Nalini, & Veeresh. (2017). Energy efficient WSN using NN smart sampling and reliable routing protocol. *IEEE WISPNET-2017.*

Cai, X., Duan, Y., He, Y., Yang, J., & Li, C. (2015). Bee-Sensor-C: An energy-efficient and scalable multipath routing protocol for wireless sensor networks. *International Journal of Distributed Sensor Networks, 26,* 1–14.

Camilo, Carreto, Silva, & Boavida. (2006). An Energy-Efficient Ant-Based Routing Algorithm for Wireless Sensor Networks. *LNCS, 4150,* 49-59.

Cao, Li, Dai, & Chen. (2014). Weirong Improved Low Energy Adaptive Clustering Hierarchy Protocol Based on Local Centroid Bat Algorithm. *Sensor Letters, 12*(9), 1372-1377.

Chao, H., & Chang, C. (2008). A Fault-Tolerant Routing Protocol in Wireless Sensor Networks. *Sensor Networks, 2*(2), 66–73. doi:10.1504/IJSNET.2008.016463

Chen, G., Branch, M. J., Pflug, L. Z., & Szymanski, B. (2004). *Sense: A sensor network simulator.* Advances in Pervasive Computing & Networking.

Chen, M., Leung, V., & Mao, S. (2009). Directional Controlled Fusion in Wireless Sensor Networks. *Mobile Networks and Applications, 14*(2), 220–229. doi:10.100711036-008-0133-6

Cherian, M., & Nair, T. R. G. (2011). Multipath Routing With Novel Packet Scheduling Approach In Wireless Sensor Networks. *International Journal of Computer Theory and Engineering, 3*(5), 666–670. doi:10.7763/IJCTE.2011.V3.389

Clausen, T., Jacquet, P., Laouiti, A., Muhlethaler, P., Qayyum, A., & Viennot, L. (2001). *Optimized Link State Routing Protocol. IEEE INMIC.*

Couto, D. S. J. D., Aguayo, D., Bicket, J., & Morris, R. (2003). A High-Throughput Path Metric for Multi-Hop Wireless Routing. *9th annual international conference on Mobile computing and networking (MobiCom '03),* 134 – 146. 10.1145/938985.939000

Devika, G., & Asha, G. K. (2015, Feb.). A pragmatic study of LEACH and its descendant routing protocols in WSN. National conference on research issues in image analysis and mining intelligence. *International Journal of Computation Intelligence and Informatics.*

Devika, G., & Asha, G. K. (2015). Performance enhancement of LEACH, V-LEACH and MOD-LEACH clustering routing protocols for wireless sensor networks. *International Conference on Research in Business Management & Information Technology (ICRBIT – 2015).*

Devika, G., Asha, G. K., & Premshudha, B. G. (2015). A pragmatic study of evolutionary techniques based energy efficient hierarchical routing protocols-LEACH and PEGASIS. *Int J Appl Eng Res, 10*(5), 3979–82.

Dijkstra, E. W. (1959). A note on two problems in connexion with graphs. *Numerische Mathematik, 1*(1), 269–271. doi:10.1007/BF01386390

Ding, P., Holliday, J., & Celik, A. (2015). Distributed Energy-E_cient Hierarchical Clustering for Wireless Sensor Networks. *Lecture Notes in Computer Science,* 3560, 322-339.

Ehsan, S., & Hamdaoui, B. (2012). A Survey on Energy-Efficient Routing Techniques with QoS Assurances for Wireless Multimedia Sensor Networks. *IEEE Communications Surveys and Tutorials, 14*(2), 265–278. doi:10.1109/SURV.2011.020211.00058

Ahvar, Pourmoslemi, & Piran. (2011). FEAR: A Fuzzy-Based Energy-Aware Routing Protocol For Wireless Sensor Networks. *International Journal of Grid Computing & Applications, 2*(2).

Ephremides, A., Wieselthier, J. E., & Baker, D. J. (1987). A design concept for reliable mobile radio networks with frequency hopping signaling. *Proceedings of the IEEE, 75*(1), 56–73. doi:10.1109/PROC.1987.13705

Eslaminejad, M. R., Sookhak, M., Razak, S. A., & Haghparast, M. (2011). A Review of Routing Mechanisms in Wireless Sensor Networks. *International Journal of Computer Science and Telecommunications, 2,* 1–9.

Felemban, E., Lee, C., & Ekici, E. (2006). MMSPEED: Multipath Multi-SPEED Protocol for QoS Guarantee of Reliability and Timeliness in Wireless Sensor Networks. *IEEE Transactions on Mobile Computing, 5*(6), 738–754. doi:10.1109/TMC.2006.79

Forster & Murphy. (2009). CLIQUE: Role-Free Clustering with Q-Learning for Wireless Sensor Networks. *Proc. 29th Int. Conf. on Distributed Computing Systems (ICDCS).*

Fu, B., Li, R., Xiao, X., Liu, C., & Yang, Q. (2009). Non-interfering multipath geographic routing for wireless multimedia sensor networks. *Proc. 2009 IEEE Int'l Conf. Multimedia Information Networking and, Security*, 254–258. 10.1109/MINES.2009.139

Gandotra, N. (2019). Exploration of HEED clustering algorithm for performance improvement in heterogeneous environment. iManager Publications.

Ganesan, D., Govindan, R., Shenker, S., & Estrin, D. (2001). Highly-resilient Energy-Efficient Multipath Routing in Wireless Sensor Networks. *2nd ACM international symposium on Mobile ad hoc networking & computing, Ser. MobiHoc '01*, 251 – 254. 10.1145/501416.501452

Garg, Rani, & Singh. (2014). Achieving Energy Efficiency in WSN using GSA. *International Journal of Advanced Research in Computer Science and Software Engineering, 4*(4), 168-174.

Ghawy & Al-Sanabani. (n.d.). Application and Performance Analysis of DSDV Routing Protocol in Ad-Hoc Wireless Sensor Network with Help of NS2 Knowledge. *Global Journal of Computer Science and Technology.*

Godbole. (2012). Performance Analysis of Clustering Protocol Using Fuzzy Logic for Wireless Sensor Network. *IAES International Journal of Artificial Intelligence, 1*(3), 103-111.

Gong, B., Li, L., Wang, S., & Zhou, X. (2008). Multihop routing protocol with unequal clustering for wireless sensor networks. *ISECS International Colloquium on Computing, Communication, Control, and Management, 2*, 552-556.

Gupta, D. R., & Sampalli, S. (2005). Cluster-head election using fuzzy logic for wireless sensor networks. *Proc. 3rd Annual Communication Networks and Services Research Conf.*, 255–260. 10.1109/CNSR.2005.27

Bhatti & Raina. (2014). Cuckoo based Energy Effective Routing in Wireless Sensor Network. *International Journal of Computer Science and Communication Engineering, 3*(1), 92-95.

Guru, S., Halgamuge, S., & Fernando, S. (2005). Particle swarm optimizers for cluster formation in wireless sensor networks. *Proc. Int. Conf. on Intelligent Sensors, Sensor Networks and Information Processing*, 319–324.

Hancke, G. P., & Leuschner, C. J. (2007). SEER: A simple energy efficient routing protocol for wireless sensor networks. *South African Computer Journal, 39*, 17–24.

He, T., Stankovic, J., Lu, C., & Abdelzaher, T. (2003). SPEED: A Stateless Protocol for Real-Time Communication in Sensor Networks. *Proc. 23ʳᵈ International Conference on Distributed Computing Systems*, 46-55. 10.21236/ADA436741

Heinzelman, W. R., Chandrakasan, A., & Balakrishnan, H. (2000). Energy-Efficient Communication Protocol for Wireless Microsensor Networks. *Proceedings of the 33rd Hawaii International Conference on System Sciences*, 1-10. 10.1109/HICSS.2000.926982

Hui, J., & Kelsey, R. (2018). *Multicast Protocol for Low-Power and Lossy Networks (MPL)*. Available online: https://tools.ietf.org/html/rfc7731

Hussain, S., Matin, A. W., & Islam, O. (2007). Genetic algorithm for energy efficient clusters in wireless sensor networks. *Proc. 4th Int. Conf. on Information Technology ITNG*, 147–154. 10.1109/ITNG.2007.97

Intanagonwiwat, C., Govindan, R., & Estrin, D. (2000). Directed diffusion: a scalable and robust communication paradigm for sensor networks. In *Proceedings of the 6th Annual International Conference on Mobile Computing and Networking (MobiCom '00)*. ACM. 10.1145/345910.345920

Ishaq, I., Hoebeke, J., Moerman, I., & Demeester, P. (2016). Experimental Evaluation of Unicast and Multicast CoAP Group Communication. *Sensors (Basel)*, *16*, 1137.

Islam, M., Thulasiraman, P., & Thulasiram, R. (2003). A parallel ant colony optimization algorithm for all-pair routing in MANETs. *Proc. Int. Parallel and Distributed Processing Symposium*. 10.1109/IPDPS.2003.1213470

Islam, O., & Hussain, S. (2006). An intelligent multi-hop routing for wireless sensor networks. *Proc. WI-IAT Workshops Web Intelligence and Int. Agent Technology Workshops*, 239–242 10.1109/WI-IATW.2006.42

Iyengar, S. S., Prasad, L., & Min, H. (1995). *Advances in distributed sensor technology*. Englewood Cliffs, NJ: Prentice Hall.

Iyengar, S. S., Wu, H.-C., Balakrishnan, N., & Chang, S. Y. (2007). Biologically inspired cooperative routing for wireless mobile sensor networks. *IEEE Systems Journal*, *1*(1), 29–37. doi:10.1109/JSYST.2007.903101

Jacson. (2017). Application of WSN- A survey. *IEEE, International Conference ICEEIMT*.

Jin, Y., Gormus, S., Kulkarni, P., & Sooriyabandara, M. (2016). Content Centric Routing in IoT Networks and Its Integration in RPL. *Computer Communications*, *89*, 87–104. doi:10.1016/j.comcom.2016.03.005

Lee & Cheng. (2012). Fuzzy-Logic-Based Clustering Approach for Wireless Sensor Networks Usmg Energy Predication. *IEEE Sensors Journal, 12*(9).

Kim, Park, Han, & Chung. (2008). CHEF: Cluster Head Election mechanism using Fuzzy logic in Wireless Sensor Networks. *ICACT*.

Kahn, J. M., Katz, R. H., & Pister, K. S. J. (1999). Next century challenges: Mobile networking for smart dust. *Proceedings of ACM/IEEE Internatonal Conference on Mobile Computing Networks*, 271–278. 10.1145/313451.313558

Karp, B., & Kung, H. T. (2000). GPSR[1]: greedy perimeter stateless routing for wireless networks. Proc. 2000 ACM Mobile Computing and Networking, 243–254.

Kim, Sharma, Kumar, Tomar, Berry, & Lee. (2014). Intercluster Ant Colony Optimization Algorithm for Wireless Sensor Network in Dense Environment. *International Journal of Distributed Sensor Networks*, 1-10.

Ko, Y.-B., & Vaidya, N. H. (1998). Location-Aided Routing (LAR) in Mobile Ad-networks. *Proceedings of the 4th Annual ACM/IEEE International Conference on Mobile Computing and Networking*, 66-75. 10.1145/288235.288252

Kumar, A., & Pahuja, S. (2014). A Comparative Study of Flooding Protocol and Gossiping Protocol in WSN. int.J. *Computer Technology and Application, 5*(2), 797–800.

Kumar, Aseri, & Patel. (2009). EEHC: Energy efficient heterogeneous clustered scheme for wireless sensor networks. *Computer Communications, 32*(4), 662-667.

Latiff, Tsimenidis, & Sharif. (2007). *Energy-Aware Clustering for Wireless Sensor Networks using Particle Swarm Optimization*. IEEE.

Leela & Yogitha. (2014). Hybrid Approach for Energy Optimization in Wireless Sensor Networks. *International Journal of Innovative Research in Science, Engineering and Technology, 3*(3), 959-964.

Li, C., Ye, M., Chen, G., & Wu, J. (2005). An energy efficient unequal clustering mechanism for wireless sensor networks. *Proceedings of IEEE International Conference on Mobile Adhoc and Sensor Systems*, 604-611.

Lin, C. R., & Gerla, M. (1997). Adaptive clustering for mobile wireless networks. *IEEE Journal on Selected Areas in Communications, 15*(7), 1265–1275. doi:10.1109/49.622910

Lindsey, S., & Raghavendra, C. (2003). PEGASIS: power-efficient gathering in sensor information systems. In *Aerospace Conference Proceedings*. IEEE.

Liu, J. J., Liu, J., Reich, J., Cheung, P., & Zhao, F. (2003). Distributed Group Management for Track Initiation and Maintenance in Target Localization Applications. Proc. Second Int"l Workshop Information Processing in Sensor Networks (IPSN '03), 113-128. doi:10.1007/3-540-36978-3_8

Liu, T., Li, Q., & Liang, P. (2012). An energy-balancing clustering approach for gradient-based routing in wireless sensor networks. *Computer Communications, 35*(17), 2150–2161. doi:10.1016/j.comcom.2012.06.013

Locke, D. (n.d.). *MQ Telemetry Transport (MQTT) V3.1 Protocol Specification.* Available online: https://www.ibm.com/developerworks/webservices/library/ws-mqtt/

Long, Zhou, Sha, & Zhang. (2014). An Improved LEACH Multi-hop Routing Protocol Based on Genetic Algorithms for Heterogeneous Wireless Sensor Networks. *Journal of Information & Computational Science, 11*(2), 415–424.

Lu, Y. M., & Wong, V. W. S. (2007). An energy-efficient multipath routing protocol for wireless sensor networks. *International Journal of Communication Systems, 20*, 747–766. doi:10.1002/dac.843

Lu, Y. M., & Wong, V. W. S. (2007, July). An Energy-Efficient Multipath Routing Protocol for Wireless Sensor Networks. *International Journal of Communication Systems, 20*(7), 747–766. doi:10.1002/dac.843

Maimour, M. (2008). Maximally Radio-Disjoint Multipath Routing for Wireless Multimedia Sensor Networks. *4th ACM workshop on Wireless Multimedia Networking and Performance Modelling*, 26 – 31. 10.1145/1454573.1454579

Maksimovic, M., Vujovic, V., & Milosevic, V. (2014). Fuzzy logic and wireless sensor networks-a survey. *Journal of Intelligent & Fuzzy Systems*.

Manjeshwar, A., & Agrawal, D. P. (2001). TEEN: A protocol for enhanced efficiency in wireless sensor network. *1st International workshop on parallel and distributed computing issues in wireless networks and mobile computing*, 189.

Manjeshwar, A., & Agrawal, D. P. (2002). APTEEN: A hybrid protocol for efficient routing and comprehensive information retrieval in wireless sensor networks. *2nd international workshop on parallel and distributed computing issues in wireless networks and mobile computing*, 195–202.

Mao & Zhu. (2013, Nov.). A source initiated on-demand routing algorithm based on the throrup-zwick theory fro wireless sensor networks. *Scientific World Journal*.

Sharawi, Emary, Saroit, & El-Mahdy. (2014). Flower Pollination optimization Algorithm for Wireless Sensor Network Lifetime Global Optimization. *International Journal of Soft Computing and Engineering, 4*(3), 54-59.

Mauve, M., Widmer, J., & Hartenstein, H. (2001). A Survey on Position Based Routing in Mobile Ad Hoc Networks. *IEEE Network, 15*(6), 30–33. doi:10.1109/65.967595

Miao, L., Djouani, K., Kurien, A., & Noel, G. (2010). Energy-efficient algorithm based on gradient based routing in wireless sensor networks. *Proc. Southern Africa Telecommunication Networks and Applications Conference (SATNAC)*.

Muraleedharan, R., & Osadciw, L. A. (2004). A predictive sensor network using ant system. *Proc. Int. Society For Optical Engineering Symposium*, 5440, 181–192. 10.1117/12.542635

Neamatollahi, P., Taheri, H., Naghibzadeh, M., & Yaghmaee, M. (2011). A hybrid clustering approach for prolonging lifetime in wireless sensor networks. *International Symposium on Computer Networks and Distributed Systems (CNDS)*, 170-174. 10.1109/CNDS.2011.5764566

Norouzi, Babamir, & Zaim. (2011). A New Clustering Protocol for Wireless Sensor Networks Using Genetic Algorithm Approach. *Wireless Sensor Network, 3*, 362-370.

Ouafaa, Mustapha, Salah-Ddine, & Said. (2016). Performance analysis of SLEACH, LEACH and DSDV protocols for wireless sensor networks (wsn). *Journal of Theoretical and Applied Information Technology, 94*(2).

Pawar, K., & Kelkar, Y. (2012). A survey of hierarchical routing protocols in wireless sensor network. *Int J Eng Innovative Technol, 1*(5), 50–54.

Perkins, C. E., & Bhagwat, P. (1994). Highly dynamic destination-sequenced Distance-Vector routing (DSDV) for mobile computers. *Proc. of the conference on Communications architectures, protocols and applications (SIGCOMM)*, 234-244. 10.1145/190314.190336

Perkins, C. E., & Royer, E. M. (1999). Ad-hoc on-demand distance vector routing. *Proc. of Second IEEE Workshop on Mobile Computing Systems and Applications (WMCSA)*, 90(100), 25-26.

Perkins, & Das. (2003). *RFC 3561: Ad-hoc on-demand distance vector (AODV) routing*.

Pottie, G., & Kaiser, W. (2000, May). Wireless integrated network sensors. *ACM Communications, 43*(5), 51–58. doi:10.1145/332833.332838

Prasad, V., & Son, S. H. (2007). Classification of analysis techniques for wireless sensor networks. *Proceedings of Int'l Conf. Networked Sensing Systems (INSS'07)*, 93–97. 10.1109/INSS.2007.4297397

Prasan, U. D., & Murugappan, S. (2012). Energy Efficient and QOS aware Ant Colony Optimization (EQ-ACO) Routing Protocol for Wireless Sensor Networks. *International Journal of Distributed and Parallel Systems, 3*(1), 257–268. doi:10.5121/ijdps.2012.3122

Qing, L., Zhu, Q., & Wang, M. (2006). Design of a distributed energy-efficient clustering algorithm for heterogeneous wireless sensor networks. *Computer Communications, 29*(12), 2230–2237. doi:10.1016/j.comcom.2006.02.017

Radi, M., Dezfouli, B., Bakarand, K. A., Razak, S. A., & Nematbakhsh, M. A. (2013). Interference-Aware Multipath Routing Protocol for QoS Improvement in Event-Driven Wireless Sensor Networks. *Tsinghua Science and Technology, 16*(5), 475–490. doi:10.1016/S1007-0214(11)70067-0

Rahman, A., & Dijk, E. (n.d.). *Group Communication for the Constrained Application Protocol (CoAP)*. Available online: https://tools.ietf.org/html/rfc7390

Rahmanian, A., Omranpour, H., Akbari, M., & Raahemifar, K. (2011). A novel genetic algortim in LEACH-C routing protocol for sensor networks. *IEEE, CCECE*, 1096 – 1100.

Rathi. (2015). An Enhanced LEACH Protocol using Fuzzy Logic for Wireless Sensor Networks. *International Journal of Computer Science and Information Security, 8*(7), 189-194.

Ren, Z., Hail, M. A., & Hellbrück, H. (2013). CCN-WSN—A lightweight, flexible Content-Centric Networking protocol for wireless sensor networks. *Proceedings of the 2013 IEEE Eighth International Conference on Intelligent Sensors, Sensor Networks and Information Processing*, 123–128.

Sandeep Kumar, E. (2014). Fire-LEACH: A Novel Clustering Protocol for Wireless Sensor Networks based on Fire fly Algorithm. *International Journal of Computer Science: Theory and Application, 1*(1), 12-17.

Kumar, Mohanraj, & Gouda. (2014). Clustering approach for Wireless Sensor Networks based on Cuckoo Search Strategy. *International Journal of Advanced Research in Computer and Communication Engineering, 3*(6), 6966-6970.

Bayrakl & Erdogan. (2012). *Genetic Algorithm Based Energy Efficient Clusters (GABEEC) in Wireless Sensor Networks*. Elsevier.

Dastgheib, Oulia, & Ghassami. (2011). An Efficient Approach for Clustering in Wireless Sensor Network Using Fuzzy Logic. In *International Conference on Computer Science and Network Technology*. IEEE.

Shafiullah, G., & Agyei, A. (2008). A Survey of Energy-Efficient and QoS-Aware Routing Protocols for Wireless Sensor Networks. In *Novel Algorithms and Techniques* (pp. 352–357). Automation and Industrial Electronics.

Shaoqiang, D., Agrawal, P., & Sivalingam, K. (2007). Reinforcement learning based geographic routing protocol for UWB wireless sensor network. *Proc. IEEE Global Telecommunications Conf. (GLOBECOM)*, 652–656.

Sharma, S., & Jena, S.K. (2011). *A survey on secure hierarchical routing protocols in wireless sensor networks*. ACM.

Shi, L., Zhang, B., Mouftah, H. T., & Ma, J. (2012). DDRP: An Efficient Data-Driven Routing Protocol for Wireless Sensor networks with Mobile Sinks. *International Journal of Communication Systems*, 26, 1341–1355.

Shu, L., Zhang, Y., Yang, L. T., Wang, Y., & Hauswirth, M. (2008). Geographic routing in wireless multimedia sensor networks. *Proc. 2008 Second Int'l Conf. Future Generation Communication and Networking*, 68–73. 10.1109/FGCN.2008.17

Siew, Bono, Yoong, Yeo, & Teo. (2013). Cluster Formation of Wireless Sensor Nodes using Adaptive Particle Swarm Optimization. *IJSSST, 13*(3B), 38-44.

Sim, K. M., & Sun, W. H. (2003). Ant colony optimization for routing and load-balancing: Survey and new directions. *IEEE Trans. Syst., Man. Cybern. A, 33*(5), 560–572.

Singh, A. K., Purohit, N., & Varma, S. (2013). Purohit N, Varma S. Fuzzy logic based clustering in wireless sensor networks: A survey. *International Journal of Electronics, 100*(1), 126–141. doi:10.1080/00207217.2012.687191

Sohrabi, K., Gao, J., Ailawadhi, V., & Pottie, G. (1999). Protocols for Self-Organization of a Wireless Sensor Network. *IEEE Pers. Commun., 7*(5), 16–27. doi:10.1109/98.878532

Soliman, & Al-Otaibi. (2011). Enhancing AODV Routing Protocol over Mobile ad hoc Sensor Networks. Sensor Networks, 10(2), 36–41.

Suhonen, J., Kuorilehto, M., Hannikainen, M., & Hamalainen, T. D. (2006). Cost-Aware Dynamic Routing Protocol for Wireless Sensor Networks - Design and Prototype Experiments. In *Personal, Indoor and Mobile Radio Communications, 2006 IEEE 17th International Symposium on*. IEEE.

Voigt, T., Dunkels, A., & Braun, T. (2010). On-demand construction of non-interfering multiple paths in wireless sensor networks. *Proc. 2nd Workshop Sensor Networks Informatik*, 277–285.

Wang, P., & Wang, T. (2006). Adaptive routing for sensor networks using reinforcement learning. In *Proc. 6th IEEE Int. Conf. on Computer and Information Technology (CIT)*. Washington, DC: IEEE Computer Society. 10.1109/CIT.2006.34

Wang, X., & Zhang, G. (2007). Decp: A distributed election clustering protocol for heterogeneous wireless sensor networks. *Proceedings of the 7th international conference on Computational Science, Part III*, 105-108. 10.1007/978-3-540-72588-6_14

Wang, Z., Bulut, E., & Szymanski, B. K. (2009). Energy Efficient Collision Aware Multipath Routing for Wireless Sensor Networks. IEEE International Conference on Communications, 91 – 95. doi:10.1109/ICC.2009.5198989

Wazed, S., Bari, A., Jaekel, A., & Bandyopadhyay, S. (2007). Genetic algorithm based approach for extending the lifetime of two-tiered sensor networks. *Proc. 2nd Int. Symposium on Wireless Pervasive Computing ISWPC*. 10.1109/ISWPC.2007.342578

Winter, T., Thubert, P., Brandt, A., Clausen, T., Hui, J., Kelsey, R., . . . Vasseur, J. P. (2011). *Internet draft*. Retrieved from http://tools.ietf.org/html/draft-ietf-roll-rpl-18

Xu, K., & Gerla, M. (2002). A heterogeneous routing protocol based on a new stable clustering scheme. *Proceedings of Military communications conference (MILCOM'02)*, 2, 838-843. 10.1109/MILCOM.2002.1179583

Xu, Y., Heidemann, J., & Estrin, D. (2001). Geography informed energy conservation for ad hoc routing. *Proceedings of the 7th Annual ACM/IEEE International Conference on Mobile Computing and Networking (MobiCom'01)*. 10.1145/381677.381685

Xue, F., Sanderson, A., & Graves, R. (2006). Multi-objective routing in wireless sensor networks with a differential evolution algorithm. *Proc. IEEE Int. Conf. on Networking, Sensing and Control ICNSC*, 880–885.

Xue, Q., & Ganz, A. (2006). On the lifetime of large scale sensor networks. *Computer Communications*, 29(4), 502–510. doi:10.1016/j.comcom.2004.12.033

Yang & Kull. (2013). Performance analysis of WSN for different speeds of sink and sensor nodes. *International Conference on Complex, Intelligent and Software Systems Intensive Systems CICIS*.

Yang, H., & Sikdar, B. (2003). A Protocol for Tracking Mobile Targets Using Sensor Networks. *Proc. First IEEE Int"l Workshop Sensor Network Protocols and Applications (SNPA'03)*, 71-81. 10.1109/SNPA.2003.1203358

Ye, M., Li, C., Chen, G., & Wu, J. (2005). EECS: An energy efficient clustering scheme in wireless sensor networks. *Proceedings of the IEEE Conference on International conference on Performance Computing and Communications*, 535-540.

Ye, M., Li, C., Chen, G., & Wu, J. (2012). EECS: An energy efficient clustering scheme in wireless sensor networks. In *National laboratory of novel software technology*. Nanjing University.

Younis, O., & Fahmy, S. (2004). HEED: a hybrid energy-efficient distributed clustering approach for ad hoc sensor networks. *IEEE Trans Mob Comput, 3*(4).

Yu, B., Scerri, P., Sycara, K., Xu, Y., & Lewis, M. (2006). Scalable and reliable data delivery in mobile ad hoc sensor networks. *Proc. 4th Int. Conf. on Autonomous Agents and Multiagent Systems (AAMAS)*. 10.1145/1160633.1160825

Yu, Estrin, & Govindan. (2001). *Geographical and Energy-Aware Routing: A Recursive Data Dissemination Protocol for Wireless Sensor Networks*." UCLA Computer Science Department Technical Report, UCLA-CSD TR-01-0023.

Yunxia, Z. Q. C. (2005). On the lifetime of wireless sensor networks (Vol. 9). Academic Press.

Zhang, W., & Cao, G. (2004). *DCTC: Dynamic Convoy Tree-Based Collaboration for Target Tracking in Sensor Networks. IEEE Trans. Wireless Comm.*

Zhang, Y., & Fromherz, M. P. J. (2006). A robust and efficient flooding-based routing for wireless sensor networks. *Journal of Interconnection Networks, 7*(4), 549–568. doi:10.1142/S0219265906001855

Zhou, H., Wu, Y., Hu, Y., & Xie, G. (2010). A novel stable selection and reliable transmission protocol for clustered heterogeneous wireless sensor networks. Comput. Commun., 33(15), 1843-1849.

Zohre & Khodaei. (2010). HERF: A Hybrid Energy Efficient Routing using a Fuzzy Method in Wireless Sensor Networks. *International Journal of Distributed and Parallel Systems, U*(1).

Chapter 8
The Efficient Managemnet of Renewable Energy Resources for Vanet– Cloud Communication

Nitika Kapoor
Chandigarh University, Gharuan, India

Yogesh Kumar
Chandigarh Engineering College, Landran, India

ABSTRACT

Vehicular ad hoc networks (VANET) are networks that interconnect road and vehicles. The mobile nodes are used to connect themselves in self-organized manner. VANET is valuable that gives better performance and assures safe transportation system in prospect. Few of them are covered that helps in knowing the best protocol to be used in particular work. Initially, renewable energy is considered to be those sources that are derived either directly or indirectly from solar energy. Due to emission of harmful gases, in VANET, use of renewable resources come in existence. In another section of the chapter, various energy issues in VANET have been highlighted and added the concept of VANET-CLOUD. As cloud computing technologies have potential to improve the travelling experience and safety of roads by giving provision of various solutions like traffic lights synchronization, alternative routes, etc., VANET-CLOUD has been added at the end of the chapter.

DOI: 10.4018/978-1-7998-1626-3.ch008

INTRODUCTION

Vehicular Ad hoc Networks (VANETs) are networks that interconnect road and vehicles. The mobile nodes are used to connect themselves in self-organized and decentralized manner in case of mobile ad hoc network (MANET). Multi-hop routes may also be established by it. If mobile nodes are cars than it is called vehicular ad hoc network (Watfa et al, 2010). To create a mobile network moving cars are used as nodes in technology used by VANET. It turns every cars in a network act as wireless node or router allow to connect them in between the area of 100 to 300 meters or a network is created in a wide range. In order to create a mobile internet other cars can join in connecting vehicles to one another if any cars drop out of the network or can say it fall out of the signal range. Fixed equipment can belong to the government or private network operators or service providers (Khekare et al, 2012).

Firstly fire and police vehicles are integrated to this technology so that they can communicate with each other for safety purposes. Between vehicles and nearby fixed roadside equipment and between nearby vehicles a number of deployment architectures are allowed by advancing trends in ad hoc network scenarios. Dedicated short range communication (DSRC) like Wi-Fi type of wireless technology is expected to be implement by VANET. Satellite, WiMAX and Cellular are other wireless technologies. It can also be viewed as Intelligent Transportation Systems (ITS) component (Kumar et al, 2012). In VANETs several different applications include safety applications that are concern with making driving much safer, mobile commerce and other information services that helps driver in getting information about accidents, congestion, traffic jams and driving hazards.

As compared to MANETs, VANETs have several different aspects such as there is rapid change in topology due to high velocity movement of nodes. In case of VANETs security is indispensable because it is more prone to several attacks.

I: Infrastructure

V: Vehicle

The aim of this paper is to give brief details about VANET, their characteristics and various routing protocols related to it. VANET is not a new topic but still it provide new research challenges and problems and its main objective is to help group of vehicles in setting and maintaining a communication network among them without the use of any controller and central base station (Zeadally et al, 2010). Main motive of this survey paper is to check that which protocols has good performance. The other objective of this paper is to give review on renewable resources for VANET. Technologies used for supply of renewable energy and various energy routing protocol. An energy issue in VANET also has been highlighted. The next section of this paper covers the communication model of VANET-CLOUD then ended this work with various future applications of VANET (Yan et al, 2008).

Figure 1. Architecture of VANET

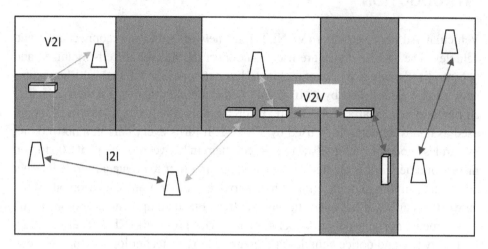

Figure 2. Types of communication in VANETs

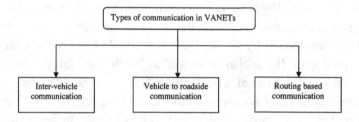

Different Communication Types

There are mainly three types of communication available using VANETs are:

- Inter-vehicle communication: In its configuration a multi-hop broadcast or multicast is used in order to transmit the information related to traffic over multiple hops to a group of receivers (Zeadally et al, 2010)
- Vehicle-To-Roadside Communication: In its configuration a single hop broadcast is represented in which broadcast message is sent by roadside unit. This message is broadcast to all the equipped vehicles in the vicinity (Jindal et la, 2016).
- Routing-Based Communication: In its configuration multihop fashion is used to propagate the message until the desired data carried by vehicle is not reached.

Characteristics of VANET

VANETs is an application of MANET but still it have their own characteristics that is given below:

- First characteristic of VANET is high mobility as speed of moving nodes in VANETs is high. Due to which prediction of nodes position and node privacy protection has become harder (Jain et al, 2016).
- Second characteristic of VANET is network topology: There is frequent change in node position due to random speed of vehicles and high node mobility. This results in frequent change of its network topology.
- Third characteristic of VANET is unbounded network size: VANET can be implemented for one city, several cities and countries or it can be said that its size of network is geographically unbounded (Lobiyal et la, 2011).
- Fourth characteristic of VANET is frequent change of information: The information can be gathered from road side units and other vehicles due to ad hoc nature of VANET. This makes frequent exchange of information among node (Kolte et al, 2014).
- Fifth characteristic of VANET is wireless communication: VANET is designed for wireless environment. Through wireless information are exchanged between nodes thats create a need of security measure in communication.
- Sixth characteristic of VANET is sufficient energy: In this there is no issue of communication and energy resources that allow VANET to use ECDSA, RSA implementation of demanding techniques and also provide unlimited transmission power.
- Seventh characteristic of VANET is time critical: There is exchange of information with in time limit so that action can be performed according to the decision made bt the nide (Kolte et al, 2014).
- Eighth characteristic of VANET is better physical protection: The nodes or VANET are physically better protected thats make its nodes more difficult to compromise physically and reduces infrastructure attack effect.

Routing Protocols in VANET

Ad-hoc networks are used for communication that was initially used for MANETs but now they are also being used for VANET. VANET routing protocols are classified into various types as given below (Bernsen et al, 2008).

Topology Based Routing Protocols: The links information is used by it to forward the incoming packets to next node in the system. The routing table are used for stroing information and there is break in route due to very frequent change in link information and mobility of the vehicles. It is further classified into two types:

Proactive Routing Protocol: Its another name is table driven routing protocols because there it different routing table for each router. In the network each destination node routes are discovered by category routes in advance (Perkins et al, 2003). Unused path is occupy by them that occupy a significant part of available bandwidth that is the main problem associated with these protocols. Some of proactive routing protocols are:

- **Destination Sequenced Distance Vector (DSDV):** This protocol was developed in 1994 to solve the problem related to routing loop. Sequence number is contain by routing table with each entry. It have even sequence number when link is present on other hand number is odd and this is generated by destination node. Then route are selected by using latest sequence number routing table entry.
- **Fisheye State Routing (FSR):** Thus is link state routing based protocol and at each node topology map is maintained so that instant route information is provided by it. In this case link state table is used to update the routing information from neighbour node. And a Fisheye technique is used in it in which geographical data is represented by information size that is reduced before storing to only relevant information.

Reactive Routing Protocol: Its another name is on-demand protocols and reduces the overhead and congestion in the network. For new route for the destination a network discovery process is carried out by source node and temporarily stores the routes (Mishra et la, 2005). When it gets the route then it stop the discovery process. In the network excessive flooding is the main problem that occurs due to message for discovery of a new route and cause overloading of nodes. Some of the reactive protocols are:

- Dynamic Source Routing (DSR)
- Ad-hoc On demand Distance Vector (AODV)
- Temporally Ordered Routing Algorithm (TORA)

Position Based Routing Protocols: Its another name is Geographical protocol as its routing mechanism is depends on the position of destination node. So, on the basis of location data packets are forwarded instead of network address. In this geographical positioning system is used by every node to find its position and their neighboring nodes. In packet header location of destination node is saved when there is need to send a packet by node. It not require any awareness of topology and route discovery (Ryu et al, 2011). This makes it suitable for highly mobile VANET. It is further categorized into:

Delay Torrent Network (DTN): When nodes have no contact with other nodes then packets are stored by nodes that help in improvement of packet delivery. So, until the nodes don't discover another node then packets are hold by them for some distance.

Non-DTN Protocol: Greedy approach is followed by it in which packet is forward to closest neighbour by node. The problem related to it is local maxima. Further this protocol is divided into:

- **Beacon:** Further divided into Overlay and non overlay protocols. In overlay protocol any routing protocol works on a set of selected nodes overlapped on the whole network. Greedy Perimeter Coordinator Routing protocol comes under the category of beacon protocols. In non-overlay protocols main principle used is greedy approach in which packet is forward to the node closest to destination. Greedy Perimeter Stateless Routing (GPSR) comes under this protocol category.
- **Non-Beacon:** Contention-Based Forwarding (CBF) protocol is the example of non-beacon protocol in which next node is selected by using biased timers based distributed contention process concept (Suthaputchakun et al, 2011).
- **Hybrid Protocols:** This is the combination of both Beacon and Non-beacon protocols. In which advantages of both protocols are taken into consideration for taking decision for relaying packet.

Hybrid Protocols (DTN and Non-DTN Protocols: In this both the advantages of DTN and Non DTN is combined to exploit the partial connectivity of network. In this DTN, Non-DTN and perimeter mode is combined. On the basis of network connectivity and number of hops travelled by packet, neighbour direction and delivery quality a non-DTN mode is switch to DTN mode.

Forwarding: Various remote jumps are used to transport bundle between two hubs by geographic uncast transports. When there is need to send a unicast parcel by hub then a gander at the area table is used to discover goal hub position. After that bundle of hubs or neighboring vehicle is used to send bundle using avaricious sending calculation .

RENEWABLE ENERGY RESOURCES FOR VANET

Initially renewable energy are considered to be those sources that are derived either directly or indirectly from solar energy. In broadcast sense all the used energy in today world including fossil fuels are considered in a form of solar energy (Su et al, 2012). All gas, coal, oil and wood like forms of energy are embodied forms of gathered, stored and natural processes transformed solar energy.

In near future transportation a system is dominating by envisaging of electric vehicles. There is less emission of green house and carbon dioxide gases by increase in dependency on fossil fuels. Possibility of charge vehicles from renewable energy sources and higher efficiency of electric vehicle engines are few of the key benefits of electric vehicle systems (Wang et al,2013). The conventional energy resources consumption can be reduced by use of electric vehicles for travelling that result in increase of other energy sources life time and help in mitigating any future crisis related to energy. In the world most of the percentage of source of green house gas is vehicles and towards cleaner environment electric vehicles play a big role (Uhrig et al, 2006). In terms of efficiency of fuel use of electric vehicle engine is more efficient and its other advantage is that it can be use in conjunction with many renewable sources that results in improvement of dependency on only one source of fuel.

ENERGY HARVESTING ARCHITECTURE

Solar, winds like ambient energy are presented in architecture these are used as input to the energy management unit (Imai et al, 1997). The energy is provided to energy storage through energy management unit. Then in the form of regulated power supply energy is transformed to output energy management unit after storing the energy for usage purpose (Jin et al, 2014)

Renewable Energy Supply Technologies

Some of the renewable energy sources are (Santhiya et al, 2017)

- **Solar Energy:** In this case energy is generated for transportation, buildings and industrial processes by directly using sun's energy along with the generation of electricity for general consumption in all three of these end-use sectors. These technologies are not constrained by feedstock requirements

Figure 3. Architecture of renewable harvesting

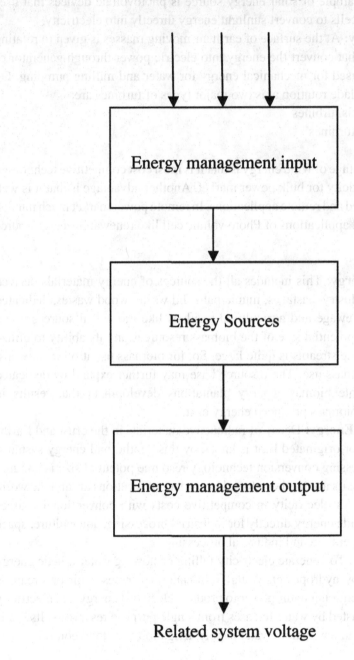

Solar, Wind, RF energy

Energy management input

Energy Sources

Energy management output

Related system voltage

even after the large amount of availability of solar resource. On other hand it is constrained by costs and operation, siting issues and perceived like obstacles. Example of solar energy source is photovoltaic devices that uses multiple PV cells to convert sunlight energy directly into electricity.

- **Wind Energy:** At the surface of earth air moving masses is given to rotating shaft power that convert the energy into electric power through generator or can directly used for mechanical energy for water and milling pumping. On the basis of blade rotation axis two major types of turbines are:
- Horizontal axis turbines
- Vertical axis turbines

The main advantage of wind energy is that it is most cost competitive technology of renewable electricity for bulk power market. Another advantage is that it is well suited for distributed and remote applications. In remote power market much interest is gained by hybrid applications of Photo voltaic cell like renewable energy source with wind turbine.

- **Biomass Energy:** This includes all the sources of energy materials derived from food industry wastages, municipal solid waste, wood wastes, dedicated herbaceous, sewage and agricultural residues like biological sources. On a global scale, potential size of the biomass resources and its ability to utilize existing residue streams is quite large. So, for biomass use it offers low cost attractive biomass use. The resource base may further expand by dedicated and sustainable biomass energy plantations development that results in reduction of biomass produced energy cost.
- **Geothermal Energy:** Decay of radioactive materials in the crust and Earths molten interior originated heat is knock by this geothermal energy systems. For fully accessing conversion technology resource potential size is hundred million quads. Its use has been found in number of locations around the world in production of electricity in competitive costs with conventional sources and also provide energy directly for industrial processing, aquaculture, space heating, refrigeration and industrial processing.
- **Hydropower:** To generate electricity falling or flowing water kinetic energy is exploited by hydropower. Water from canal, river, reservoir or stream is used by conventional hydropower to produce electrical energy and electricity loads are adjusted by water releases from single purpose reservoirs. Its use is mostly found in navigation, water supply, irrigation and flood control.

Different Types of Energy-Aware Routing Protocols

The main task of energy aware routing is to find the routes that minimize the energy cost for packet travelling from one end to another. In this case while selecting routes both the enrgy cost of routes and reliability is considered. There is increase in the probability of packet retransmission if routes are not much reliable that need a more amount of energy for retransmission of packet. Various energy routing are designed by different researchers to find the reliable route cost. Some of the work done for energy efficient or aware routing protocol is given in this section.

Routing is used by VANET for exchanging data between vehicles and vehicles to roadside infrastructures. Energy is consumed when data is transferred through routing due to which number of researchers has proposed various routing protocols for saving energy. But still routing is a very challenging issue in VANET that consist of various road obstacles, dynamical road topology and high vehicle movement along with the fact that traffic and roads conditions constrained movement of vehicle. Categories of vehicle and behaviours of driver much influence the movement thats why we route them in a proper way by proposing an energy efficient routing protocol. Daqiang Zhang et al (2013), have proposed energy efficient routing using movement trends (ERBA) for VANETs which classify vehicles into number of categories and to make routing recommendation it leverages the movement of vehicle. After going through intersections of road, next and current directions movement is predicted. The energy consume by propagation of vehicles is reduces with the use of categories vehicular information of distance between current and next intersections, pattern behaviour of driving. Shanghai Grid project extracted urban scenarios is to validate the proposed scheme and tested it in terms of path duration time, packet delivery ratio and end to end delay. The comparison result shows that proposed routing protocol is efficient as compared to other existing routing protocols. In vehicular networks OLSR routing protocol power consumption reduction is handle by **Alba Enrique, et. al, (2013).** Green communication and energy aware protocols are consider as important topic for research mainly in the case of wireless mobile networks deployment. **Alba Enrique** have used parallel evolutionary algorithm based fast automatic methodology that increases the speed of searching energy efficient OLSR configurations. The proposed approach is tested in terms of power consumption, QoS and as compared to other standard configurations there is less loss.

In animal monitoring, environmental monitoring, smart building and infrastructure monitoring Heterogeneous WSN is widely used. In order to make network more energy efficient, robust, reliable and simple nodes are become heterogeneity by routing protocol due to different operational capability and power supply. Still existing protocols are not able to achieve all goals. For data collection a beaconing based reliable protocol is provided by collection tree protocol (CTP) but energy balance is not considered in it. It was also not able to provide an efficient dissemination scheme. So for heterogeneous WSN a beaconing based routing protocol has been presented in their work. The proposed Energy-Aware Routing Based on Beaconing introduced by **Li Ya, et.al, (2014)** is more efficient routing scheme for both dissemination and collection with beaconing packets exchanged between nodes and their neighbour. Beside of node to sink routing scheme a node to node routing scheme is also supported by EARBB. The results conducted to test proposed scheme show that a reliable network is establish by it that can quickly recover from any failure of node and also increase the average lifetime. Amount of energy required for forwarding packet is potentially reduce by energy efficient routing protocols. However, existing literature lacks studies on improving green performance of geocast routings for the Internet of Vehicles. So, a geocast routing protocol has been proposed by **Li-Der CHOU, et. al., (2015),** that is based on energy efficient min delay (EEMD). The green protocol model is presented by them and also analyzes the green networking performance in forwarding of packet. The proposed protocol is tested under various traffic conditions and results show that it is more efficient in energy saving data forwarding.

Zhongwei CUI, et. al., (2015), have proposed a opportunity route based on real time information (VORI) by taking into account the important role of mobile nodes. In this real time area information is collected by VORI using mobile nodes and with the help of delivery message a hot area is constructed for selecting best inter-area. Both data transmission and node position query is consist in VORI and number of query copies with the net is reduced. Along with this it dynamically select hot area message delivery works. Then for wireless ad-hoc network an energy aware routing algorithm Reliable Minimum Energy Routing (RMER) is proposed by **Priyanka R. More, et. al.** Nodes of ad-hoc networks are completely work on the power of battery and wireless ad-hoc network energy efficiency is one of the challenge. There is minimization of energy required to transfer the packet from one point to another by finding the routes using energy efficient routing algorithm RMER. In this work they have used optimized link state routing protocol.

Energy Issues in VANET

In VANET energy get minimized by finding the best routes for sending packets from one end to another. While selecting routes energy cost, reliability and energy consumption is considered as main parameters. There is increase in packet

Table 1. Review on various issues related to Energy in VANET

Issue	Solution
Position, direction and speed like mobility parameter are used for working of existing system. But during transmission of data more energy is consumed by it.	So a system is proposed by Prerana Deshmukh, et.al, (2014), in which mobility parameter is used as distance between node in a base station and cluster. This also helps in minimizing the energy consumption. In this data discovery phase of AODV routing protocol is improved by using cluster head selection and location based cluster mechanism. In this two tier data delivery mechanism is used to improve the VANET energy efficiency.
The shortage of resources has become a serious issue with the development of vehicular ad hoc networks. An packet vehicles has been used by various researchers to red rid of the problem given about but these type of vehicles cant continue charging when they are turned off. This problem is termed as problem of limited energy.	Parked vehicles are used as relay nodes and in most energy efficient manner services are provided by introducing optimal method of enabling parked vehicles. Gang Sun, et.al, (2018), has divided their method into two steps as given below: On the basis of communication coverage a clustering of moving vehicles is considered and relay nodes are used to select the parked vehicles between clusters. This ensures the communication among driving vehicles. Secondly for achieving energy conservation a external environmental dynamic factors are used Their results show that an improvement is achieved using proposed energy saving method as compared to other parked vehicles based methods.
To deploy intelligent transportation systems a communications is provided by VANETs. Very less researchers have worked on green communications or energy efficiency. In VANET design, power consumption has become a major issue due to the possible interaction with devices that are fed with different electrical sources and the proliferation of electrical vehicles	By means of Differential Evolution (DE-OLSR) a quality-of-service optimized version of OLSR energy efficiency is studied by Jamal Toutouh, et.al, (2011). DE-OLSR is compared with the standard version of OLSR in terms of QoS and Power consumtion. To do this number of VANET simulations are conducted. The performance evaluation shows that DE-OLSR gives better results as compared to other standard version.

retransmission when routes are less reliable so need more amount of energy. In this section we have covered some of the energy related issues focused by various researcher. We have also given the solution to solve those problems.

Energy Management used in VANET

User has basic skills to carry a smart devices by energy management. For example while communication there is need to serve a better optimization of energy management. In fact, the user is who can parameterize the data concerning the EV as SOC, ton, toff, plus programming the appliances (Lateef et al, 2016). Designing of charging and energy management systems is the key issue related to deployment of EV. As compared to refuelling of a conventional vehicle a longer time is taken by EV for recharging so there is need of charging infrastructure management systems based on city wide or an area. This creates a need to develop an information system that is able to interact with mobile EV fleet and spatially distributed charging stations with different occupancy levels.

In future charging stations may provide a supply energy using multiple sources where there is location and time dependent availability of price and energy. In certain areas when consumption load of peak/average generation is exceeded then energy storage task can be done by EV. Efficiently and timely provision of electric vehicle information system (EVIS) is primary challenge. The task is to provide low cost station, nearest charging station location and availability of quicker charging. So, there is need to develop an electric vehicle information system (EVIS) to enable these energy management services in which EVIS interact with the spatially distributed information/control servers and mobile EV fleet. These system should be able to support the exchange of data from infrastructure to vehicles (I2V) on the downlink channel and vehicles to infrastructure (V2I) on the uplink Channel.

In a macro-relay heterogeneous network for load balancing and optimizing relay placement an analytical model is presented by **Hafiz Yasar Lateef, et.al,** that helps in minimizing the energy consumption. Base station sleep modes is studied by Marsan, M. A., et.al, (2012), that is considered as viable approach for improving the energy efficiency of cellular access networks. In this power consumption is reduced in periods of low traffic in which base stations take care of service provisioning and radio coverage when base some of the base stations are switched off. It is assumed and guarantees that whole the times service is available in it. In case of urban areas dense base station layouts this is realistic assumptions that consumes most of the energy of network. Identification of optimal base station switch off times is allowed by the development of simple analytical models as patterns of daily traffic function.

Managing Energy Resources in Vehicles-To-Home Communications

In large number of countries there is increase in installed capacity of RES that impact in the electricity distribution network (Hussain et al, 2012) This problem can be partially solved by EV and its main feature is the possibility of a transfer of energy bidirectional. When there is need to implement systems to support natural disaster situations detected by different areas with long time supply outages in these cases use of vehicle to home (V2H) concept is important. They are designed to implement smart homes with devices that can manage energy that consist of single EV in a home and in terms of configuration it is easy and simple. Further to install it in a home there is no need to change the existing home network.

With the supply of reactive power and active power exchange to the home daily load profile of households can be smoothen using V2H system. It can also interact with vehicle to grid (V2G) and vehicle to building (V2B) systems and it also improves the efficiency of the RES and minimized the losses (Martinez et al, 2017). In short, V2H concept aims to harness all the resources and possibilities of the EV. So for household loads feeding better integration of micro renewable resources can be achieved by using energy stored in the EV.

There are systems for home as given below:

One is with access to the network or deferred injection, zeros injection and grid connected

Another is systems for homes without access to the network or isolated. An ESS system is incorporated by deferred injection system to store energy from RES. Along with this there are some already available commercial devices (Li et al, 2017).

EV is managed by user and prediction of network behaviour is done by demand forecast using historical data and then it act according to the higher profit. Mobile devices application can be used to do active energy management at home in which users have their own credentials.

VANET-CLOUD

A new vehicular cloud computing model name as VANET-CLOUD comes in existence. To the edge of server a workstations, servers like stationary nodes exist in conventional cloud infrastructure model. On vehicles computers like new computing resources are integrated to achieve extension that helps vehicular drivers to access computing resources using both stationary and mobile nodes in virtualized manner with improvement in costs. The computing resources is provided to vehicular drivers along with other users (Li et al, 2017). While executing the application of road safety its get improved by model that is based on client, communication and cloud three layers.

VANET cloud are divided into three major architectures namely Vehicular Clouds (VC), Vehicles using Clouds (VuC), and Hybrid Clouds (HC).

Figure 4. Vehicular Clouds (VC)

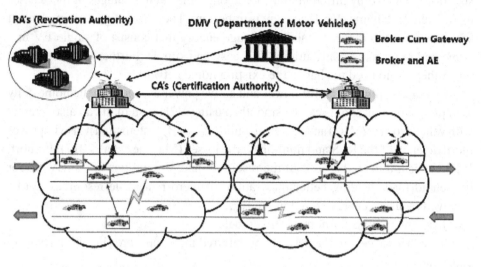

Vehicular Clouds (VC):

VANET infrastructure, gateway is main players in VC where in this paradigm a service is provided by vehicular nodes.

In this firstly a protocol is initiated to select brokers among them and authorized entity (AE) is selected among the brokers to identify the clouds boundaries to form a cloud by taking authorization (Martinez et al, 2017). After that vehicular node is invited by AE after electing the AE and brokers and an ack is received from interested vehicles. To provide potential resources and form a cloud permission is taken from higher authorities when number of interested vehicles becomes higher than threshold (Li et al, 2017). So, in order to form a rich virtual environment a resources are grouped by cloud participants when they get a permission.

OPTIMIZATION METHODS USED FOR ENERGY EFFICIENCY IN VANET

Table 2. Review on various optimization methods used for energy efficient in VANET

Author name	Optimization algorithm	Description
Jamal Toutouh, et.al, (2012),	Differential Evolution algorithm	Involved terminals energy consumption is rely on limited battery power that creates a need to design a energy efficient communications. In VANETs OLSR routing protocol energy consumption is reduced using Differential Evolution algorithm that search for energy efficient configurations. They have tested their proposed work and its results show a significant improvement in terms of energy saving without degrading QoS as compared to other standard configuration.
Santanu Majumdar, et.al, (2016),	Ant Colony Optimization (ACO)	In VANET structure the disconnection of high mobile nodes is a problem and vehicles or nodes in a this can move with a speed of 186.41 miles/h or 300 km/h due to which loss of information will become very critical. For these mobile nodes a fixed topology is used by earlier protocols and various algorithms like moving directional or greedy approach and beaconing ignored the changes in environment that plays an important role in information regulation. So, Santanu Majumdar, have proposed ACO that helps in achieving information transfer and efficient path establishment. The discovered paths are evaluated by using delay time and path availability and also consider environment changes. The experiment results show the improvement in terms of throughput that is achieved through various environmental modifications.
F. Aadil, et.al, (2016),	Clustering algorithm based on Ant Colony Optimization (ACO) for VANETs (CACONET)	VANETs communication efficiency gets improved by using vehicular node clustering, data aggregation and message ferrying techniques. F. Aadil, et.al, have proposed a Clustering algorithm based on Ant Colony Optimization (ACO) for VANETs (CACONET). For robust communication a optimize clusters are made by CACONET that is compared with Comprehensive Learning Particle Swarm Optimization (CLPSO) and Multi-Objective Particle Swarm Optimization (MOPSO). For experiment purpose a number of nodes, transmission range of nodes and network size of grid is varied to check the effectiveness of algorithms and results show that proposed algorithm gives better results as compared to other existing algorithms.
J. Rangaraj, et.al, (2017),	Ant Colony Optimization (ACO) and Fitness Distance Ratio based Particle Swarm Optimization (FDR PSO)	In order to improve efficiency of the central administration lacking network a vital role is played by network performance enhancement. J. Rangaraj, et.al, have proposed a hybrid of Ant Colony Optimization (ACO) and Fitness Distance Ratio based Particle Swarm Optimization (FDR PSO). Where on the basis of ant information a higher enduring energy efficient path is discovered by ACO that optimize a energy utilization of the nodes in the network. On other hand nodes life span is extended by FDR-PSO. To do this a expenditure of energy over transmission is minimized and a duty cycle process coupled with the hybrid technique can prevent nodes being active all the time.100 node network is used to implement the proposed hybrid technique that is tested in terms of delay, packet delivery ratio, throughput and energy utilization like metrics.
X. Zhang, et.al, (2017	Micro artificial bee colony (MABC) algorithm	X. Zhang, et.al, have studied a QoS constrained multicast routing problem. This is NP-complete problem and use of swarm intelligence algorithm is prove to be more suitable than other classical algorithms. The problem is solved by using micro ACO and minimizing delay cost and network lifetime is included in QoS constraints. Multicast routing is abstracted to a continuous optimization problem. Then, it is linked with MABC. Three instances with traffic scenario is used for implementation of numerical simulation. Use of MABC algorithm gives optimal routes and there is no frequent change when outing framework is applied in real time.

continued on the following page

Table 2. Continued

Author name	Optimization algorithm	Description
R. Aravinth, et.al, (2018),	fuzzy optimization routing logic	Distance, direction and position based Vehicle localization and opportunistic neighbour selection routing logic suffers from drain of energy. In order to get rid of those problems R. Aravinth, et.al, have proposed a fuzzy optimization routing logic. Vehicular communication is influenced by factors like link acceptance and energy. A fuzzy based decision making system is used to decide upon fluctuating factors of energy and data acceptance rate to ensure reliable routing and relevant neighbor selection. Simulation results show that a less energy consumption and high throughput and packet delivery ratio is achieved using proposed algorithm as compared to existing routing logic.
Muhammad Fahad Khan, et.al, (2018),	Intelligent Clustering using Gray Wolf Optimization (ICGWO)	For creating clusters in VANET various methods have been developed. In order to increase the network performance cluster lifetime should be longer and efficient communication is achieved if number of cluster heads is lesser. Muhammad Fahad Khan, et.al, have proposed a Intelligent Clustering using Gray Wolf Optimization (ICGWO) for clustering. This clustering based algorithm provides the optimized solution for smooth and robust communication in the VANETs. Direction, load balance factor, Transmission range and grid size are key parameters of proposed algorithm. CLPSO and MOPSO are used for comparing ICGWO effectiveness in terms of optimization of number of cluster with respect to transmission range, grid size and number of nodes.

FUTURE APPLICATIONS OF VANETS

Main future applications of VANETs are its role towards green environment, vehicular cyber physical system, VANETs and smart grid and applications of vehicular grid. In this section we have given review on various future applications of VANETs.

Cooperative Systems for Road Transportation: A State of the Art

Typical working areas include improving road safety and traffic efficiency, traffic management and control, video delivery, intersection management, and so on. There are VANETs based ITS application pilots and applications is to assist drivers for a better information awareness by utilizing limited capabilities of VANETs. Other applications in research are VRU protection, cooperative intersection for urban traffic and platooning for high way automation. The future applications that fully explore the VANETs capabilities are:

- **Traffic Management and Control:** Traffic congestion gets eliminated with the help of ITS and through efficient traffic control and management that reduces environmental impacts and improves the traffic safety and comfort. At vehicle information and communication system (VICS) center vehicle road traffic information is processes using VICS. It enables users to get regulation or congestion like real time road traffic information.

- **Platooning:** This concept comes in existing in new York 1939 when vision of driverless vehicles are presented by general motors and automatic radio control is used to maintain the safe distance to each other. *GCDC (2011).* The Grand Cooperative Driving Challenge 2011 was a competition where the main goal was to accelerate the development, integration, demonstration, and deployment of cooperative mobility. In GCDC both the scenario of highway and urban is demonstrated where traffic coordination in a traffic light controlled intersection is the urban scenario where two platoons are joined in the same lane. How traffic shockwaves is demonstrated by highway part. There is need of common interaction and communication protocol is used to implement number of followed by team. In this there is no centralized controlling vehicle.

- **Cooperative Intersection:** It is the concept of integrating multiple elements operating at intersection through coordination and communication that enable smooth and safe flow of traffic at the intersection. In order to improve the intersection safety a vehicle collision avoidance and warning systems is introduced on other hand comfort and smooth intersection passing is done by introducing the Cooperative Intersection Management (CIM) traffic management methods. The future intersections will be traffic light free by the introduction of VANETs in which automated algorithms and sensors are used to control vehicles by humans with assistance from on-board systems. V2I or V2V techniques are used for vehicle communication with infrastructure or vehicle that negotiate the optimal passing sequence of the intersection. Each vehicle will individually receive the personalized right of way to cross the intersection after negotiation.

- **Vulnerable Road Users:** Communication with other road users is also included in the applications of vanet. In japan a pedestrian-to-vehicle (P2V) communication device is presented by Panasonic (Ferreira et al, 2012) and pedestrians crossing a road intersection system wasted for overcoming the traffic from all directions. So to give disseminate information about its presence a P2V is able to communicate with other road users that is demonstrated by the real life experiments conducted on it. For communication between bicyclist and vehicles POC and Volvo cars are two Swedish companies collaborated as another example of VANETs within road safety.

VANET Applications for Future Cooperative Mobility: After the release of standards various applications are expected to be deployed within a time frame of 3 years. Active road, global internet services, cooperative traffic efficiency and local services are categorization of applications. Certain warnings or necessary information is provided to the driver so that actions can be taken accordingly. By applications simple information can be easily interpreted that directly creates an interface to deliver the message.

- **VANETs for Enabling a Safer, More Efficient, and Sustainable Road Transportation:** Number of communication vehicles grow fast by equipping the vehicles with communication capabilities by automakers. VANETs become advanced and reality cooperative applications by traffic system are populated by more and more vehicles that give the benefits of vehicle coordination. Fr enabling advanced cooperative applications new features have been utilized by VANET enabled traffic systems. Some of the key enabling concepts are given below:

Cooperative context awareness: Vehicles have awareness of bridge ahead, congestion level, road states, tunnel and traffic information like both global and local environments. Vehicles perception is extended from local to global level that goes beyond the current deployment.

Virtual Infrastructure: To improve efficiency and safety a negotiation is done between vehicles and with infrastructure that results in reduction of environmental impact. Maintenance and installation cost is reduced by gradual virtualization of road infrastructure. In future transportation system there will be no traffic lights, marks and road signs. Through VANET vehicles have full awareness and all information will be provided virtually.

VANET Big Data (Nunen eta l, 2012): In real time large amount of data is generated by VANET. For traffic improvement all aspects from CO2 emission to comfort, efficiency and safety aspects are enabled by utilization of VANET data. Loop detectors and road camera are traditional road data collected and then much more detailed information is provided by VANET data.

Energy Aspects: Much more sustainable transportation system is enable by VANETs. Inefficient behaviour of driving can be avoided by intelligent decision modules and fusion methods in vehicle along with VANETs real time information. Transportation network of two of the biggest parts of future are grid and electric vehicles gap is bridge by VANETs that is an innovative applications in both of the areas.

Enhancement Via Live Video Delivery: Before platooning comes in existence on our public roads there is need to solve the acceptance, liability and policy like open issues. Use of platooning application is not suitable for car passengers and drivers which is following the truck in 10m distance. Its use can be increased by using live video streaming between the vehicles. Ahead to all vehicles in the platoon a leader of platoon and installed camera in windshield is used to distribute the current view of road.

- **Pedestrian Crossing Assistance:** Live video is exchanged between the vehicles approaching a pedestrian crossing for protecting VRUs.
- **Public Transportation Assistance:** Live video is delivered from the bus at the stop

to the vehicles passing by for protecting disembarking passengers.

- **Enhanced Road Safety:** A fully context awareness for the drivers is enabled by extended the vision of the vehicle beyond the sensors. The use of VANETs gives significant enhancement in future driving assistance system. To avoid potential dangerous situations a warnings and safety related information is provided to driver by utilizing the information of both the surrounding environments. Potential applications in this area are:
- **Advanced Danger Warning:** Before vehicle arrive on sites a road dangers can be sent that allow vehicles to take actions ahead of time. Bridges, slippery road, tunnels and uneven road are some of the warning messages that is sent to warn other vehicles with information of correct location.

Cooperative Overtaking and Merging: Efficient road merging and overtaking is possible by VANETs and cooperatively merging and overtaking is done. Future road manoeuvring such as overtaking and merging will be done cooperatively. The communication and coordination is done with relevant vehicles when any manoeuvre is planned by vehicles.

Vehicle Cloud: The integration of transportation network and VANETs along with fast development of cloud computing make vehicle cloud a promising method. It provide services for both emerging and traditional purposes. Real time information distribution, control and conventional traffic management like enhancing platform is provided by vehicle cloud.

Green Transportation: For planning of future transportation reduction of greenhouse emission is one of the key challenges. In advanced traffic management, data provision and guidance process a key role is played by VANETs. Examples: Eco-driving, Green goods transportation.

CONCLUSION

This research is on VANET and various aspects related to it. Whole chapter is divided into various sections in which first section covers brief introduction about VANET and various characteristics, routing protocols used in it. There are number of characteristics that makes VANET different and mostly used and growing technology. For sending information there is need of routing to get efficient results so we have covered some of main routing protocols used in VANET that helps other researchers in choosing the best one according to their application. Next sections covers renewable energy resources in which we have covered most of the available renewable energies that can be used to protect the environment from harmful gases. That's why in near future transportation a system is dominating by envisaging of electric vehicles. There is less emission of green house and carbon dioxide gases by increase in dependency on fossil fuels. Other focus is given work on various energy resources and issues related to energy along with their solutions concluded by various researchers. When there is need to implement systems to support natural disaster situations detected by different areas with long time supply outages in these cases use of vehicle to home (V2H) concept is important. Due to which a brief about energy management in V2H is highlighted and introduced a new concept of VANET-CLOUD as Cloud computing has potential to improve the experience of travelling and safety of road by providing flexible solutions. To further improve the energy efficiency of VANET various optimization algorithms has been used by number of researchers that gives efficient results and improved output. The use of VANET is getting increased in various existing and new applications and main future applications of VANETs are its role towards green environment, vehicular cyber physical system, VANETs and smart grid and applications of vehicular grid.

REFERENCES

Aadil, F., Bajwa, K. B., Khan, S., Chaudary, N. M., & Akram, A. (2016). CACONET: Ant Colony Optimization (ACO) Based Clustering Algorithm for VANET. *PLoS One*, *11*(5). doi:10.1371/journal.pone.0154080 PMID:27149517

Aravinth, R., & Jothy, N. (2018). *Enhancement of energy efficient routing and Minimized outage based on fuzzy optimization in VANET*. International Journal of Engineering Science and Computing.

Association of Radio Industries and Businesses (ARIB). (2012). Dedicated short-range communication (DSRC) basic application interface. *ARIB STD, T110*, 2012.

Bernsen, J., & Manivannan, D. (2008). Greedy Routing Protocols for Vehicular Ad Hoc Networks. *Wireless Communications and Mobile Computing Conference IWCMC, 632*(637), 6–8.

Chou, L.-D., & Li, D. C. (2015). Energy-Efficient Min Delay-based Geocast Routing Protocol for Internet of Things. *Journal of Information Science and Engineering*, *31*, 1903–1918.

Cui, Zhao, & Xu, . (2015). *An energy-efficient routing for vehicular ad hoc networking using real-time perception of node information* (Vol. 8). International Journal on Smart Sensing and Intelligent System.

Deshmukh, P. (2014). *Improving Energy and Efficiency in cluster based VANETs through AODV Protocol*. International Journal of Computer Science and Information Technologies.

Englund, C., Chen, L., Vinel, A., & Lin, S. Y. (2015). *Future Applications of VANETs. In Vehicular ad hoc Networks* (pp. 525–544). Springer. doi:10.1007/978-3-319-15497-8_18

Ferreira, M., & d'Orey, P. M. (2012). On the impact of virtual traffic lights on carbon emissions mitigation. *IEEE Transactions on Intelligent Transportation Systems*, *13*(1), 284–295. doi:10.1109/TITS.2011.2169791

Hussain, R., Son, J., Eun, H., Kim, S., & Oh, H. (2012). Rethinking Vehicular Communications: Merging VANET with Cloud Computing. *2012 IEEE 4th International Conference on Cloud Computing Technology and Science*, 606-609. 10.1109/CloudCom.2012.6427481

Imai, S., Takeda, N., & Horii, Y. (1997). Total efficiency of a hybrid electric vehicle. *Proc. IEEE Power Conversion Conference, 2*, 947–950. 10.1109/PCCON.1997.638381

Jain, J., & Chahal, N. (2016). A review on vanet, types, characteristics and various approaches. International Journal of Engineering Sciences & Research Technology, 239-245.

Jin, C., Sheng, X., & Ghosh, P. (2014). Optimized electric vehicle charging with intermittent renewable energy sources. *IEEE Journal of Selected Topics in Signal Processing, 8*(6), 1063–1072. doi:10.1109/JSTSP.2014.2336624

Jindal, V. (2016). *Vehicular Ad-Hoc Networks: Introduction.* Standards, Routing Protocols and Challenges.

Khan, M. F., Aadil, F., Maqsood, M., Khan, S., & Bukhari, B. H. (2018). An Efficient Optimization Technique for Node Clustering in VANETs Using Gray Wolf Optimization. *Transactions on Internet and Information Systems (Seoul)*, 4228–4247.

Khekare, G. S., & Sakhare, A. V. (2012). Intelligent Traffic System for VANET: A Survey. *International Journal of Advanced Computer Research, 2*, 99–102.

Kolte, S. R., & Madankar, M. S. (2014). Adaptive congestion control for transmission of safety messages in VANET. *2014 Int. Conf. Converg. Technol. I2CT 2014*, 1–5. 10.1109/I2CT.2014.7092177

Kumar, R., & Dave, M. (2012). A Review of Various VANET Data Dissemination Protocols. *International Journal of u- and e-Service Science and Technology, 5*(3), 27–44.

Lateef, H. Y., Dohler, M., Mohammed, A., Guizani, M. M., & Chiasserini, C. F. (2016). Towards Energy-Aware 5G Heterogeneous Networks. Energy management in wireless cellular and Ad-hoc networks, 31-44. doi:10.1007/978-3-319-27568-0_2

Li, C., Luo, F., Chen, Y., Xu, Z., An, Y., & Li, X. (2017). Smart Home Energy Management with Vehicle-to-Home Technology. *2017 13th IEEE International Conference on Control & Automation (ICCA)*, 136-142. 10.1109/ICCA.2017.8003048

Lobiyal. (2011). *Performance Evaluation of VANET using realistic Vehicular Mobility* (M.Tech Dissertation). Jawaharlal Nehru University, New Delhi, India.

Marsan, M. A., Chiaraviglio, L., Ciullo, D., & Meo, M. (2012). Multiple daily base station switch-offs in cellular networks. *Proceedings of IEEE International Conference on Communications and Electronics (ICCE 2012)*, 245–250. 10.1109/CCE.2012.6315906

Martinez, Garcia-Villalobos, Zamora, & Eguia. (2017). Energy management of micro renewable energy source and electric vehicles at home level. *J. Mod. Power Syst. Clean Energy*, 979-990.

Mishra, R., & Mandal, C. R. (2005). *Performance comparison of AODV/DSR On-demand Routing Protocols for Ad hoc Networks in Constrained Situation*. ICPWC.

Nagai, M. (2012). *Pedestrian-to-vehicle communication access method and field test results. In 2012 international symposium on antennas and propagation (ISAP)* (pp. 712–715). New York: IEEE.

Perkins, Royer, & Das. (2003). *Ad hoc On Demand Distance Vector (AODV) Routing*. RFC 3561.

Priyanka & Sankpal. (2016). Energy Aware Routing using Energy Efficient Routing Protocol in Wireless Ad hoc Network. *International Conference on Electrical, Electronics, and Optimization Techniques (ICEEOT)*, 1258-1261. 10.1109/ICEEOT.2016.7754885

Rangaraj, J. (2017). *Implementing Energy Optimization by a Novel Hybrid Technique for Performance Improvement in Mobile Ad Hoc Network*. International Journal of Applied Engineering Research.

Ryu, Jha, Koh, & Cho. (2011, Aug.). Position-based routing algorithm improving reliability of inter-vehicle communication. *Transaction on Internet and Information Systems (TIIS)*.

Santhiya & Kala. (2017). Energy Harvesting in vehicular Environment using Sources and Techniques. International Journal for Trends in Engineering & Technology, 19-22.

Shivashankar, Prasad, Kumar, & Kumar. (2016). An Efficient Routing Algorithm based on Ant Colony Optimisation for VANETs. *IEEE International Conference On Recent Trends In Electronics Information Communication Technology*, 436-440.

Su, H., Qiu, M., & Wang, H. (2012, August). Secure wireless communication system for smart grid with rechargeable electric vehicles. *IEEE Communications Magazine*, *50*(8), 62–68. doi:10.1109/MCOM.2012.6257528

Sun, G., Yu, M., Dan, L., & Chang, V. (2018). Analytical Exploration of Energy Savings for Parked Vehicles to Enhance VANET Connectivity. *IEEE Transactions on Intelligent Transportation Systems*, 1–13.

Suthaputchakun, C., & Sun, Z. (2011, December). Routing Protocol in Inter-vehicle Communication Systems: A Survey. *IEEE Communications Magazine*, *49*(12), 150–156. doi:10.1109/MCOM.2011.6094020

Toutouh, J., & Alba, E. (2011). An Efficient Routing Protocol for Green Communications in Vehicular Ad-hoc Networks. *13th Annual Genetic and Evolutionary Computation Conference, GECCO 2011*, 719-725. 10.1145/2001858.2002076

Toutouh, J., & Alba, E. (2012). Green OLSR in VANETs with Differential Evolution. GECCO'12 Companion, 11-18. doi:10.1145/2330784.2330787

Toutouh, J., Nesmachnow, S., & Alba, E. (2012). Fast energy-aware OLSR routing in VANETs by means of parallel evolutionary algorithm. *Cluster Computing*.

Uhrig, R. (2006). Greenhouse gas emissions from gasoline, hybrid-electric, and hydrogen-fueled vehicles. *Proc. IEEE EIC Climate Change Technology*, 1–6. 10.1109/EICCCC.2006.277196

Van Nunen, E., Kwakkernaat, M., Ploeg, J., & Netten, B. D. (2012). Cooperative competition for future mobility. *IEEE Transactions on Intelligent Transportation Systems*, *13*(3), 1018–1025. doi:10.1109/TITS.2012.2200475

Wang, M., Liang, H., Deng, R., Zhang, R., & Shen, X. S. (2013). VANET based online charging strategy for electric vehicles. *Proc. IEEE Global Telecommunications Conference Workshops*, 4804-4809.

Watfa, M. (2010). *Advances in Vehicular Ad-Hoc Networks: Developments and Challenges*. IGI Global. doi:10.4018/978-1-61520-913-2

Ya, L., Wang, P., Rong, L., Yang, H., & Wei, L. (2014). *Reliable Energy-Aware Routing Protocol for Heterogeneous WSN Based on Beaconing*. IEEE. doi:10.1109/ICACT.2014.6778931

Yan, G., Wang, Y., Weigle, M., Olariu, S., & Ibrahim, K. (2008). Wehealth: a secure and privacy preserving ehealth using notice. *Proc. Int. Conf. Wireless Access in Vehicular Environments (WAVE)*.

Zeadally, S., Hunt, R., Chen, Y. S., Irwin, A., & Hassan, A. (2010). *Vehicular ad hoc networks (VANETS): Status, results and challenges*. Springer.

Zeadally, S., Hunt, R., Chen, Y. S., Irwin, A., & Hassan, A. (2010). Vehicular ad hoc networks (VANETS): Status, results, and challenge. *Telecommunication Systems*, *50*(4), 217–241. doi:10.100711235-010-9400-5

Zhang, D., Yang, Z., Raychoudary, V., Chen, Z., & Lloret, J. (2013). An Energy-Efficient Routing Protocol Using Movement Trends in Vehicular Ad-Hoc Networks. *The Computer Journal*, *56*(8), 938–946. doi:10.1093/comjnl/bxt028

Zhang, J., Wang, F. Y., Wang, K., Lin, W. H., Xu, X., & Chen, C. (2011). Data-driven intelligent transportation systems: A survey. *IEEE Transactions on Intelligent Transportation Systems*, *12*(4), 1624–1639. doi:10.1109/TITS.2011.2158001

Zhang, X., Zhang, X., & Gu, C. (2017). A micro-artificial bee colony multicast routing in vehicular ad hoc networks. *Ad Hoc Networks*, *58*, 213–221. doi:10.1016/j.adhoc.2016.06.009

Chapter 9
Performance Analysis of Multi–Hop Routing Protocol With Optimized Grid–Based Clustering for Wireless Sensor Network

Saloni Dhiman
Dr. B. R. Ambedkar National Institute of Technology, Jalandhar, India

Deepti Kakkar
iD https://orcid.org/0000-0002-9681-1291
Dr. B. R. Ambedkar National Institute of Technology, Jalandhar, India

Gurjot Kaur
Dr. B. R. Ambedkar National Institute of Technology, Jalandhar, India

ABSTRACT

Wireless sensor networks (WSNs) consist of several sensor nodes (SNs) that are powered by battery, so their lifetime is limited, which ultimately affects the lifespan and hence performance of the overall networks. Till now many techniques have been developed to solve this problem of WSN. Clustering is among the effective technique used for increasing the network lifespan. In this chapter, analysis of multi-hop routing protocol based on grid clustering with different selection criteria is presented. For analysis, the network is divided into equal-sized grids where each grid corresponds to a cluster and is assigned with a grid head (GH) responsible for collecting data from each SN belonging to respective grid and transferring it to the base station (BS) using multi-hop routing. The performance of the network has been analyzed for different position of BS, different number of grids, and different number of SNs.

DOI: 10.4018/978-1-7998-1626-3.ch009

WIRELESS SENSOR NETWORKS

Wireless Sensor Networks (WSNs) have become popular recently, mainly due to the advancements in the Micro-Electro-Mechanical Systems (MEMS) technology that has prompted the improvement in smart sensors. This type of network consists of tiny sensors which are equipped with limited computing and processing resources. Typically, WSNs comprise of huge number of Sensor Nodes (SNs). These SNs are able to communicate with each other or with the Base Station (BS) depending upon the structure and functionality of network. Each SN performs the function of sensing, processing and communication within the network. Information is gathered by SN and transmitted periodically to other SNs or BS. The sensed collected data is transmitted to the BS via intermediate nodes using wireless transmission techniques (S.K. Singh et al. 2017).

Architecture of a Sensor Node

SNs have four basic components: a sensing unit, a processing unit, a transceiver unit and a power unit. Location finding system, a power generator and a mobilizer are its additional components that are application dependent (Akyildiz et al. 2002).

- **Sensing Unit:** Sensing unit usually has two sub-units: Sensors and Analog to Digital Converters (ADCs). Analog signals are obtained by the sensors which are then converted to digital signals by ADC and then given to the processing unit.
- **Processing Unit:** It also has two sub-units: processor and storage unit. It manages the procedures needed for collaboration of SNs with each other to perform required sensing operations.
- **Transceiver:** It is responsible for connecting the SN with each other and to the other parts of the network.
- **Power Unit:** Power unit supplies the energy required by all the board components. The power unit determines the lifetime of the entire network. Energy efficiency is the primary challenge since the battery of the SNs cannot be easily re-charged after the deployment of the SNs.

Other application dependent components of an SN are:

- **Location Finding System:** Position finding system like Global Positioning System (GPS) device helps the nodes to locate other nodes. It is useful in obtaining the location accurately as is required by various routing techniques in sensor networks.

- **Mobilizer:** It is providing mobility to SNs for completing the assigned task.

Protocol Stack Architecture

In WSN, the protocol stack is made up of the application layer, transport layer, network layer, data link layer, physical layer, power management plane, mobility management plane and task management plane. The responsibilities of physical layer include transmitting and receiving a signal over a physical medium. It determines various characteristics like frequency of operation, modulation technique, data encryption, etc. The main functions of data link layer are multiplexing of the data stream, transmission and reception of data frame, medium access and error check. The network layer is concerned with routing. It routes the data from source to destination which is managed by the transport layer. This layer maintains the data flow when required by the application layer. Application layer is required when the system is to be accessed via internet or other external network. Application layer develops several application softwares depending upon the sensing task requirement. Also, the power, mobility and task management planes make SNs work collectively, route data, share resources and distribute task among them so as to make use of power efficiently. The power management plane optimizes the power usage by the SN. The mobility management plane tracks the SN's movement to maintain a returning route to the user, and also find out neighbors of the SNs. For balancing the load, task management plane distributes the sensing duties among several SNs.

Communication in WSN

There are two types of communication in WSN i.e., single-hop and multi-hop communication. Using either of this communication type, data is sensed, collected and forwarded to the BS.

The ways of communication in WSNs (Tsitsigkos et al. 2012; Dargie and Poellabauer, 2010) are:

- **Single-hop:** The SNs send aggregated data to the BS directly in single-hop communication.
- **Multi-hop:** The SNs send the aggregated data to the BS via one or more intermediate nodes in multi-hop communication.

For the small-scale network, single-hop communication is preferred mainly, whereas multi-hop communication is preferred for large scaled WSNs. This is because the BS is usually situated at a longer distance from the SNs in large scale network and the long distance transmission consumes more power. In this case, SNs sense and aggregate their data as well as act as relay nodes for the other SNs. WSNs have numerous applications (Ramson and Moni, 2017; S. Zhang and H. Zhang, 2012; Othman and Shazali, 2012) in different fields like health care monitoring, military, agriculture, environmental monitoring, industrial monitoring, etc. Some of them are mentioned below:

- **Health Care Monitoring:** It includes monitoring of the patient, diagnosis of disease, hospital drug management, various physiological data monitoring of patient, tracking and monitoring of hospital doctors and the patient's activities, smart hospitalization, etc.
- **Military Applications:** Sensor networks play a vital role in battlefield surveillance, monitoring and guidance systems, prediction and communications and intelligence systems.
- **Environmental Monitoring:** Sensor networks could be very helpful for prevention measures in case of natural disasters like earth quakes, tsunamis, water level and quality monitoring, tornadoes, volcanic eruptions, flood detection, forest fire prediction, rain level monitoring, pollution monitoring, weather monitoring, etc.
- **Agricultural Monitoring:** It includes monitoring the effects of environmental conditions over the crops, precision agriculture monitoring, greenhouse monitoring, etc.
- **Smart Home Application:** The SNs can be built into various appliances at home so as to make them remote-controlled and makes them able to interact with each other.

Routing Protocol

The greatest challenge in the WSN set up is the constrained battery source of the sensors to be employed (Jannu, and Jana, 2014). This problem can be dealt with the help of efficient routing that can enhance the network lifespan by finding out the best possible route between the source node and destination node (C. Wang et al. 2018; Liu, 2015).Categorization of routing protocols is mainly performed by considering next hop selection, protocol operation, path establishment and structure of the network (Misra and Kumar, 2016; Bazzi et al. 2015). Bases on the network structure, the routing protocols are classified as flat, location-based and hierarchical protocols which are as described below:

- **Flat Routing Protocols:** Each node in the network performs same function in flat routing. Whenever the SN has to send data to BS, the node finds out the route hop-by-hop by using some form of flooding.
- **Location-Based Protocols:** In this, nodes are addressed with the help of their location. The distance between the neighboring nodes is estimated based on the strength of the incoming signal. In this case, nodes may also be equipped with low-power GPS receiver
- **Hierarchical Routing Protocols:** Hierarchical approach is primarily a two layer approach, in which the function of one layer is sensing and that of other layer is routing (Othman and Shazali, 2012). This protocol is further categorized as typical and atypical routing (Liu, 2015). Typical hierarchical protocol is mainly a clustering protocol. In this protocol, division of the network is done into multiple clusters and a CH is chosen from every cluster. The nodes in the cluster sense data from the surrounding and forward it to the CH. Then CH has to send this collected data to the BS via hierarchical routing. These protocols are further categorized as:
  - ○ Typical Hierarchical Protocols: Typical hierarchical routing is a cluster based routing in which division of network is done into number of clusters and nodes are assigned two different tasks. After sensing data, normal node sends it to the cluster head and cluster head acquire data from normal nodes and passes it to the sink through hierarchical routing.
  - ○ Atypical Hierarchical Protocols: These are variants of cluster based routing (Liu, 2015). These are classified as:
- **Chain-Based:** For data transmission, SNs are connected by constructing a chan. Data aggregation is performed during the transmission process where gathered information is sent to the leader node along the chain.
- **Tree-Based:** Logical tree is constructed by all the SNs. Each node performs the data aggregation possibly and data is sent from leaf node to parent nodes towards the root.
- **Grid-Based:** Division of complete network into virtual grids is done. From every grid, a grid head is chosen that aggregates the collected data of the other SNs present in the same grid and the send it to the sink.
- **Area-Based:** Some SNs are deployed in a particular area and are designated as high-tier nodes in area-based routing. Mainly, these nodes are in charge of data aggregation and forwarding in the network.

Design Challenges of Routing Protocols

The routing protocol designing in WSNs is affected by many challenges (Al-Karaki and Kamal, 2004; Sohraby et al. 2007). For achieving efficient communication, these designing challenges must be overcome. Some of these designing challenges are listed below:

- **Energy Consumption:** The sensor network's lifetime is heavily dependent over the battery life. So, it is essential to have energy efficient communication in the sensor network.
- **Transmission Channel:** WSNs have to perform mainly in a bandwidth and performance constrained wireless communication medium. The problems linked with wireless channels like fading, high error rate, etc. can hamper the performance of WSNs.
- **Scalability:** WSN consists of a huge number (hundreds or thousands) of SNs. Therefore, any routing protocol must be able to control these huge numbers of SNs and should be able balance the load.
- **Quality of Service (QoS):** Some of the applications require that the sensed data should reach its destination within certain time period otherwise it loses its significance. On the other hand, some application has the requirement of energy conservation relatively more than that of quality of data sent.
- **Data Aggregation:** It is the combination of information collected from various sources on the basis of some aggregation function (e.g., maxima, average, minima etc.). Data aggregation is used to aggregate similar packets that are generated multiple time times by SNs.
- **Coverage:** Each SN has a specific range up to which it can sense data. So, it has limited range and accuracy.
- **Fault Tolerance:** Lack of energy supply, some damage or environmental interference may cause the SN failure. It may hamper the performance of the network.
- **Connectivity and Topology:** Large number of SNs can be deployed in the sensor network that accounts for its high node density and hence high connectivity. But after deployment, due to alteration in SN position, power availability, malfunctioning, jamming and so on, the network topology may vary.

BACKGROUND

MCDM Techniques

MCDM techniques belong to the field of decision making. It is used for making decision when various sets of alternatives are available for different criteria (Mulliner et al. 2016). This class of decision making is further categorized as Multi Objective Decision Making (MODM) and Multi Attribute Decision Making (MADM) (Pohekar and Ramachandran, 2004).

MCDM techniques follow different stages: (Mulliner et al. 2016) Creating decision matrix by determining the relevant criteria and alternatives; assigning weights to the criteria according to its importance; and processing the matrix obtained for determining the ranking of the alternatives available to every criterion.

There are many MCDM techniques which can be used for decision making. In this chapter, TOPSIS has been used for decision making with multiple criteria. Next section provides the description of TOPSIS method.

Technique for Order Preference by Similarity to Ideal Solution

Technique for Order Preference by Similarity to Ideal Solution (TOPSIS) is a type of MCDM technique. TOPSIS was presented (Hwang and Yoon, 1981) to decide the best possible option or solution from the pool of available solutions. The best solution is basically determined as the solution which has the shortest Euclidean distance from Positive Ideal Solution (PIS) and the longest Euclidean distance from the Negative Ideal Solution (NIS). It includes following steps:

- Decision Matrix creation.
- Normalizing the Decision Matrix.
- Determining PIS and NIS.
- Getting the separation measure of existing choices from PIS and NIS through euclidean distance.
- Determining relative closeness to the ideal solution.
- Rank the alternatives and their preference in descending order of CC_i.

Till now various methods have been put forward for reducing the energy consumption of the sensors and enhancing the network's lifespan. These works include routing algorithm, clustering protocols, etc. Different techniques have been proposed for routing and CH selection in WSN for effective communication. Manjeshwar and Agrawal (2001): In this paper, authors proposed threshold sensitive protocol. During cluster formation, CH broadcasts two types of threshold viz. hard threshold and soft threshold. Hard threshold provides the minimum value of parameter for an attribute after which SN turns on its transmitter and forwards the sensed. An internal variable called Sensed Value (SV) in the node is used to store this sensed. If the value is greater than hard threshold, only at that time the node can transmit it after making sure that there is difference in sensed attribute from SV greater than or equal to the value of soft threshold. Heinzelman et al. (2000): This paper proposed a cluster-based routing protocol. In it, CHs are arbitrarily rotated and the protocol operates in rounds with the set-up phase at start and followed by the steady-state phase. In set-up phase clusters are organized whereas in steady-state phase data is transferred to BS. Without taking into account the distance between the BS and CHs, all the CHs communicate directly with the BS in this case which results in more consumption of energy if distance between these two is large. Lindsey and Raghavendra (2002): In this paper, the authors proposed another hierarchical approach based on creating a chain of sensor nodes where each node can send and receive information from its neighbor. Data is aggregated at the SN when it moves from one node to the other and hence only designated nodes can send the data to the BS at a time. G. Smaragdakis et. al (2004): In this paper, author proposed heterogeneous network model called as Stable Election Probability protocol. It is a two-level hierarchical heterogeneous network. The CH is independently selected based on its initial energy relative to that of other SNs. Xiangning and Yulin (2007): In this paper, the authors proposed Energy-LEACH protocol that has enhanced the method of selection of CH as compared to LEACH protocol in which nodes with more energy have the higher probability of being chosen as the CH. Like LEACH protocol, Energy-LEACH works in rounds where each round has cluster formation and steady-state phase. They also proposed multi-hop LEACH in the same paper that uses multi-hop communication between CHs and BS. Kumar et al. (2009): In this paper, authors proposed Energy Efficient Heterogeneous Clustered (EEHC) protocol. This approach is based on weighted probabilities of selecting a CH depending upon their residual energy. Three-level of heterogeneity based on initial energy of nodes are used in this method. Many of the proposed woks consider only single criteria for CH selection. Most of the time such methods based on single criteria are not sufficient in complicated WSNs environment. To overcome such problems, the CH selection can be made on the basis of multiple criteria. Also for routing, in case of multi-hop communication, decision criteria for selecting next-hop play an important.

For this purpose decision can be made on the basis of either single criteria or multiple criteria. Yin et al. (2006): In this paper authors proposed a centralized CH selection method based on MCDM technique. Three criteria i.e., residual energy, distance to the centroid of the involved cluster and mobility are considered as the contributing factor to the lifetime of the network. Re-selection of CH is on the basis of mobility and the residual energy of the nodes. Ahmed et al. (2008): The authors proposed a method to select CH based on four criteria namely, the distance of a node from the centroid of cluster, the residual battery power, the degree of mobility of nodes and the vulnerability index in this paper. Using these four criteria, Decision Tree algorithm is run by the BS in every round to find out the nodes suitable to be CHs. The nodes having low mobility, low vulnerability, high energy and close to cluster centroids are elected as CHs. Suh et al. (2015): In this paper, authors proposed traffic aware routing algorithm that uses MCDM method for selecting next-hop for routing. For deciding the next-hop three criteria are used. In this work, the hybrid virtual potential field which represents communication distance, length of queue, and residual energy of every node is used for decision making in the MCDM.

Many clustering techniques have been put forward in the literature to carry out cluster based routing. One of the clustering techniques is grid-based clustering which is more effective because of its feasible, simple, straight forward and uniform method for structure handling that helps in reducing the overhead in case of routing. Liu et al. (2010): The proposed work in this paper divides the network into various grids as per the node location information. The nodes are organized in the grid in a clustering way. CH is chosen dynamically based on residual energy of the SN, and afterwards communication between BS and SN is by the way of a relay node. It compared results with EBCA (Li et al. 2009). Yuea et al. (2012): The authors purposed a method that divides the complete sensing area into rectangular grids called swim lanes. These swim lanes are further divided into different sized grids, the size of the grid lying away from the BS is larger. CHs are rotated among sensor nodes in every grid and are chosen on the basis of energy of the nodes. Those grids in which the cluster heads consume more energy are provided with greater number of SNs to participate in CHs selection. Nadeem et al. (2013): In this paper, authors proposed M-GEAR protocol. In this method, based on the location of SNs in the network, they are divided into four logical regions. BS is installed outside of the sensing area and a gateway is placed at the centre of the sensing area. Each of the divided regions uses different type of communication hierarchy. Two out of four regions make use of direct communication and other two regions are further sub-divided into clusters and they make use of multi-hop communication. Both clusters elect their CH on the basis of probability independent of other regions. Then the SNs in these two regions transmit their data to gateway via these CHs. Patra and Chouhan (2013): In this paper, author proposed multi-hop scheme for area divided into zone where optimum number of CHs are chosen by the BS. The criteria used for CH selection purpose are remaining energy of SNs, number of neighbors and minimum separation distance between CHs. For transmitting data, numbers of CH are used as intermediate relay nodes for saving the energy of the node. Chakraborty and Khan (2014): In this paper, the author proposed two hop low power data transmission between CHs and BS for cluster based routing. The data is transmitted by a CH to other CH at a distance less than d_0 from itself and also the distance between receiver CH and BS should be less than d_0. Liu (2015): In this paper, author presented a review on atypical hierarchical routing protocol and compared the hierarchical routing protocols. Here the hierarchical routing for WSNs is categorized as cluster-based routing, tree-based routing, chain-based routing, grid-based routing and area-based routing. Pant et al. (2015): In this paper, author presented a multi-hop routing protocol. It uses grid clustering and divide the complete sensing area into grids of different sizes in such a way that grid lying at a greater distance from the BS has bigger size and greater number of sensor nodes. Rotation of CH is carried out in every grid on the basis of residual energy. After cluster formation, CH collects data sensed by the nodes present in every grid and forwards it to its next level neighboring grid and selects CH for next hop data transmission.

Nuray and Daraghma (2015):The protocol in this paper makes use of channel state information for selecting CHs. In every cluster, CHs are selected on the basis of residual energy of the node and the best channel. It considers SNs with different energy levels leading to heterogeneity in the network. For both intra-cluster and inter-cluster communication, single-hop transmission method is used. Thulasiraman and White (2016): Authors proposed EZone protocol in this paper. It is a clustering algorithm that divides nodes into particular zones. In this method, node with highest energy is chosen as CH from each zone so as to make efficient use of energy. Jannu and Jana (2014): In this paper, authors presented grid based clustering and routing algorithms to balance consumption of energy among sensor nodes. The complete region in this case is divided into a number of grids of same size. Each grid is treated as a cluster from which a CH is chosen among the normal nodes on the basis of minimal distance from other SN within the cluster. The data is transmitted to the BS by using multi-hop routing. Rajathi and Jayashree (2016): In this paper, a distance based grid clustering approach (DC) is presented. It divides the monitoring field into equal sized grid and a leader node from each grid is selected which is responsible for routing and aggregation of data. In the grid, every node calculates the sum of distance to other nodes and this is also broadcasted to other nodes. A node having minimum sum of the distance from other nodes in the grid is chosen as a grid leader. A leader list is constructed on the basis of received values by each node in which the node with smallest mean distance is placed first. The first leader is then responsible for data aggregation and transmission to the BS. It has been assumed that the communication between the CHs and BS is direct. When the energy of the grid leader reaches the specified threshold value then second leader in the list is selected as the leader. Tripathi et al. (2017): Authors proposed Semi Grid-Based Clustering method (EESGBC) for Heterogeneous WSN in this paper. In EESGBC, complete area is divided into blocks and CHs are chosen from every grid. The SN covering most of the area is selected as CH from every block. Any node closer to the block, not necessarily from similar block is considered as cluster member. The CHs are not same in each block. Wang et al. (2018): In this paper, author proposed a protocol that divided the monitoring region into a number of zones. This method adopted single chain structure in the cluster and the region minimum spanning tree algorithm for communication among the CHs. Based on the residual energy of the nodes, CHs are selected during the transmission. Logambigai et al. (2018): In this paper, authors proposed grid-based routing protocol to overcome hotspot problem. This protocol is divided into three phases i.e., grid formation, Grid Coordinator (GC) election and grid-based routing. For GC selection it used Fuzzy logic, in which the fuzzy variables used are based on the residual energy of the nodes, mobility pattern of nodes and the distance of the nodes from the BS. The data is transmitted to BS by GC by using the neighboring grid coordinators that act as relay nodes along the route. The selection of next relay node from the neighboring GC is done by applying the fuzzy logic among them and selecting one with maximum fuzzy value. The fuzzy system which is proposed uses the residual energy of the node, the distance to the sink and the degree of the GC as the deciding criteria for selecting the next relay node. In the same way next relay node applies fuzzy logic for selecting its next relay node and so on. The selection process goes on until the data reaches the BS.

Grid Based Clustering

In grid-based clustering, complete sensing field is divided into smaller area of certain length called grids and each grid is considered as a cluster. From every grid, one SN is selected as the Grid Head (GH) based on some criteria (Liu et al. 2010). GH is responsible for aggregating the data sensed by other SNs of the same grid and then routing it to the BS. The nodes of the grid near to the BS are over-burdened due to subsequent data arrival from the nodes of the grids lying far from the BS. Therefore, the energy of the grids lying near to the BS is depleted faster in comparison to the nodes of other grids leading to disconnection in the system. This phenomenon is termed as hot spot problem. So to optimization the energy usage in the network, the various ways are:

- Formulation of an optimal method for selecting GH for improving the performance of grid-based clustering.
- Making inter-cluster long distance communication energy efficient by making use of either dual or multi- hop communication instead of direct communication.
- Making next-hop selection criteria energy efficient by using appropriate criteria.

Figure 1 shows the steps that are followed for the implementation of the TOPSIS method for obtaining the optimal solution. Decision matrix is created by considering the different attributes of all the possible solution available and then further steps are carried out which gives ranking to all the solution available and the one with highest rank is selected as the best alternative solution.

In this chapter, this method has been applied in the cases where a selection has to be made on the basis of multiple criteria i.e., either for multiple criteria based GH selection or for multiple criteria based next hop selection or for both (as required for the case 4). While considering the multiple criteria based selection in this chapter, three criteria have been used that are: number of neighbouring nodes; distance from BS; and residual energy of the SNs located in particular grid. Using these three criteria, decision matrix is formed first. Then the decision matrix so formed is normalised and then other steps of TOPSIS method are carried out to obtain the optimal node. After this, the node which corresponds to the highest rank is chosen as the optimal node for further processing.

NETWORK ASSUMPTIONS WITH DETAILED METHODOLOGY

Network Model Assumptions

This section presents the various assumptions made in the presented work and presents the network model taken into consideration while evaluating the performance of all the four cases.

Figure 1. Steps followed for implementation of TOPSIS method

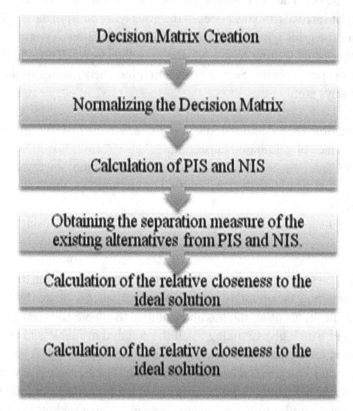

The assumptions for the network presented in the chapter are as follows:

1. The whole area is divided into equal sized grids and SNs are distributed randomly in each grid.
2. Every grid has same number of nodes and each node has its unique identity number. The nodes also have a grid number which represents the grid to which a particular node belongs.
3. The BS is stationary and does not have any constraint on resources while all the SNs are identical, fixed after deployment and have limited resources.
4. The BS has the information of the grid identity number and location of each SN.
5. Normal nodes cannot communicate with SNs of other GHs. They can only communicate with SNs of same grid.
6. GH can setup communication with other GH irrespective of the grid identity number.

Energy Model Followed

The energy model as discussed in (Heinzelman et. al, 2000) is being used here. This model includes free space and multi-path model based on the distance (d) between the receiver and transmitter. If the distance, d is less than or equal to threshold, free space (f_s) model is used. For the calculation of energy used for transmitting $(E_{Tx\,(n,d)})$ and receiving $(E_{Rx(n,d)})$, n bit message at distance d, "(1)" and "(2)" are used respectively.

$$E_{Tx(n,d)} = n*E_{elec} + E_{amp}\left(n,d\right)$$

$$E_{Tx(n,d)} = \begin{cases} n*E_{elec} + n*\varepsilon_{fs}*d^2, d \leq d_o \\ n*E_{elec} + n*\varepsilon_m*d^4, d > d_o \end{cases} \tag{1}$$

$$E_{Rx(n,d)} = n*E_{elec} \tag{2}$$

$$d_o = \sqrt{\frac{\varepsilon_{fs}}{\varepsilon_m}} \tag{3}$$

E_{elec} is the energy dissipated per bit to run the transmitter or receiver circuitry. ε_{fs} is the amplifier energy consumption of free space model and ε_m is the amplifier energy consumption of multiple attenuation model.

Methodology Followed

This section presents the general methodology followed for implementing the four cases of multi-hop routing with optimized grid-clustering for the purpose of evaluating the performance of all the four cases. Figure 2 shows the diagrammatic representation of the methodology followed.

The whole area is firstly divided into various grids of same size and equal numbers of SNs are arbitrarily deployed in each grid. A single grid corresponds to a particular cluster and from each grid, a head called as GH is chosen from the distributed nodes, which is responsible for gathering data from all the members of the grid and forward it to BS using multi-hop routing protocol. SNs within the same grid are permitted to communicate with each other and the GH of that specific grid only and SNs of a particular grid cannot communicate with SNs of other grids.

Figure 2. Representation of followed methodology

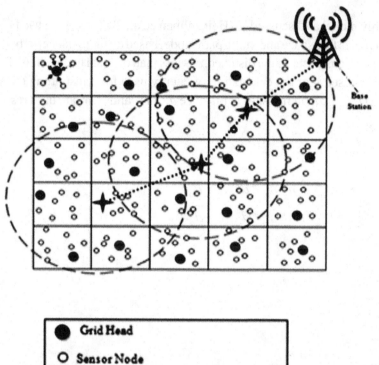

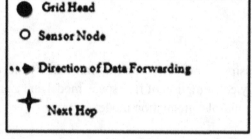

The methodology followed for performance analysis in this chapter works in three phases. Figure 3 shows the phase description of the methodology followed. Three phases are considered i.e., grid formation phase, GH election phase and data transmission phase. In the first phase, grids are formed in the sensing region. The grids so formed have same size and SNs are arbitrarily deployed in every grid. The numbers of SNs deployed are equal in every region. In the next phase, the GH is elected from every grid. The selection of the GH in every grid may be based on single criteria or multiple criteria. Third phase is the phase in which data from source to destination is transmitted and called data transmission.

Figure 3. Phase Description of the Methodology followed

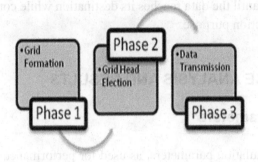

Phase 1: Grid Formation Phase

At the starting of simulation of presented work, the complete sensing area is divided into equal size square shaped grids. Then *n* numbers of nodes are randomly deployed in these grids. There is equal number of nodes in every grid. The process of grid formation is executed only once in entire lifetime of presented work.

Phase 2: GH Election Phase

After the grid formation phase, the presented work then initiates the GH election phase. In this phase, for carrying out communication among SNs, one of the nodes from every grid is elected as GH to aggregate and forward the sensed data toward sink node or BS. GH selection is based either on single criteria or on multiple criteria. When multiple criteria are considered for GH election then TOPSIS method is used for decision making with three criteria being taken into consideration. The node that gets the highest rank in TOPSIS method is selected as GH. The same procedure is carried out for every grid while considering multiple criteria for GH election purpose.

Phase 3: Data Transmission Phase

Energy is utilized more in single hop than multi-hop communication. Therefore to overcome this issue, presented work adopts multi-hop communication model for data forwarding towards BS. Whenever GH needs to send data, it determines the neighbouring GHs. It finds the distance with BS and closest surrounding GH. Depending upon the selection criteria of next hop, data is forwarded towards destination i.e., either through closest hop or directly to BS. If the selection criterion is based on multiple criteria then decision making is done by using TOPSIS method with three criteria being taken into consideration. The node that gets the highest rank in TOPSIS method is selected as next hop. The same procedure is carried out for next hop selection until the data reaches its destination while considering multiple criteria for GH election purpose.

PERFORMANCE ANALYSIS AND RESULTS

Simulation Parameters

In this section, simulation parameters, as used for performance analysis has been given. Complete network has been divided into grids of same size and all of these grids have same number of SNs deployed randomly. The SNs so deployed are having same initial energy. The different parameters used for simulation are given in Table 1.

The performance of the proposed method is evaluated with respect to the following performance metrics:

- **Stability Period:** The number of rounds from the starting of the network operation to the First Node Dead (FND).
- **Instability Period:** The number of rounds from FND to the Last Node Dead (LND).
- **Network Lifetime:** The number of rounds from the starting of the network operation to the LND.
- **Number of Alive Nodes:** The number of SNs whose energy has not been depleted yet.
- **Number of Dead Nodes:** The number of SNs whose energy has been depleted completely.
- **Half Node Dead (HND):** When the total nodes that are dead are exactly half of the total.

Table 1. Values of parameters used for simulation

Simulation Parameters	Values
Initial energy, E_o	0.5J
ε_{fs} (free space model)	10nJ/bit/m^2
ε_m (multi-path model)	0.0013 pJ/bit/m4
E_{DA}	5nj/bit/signal
E_{Tx}	50nj/bit
E_{Rx}	50nj/bit
Message size	4000 bit

Performance Analysis

Here, the performance analysis has been presented for SNs deployed in an area of 100m×100m which is divided into equal sized grids. Each grid contains same number of SNs that are distributed arbitrarily in every grid. MATLAB has been used to evaluate the performance of the grid clustering based protocol.

Performance of grid clustering based multi-hop routing protocol has been evaluated for four different cases:

Case 1: Both GH selection and multi-hop communication between GH and BS are based on single criteria.

Case 2: GH selection is based on single criteria and multi-hop communication between GH and BS is based on multiple criteria.

Case 3: GH selection is based on multiple criteria and multi-hop communication between GH and BS is based on single criteria.

Case 4: Both GH selection and multi-hop communication between GH and BS are based on multiple criteria.

Evaluation and simulation has been carried out for different location of BS, different node density and different number of grids for all the four cases.

Evaluation for Different Location of BS

For evaluating the performance for different location of BS, 100m×100m network has been considered. Then this network is divided into 16 equal sized grids. It has been considered that each grid contains same number of SNs which have been arbitrarily deployed and the network has total of 400 SNs deployed in it. The performance has been evaluated for BS location of (50, 50) and (100,100) for all the four cases. Figure 4 shows the performance analysis in terms of FND, HND and LND respectively for all four cases.

It can be observed from Figure 4 that performance of all four cases is better when the BS is placed at the centre in comparison to that of corner position of BS. Also, the performance is better when the next hop for multi-hop communication is selected on the basis of multiple criteria.

Evaluation for Different Node Densities

For evaluating the performance for different node density, 100m×100m network has been considered. This network is then divided into 16 equal sized grids. It has been considered that each grid contains same number of SNs arbitrarily deployed

Figure 4. Performance analysis for different locations of BS in terms of FND, HND and LND

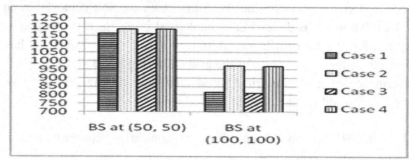

Performance analysis for different locations of BS in terms of FND.

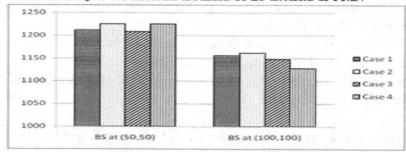

Performance analysis for different locations of BS in terms of HND.

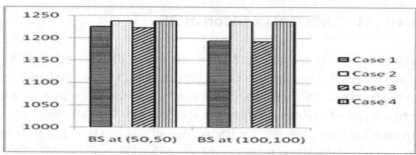

Performance analysis for different locations of BS in terms of LND.

in it. The performance has been evaluated for BS location of (50, 50) by varying the node density for all the four cases. Figure 5 shows the performance analysis in terms of FND, HND and LND respectively for all four cases.

It can be observed from the Figure 5 that the performance is better for the cases when the next hop for multi communication is selected on the basis of multiple criteria. Also, the stability period of all the four cases is better when the node density is higher.

Figure 5. Performance analysis for different node densities in terms of FND, HND and LND

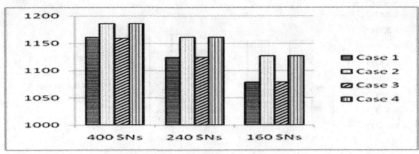

Performance analysis for different node densities in terms of

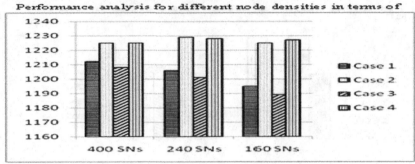

Performance analysis for different node densities in terms of HND.

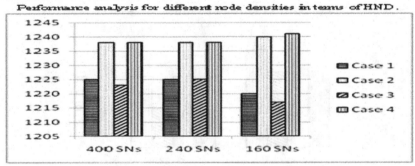

Performance analysis for different node densities in terms of LND.

Evaluation For Different Number Of Grids

For evaluating the performance for different number of grids, 100m×100m network has been taken into consideration. This network is then divided into equal sized grids with the number of nodes equally distributed in each grid. The performance has been evaluated for BS location of (50, 50) by varying the number of grids for all the four cases. Figure 6 shows the performance analysis in terms of FND, HND and LND respectively for all four cases.

Figure 6. Performance analysis for different number of grids in terms of FND, HND and LND

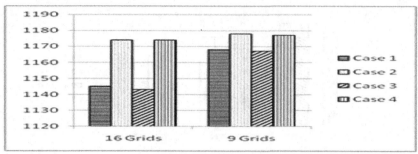

Performance analysis for different number of grids in terms of FND.

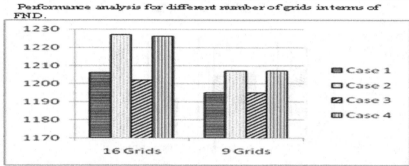

Performance analysis for different number of grids in terms of HND.

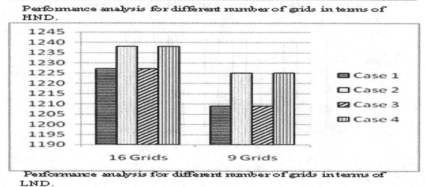

Performance analysis for different number of grids in terms of LND.

It can be noted from the Figure 6 that in all the four cases the lifetime is better when the number of grids is more while stability period is better for network with less number of grids. Also, the performance is better when the next hop for multi-hop communication is selected on the basis of multiple criteria.

Comparison with Other Existing Methods

Figure 7 shows the comparison for BS location at (50, 50) of FND, HND and LND with node density of 400, 240 and 160 respectively when the network is divided into 16 grids.

It can be observed from the figures that performance of all the four cases with 16 grids is better than Ezone. Also, the performance is better for cases when the next hop for multi-hop communication is selected on the basis of multiple criteria.

Figure 7. Comparison of FND, HND and LND for node density of 400, 240 and 160

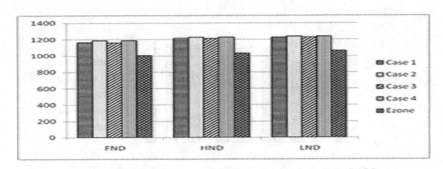

Comparison of FND, HND and LND for node density of 400.

Comparison of FND, HND and LND for node density of 240.

Comparison of FND, HND and LND for node density of 160.

Figure 8 shows the comparison for BS location at (100, 100) of FND, HND and LND with node density of 400, 240 and 160 respectively when the network is divided into 16 grids.

It can be observed from the Figure 8 that stability of Ezone is better than all other four cases with 16 grids while lifetime of other four cases is better than Ezone. Also, the performance is better for cases when the next hop for multi-hop communication is selected on the basis of multiple criteria.

Figure 8. Comparison of FND, HND and LND for node density of 400, 240 and 160

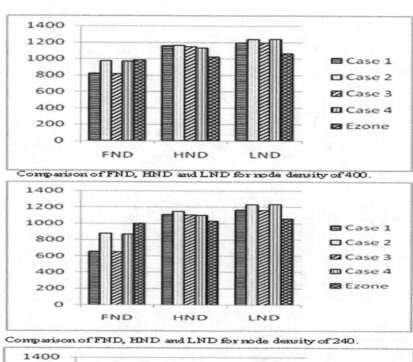

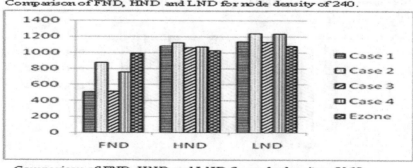

Comparison of FND, HND and LND for node density of 160.

FUTURE RESEARCH DIRECTIONS

TOPSIS is used as one of the MCDM techniques for the selection purposes. In future, performance of other MCDM techniques for selection could be analyzed and the comparison of these techniques could be made based on their performance in WSNs.

CONCLUSION

In this chapter the analysis of performance of the multi-hop routing protocol with grid-based clustering has been done for four different kinds of cases. These four cases are:

- **Case 1:** Both GH selection and multi-hop communication between GH and BS are based on single criteria.
- **Case 2:** GH selection is based on single criteria and multi-hop communication between GH and BS is based on multiple criteria.
- **Case 3:** GH selection is based on multiple criteria and multi-hop communication between GH and BS is based on single criteria.
- **Case 4:** Both GH selection and multi-hop communication between GH and BS are based on multiple criteria.

These cases include selection of next hop and GH either on the basis of multiple criteria or on the basis of single criteria. In any of the cases, while multiple criteria have been taken into consideration, TOPSIS method has been used for the selection purpose. TOPSIS is one of the methods of MCDM techniques. While considering the multiple criteria based selection in this chapter, three criteria that have been used are: number of neighbouring nodes; distance of the nodes from the BS; and residual energy of SNs located in a particular grid. The performance analysis has been made in terms of FND, HND and LND and has been carried out by using MATLAB for all the four cases.

The performance of the multi-hop routing protocol using grid-based clustering has been analyzed for different BS location, different node density and different number of grids.

In this work, for different BS location, stability period as well as lifetime is more for BS location at (50, 50). For different node density, stability period is more for large node density. For different number of grids, stability period is more for less number of grids whereas lifetime is large for greater number of grids.

Also, out of all the four scenarios for which performance has been analyzed in this chapter, in most of the cases, the performance of the scenarios, in which next hop is decided based on the best selection through multiple criteria using TOPSIS method, has significantly improved in comparison to other two scenarios.

REFERENCES

Ahmed, G., Khan, N. M., Khalid, Z., & Ramer, R. (2008, December). Cluster head selection using decision trees for wireless sensor networks. In *Intelligent Sensors, Sensor Networks and Information Processing, 2008. ISSNIP 2008. International Conference on* (pp. 173-178). IEEE. 10.1109/ISSNIP.2008.4761982

Akyildiz, I. F., Su, W., Sankarasubramaniam, Y., & Cayirci, E. (2002). A survey on sensor networks. *IEEE Communications Magazine, 40*(8), 102–114. doi:10.1109/MCOM.2002.1024422

Al-Karaki, J. N., & Kamal, A. E. (2004). Routing techniques in wireless sensor networks: A survey. *IEEE Wireless Communications, 11*(6), 6–28. doi:10.1109/MWC.2004.1368893

Bazzi, H. S., Haidar, A. M., & Bilal, A. (2015, January). Classification of routing protocols in wireless sensor network. In *Computer Vision and Image Analysis Applications (ICCVIA), 2015 International Conference on* (pp. 1-5). IEEE. 10.1109/ICCVIA.2015.7351790

Chakraborty, S., & Khan, A. K. (2014, April). Locoduo-low cost dual hop clustering based routing protocol for wireless sensor network. In *Communication Systems and Network Technologies (CSNT), 2014 Fourth International Conference on* (pp. 168-172). IEEE. 10.1109/CSNT.2014.41

Dargie, W., & Poellabauer, C. (2010). *Fundamentals of wireless sensor networks: theory and practice*. John Wiley &Sons. doi:10.1002/9780470666388

Heinzelman, W. R., Chandrakasan, A., & Balakrishnan, H. (2000, January). Energy-efficient communication protocol for wireless microsensor networks. In *System sciences, 2000. Proceedings of the 33rd annual Hawaii international conference on* (pp. 10-pp). IEEE. 10.1109/HICSS.2000.926982

Hwang, L., & Yoon, K. (1981). *Multiple attribute decision making: Methods and applications*. New York: Springer. doi:10.1007/978-3-642-48318-9

Jannu, S., & Jana, P. K. (2014, April). Energy efficient grid based clustering and routing algorithms for wireless sensor networks. In *Communication Systems and Network Technologies (CSNT), 2014 Fourth International Conference on* (pp. 63-68). IEEE. 10.1109/CSNT.2014.245

Kumar, D., Aseri, T. C., & Patel, R. B. (2009). EEHC: Energy efficient heterogeneous clustered scheme for wireless sensor networks. *Computer Communications, 32*(4), 662-667.

Li, L. Y., Jiang, X. L., Zhong, S., & Hu, L. (2009, April). Energy balancing clustering algorithm for wireless sensor network. In *Networks Security, Wireless Communications and Trusted Computing, 2009. NSWCTC'09. International Conference on* (Vol. 1, pp. 61-64). IEEE. 10.1109/NSWCTC.2009.97

Lindsey, S., & Raghavendra, C. S. (2002). PEGASIS: Power-efficient gathering in sensor information systems. In *Aerospace conference proceedings, 2002. IEEE* (Vol. 3, pp. 3-3). IEEE.

Liu, W. D., Wang, Z. D., Zhang, S., & Wang, Q. Q. (2010, July). A low power grid-based cluster routing algorithm of wireless sensor networks. In Information technology and applications (IFITA), 2010 international forum on (Vol. 1, pp. 227-229). IEEE. doi:10.1109/IFITA.2010.254

Liu, X. (2015). Atypical hierarchical routing protocols for wireless sensor networks: A review. *IEEE Sensors Journal, 15*(10), 5372–5383. doi:10.1109/JSEN.2015.2445796 PMID:27761103

Logambigai, R., Ganapathy, S., & Kannan, A. (2018). Energy–efficient grid–based routing algorithm using intelligent fuzzy rules for wireless sensor networks. *Computers & Electrical Engineering, 68*, 62–75. doi:10.1016/j.compeleceng.2018.03.036

Manjeshwar, A., & Agrawal, D. P. (2001, April). TEEN: a routing protocol for enhanced efficiency in wireless sensor networks. In null (p. 30189a). IEEE. doi:10.1109/IPDPS.2001.925197

Misra, S., & Kumar, R. (2016, November). A literature survey on various clustering approaches in wireless sensor network. In *Communication Control and Intelligent Systems (CCIS), 2016 2nd International Conference on* (pp. 18-22). IEEE. 10.1109/CCIntelS.2016.7878192

Mulliner, E., Malys, N., & Maliene, V. (2016). Comparative analysis of MCDM methods for the assessment of sustainable housing affordability. *Omega, 59*, 146–156. doi:10.1016/j.omega.2015.05.013

Nadeem, Q., Rasheed, M. B., Javaid, N., Khan, Z. A., Maqsood, Y., & Din, A. (2013, October). M-GEAR: Gateway-based energy-aware multi-hop routing protocol for WSNs. In *Broadband and Wireless Computing, Communication and Applications (BWCCA), 2013 Eighth International Conference on* (pp. 164-169). IEEE.

Nuray, A. T., & Daraghma, S. M. (2015). A New Energy Efficient Clustering-based Protocol for Heterogeneous Wireless Sensor Networks. *Journal of Electrical & Electronics, 4*(3), 1.

Othman, M. F., & Shazali, K. (2012). Wireless sensor network applications: A study in environment monitoring system. *Procedia Engineering, 41*, 1204–1210. doi:10.1016/j.proeng.2012.07.302

Pant, M., Dey, B., & Nandi, S. (2015, February). A multihop routing protocol for wireless sensor network based on grid clustering. In *Applications and Innovations in Mobile Computing (AIMoC), 2015* (pp. 137–140). IEEE. doi:10.1109/AIMOC.2015.7083842

Patra, A., & Chouhan, S. (2013, December). Energy Efficient Hybrid multihop clustering algorithm in wireless sensor networks. In *Communication, Networks and Satellite (COMNETSAT), 2013 IEEE International Conference on* (pp. 59-63). IEEE. 10.1109/COMNETSAT.2013.6870861

Pohekar, S. D., & Ramachandran, M. (2004). Application of multi-criteria decision making to sustainable energy planning—A review. *Renewable & Sustainable Energy Reviews, 8*(4), 365–381. doi:10.1016/j.rser.2003.12.007

Rajathi, N., & Jayashree, L. S. (2016, November). Energy efficient grid clustering based data aggregation in Wireless Sensor Networks. In Region 10 Conference (TENCON), 2016 IEEE (pp. 488-492). IEEE. doi:10.1109/TENCON.2016.7848047

Ramson, S. J., & Moni, D. J. (2017, February). Applications of wireless sensor networks—A survey. In *Innovations in Electrical, Electronics, Instrumentation and Media Technology (ICEEIMT), 2017 International Conference on* (pp. 325-329). IEEE.

Singh, S. K., Kumar, P., Singh, J. P., & Alryalat, M. A. A. (2017, November). An energy efficient routing using multi-hop intra clustering technique in WSNs. In Region 10 Conference, TENCON 2017-2017 IEEE (pp. 381-386). IEEE. doi:10.1109/TENCON.2017.8227894

Smaragdakis, G., Matta, I., & Bestavros, A. (2004). *SEP: A stable election protocol for clustered heterogeneous wireless sensor networks*. Boston University Computer Science Department.

Sohraby, K., Minoli, D., & Znati, T. (2007). *Wireless sensor networks: technology, protocols, and applications*. John Wiley & Sons. doi:10.1002/047011276X

Suh, Y. H., Kim, K. T., Shin, D. R., & Youn, H. Y. (2015, August). Traffic-Aware Energy Efficient Routing (TEER) Using Multi-Criteria Decision Making for Wireless Sensor Network. In *IT Convergence and Security (ICITCS), 2015 5th International Conference on* (pp. 1-5). IEEE.

Thulasiraman, P., & White, K. A. (2016). Topology control of tactical wireless sensor networks using energy efficient zone routing. *Digital Communications and Networks*, 2(1), 1–14. doi:10.1016/j.dcan.2016.01.002

Tripathi, M., Naidu, K., & Biswas, M. (2017, March). Energy efficient semi grid based clustering in heterogeneous Wireless Sensor Network. In *Wireless Communications, Signal Processing and Networking (WiSPNET), 2017 International Conference on* (pp. 278-282). IEEE. 10.1109/WiSPNET.2017.8299762

Tsitsigkos, A., Entezami, F., Ramrekha, T. A., Politis, C., & Panaousis, E. A. (2012, April). A case study of internet of things using wireless sensor networks and smartphones. In *Proceedings of the Wireless World Research Forum (WWRF) Meeting: Technologies and Visions for a Sustainable Wireless Internet, Athens, Greece* (Vol. 2325). Academic Press.

Wang, C., Zhang, Y., Wang, X., & Zhang, Z. (2018). Hybrid Multihop Partition-Based Clustering Routing Protocol for WSNs. *IEEE Sensors Letters*, 2(1), 1–4. doi:10.1109/LSENS.2018.2803086

Xiangning, F., & Yulin, S. (2007, October). Improvement on LEACH protocol of wireless sensor network. In *Sensor Technologies and Applications, 2007. SensorComm 2007. International Conference on* (pp. 260-264). IEEE. 10.1109/SENSORCOMM.2007.4394931

Yin, Y. Y., Shi, J. W., Li, Y. N., & Zhang, P. (2006). Cluster head selection using analytical hierarchy process for wireless sensor networks. In *International Symposium on Personal, Indoor and Mobile Radio Communications, PIMRC2006* (pp. 11–14). IEEE 10.1109/PIMRC.2006.254181

Yuea, J., Zhang, W., Xiao, W., Tang, D., & Tang, J. (2012). Energy efficient and balanced cluster-based data aggregation algorithm for wireless sensor networks. *Procedia Engineering*, 29, 2009–2015. doi:10.1016/j.proeng.2012.01.253

Zhang, S., & Zhang, H. (2012, August). A review of wireless sensor networks and its applications. In *Automation and Logistics (ICAL), 2012 IEEE International Conference on* (pp. 386-389) IEEE. 10.1109/ICAL.2012.6308240

Compilation of References

(2016). Dashuang Li · Chaoyong Zhang · Xinyu Shao ·Wenwen Lin.,2016. A multi-objective TLBO algorithm for balancing two-sided assembly line with multiple constraints. *Journal of Intelligent Manufacturing, 27,* 725–739.

Aadil, F., Bajwa, K. B., Khan, S., Chaudary, N. M., & Akram, A. (2016). CACONET: Ant Colony Optimization (ACO) Based Clustering Algorithm for VANET. *PLoS One, 11*(5). doi:10.1371/journal.pone.0154080 PMID:27149517

Abramson, N. (1970). The Aloha System: another alternative for computer Communications. *Proceedings of November 17-19, 1970, Fall Joint computer conference,* 281-285. 10.1145/1478462.1478502

Aceto, G., Botta, A., De Donato, W., & Pescapè, A. (2013). Cloud monitoring: A survey. *Computer Networks, 57*(9), 2093–2115. doi:10.1016/j.comnet.2013.04.001

Agpak, K., Yegul, M. F., & Gokcen, H. (2012). Two-sided U-type assembly line balancing problem. *International Journal of Production Research, 50*(18), 5035–5047. doi:10.1080/00207543.2011.631599

Agpak, K., & Zolfaghari, S. (2015). Mathematical models for parallel two-sided assembly line balancing problems and extensions. *International Journal of Production Research, 53*(4), 1242–1254.

Agrawal, V., Rastogi, R., & Tiwari, D. C. (2018). Spider Monkey Optimization: A survey. *International Journal of System Assurance Engineering and Management, 9*(4), 929–941. doi:10.100713198-017-0685-6

Ahmed, G., Khan, N. M., Khalid, Z., & Ramer, R. (2008, December). Cluster head selection using decision trees for wireless sensor networks. In *Intelligent Sensors, Sensor Networks and Information Processing, 2008. ISSNIP 2008. International Conference on* (pp. 173-178). IEEE. 10.1109/ISSNIP.2008.4761982

Ahvar, Pourmoslemi, & Piran. (2011). FEAR: A Fuzzy-Based Energy-Aware Routing Protocol For Wireless Sensor Networks. *International Journal of Grid Computing & Applications, 2*(2).

Akkaya, K., & Younis, M. (2005). A survey on routing protocols for wireless sensor networks. *Ad Hoc Networks, 3*(3), 325–349. doi:10.1016/j.adhoc.2003.09.010

Akkaya, M. Y., & Younis, M. (2005). Energy and QoS Routing for Wireless Sensor Networks. *Cluster Computing, 8*(2), 179–188. doi:10.100710586-005-6183-7

Aksher. (2019). *A new neural network based energy efficient clustering protocol for WSN.* Academic Press.

Akyildiz, F., Weilian, S., Sankarasubramania, Y., & Cayirci, E. (2002). A survey on sensor networks. *IEEE Communications Magazine, 40*(8), 102–114. doi:10.1109/MCOM.2002.1024422

Akyildiz, I. F., Su, W., Sankarasubramaniam, Y., & Cayirci, E. (2002). Wireless sensor networks: A survey. *Computer Networks, 38*(4), 393–422. doi:10.1016/S1389-1286(01)00302-4

Al-Fuqaha, A., Guizani, M., Mohammadi, M., Aledhari, M., & Ayyash, M. (2015). Internet of things: A survey on enabling technologies, protocols, and applications. *IEEE Communications Surveys and Tutorials, 17*(4), 2347–2376. doi:10.1109/COMST.2015.2444095

Al-Karaki, J. N., & Kamal, A. E. (2004). Routing techniques in wireless sensor networks: A survey. *IEEE Wireless Communications, 11*(6), 6–28. doi:10.1109/MWC.2004.1368893

Alliance, Z.-W. (n.d.). *Z-Wave.* Available: https://www.z-wave.com

Amiri, E., Keshavarz, H., Heidari, H., Mohamadi, E., & Moradzadeh, H. (2013). Intrusion detection systems in MANET: a review. *Proceedings of the International Conference on Innovation, Management and Technology Research,* 1–6.

Amiri, Keshavarz, & Alizadeh, Zamani, & Khodadadi. (2014). Energy Efficient Routing in Wireless Sensor Networks Based on Fuzzy Ant Colony Optimization. *International Journal of Distributed Sensor Networks.*

Anjali, S., & Garg, A. (2013). Location aided destination initiated data tranfe in WSN. *4th International Conference on Reliability.*

Arabshahi, P., Gray, A., Kassabalidis, I., El-Sharkawi, M. A., Marks, R. J., Das, A., & Narayanan, S. (2001). Adaptive routing in wireless communication networks using swarm intelligence. *Proc. the 9th AIAA Int. Communications Satellite Systems Conf.*

Aravinth, R., & Jothy, N. (2018). *Enhancement of energy efficient routing and Minimized outage based on fuzzy optimization in VANET.* International Journal of Engineering Science and Computing.

Archana. (2014). A New BBC based LEACH Algorithm for Energy Efficient Routing in WSN. *International Journal of Engineering and Computer Science, 3*(2), 3914-3918.

Arjunan, S., & Sujatha, P. (2018). Lifetime maximization of the wireless sensor network using fuzzy-based unequal clustering and ACO based routing hybrid protocol. *Applied Intelligence, 48*(8), 2229–2246. doi:10.100710489-017-1077-y

Arora, S., & Singh, S. (2017). An improved butterfly optimization algorithm with chaos. *Journal of Intelligent & Fuzzy Systems*, *32*(1), 1079–1088. doi:10.3233/JIFS-16798

Association of Radio Industries and Businesses (ARIB). (2012). Dedicated short-range communication (DSRC) basic application interface. *ARIB STD*, *T110*, 2012.

Atzori, L., Iera, A., & Morabito, G. (2010). The internet of things: A survey. *Computer Networks*, *54*(15), 2787–2805. doi:10.1016/j.comnet.2010.05.010

Bandyopadhyay, S., & Coyle, E. (2003). An energy efficient hierarchical clustering algorithm for wireless sensor networks. *Proceedings of the 22nd Annual Joint Conference of the IEEE Computer and Communications Societies (INFOCOM 2003)*. 10.1109/INFCOM.2003.1209194

Bandyopadhyay, D., & Sen, J. (2011). Internet of things: Applications and challenges in technology and standardization. *Wireless Personal Communications*, *58*(1), 49–69. doi:10.100711277-011-0288-5

Bansal, J.C., Sharma, H., Jadon, S.S., & Clerc, M. (2014). Spider monkey optimization algorithm for numerical optimization. *Memetic Computing, 6*(1), 31-47.

Baronti, P., Pillai, P., Chook, V. W., Chessa, S., Gotta, A., & Hu, Y. F. (2007). Wireless sensor networks: A survey on the state of the art and the 802.15. 4 and ZigBee standards. *Computer Communications*, *30*(7), 1655–1695. doi:10.1016/j.comcom.2006.12.020

Bashyal, S., & Venayagamoorthy, G. K. (2007). Collaborative routing algorithm for wireless sensor network longevity. *Proc. 3rd Int. Conf on Intelligent Sensors, Sensor Networks and Information Processing*. 10.1109/ISSNIP.2007.4496896

Baykasoglu, A., & Dereli, T. (2008). Two-sided assembly line balancing using an ant– colony-based heuristic. *International Journal of Advanced Manufacturing Technology*, *36*(5), 582–588. doi:10.100700170-006-0861-3

Bayrakl & Erdogan. (2012). *Genetic Algorithm Based Energy Efficient Clusters (GABEEC) in Wireless Sensor Networks*. Elsevier.

Bazan, O., & Jaseemuddin, M. (2011). A survey on MAC protocols for wireless adhoc networks with beamforming antennas. *IEEE Communications Surveys and Tutorials*, *14*(2), 216–239. doi:10.1109/SURV.2011.041311.00099

Bazzi, H. S., Haidar, A. M., & Bilal, A. (2015, January). Classification of routing protocols in wireless sensor network. In *Computer Vision and Image Analysis Applications (ICCVIA), 2015 International Conference on* (pp. 1-5). IEEE. 10.1109/ICCVIA.2015.7351790

Bergh, F. V. D., & Engelbrecht, A. (2006). A study of particle swarm optimization particle trajectories. *Information Sciences*, *176*(8), 937–971. doi:10.1016/j.ins.2005.02.003

Bernsen, J., & Manivannan, D. (2008). Greedy Routing Protocols for Vehicular Ad Hoc Networks. *Wireless Communications and Mobile Computing Conference IWCMC*, *632*(637), 6–8.

Bhatti & Raina. (2014). Cuckoo based Energy Effective Routing in Wireless Sensor Network. *International Journal of Computer Science and Communication Engineering, 3*(1), 92-95.

Bonabeau, E., Dorigo, M., & Theraulaz, G. (1999). *Swarm Intelligence: From Natural to Artificial Systems.* New York: Oxford University Press.

Bormann, C., Castellani, A. P., & Shelby, Z. (2012). CoAP: An Application Protocol for Billions of Tiny Internet Nodes. *IEEE Internet Computing, 16*(2), 62–67. doi:10.1109/MIC.2012.29

Brandt, A., & Buron, J. (2015). *Transmission of IPv6 packets over ITU-T G. 9959 Networks* (No. RFC 7428).

Bulusu, N., Heidemann, J., & Estrin, D. (2000). GPS-less low-cost outdoor localization for very small devices. *IEEE Personal Communications, 7*(5), 28-34.

Cai, X., Duan, Y., He, Y., Yang, J., & Li, C. (2015). Bee-Sensor-C: An energy-efficient and scalable multipath routing protocol for wireless sensor networks. *International Journal of Distributed Sensor Networks, 26*, 1–14.

Camilo, Carreto, Silva, & Boavida. (2006). An Energy-Efficient Ant-Based Routing Algorithm for Wireless Sensor Networks. *LNCS, 4150*, 49-59.

Camilo, T., Carreto, C., Silva, J., & Boavida, F. (2006). An Energy-Efi cient Ant Base Routing Algorithm for Wireless Sensor Networks. *ANTS 2006 – Fifth International Workshop on Ant Colony Optimization and Swarm Intelligence*, 49-59.

Cao, Li, Dai, & Chen. (2014). Weirong Improved Low Energy Adaptive Clustering Hierarchy Protocol Based on Local Centroid Bat Algorithm. *Sensor Letters, 12*(9), 1372-1377.

Cardell-Oliver, R. (2005). *Soil Moisture Monitoring with Wireless Sensor Networks.* University of Western Australia. Retrieved from www.csse.uwa.edu.au/adhocnets/WSNgroup/soilwater-proj

Chakraborty, S., & Khan, A. K. (2014, April). Locoduo-low cost dual hop clustering based routing protocol for wireless sensor network. In *Communication Systems and Network Technologies (CSNT), 2014 Fourth International Conference on* (pp. 168-172). IEEE. 10.1109/CSNT.2014.41

Chao, H., & Chang, C. (2008). A Fault-Tolerant Routing Protocol in Wireless Sensor Networks. *Sensor Networks, 2*(2), 66–73. doi:10.1504/IJSNET.2008.016463

Cheng, X., Thaeler, A., Xue, G., & Chen, D. (2004, March). TPS: A time-based positioning scheme for outdoor wireless sensor networks. In IEEE INFOCOM 2004 (Vol. 4, pp. 2685-2696). IEEE.

Chen, G., Branch, M. J., Pflug, L. Z., & Szymanski, B. (2004). *Sense: A sensor network simulator.* Advances in Pervasive Computing & Networking.

Chen, M., Leung, V., & Mao, S. (2009). Directional Controlled Fusion in Wireless Sensor Networks. *Mobile Networks and Applications, 14*(2), 220–229. doi:10.100711036-008-0133-6

Chen, X., & Zhang, B. (2012). Improved DV-Hop node localization algorithm in wireless sensor networks. *International Journal of Distributed Sensor Networks*, 8(8), 213980. doi:10.1155/2012/213980

Chen, X., & Zhang, B. (2014). 3D DV-hop localisation scheme based on particle swarm optimisation in wireless sensor networks. *International Journal of Sensor Networks*, 16(2), 100–105. doi:10.1504/IJSNET.2014.065869

Cherian, M., & Nair, T. R. G. (2011). Multipath Routing With Novel Packet Scheduling Approach In Wireless Sensor Networks. *International Journal of Computer Theory and Engineering*, 3(5), 666–670. doi:10.7763/IJCTE.2011.V3.389

Chiang, W.-C., Urban, T. L., & Luo, C. (2015). Balancing stochastic two-sided assembly lines. *International Journal of Production Research*, 54(20), 6232–6250. doi:10.1080/00207543.2015.1029084

Chou, L.-D., & Li, D. C. (2015). Energy-Efficient Min Delay-based Geocast Routing Protocol for Internet of Things. *Journal of Information Science and Engineering*, 31, 1903–1918.

Cho, Y. S., Kim, J., Yang, W. Y., & Kang, C. G. (2010). *MIMO-OFDM wireless communications with MATLAB*. John Wiley & Sons. doi:10.1002/9780470825631

Chutima, P., & Chimklai, P. (2012). Multi-objective two-sided mixed-model assembly line balancing using particle swarm optimisation with negative knowledge. *Computers & Industrial Engineering*, 62(1), 39–55. doi:10.1016/j.cie.2011.08.015

Cimini, L. J., & Sollenberger, N. R. (2000). Peak-to-Average Power Ratio reduction of an OFDM signal using partial transmit sequences. *IEEE Communications Letters*, 4(3), 86–88. doi:10.1109/4234.831033

Clausen, T., Jacquet, P., Laouiti, A., Muhlethaler, P., Qayyum, A., & Viennot, L. (2001). *Optimized Link State Routing Protocol. IEEE INMIC*.

Couto, D. S. J. D., Aguayo, D., Bicket, J., & Morris, R. (2003). A High-Throughput Path Metric for Multi-Hop Wireless Routing. *9th annual international conference on Mobile computing and networking (MobiCom '03)*, 134 – 146. 10.1145/938985.939000

Cui, X. (2016). The internet of things. In *Ethical Ripples of Creativity and Innovation* (pp. 61–68). London: Palgrave Macmillan.

Cui, Zhao, & Xu, . (2015). *An energy-efficient routing for vehicular ad hoc networking using real-time perception of node information* (Vol. 8). International Journal on Smart Sensing and Intelligent System.

Dargie & Poellabauer. (2010). *Fundamental of Wireless Sensor Networks: Theory and Practice*. John Wiley & Sons.

Dargie, W., & Poellabauer, C. (2010). *Fundamentals of wireless sensor networks: theory and practice*. John Wiley &Sons. doi:10.1002/9780470666388

Dasgupta, D., & Michalewicz, Z. (Eds.). (2013). *Evolutionary algorithms in engineering applications*. Springer Science & Business Media.

Dastgheib, Oulia, & Ghassami. (2011). An Efficient Approach for Clustering in Wireless Sensor Network Using Fuzzy Logic. In *International Conference on Computer Science and Network Technology*. IEEE.

Delice, Y., Aydogan, E.K., Ozcan, U., & Ilkay, M.S. (2017). Balancing two-sided U–type assembly lines using modified particle swarm optimization algorithm. *4 OR, 15*(1), 35–66.

Delice, Y., Kızılkaya Aydogan, E., & Ozcan, U. (2016). Stochastic two-sided U-type assembly line balancing: A genetic algorithm approach. *International Journal of Production Research, 54*(11), 3429–3451. doi:10.1080/00207543.2016.1140918

Delice, Y., Kızılkaya Aydogan, E., Ozcan, U., & Ilkay, ˙. M. S. (2017). A modified particle swarm optimization algorithm to mixed-model two-sided assembly line balancing. *Journal of Intelligent Manufacturing, 28*(1), 23–36. doi:10.100710845-014-0959-7

Deshmukh, P. (2014). *Improving Energy and Efficiency in cluster based VANETs through AODV Protocol*. International Journal of Computer Science and Information Technologies.

Devika, G., & Asha, G. K. (2015). Performance enhancement of LEACH, V-LEACH and MOD-LEACH clustering routing protocols for wireless sensor networks. *International Conference on Research in Business Management & Information Technology (ICRBIT – 2015)*.

Devika, G., & Asha, G. K. (2015, Feb.). A pragmatic study of LEACH and its descendant routing protocols in WSN. National conference on research issues in image analysis and mining intelligence. *International Journal of Computation Intelligence and Informatics*.

Devika, G., Asha, G. K., & Premshudha, B. G. (2015). A pragmatic study of evolutionary techniques based energy efficient hierarchical routing protocols-LEACH and PEGASIS. *Int J Appl Eng Res, 10*(5), 3979–82.

Dhar, J., & Arora, S. (2017). Designing fuzzy rule base using spider monkey optimization algorithm in cooperative framework. *Future Computing and Informatics Journal, 2*(1), 31–38. doi:10.1016/j.fcij.2017.04.004

Dhivya, M., & Sundarambal, M. (2011). Cuckoo Search for data gathering in Wireless Sensor Networks. *International Journal of Mobile Communications, 9*(6), 642–656. doi:10.1504/IJMC.2011.042781

Dhivya, M., Sundarambal, M., & Anand, L. N. (2011). Energy efficient computation of data fusion in wireless sensor networks using cuckoo based particle approach (CBPA), International Journal of Communications. *Network and System Sciences, 4*(4), 249–255. doi:10.4236/ijcns.2011.44030

Dijkstra, E. W. (1959). A note on two problems in connexion with graphs. *Numerische Mathematik, 1*(1), 269–271. doi:10.1007/BF01386390

Ding, N., & Liu, P. X. (2005). A centralized approach to energy-efficient protocols for wireless sensor networks. In *Mechatronics and Automation, 2005 IEEE International Conference (Vol. 3*, pp. 1636-1641). IEEE.

Ding, P., Holliday, J., & Celik, A. (2015). Distributed Energy-E_cient Hierarchical Clustering for Wireless Sensor Networks. Lecture Notes in Computer Science, 3560, 322-339.

Dorigo, M. (1992). *Optimization, learning and natural algorithms* (Ph.D. thesis). Politecnico di Milano, Milan, Italy.

Dorigo, M., & Stützle, T. (Eds.). (2004). Ant Colony Optimization. MIT Press.

Dorigo, M., & Birattari, M. (2010). *Ant colony optimization.* Springer.

Dorigo, M., & Di Caro, G. A. (1999). The ant colony optimization metaheuristic. In D. Corne & M. Dorigo (Eds.), *New Ideas in Optimization* (pp. 11–32). McGraw-Hill.

Dorigo, M., Montes de Oca, M. A., & Engelbrecht, A. (2008). Particle swarm optimization. *Scholarpedia, 3*(11), 1486. doi:10.4249cholarpedia.1486

Ehsan, S., & Hamdaoui, B. (2012). A Survey on Energy-Efficient Routing Techniques with QoS Assurances for Wireless Multimedia Sensor Networks. *IEEE Communications Surveys and Tutorials, 14*(2), 265–278. doi:10.1109/SURV.2011.020211.00058

El Alami, H., & Najid, A. (2017). Gateways Selection for Integrating Wireless Sensor Networks into Internet of Things. In *Europe and MENA Cooperation Advances in Information and Communication Technologies* (pp. 423–430). Cham: Springer. doi:10.1007/978-3-319-46568-5_43

El Alami, H., & Najid, A. (2018). MS-routing-G i: Routing technique to minimise energy consumption and packet loss in WSNs with mobile sink. *IET Networks, 7*(6), 422–428. doi:10.1049/iet-net.2017.0258

El Alami, H., & Najid, A. (2019). ECH: An Enhanced Clustering Hierarchy Approach to Maximize Lifetime of Wireless Sensor Networks. *IEEE Access: Practical Innovations, Open Solutions, 7*, 107142–107153. doi:10.1109/ACCESS.2019.2933052

Englund, C., Chen, L., Vinel, A., & Lin, S. Y. (2015). *Future Applications of VANETs. In Vehicular ad hoc Networks* (pp. 525–544). Springer. doi:10.1007/978-3-319-15497-8_18

Ephremides, A., Wieselthier, J. E., & Baker, D. J. (1987). A design concept for reliable mobile radio networks with frequency hopping signaling. *Proceedings of the IEEE, 75*(1), 56–73. doi:10.1109/PROC.1987.13705

Ercin, Ö., & Coban, R. (2012). Identification of linear dynamic systems using the artificial bee colony algorithm. *Turkish Journal of Electrical Engineering & Computer Sciences, 20*(Sup. 1), 1175-1188. doi:10.3906/elk-1012-956

Eslaminejad, M. R., Sookhak, M., Razak, S. A., & Haghparast, M. (2011). A Review of Routing Mechanisms in Wireless Sensor Networks. *International Journal of Computer Science and Telecommunications*, 2, 1–9.

Farooq-i-Azam, M., & Ayyaz, M. N. (2016). Location and position estimation in wireless sensor networks. In Wireless Sensor Networks: Current Status and Future Trends (pp. 179-214). CRC Press.

Fattahia, P., Samoueib, P., & Zandiehc, M. (2016). *Simultaneous Multi-skilled Worker Assignment and Mixed-model Two-sided Assembly Line Balancing. International Journal of Engineering*, 29(2), 211–221.

Felemban, E., Lee, C., & Ekici, E. (2006). MMSPEED: Multipath Multi-SPEED Protocol for QoS Guarantee of Reliability and Timeliness in Wireless Sensor Networks. *IEEE Transactions on Mobile Computing*, 5(6), 738–754. doi:10.1109/TMC.2006.79

Fernandez, P. M. (2003). *Circuit switching in the Internet* (Ph.D. thesis). Stanford University.

Ferreira, M., & d'Orey, P. M. (2012). On the impact of virtual traffic lights on carbon emissions mitigation. *IEEE Transactions on Intelligent Transportation Systems*, 13(1), 284–295. doi:10.1109/TITS.2011.2169791

Fleisch, E. (2010). What is the internet of things? An economic perspective. *Economics, Management & Financial Markets, 5*(2).

Forster & Murphy. (2009). CLIQUE: Role-Free Clustering with Q-Learning for Wireless Sensor Networks. *Proc. 29th Int. Conf. on Distributed Computing Systems (ICDCS)*.

Frey, H., R¨uhrup, S., & Stojmenovi'c, I. (2009). *Routing in wirelesssensor networks. In Guide to Wireless Sensor Networks* (pp. 81–111). Berlin, Germany: Springer. doi:10.1007/978-1-84882-218-4_4

Fu, B., Li, R., Xiao, X., Liu, C., & Yang, Q. (2009). Non-interfering multipath geographic routing for wireless multimedia sensor networks. *Proc. 2009 IEEE Int'l Conf. Multimedia Information Networking and, Security*, 254–258. 10.1109/MINES.2009.139

Gandotra, N. (2019). Exploration of HEED clustering algorithm for performance improvement in heterogeneous environment. iManager Publications.

Ganesan, D., Govindan, R., Shenker, S., & Estrin, D. (2001). Highly-resilient Energy-Efficient Multipath Routing in Wireless Sensor Networks. *2nd ACM international symposium on Mobile ad hoc networking & computing, Ser. MobiHoc '01*, 251 – 254. 10.1145/501416.501452

Gansterer, M., & Hartl, R. F. (2018). One- and two-sided assembly line balancing problems with real-world constraints. *International Journal of Production Research*, 56(8), 3025–3042. doi:10.1080/00207543.2017.1394599

Gao, W. (2011). *Intelligent processing in wireless communications using particle Swarm based methods* (PhD. Dissertation). Syracuse University.

Garg, Rani, & Singh. (2014). Achieving Energy Efficiency in WSN using GSA. *International Journal of Advanced Research in Computer Science and Software Engineering, 4*(4), 168-174.

Ghawy & Al-Sanabani. (n.d.). Application and Performance Analysis of DSDV Routing Protocol in Ad-Hoc Wireless Sensor Network with Help of NS2 Knowledge. *Global Journal of Computer Science and Technology.*

Girod, L., Bychkovskiy, V., Elson, J., & Estrin, D. (2002, September). Locating tiny sensors in time and space: A case study. In *Proceedings. IEEE International Conference on Computer Design: VLSI in Computers and Processors* (pp. 214-219). IEEE. 10.1109/ICCD.2002.1106773

Godbole. (2012). Performance Analysis of Clustering Protocol Using Fuzzy Logic for Wireless Sensor Network. *IAES International Journal of Artificial Intelligence, 1*(3), 103-111.

Gong, B., Li, L., Wang, S., & Zhou, X. (2008). Multihop routing protocol with unequal clustering for wireless sensor networks. *ISECS International Colloquium on Computing, Communication, Control, and Management, 2,* 552-556.

Goyal, S., & Patterh, M. S. (2014). Wireless sensor network localization based on cuckoo search algorithm. *Wireless Personal Communications, 79*(1), 223–234. doi:10.100711277-014-1850-8

Granjal, J., Monteiro, E., & Silva, J. S. (2015). Security in the integration of low-power Wireless Sensor Networks with the Internet: A survey. *Ad Hoc Networks, 24,* 264–287. doi:10.1016/j.adhoc.2014.08.001

Gupta, G. P., & Jha, S. (2018). Integrated clustering and routing protocol for wireless sensor networks using Cuckoo and Harmony Search based metaheuristic techniques. *Engineering Applications of Artificial Intelligence, 68,* 101–109. doi:10.1016/j.engappai.2017.11.003

Gupta, D. R., & Sampalli, S. (2005). Cluster-head election using fuzzy logic for wireless sensor networks. *Proc. 3rd Annual Communication Networks and Services Research Conf.,* 255–260. 10.1109/CNSR.2005.27

Gupta, G. P. (2018). Improved Cuckoo Search-based Clustering Protocol for Wireless Sensor Networks. *Procedia Computer Science, 125,* 234–240. doi:10.1016/j.procs.2017.12.032

Gupta, K., Deep, K., & Bansal, J. C. (2017). Spider monkey optimization algorithm for constrained optimization problems. *Soft Computing, 21*(23), 6933–6962. doi:10.100700500-016-2419-0

Guru, S., Halgamuge, S., & Fernando, S. (2005). Particle swarm optimizers for cluster formation in wireless sensor networks. *Proc. Int. Conf. on Intelligent Sensors, Sensor Networks and Information Processing,* 319–324.

Haidar, Ghassempour, & Braun. (2012, Mar.). Nature-inspired routing algorithm for wireless sensor networks. *Australian Journal of Electrical and Electronics Engineering.*

Hamdi, Essaddi, & Boudriga. (2008). *Energy-Efficient Routing in Wireless Sensor Networks Using Probabilistic Strategies.* IEEE Communications Society.

Hancke, G. P., & Leuschner, C. J. (2007). SEER: A simple energy efficient routing protocol for wireless sensor networks. *South African Computer Journal, 39*, 17–24.

Han, G., Xu, H., Duong, T. Q., Jiang, J., & Hara, T. (2013). Localization algorithms of wireless sensor networks: A survey. *Telecommunication Systems, 52*(4), 2419–2436. doi:10.100711235-011-9564-7

Han, S. H., & Lee, J. H. (2004). PAPR reduction of OFDM signals using a reduced complexity PTS technique. *IEEE Signal Processing Letters, 11*(11), 887–890. doi:10.1109/LSP.2004.833490

Han, S. H., & Lee, J. H. (2005). An overview of peak-to-average power ratio reduction techniques for multicarrier transmission. *IEEE Wireless Communications, 12*(2), 56–65. doi:10.1109/MWC.2005.1421929

Harter, A., Hopper, A., Steggles, P., Ward, A., & Webster, P. (2001). The anatomy of a context-aware application. *Wireless Networks, 1*(1).

He, T., Stankovic, J., Lu, C., & Abdelzaher, T. (2003). SPEED: A Stateless Protocol for Real-Time Communication in Sensor Networks. *Proc. 23rd International Conference on Distributed Computing Systems*, 46-55. 10.21236/ADA436741

Heinzelman, W. R., Chandrakasan, A., & Balakrishnan, H. (2000). Energy-efficient communication protocol for wireless microsensor networks. In *System sciences, 2000. Proceedings of the 33rd annual Hawaii international conference on*. IEEE. 10.1109/HICSS.2000.926982

Heinzelman, W. R., Chandrakasan, A., & Balakrishnan, H. (2005). *Energy-efficient communication protocol for wireless microsensor networks*. doi:10.1109/hicss.2000.926982

Heinzelman, W. B., Chandrakasan, A. P., & Balakrishnan, H. (2002). An application-specific protocol architecture for wireless microsensor networks. *IEEE Transactions on Wireless Communications, 1*(4), 660–670. doi:10.1109/TWC.2002.804190

He, T., Huang, C., Blum, B. M., Stankovic, J. A., & Abdelzaher, T. (2003, September). Range-free localization schemes for large scale sensor networks. In *Proceedings of the 9th annual international conference on Mobile computing and networking* (pp. 81-95). ACM. 10.1145/938985.938995

Holger Karl and Andreas Willig. (2005). *Protocols and Architectures for Wireless Sensor Networks*. John Wiley & Sons, Ltd.

Hui, J., & Kelsey, R. (2018). *Multicast Protocol for Low-Power and Lossy Networks (MPL)*. Available online: https://tools.ietf.org/html/rfc7731

Hussain, R., Son, J., Eun, H., Kim, S., & Oh, H. (2012). Rethinking Vehicular Communications: Merging VANET with Cloud Computing. *2012 IEEE 4th International Conference on Cloud Computing Technology and Science*, 606-609. 10.1109/CloudCom.2012.6427481

Hussain, S., Matin, A. W., & Islam, O. (2007). Genetic algorithm for energy efficient clusters in wireless sensor networks. *Proc. 4th Int. Conf. on Information Technology ITNG*, 147–154. 10.1109/ITNG.2007.97

Hu, X., & Wu, C. (2018). Workload smoothing in two-sided assembly lines. *Assembly Automation*, *38*(1), 51–56. doi:10.1108/AA-09-2016-112

Hwang, L., & Yoon, K. (1981). *Multiple attribute decision making: Methods and applications*. New York: Springer. doi:10.1007/978-3-642-48318-9

Imai, S., Takeda, N., & Horii, Y. (1997). Total efficiency of a hybrid electric vehicle. *Proc. IEEE Power Conversion Conference*, 2, 947–950. 10.1109/PCCON.1997.638381

Intanagonwiwat, C., Govindan, R., & Estrin, D. (2000). Directed diffusion: a scalable and robust communication paradigm for sensor networks. In *Proceedings of the 6th Annual International Conference on Mobile Computing and Networking (MobiCom '00)*. ACM. 10.1145/345910.345920

Ishaq, I., Hoebeke, J., Moerman, I., & Demeester, P. (2016). Experimental Evaluation of Unicast and Multicast CoAP Group Communication. *Sensors (Basel)*, *16*, 1137.

Islam, O., & Hussain, S. (2006). An intelligent multi-hop routing for wireless sensor networks. *Proc. WI-IAT Workshops Web Intelligence and Int. Agent Technology Workshops*, 239–242 10.1109/WI-IATW.2006.42

Islam, M., Thulasiraman, P., & Thulasiram, R. (2003). A parallel ant colony optimization algorithm for all-pair routing in MANETs. *Proc. Int. Parallel and Distributed Processing Symposium*. 10.1109/IPDPS.2003.1213470

Iwata, A., Chiang, C.-C., Pei, G., & Gerla, M. (1999, August). Scalable routing strategies for ad hoc wireless networks. *IEEE Journal on Selected Areas in Communications*, *17*(8), 1369–1379. doi:10.1109/49.779920

Iyengar, S. S., Prasad, L., & Min, H. (1995). *Advances in distributed sensor technology*. Englewood Cliffs, NJ: Prentice Hall.

Iyengar, S. S., Wu, H.-C., Balakrishnan, N., & Chang, S. Y. (2007). Biologically inspired cooperative routing for wireless mobile sensor networks. *IEEE Systems Journal*, *1*(1), 29–37. doi:10.1109/JSYST.2007.903101

Jacson. (2017). Application of WSN- A survey. *IEEE, International Conference ICEEIMT*.

Jain, J., & Chahal, N. (2016). A review on vanet, types, characteristics and various approaches. International Journal of Engineering Sciences & Research Technology, 239-245.

Jang, W. S., & Healy, W. M. (2009, September). Assessment of Performance Metrics for Use of Wireless Sensor Networks in Buildings. *The International Symposium on Automation and Robotics in Construction (ISARC 2009)*.

Jannu, S., & Jana, P. K. (2014, April). Energy efficient grid based clustering and routing algorithms for wireless sensor networks. In *Communication Systems and Network Technologies (CSNT), 2014 Fourth International Conference on* (pp. 63-68). IEEE. 10.1109/CSNT.2014.245

Jiang, T., Xiang, W., Richardson, P. C., Guo, J., & Zhu, G. (2007). PAPR Reduction of OFDM Signals Using Partial Transmit Sequences with Low Computational Complexity. *IEEE Transactions on Broadcasting, 53*(3), 719–724. doi:10.1109/TBC.2007.899345

Jietai, W., Jiadong, X. U., & Mantian, X. (2009). EAQR: An energy-efficient ACO basedQoS routing algorithm in wireless sensor networks. *Chinese Journal of Electronics, 18*, 113–116.

Jin, C., Sheng, X., & Ghosh, P. (2014). Optimized electric vehicle charging with intermittent renewable energy sources. *IEEE Journal of Selected Topics in Signal Processing, 8*(6), 1063–1072. doi:10.1109/JSTSP.2014.2336624

Jindal, V. (2016). *Vehicular Ad-Hoc Networks: Introduction.* Standards, Routing Protocols and Challenges.

Jin, Y., Gormus, S., Kulkarni, P., & Sooriyabandara, M. (2016). Content Centric Routing in IoT Networks and Its Integration in RPL. *Computer Communications, 89*, 87–104. doi:10.1016/j.comcom.2016.03.005

Johnson & Maltz. (1996). *Dynamic source routing in ad hoc wireless networks. In Mobile Computing* (pp. 153–181). NewYork, NY: Springer.

Jovanov, E., Milenkovic, A., Otto, C., & De Groen, P. C. (2005). A wireless body area network of intelligent motion sensors for computer assisted physical rehabilitation. *Journal of Neuroengineering and Rehabilitation, 2*(1), 6. doi:10.1186/1743-0003-2-6 PMID:15740621

Kahn, J. M., Katz, R. H., & Pister, K. S. J. (1999). Next century challenges: Mobile networking for smart dust. *Proceedings of ACM/IEEE Internatonal Conference on Mobile Computing Networks*, 271–278. 10.1145/313451.313558

Kang, S. G., Kim, J. G., & Joo, E. K. (1999). A Novel Subblock Partition Scheme for Partial Transmit Sequence OFDM. *IEEE Transactions on Broadcasting, 45*(3), 333–338. doi:10.1109/11.796276

Karp, B., & Kung, H. T. (2000). GPSR[1]: greedy perimeter stateless routing for wireless networks. Proc. 2000 ACM Mobile Computing and Networking, 243–254.

Katkar & Ghorpade. (2015). A Survey on Energy Efficient Routing Protocol forWireless Sensor Networks. *International Journal of Computer Science and Information Technologies, 6.*

Kaur, A., Kumar, P., & Gupta, G. P. (2017). A weighted centroid localization algorithm for randomly deployed wireless sensor networks. *Journal of King Saud University-Computer and Information Sciences.*

Kaur, A., Kumar, P., & Gupta, G. P. (2018). Nature inspired algorithm-based improved variants of DV-Hop algorithm for randomly deployed 2D and 3D wireless sensor networks. *Wireless Personal Communications, 101*(1), 567–582. doi:10.100711277-018-5704-7

Kaur, T., & Kumar, D. (2018). Particle Swarm Optimization-Based Unequal and Fault Tolerant Clustering Protocol for Wireless Sensor Networks. *IEEE Sensors Journal, 18*(11), 4614–4622. doi:10.1109/JSEN.2018.2828099

Kelley, R. H., Carpenter, R. C., Lunney, R. H., & Martinez, M. (2000). *U.S. Patent No. 6,088,659.* Washington, DC: U.S. Patent and Trademark Office.

Kennedy, J., Eberhart, R. C., & Shi, Y. (2001). *Swarm Intelligence.* San Francisco, CA: Morgan Kaufman.

Keshavarz, H., Noor, R. M., & Mostajeran, E. (2013). Using routing table lag to improve performance of AODV routing protocol for VANETs environment. *Proceedings of the 9th International Conference on Computing and Information Technology (IC2IT '13)*, 73–82.

Khademi, S. (2010). *OFDM Peak-to-Average-Power-Ratio Reduction in WiMAX Systems* (MSc. Thesis). Chalmers University of Technology, Goteborg, Sweden.

Khan, M. F., Aadil, F., Maqsood, M., Khan, S., & Bukhari, B. H. (2018). An Efficient Optimization Technique for Node Clustering in VANETs Using Gray Wolf Optimization. *Transactions on Internet and Information Systems (Seoul)*, 4228–4247.

Khekare, G. S., & Sakhare, A. V. (2012). Intelligent Traffic System for VANET: A Survey. *International Journal of Advanced Computer Research*, 2, 99–102.

Khorasanian, D., Hejazi, S. R., & Moslehi, G. (2013). Two-sided assembly line balancing considering the relationships between tasks. *Computers & Industrial Engineering*, 66(4), 1096–1105. doi:10.1016/j.cie.2013.08.006

Kim, Park, Han, & Chung. (2008). CHEF: Cluster Head Election mechanism using Fuzzy logic in Wireless Sensor Networks. *ICACT.*

Kim, Sharma, Kumar, Tomar, Berry, & Lee. (2014). Intercluster Ant Colony Optimization Algorithm for Wireless Sensor Network in Dense Environment. *International Journal of Distributed Sensor Networks*, 1-10.

Kim, Y. K., Song, W. S., & Kim, J. H. (2009). A mathematical model and a genetic algorithm for two-sided assembly line balancing. *Computers & Operations Research*, 36(3), 853–865. doi:10.1016/j.cor.2007.11.003

Ko, Y.-B., & Vaidya, N. H. (1998). Location-Aided Routing (LAR) in Mobile Ad- networks. *Proceedings of the 4th Annual ACM/IEEE International Conference on Mobile Computing and Networking*, 66-75. 10.1145/288235.288252

Koch, S. (2006). Home telehealth—Current state and future trends. *International Journal of Medical Informatics*, 75(8), 565–576. doi:10.1016/j.ijmedinf.2005.09.002 PMID:16298545

Kolte, S. R., & Madankar, M. S. (2014). Adaptive congestion control for transmission of safety messages in VANET. *2014 Int. Conf. Converg. Technol. I2CT 2014*, 1–5. 10.1109/I2CT.2014.7092177

Kone, C. T. (2011). *Architectural design of a large wireless sensor network* (Doctoral dissertation). Henri Poincaré-Nancy I University, France.

Kucukkoc, I. (2016). Multi-objective Optimization of Mixed-model Two-sided Assembly Lines – A Case Study. *International Conference on Computer Science and Engineering*, 20-23.

Kucukkoc, I., & Zhang, D. Z. (2014). Mathematical model and agent based solution approach for the simultaneous balancing and sequencing of mixed-model parallel two-sided assembly lines. *International Journal of Production Economics*, *158*, 314–333. doi:10.1016/j.ijpe.2014.08.010

Kucukkoc, I., & Zhang, D. Z. (2015). Type-E parallel two-sided assembly line balancing problem: Mathematical model and ant colony optimization based approach with optimised parameters. *Computers & Industrial Engineering*, *84*, 56–69. doi:10.1016/j.cie.2014.12.037

Kucukkoc, I., & Zhang, D. Z. (2015, August 18). approach for parallel two-sided assembly line balancing problem. *Production Planning and Control*, *26*(11), 874–894. doi:10.1080/0953728 7.2014.994685

Kumar, Aseri, & Patel. (2009). EEHC: Energy efficient heterogeneous clustered scheme for wireless sensor networks. *Computer Communications*, *32*(4), 662-667.

Kumar, D., Aseri, T. C., & Patel, R. B. (2009). EEHC: Energy efficient heterogeneous clustered scheme for wireless sensor networks. *Computer Communications, 32*(4), 662-667.

Kumar, Mohanraj, & Gouda. (2014). Clustering approach for Wireless Sensor Networks based on Cuckoo Search Strategy. *International Journal of Advanced Research in Computer and Communication Engineering, 3*(6), 6966-6970.

Kumar, A., & Pahuja, S. (2014). A Comparative Study of Flooding Protocol and Gossiping Protocol in WSN. int.J. *Computer Technology and Application, 5*(2), 797–800.

Kumar, R., & Dave, M. (2012). A Review of Various VANET Data Dissemination Protocols. *International Journal of u- and e-Service Science and Technology*, *5*(3), 27–44.

Lateef, H. Y., Dohler, M., Mohammed, A., Guizani, M. M., & Chiasserini, C. F. (2016). Towards Energy-Aware 5G Heterogeneous Networks. Energy management in wireless cellular and Ad-hoc networks, 31-44. doi:10.1007/978-3-319-27568-0_2

Latiff, Tsimenidis, & Sharif. (2007). *Energy-Aware Clustering for Wireless Sensor Networks using Particle Swarm Optimization*. IEEE.

Lee & Cheng. (2012). Fuzzy-Logic-Based Clustering Approach for Wireless Sensor Networks Usmg Energy Predication. *IEEE Sensors Journal, 12*(9).

Leela & Yogitha. (2014). Hybrid Approach for Energy Optimization in Wireless Sensor Networks. *International Journal of Innovative Research in Science, Engineering and Technology, 3*(3), 959-964.

Lee, T. O., Kim, Y., & Kim, Y. K. (2001). Two-sided assembly line balancing to maximize work relatedness and slackness. *Computers & Industrial Engineering*, *40*(3), 273–292. doi:10.1016/ S0360-8352(01)00029-8

Lei, D., & Guo, X. (2016). Variable neighborhood search for the second type of two-sided assembly line balancing problem. *Computers & Operations Research, 72*, 183–188. doi:10.1016/j.cor.2016.03.003

Li, C., Luo, F., Chen, Y., Xu, Z., An, Y., & Li, X. (2017). Smart Home Energy Management with Vehicle-to-Home Technology. *2017 13th IEEE International Conference on Control & Automation (ICCA)*, 136-142. 10.1109/ICCA.2017.8003048

Li, C., Ye, M., Chen, G., & Wu, J. (2005). An energy efficient unequal clustering mechanism for wireless sensor networks. *Proceedings of IEEE International Conference on Mobile Adhoc and Sensor Systems*, 604-611.

Li, L. Y., Jiang, X. L., Zhong, S., & Hu, L. (2009, April). Energy balancing clustering algorithm for wireless sensor network. In *Networks Security, Wireless Communications and Trusted Computing, 2009. NSWCTC'09. International Conference on* (Vol. 1, pp. 61-64). IEEE. 10.1109/NSWCTC.2009.97

Lin, C. R., & Gerla, M. (1997). Adaptive clustering for mobile wireless networks. *IEEE Journal on Selected Areas in Communications, 15*(7), 1265–1275. doi:10.1109/49.622910

Lindsey, S., & Raghavendra, C. S. (2002). PEGASIS: Power-efficient gathering in sensor information systems. In *Aerospace conference proceedings, 2002. IEEE* (Vol. 3, pp. 3-3). IEEE.

Lindsey, S., & Raghavendra, C. (2003). PEGASIS: power-efficient gathering in sensor information systems. In *Aerospace Conference Proceedings*. IEEE.

Lin, J. Z., Chen, X. B., & Liu, H. B. (2009). Iterative algorithm for locating nodes in WSN based on modifying average hopping distances. *Journal of Communication, 30*(10), 107–113.

Liu, J. J., Liu, J., Reich, J., Cheung, P., & Zhao, F. (2003). Distributed Group Management for Track Initiation and Maintenance in Target Localization Applications. Proc. Second Int"l Workshop Information Processing in Sensor Networks (IPSN '03), 113-128. doi:10.1007/3-540-36978-3_8

Liu, W. D., Wang, Z. D., Zhang, S., & Wang, Q. Q. (2010, July). A low power grid-based cluster routing algorithm of wireless sensor networks. In Information technology and applications (IFITA), 2010 international forum on (Vol. 1, pp. 227-229). IEEE. doi:10.1109/IFITA.2010.254

Liu, T., Li, Q., & Liang, P. (2012). An energy-balancing clustering approach for gradient-based routing in wireless sensor networks. *Computer Communications, 35*(17), 2150–2161. doi:10.1016/j.comcom.2012.06.013

Liu, X. (2015). Atypical hierarchical routing protocols for wireless sensor networks: A review. *IEEE Sensors Journal, 15*(10), 5372–5383. doi:10.1109/JSEN.2015.2445796 PMID:27761103

Li, Z., Dey, N., Ashour, A. S., & Tang, Q. (2017). Discrete cuckoo search algorithms for two-sided robotic assembly line balancing problem. *Neural Computing & Applications, 17*, 2855–2860.

Lobiyal. (2011). *Performance Evaluation of VANET using realistic Vehicular Mobility* (M.Tech Dissertation). Jawaharlal Nehru University, New Delhi, India.

Locke, D. (n.d.). *MQ Telemetry Transport (MQTT) V3.1 Protocol Specification*. Available online: https://www.ibm.com/developerworks/webservices/library/ws-mqtt/

Logambigai, R., Ganapathy, S., & Kannan, A. (2018). Energy–efficient grid–based routing algorithm using intelligent fuzzy rules for wireless sensor networks. *Computers & Electrical Engineering, 68*, 62–75. doi:10.1016/j.compeleceng.2018.03.036

Long, Zhou, Sha, & Zhang. (2014). An Improved LEACH Multi-hop Routing Protocol Based on Genetic Algorithms for Heterogeneous Wireless Sensor Networks. *Journal of Information & Computational Science, 11*(2), 415–424.

LoRa Alliance™ Technology. (n.d.). Available: https://www.lora-alliance.org/What-Is-LoRa/Technology

Lu, Y. M., & Wong, V. W. S. (2007). An energy-efficient multipath routing protocol for wireless sensor networks. *International Journal of Communication Systems, 20*, 747–766. doi:10.1002/dac.843

Mahesh, N., & Vijayachitra, S. (2019). DECSA: Hybrid dolphin echolocation and crow search optimization for cluster-based energy-aware routing in WSN. *Neural Computing & Applications, 31*(S1s1), 47–62. doi:10.100700521-018-3637-4

Maimour, M. (2008). Maximally Radio-Disjoint Multipath Routing for Wireless Multimedia Sensor Networks. *4th ACM workshop on Wireless Multimedia Networking and Performance Modelling*, 26 – 31. 10.1145/1454573.1454579

Maksimovic, M., Vujovic, V., & Milosevic, V. (2014). Fuzzy logic and wireless sensor networks-a survey. *Journal of Intelligent & Fuzzy Systems*.

Manjeshwar & Agrawal. (2001). TEEN: A routing protocol for Enhanced Efficiency in Wireless Sensor Networks. *Proceedings of 15th International Parallel and Distributed Processing Symposium* (IPDPS'01) Workshops, 2009-2015.

Manjeshwar, A., & Agrawal, D. P. (2001). TEEN: A protocol for enhanced efficiency in wireless sensor network. *1st International workshop on parallel and distributed computing issues in wireless networks and mobile computing*, 189.

Manjeshwar, A., & Agrawal, D. P. (2001). TEEN: a routing protocol for enhanced efficiency in wireless sensor networks. In *Null* (p. 30189a). IEEE.

Manjeshwar, A., & Agrawal, D. P. (2001, April). TEEN: a routing protocol for enhanced efficiency in wireless sensor networks. In null (p. 30189a). IEEE. doi:10.1109/IPDPS.2001.925197

Manjeshwar, A., & Agrawal, D. P. (2002). APTEEN: A hybrid protocol for efficient routing and comprehensive information retrieval in wireless sensor networks. *2nd international workshop on parallel and distributed computing issues in wireless networks and mobile computing*, 195–202.

Manjeshwar, A., & Agrawal, D. (2002). APTEEN: A Hybrid Protocol for Efficiency Routing and Comprehensive Information Retrieval in Wireless Sensor Networks. *Proceedings of International Parallel and Distributed Processing Symposium*, 195-202.

Mao & Zhu. (2013, Nov.). A source initiated on-demand routing algorithm based on the throrup-zwick theory fro wireless sensor networks. *Scientific World Journal*.

Marksteiner, S., Jimenez, V. J. E., Valiant, H., & Zeiner, H. (November, 2017). An overview of wireless IoT protocol security in the smart home domain. In Internet of Things Business Models, Users, and Networks, 2017 (pp. 1-8). IEEE. doi:10.1109/CTTE.2017.8260940

Marsan, M. A., Chiaraviglio, L., Ciullo, D., & Meo, M. (2012). Multiple daily base station switch-offs in cellular networks. *Proceedings of IEEE International Conference on Communications and Electronics (ICCE 2012)*, 245–250. 10.1109/CCE.2012.6315906

Martinez, Garcia-Villalobos, Zamora, & Eguia. (2017). Energy management of micro renewable energy source and electric vehicles at home level. *J. Mod. Power Syst. Clean Energy*, 979-990.

Mauve, M., Widmer, J., & Hartenstein, H. (2001). A Survey on Position Based Routing in Mobile Ad Hoc Networks. *IEEE Network*, *15*(6), 30–33. doi:10.1109/65.967595

Miao, L., Djouani, K., Kurien, A., & Noel, G. (2010). Energy-efficient algorithm based on gradient based routing in wireless sensor networks. *Proc. Southern Africa Telecommunication Networks and Applications Conference (SATNAC)*.

Mirjalili, S., Gandomi, A. H., Mirjalili, S. Z., Saremi, S., Faris, H., & Mirjalili, S. M. (2017). Salp Swarm Algorithm: A bio-inspired optimizer for engineering design problems. *Advances in Engineering Software*, *114*, 163–191. doi:10.1016/j.advengsoft.2017.07.002

Mirjalili, S., Mirjalili, S. M., & Lewis, A. (2014). Grey wolf optimizer. *Advances in Engineering Software*, *69*, 46–61. doi:10.1016/j.advengsoft.2013.12.007

Mishra, R., & Mandal, C. R. (2005). *Performance comparison of AODV/DSR On-demand Routing Protocols for Ad hoc Networks in Constrained Situation*. ICPWC.

Misra, R., & Mandal, C. (2006). Ant-aggregation: ant colony algorithm for optimal data aggregation in wireless sensor networks. In *Wireless and Optical Communications Networks, 2006 IFIP International Conference on*. IEEE. 10.1109/WOCN.2006.1666600

Misra, S., & Kumar, R. (2016, November). A literature survey on various clustering approaches in wireless sensor network. In *Communication Control and Intelligent Systems (CCIS), 2016 2nd International Conference on* (pp. 18-22). IEEE. 10.1109/CCIntelS.2016.7878192

Mittal, N. (2019). Moth Flame Optimization Based Energy Efficient Stable Clustered Routing Approach for Wireless Sensor Networks. *Wireless Personal Communications*, *104*(2), 677–694. doi:10.100711277-018-6043-4

Mohamed, B., & Mohamed, F. (2015). Qos routing rpl for low power and lossy networks. *International Journal of Distributed Sensor Networks*, *11*(11), 971545. doi:10.1155/2015/971545

Moscibroda, T., & Wattenhofer, R. (2006). The Complexity of Connectivity in Wireless Networks. In Infocom (pp. 1-13). Academic Press. doi:10.1109/INFOCOM.2006.23

Mounir, M., Youssef, M. I., & Tarrad, I. F. (2017, December). On the effectiveness of deliberate clipping PAPR reduction technique in OFDM systems. In *2017 Japan-Africa Conference on Electronics, Communications and Computers (JAC-ECC)* (pp. 21-24). IEEE. 10.1109/JEC-ECC.2017.8305769

Müller, S. H., & Huber, J. B. (1997c, Nov.). A Comparison of Peak Power Reduction Schemes for OFDM. In IEEE GLOBECOM '97 (pp. 1-5). IEEE. doi:10.1109/GLOCOM.1997.632501

Müller, S. H., & Huber, J. B. (1997a). OFDM with Reduced Peak–to–Average Power Ratio by Optimum Combination of Partial Transmit Sequences. *Electronics Letters*, *33*(5), 368–369. doi:10.1049/el:19970266

Müller, S. H., & Huber, J. B. (1997b, September). A Novel Peak Power Reduction Scheme for OFDM. In *IEEE Conference Proceedings PIMRC 1997* (pp. 1090-1094). IEEE. 10.1109/PIMRC.1997.627054

Mulliner, E., Malys, N., & Maliene, V. (2016). Comparative analysis of MCDM methods for the assessment of sustainable housing affordability. *Omega*, *59*, 146–156. doi:10.1016/j.omega.2015.05.013

Muraleedharan, R., & Osadciw, L. A. (2004). A predictive sensor network using ant system. *Proc. Int. Society For Optical Engineering Symposium*, 5440, 181–192. 10.1117/12.542635

Nabil, E. (2016). A modified flower pollination algorithm for global optimization. *Expert Systems with Applications*, *57*, 192–203. doi:10.1016/j.eswa.2016.03.047

Nadeem, Q., Rasheed, M. B., Javaid, N., Khan, Z. A., Maqsood, Y., & Din, A. (2013, October). M-GEAR: Gateway-based energy-aware multi-hop routing protocol for WSNs. In *Broadband and Wireless Computing, Communication and Applications (BWCCA), 2013 Eighth International Conference on* (pp. 164-169). IEEE.

Nagai, M. (2012). *Pedestrian-to-vehicle communication access method and field test results. In 2012 international symposium on antennas and propagation (ISAP)* (pp. 712–715). New York: IEEE.

Nagpal, R., Shrobe, H., & Bachrach, J. (2003, April). Organizing a global coordinate system from local information on an ad hoc sensor network. In *Information processing in sensor networks* (pp. 333–348). Berlin: Springer. doi:10.1007/3-540-36978-3_22

Neamatollahi, P., Taheri, H., Naghibzadeh, M., & Yaghmaee, M. (2011). A hybrid clustering approach for prolonging lifetime in wireless sensor networks. *International Symposium on Computer Networks and Distributed Systems (CNDS)*, 170-174. 10.1109/CNDS.2011.5764566

Nguyen, T. T., & Lampe, L. (2008). On Partial Transmit Sequences for PAR Reduction in OFDM Systems. *IEEE Transactions on Wireless Communications*, *7*(2), 746–755. doi:10.1109/TWC.2008.060664

Niculescu, D., & Nath, B. (2001, November). Ad hoc positioning system (APS). In *GLOBECOM'01. IEEE Global Telecommunications Conference (Cat. No. 01CH37270)* (Vol. 5, pp. 2926-2931). IEEE.

Niculescu, D., & Nath, B. (2003, March). Ad hoc positioning system (APS) using AOA. In *IEEE INFOCOM 2003. Twenty-second Annual Joint Conference of the IEEE Computer and Communications Societies (IEEE Cat. No. 03CH37428)* (Vol. 3, pp. 1734-1743). IEEE.

Norouzi, Babamir, & Zaim. (2011). A New Clustering Protocol for Wireless Sensor Networks Using Genetic Algorithm Approach. *Wireless Sensor Network, 3*, 362-370.

Nuray, A. T., & Daraghma, S. M. (2015). A New Energy Efficient Clustering-based Protocol for Heterogeneous Wireless Sensor Networks. *Journal of Electrical & Electronics, 4*(3), 1.

Oh, H., & Chae, K. (2007). An Energy-Efficient Sensor Routing with low latency. *Scalability in Wireless Sensor Networks IEEE 2007 International Conference on Multimedia and Ubiquitous Engineering,* 147-152. 10.1109/MUE.2007.75

Oh, H., Bahn, H., & Chae, K. (2005, August). An Energy-Efficient Sensor Routing Scheme for Home Automation Networks. *IEEE Transactions on Consumer Electronics, 51*(3), 836–839. doi:10.1109/TCE.2005.1510492

Othman, M. F., & Shazali, K. (2012). Wireless sensor network applications: A study in environment monitoring system. *Procedia Engineering, 41*, 1204–1210. doi:10.1016/j.proeng.2012.07.302

Ouafaa, Mustapha, Salah-Ddine, & Said. (2016). Performance analysis of SLEACH, LEACH and DSDV protocols for wireless sensor networks (wsn). *Journal of Theoretical and Applied Information Technology, 94*(2).

Ozbakır, L., & Tapkan, P. (2011). Bee colony intelligence in zone constrained two-sided assembly line balancing problem. *Expert Systems with Applications, 38*(9), 11947–11957. doi:10.1016/j.eswa.2011.03.089

Ozcan, U. (2010). Balancing stochastic two-sided assembly lines: A chance-constrained, piecewise-linear, mixed integer program and a simulated annealing algorithm. *European Journal of Operational Research, 205*(1), 81–97. doi:10.1016/j.ejor.2009.11.033

Ozcan, U., Gokcen, H., & Toklu, B. (2010). Balancing parallel two-sided assembly lines. *International Journal of Production Research, 48*(16), 4767–4784. doi:10.1080/00207540903074991

Ozcan, U., & Toklu, B. (2008). A tabu search algorithm for two-sided assembly line balancing. *International Journal of Advanced Manufacturing Technology, 43*(7), 822–829.

Ozcan, U., & Toklu, B. (2009). Balancing of mixed-model two-sided assembly lines. *Computers & Industrial Engineering, 57*(1), 217–227. doi:10.1016/j.cie.2008.11.012

Ozcan, U., & Toklu, B. (2010). Balancing two-sided assembly lines with sequence-dependent setup times. *International Journal of Production Research, 48*(18), 5363–5383. doi:10.1080/00207540903140750

Ozturk, Karaboga, & Gorkemli. (n.d.). Artificial bee colony algorithm for dynamic deployment of wireless sensor networks. *Turkish Journal of Electrical Engineering & Computer.*

Pantazis, Nikolidakis, & Vergados. (2013). Senior Member,Energy-Efficient Routing Protocols in Wireless Sensor Networks: A Survey. IEEE Communications Surveys & Tutorials, 15(2).

Pantazis, N. A., Nikolidakis, S. A., Vergados, D. D., & Member, S. (2013). Energy-efficient routing protocols in wireless sensor networks: A survey. *IEEE Communications Surveys and Tutorials, 15*(2), 551–591. doi:10.1109/SURV.2012.062612.00084

Pant, M., Dey, B., & Nandi, S. (2015, February). A multihop routing protocol for wireless sensor network based on grid clustering. In *Applications and Innovations in Mobile Computing (AIMoC), 2015* (pp. 137–140). IEEE. doi:10.1109/AIMOC.2015.7083842

Parnian, A. R., Parsaei, M. R., Javidan, R., & Mohammadi, R. (2017). Smart Objects Presence Facilitation in the Internet of Things. *International Journal of Computers and Applications, 168*(4).

Patra, A., & Chouhan, S. (2013, December). Energy Efficient Hybrid multihop clustering algorithm in wireless sensor networks. In *Communication, Networks and Satellite (COMNETSAT), 2013 IEEE International Conference on* (pp. 59-63). IEEE. 10.1109/COMNETSAT.2013.6870861

Pawar, K., & Kelkar, Y. (2012). A survey of hierarchical routing protocols in wireless sensor network. *Int J Eng Innovative Technol, 1*(5), 50–54.

Peng, S., Yang, S. X., Gregori, S., & Tian, F. (2008, June). An adaptive QoSand energy-aware routing algorithm for wireless sensor networks.In *Information and Automation, 2008. ICIA 2008. International Conference on* (pp. 578-583). IEEE

Peng, B., & Li, L. (2015). An improved localization algorithm based on genetic algorithm in wireless sensor networks. *Cognitive Neurodynamics, 9*(2), 249–256. doi:10.100711571-014-9324-y PMID:25852782

Perkins & Das. (2003). *RFC 3561: Ad-hoc on-demand distance vector (AODV) routing.*

Perkins, C. E., & Royer, E. M. (1999). Ad-hoc on-demand distance vector routing. *Proc. of Second IEEE Workshop on Mobile Computing Systems and Applications (WMCSA), 90*(100), 25-26.

Perkins, Royer, & Das. (2003). *Ad hoc On Demand Distance Vector (AODV) Routing.* RFC 3561.

Perkins, C. E., & Bhagwat, P. (1994). Highly dynamic destination-sequenced distance-vector routing (DSDV) for mobile comput-ers. *Computer Communication Review, 24*(4), 234–244. doi:10.1145/190809.190336

Perkins, C. E., & Bhagwat, P. (1994). Highly dynamic destination-sequenced Distance-Vector routing (DSDV) for mobile computers. *Proc. of the conference on Communications architectures, protocols and applications (SIGCOMM)*, 234-244. 10.1145/190314.190336

Pohekar, S. D., & Ramachandran, M. (2004). Application of multi-criteria decision making to sustainable energy planning—A review. *Renewable & Sustainable Energy Reviews, 8*(4), 365–381. doi:10.1016/j.rser.2003.12.007

Pooranian, Z., Barati, A., & Movaghar, A. (2011). Queen-bee Algorithm for Energy Efficient Clusters in Wireless Sensor Networks. *Engineering and Technology, 5*(1), 1080–1083.

Pottie, G. J., & Kaiser, W. J. (2000). Wireless integrated network sensors. *Communications of the ACM, 43*(5), 51–58. doi:10.1145/332833.332838

Prasad, V., & Son, S. H. (2007). Classification of analysis techniques for wireless sensor networks. *Proceedings of Int'l Conf. Networked Sensing Systems (INSS'07)*, 93–97. 10.1109/INSS.2007.4297397

Prasan, U. D., & Murugappan, S. (2012). Energy Efficient and QOS aware Ant Colony Optimization (EQ-ACO) Routing Protocol for Wireless Sensor Networks. *International Journal of Distributed and Parallel Systems, 3*(1), 257–268. doi:10.5121/ijdps.2012.3122

Priyanka & Sankpal. (2016). Energy Aware Routing using Energy Efficient Routing Protocol in Wireless Ad hoc Network. *International Conference on Electrical, Electronics, and Optimization Techniques (ICEEOT)*, 1258-1261. 10.1109/ICEEOT.2016.7754885

Purnomo, H. D., & Wee, H.-M. (2014). Maximizing production rate and workload balancing in a two-sided assembly line using Harmony search. *Computers & Industrial Engineering, 76*, 222–230. doi:10.1016/j.cie.2014.07.010

Purnomo, H. D., Wee, H.-M., & Rau, H. (2013). Two-sided assembly lines balancing with assignment restrictions. *Mathematical and Computer Modelling, 57*(2), 189–199. doi:10.1016/j.mcm.2011.06.010

Qing, L., Zhu, Q., & Wang, M. (2006). Design of a distributed energy-efficient clustering algorithm for heterogeneous wireless sensor networks. *Computer Communications, 29*(12), 2230–2237. doi:10.1016/j.comcom.2006.02.017

Rabbani, M., Moghaddam, M., & Manavizadeh, N. (2012). Balancing of mixed-model two-sided assembly lines with multiple U-shaped layout. *International Journal of Advanced Manufacturing Technology, 59*(9-12), 1191–1210. doi:10.100700170-011-3545-6

Rabiner, W., Chandrakasan, A., & Balakrishnan, H. (2000). Energy-Efficient Communication Protocol for Wireless Microsensor Networks. *Hawaii International Conference on System Sciences*, 10-19.

Radi, M., Dezfouli, B., Bakarand, K. A., Razak, S. A., & Nematbakhsh, M. A. (2013). Interference-Aware Multipath Routing Protocol for QoS Improvement in Event-Driven Wireless Sensor Networks. *Tsinghua Science and Technology, 16*(5), 475–490. doi:10.1016/S1007-0214(11)70067-0

Rahman, A., & Dijk, E. (n.d.). *Group Communication for the Constrained Application Protocol (CoAP).* Available online: https://tools.ietf.org/html/rfc7390

Rahmanian, A., Omranpour, H., Akbari, M., & Raahemifar, K. (2011). A novel genetic algortim in LEACH-C routing protocol for sensor networks. *IEEE, CCECE*, 1096 – 1100.

Rajathi, N., & Jayashree, L. S. (2016, November). Energy efficient grid clustering based data aggregation in Wireless Sensor Networks. In Region 10 Conference (TENCON), 2016 IEEE (pp. 488-492). IEEE. doi:10.1109/TENCON.2016.7848047

Rajesh, S. L. (2014, December). Nature Inspired Energy Efficient Wireless Sensor Networks Using Dynamic Sleep-Active Algorithm. *International Journal for Research in Applied Science and Engineering Technology, 2.*

Ramson, S. J., & Moni, D. J. (2017, February). Applications of wireless sensor networks—A survey. In *Innovations in Electrical, Electronics, Instrumentation and Media Technology (ICEEIMT), 2017 International Conference on* (pp. 325-329). IEEE.

Rangaraj, J. (2017). *Implementing Energy Optimization by a Novel Hybrid Technique for Performance Improvement in Mobile Ad Hoc Network*. International Journal of Applied Engineering Research.

Rao, P. C. S., Jana, P. K., & Banka, H. (2017). A particle swarm optimization based energy efficient cluster head selection algorithm for wireless sensor networks. *Wireless Networks, 23*(7), 2005–2020. doi:10.100711276-016-1270-7

Rao, R. S., & Malathi, P. (2019). A novel PTS: Grey wolf optimizer-based PAPR reduction technique in OFDM scheme for high-speed wireless applications. *Soft Computing, 23*(8), 2701–2712. doi:10.100700500-018-3665-0

Rappaport, T. S. (1996). *Wireless communications: principles and practice* (Vol. 2). Prentice Hall PTR.

Rathi. (2015). An Enhanced LEACH Protocol using Fuzzy Logic for Wireless Sensor Networks. *International Journal of Computer Science and Information Security, 8*(7), 189-194.

Rault, T., Bouabdallah, A., & Challal, Y. (2014). Energy Efficiency in wireless sensor networks: A top-down survey. *Computer Networks, 67*, 104–122. doi:10.1016/j.comnet.2014.03.027

Rawat, P., Singh, K. D., Chaouchi, H., & Bonnin, J. M. (2014). Wireless sensor networks: A survey on recent developments and potential synergies. *The Journal of Supercomputing, 68*(1), 1–48. doi:10.100711227-013-1021-9

Ren, Z., Hail, M. A., & Hellbrück, H. (2013). CCN-WSN—A lightweight, flexible Content-Centric Networking protocol for wireless sensor networks. *Proceedings of the 2013 IEEE Eighth International Conference on Intelligent Sensors, Sensor Networks and Information Processing*, 123–128.

Rodoplu, V., & Meng, T. H. (1999). Minimum energy mobile wireless networks. *IEEE Journal on Selected Areas in Communications, 17*(8), 1333–1344. doi:10.1109/49.779917

Roseline, R. A., & Sumathi, P. (2012). Local clustering and threshold sensitive routing algorithm for Wireless Sensor Networks. In *Devices, Circuits and Systems (ICDCS), 2012 International Conference*. IEEE.

Roshani, A., Fattahi, P., Roshani, A., Salehi, M., & Roshani, A. (2012). Cost-oriented two-sided assembly line balancing problem: A simulated annealing approach. *International Journal of Computer Integrated Manufacturing, 25*(8), 689–715. doi:10.1080/0951192X.2012.664786

Rostami & Mottar. (2014). Wireless sensor network clustering using particles swarm optimization for reducing Energy Consumption. *International Journal of Managing Information Technology, 6*(4).

Ryu, Jha, Koh, & Cho. (2011, Aug.). Position-based routing algorithm improving reliability of inter-vehicle communication. *Transaction on Internet and Information Systems (TIIS)*.

Sandeep Kumar, E. (2014). Fire-LEACH: A Novel Clustering Protocol for Wireless Sensor Networks based on Fire fly Algorithm. *International Journal of Computer Science: Theory and Application, 1*(1), 12-17.

Santhiya & Kala. (2017). Energy Harvesting in vehicular Environment using Sources and Techniques. International Journal for Trends in Engineering & Technology, 19-22.

Schott, W., Gluhak, A., Presser, M., Hunkeler, U., & Tafazolli, R. (2007). e-SENSE protocol stack architecture for wireless sensor networks. In Mobile and Wireless Communications Summit, 2007. 16th IST (pp. 1-5). IEEE.

Seetharam, Acharya, Bhattacharyya, & Naska. (2009). Energy Efficient Data Gathering Schemes in Wireless Sensor Networks Using Ant Colony Optimization. *Journal of Applied Computer Science & Mathematics, 5*(6), 1-13.

Sen, J., & Ukil, A. (2009, May). An adaptable and QoS-aware routing protocol for Wireless Sensor Networks. In *Wireless Communication, Vehicular Technology, Information Theory and Aerospace & Electronic Systems Technology, 2009. Wireless VITAE 2009. 1st International Conference on* (pp. 767-771). IEEE. 10.1109/WIRELESSVITAE.2009.5172546

Sendra, S., Parra, L., Lloret, J., & Khan, S. (2015). Systems and Algorithms for Wireless Sensor Networks Based on Animal and Natural Behavior. International Journal of Distributed Sensor Networks.

Sepahi, A., & Naini, S. G. J. (2016). Two-sided assembly line balancing problem with parallel performance capacity. *Applied Mathematical Modelling, 40*(14), 6280–6292. doi:10.1016/j.apm.2016.02.022

Shafiullah, G., & Agyei, A. (2008). A Survey of Energy-Efficient and QoS-Aware Routing Protocols for Wireless Sensor Networks. In *Novel Algorithms and Techniques* (pp. 352–357). Automation and Industrial Electronics.

Shang, Y., & Ruml, W. (2004, March). Improved MDS-based localization. In *IEEE INFOCOM 2004* (Vol. 4, pp. 2640–2651). IEEE. doi:10.1109/INFCOM.2004.1354683

Shaoqiang, D., Agrawal, P., & Sivalingam, K. (2007). Reinforcement learning based geographic routing protocol for UWB wireless sensor network. *Proc. IEEE Global Telecommunications Conf. (GLOBECOM)*, 652–656.

Sharawi, Emary, Saroit, & El-Mahdy. (2014). Flower Pollination optimization Algorithm for Wireless Sensor Network Lifetime Global Optimization. *International Journal of Soft Computing and Engineering, 4*(3), 54-59.

Sharawi, M., Emary, E., Saroit, I. A., & El-Mahdy, H. (2014). Bat Swarm Algorithm for Wireless Sensor Networks Lifetime Optimization. *International Journal of Science and Research, 3*(5), 654–664.

Sharma, S., & Jena, S.K. (2011). *A survey on secure hierarchical routing protocols in wireless sensor networks.* ACM.

Sharma, R., & Lobiyal, D. K. (2015). Dual Transmission Power and Ant Colony Optimization Based Lifespan Maximization Protocol for Sensor Networks *International Journal of Business Data Communications and Networking, 11*(1), 1–14. doi:10.4018/IJBDCN.2015010101

Shi, L., Zhang, B., Mouftah, H. T., & Ma, J. (2012). DDRP: An Efficient Data-Driven Routing Protocol for Wireless Sensor networks with Mobile Sinks. *International Journal of Communication Systems, 26*, 1341–1355.

Shivashankar, Prasad, Kumar, & Kumar. (2016). An Efficient Routing Algorithm based on Ant Colony Optimisation for VANETs. *IEEE International Conference On Recent Trends In Electronics Information Communication Technology*, 436-440.

Shi, Y. (2001, May). Particle swarm optimization: developments, applications and resources. In *Proceedings of the 2001 congress on evolutionary computation (IEEE Cat. No. 01TH8546)* (Vol. 1, pp. 81-86). IEEE. 10.1109/CEC.2001.934374

Shu, L., Zhang, Y., Yang, L. T., Wang, Y., & Hauswirth, M. (2008). Geographic routing in wireless multimedia sensor networks. *Proc. 2008 Second Int'l Conf. Future Generation Communication and Networking*, 68–73. 10.1109/FGCN.2008.17

Siew, Bono, Yoong, Yeo, & Teo. (2013). Cluster Formation of Wireless Sensor Nodes using Adaptive Particle Swarm Optimization. *IJSSST, 13*(3B), 38-44.

Sigfox. (n.d.). Available: http://www.sigfox.com

Simaria, A. S., & Vilarinho, P. M. (2009). 2-ANTBAL: An ant colony optimization algorithm for balancing two-sided assembly lines. *Computers & Industrial Engineering, 56*(2), 489–506. doi:10.1016/j.cie.2007.10.007

Sim, K. M., & Sun, W. H. (2003). Ant colony optimization for routing and load-balancing: Survey and new directions. *IEEE Trans. Syst., Man. Cybern. A, 33*(5), 560–572.

Singh, S. K., Kumar, P., Singh, J. P., & Alryalat, M. A. A. (2017, November). An energy efficient routing using multi-hop intra clustering technique in WSNs. In Region 10 Conference, TENCON 2017-2017 IEEE (pp. 381-386). IEEE. doi:10.1109/TENCON.2017.8227894

Singh, A. K., Purohit, N., & Varma, S. (2013). Purohit N, Varma S. Fuzzy logic based clustering in wireless sensor networks: A survey. *International Journal of Electronics, 100*(1), 126–141. doi:10.1080/00207217.2012.687191

Singh, M., & Patra, S. K. (2018). On the PTS Optimization Using the Firefly Algorithm for PAPR Reduction in OFDM Systems. *IETE Technical Review, 35*(5), 441–455. doi:10.1080/02 564602.2018.1505563

Sinha & Barman. (2012). Energy Efficient Routing Mechanism in Wireless Sensor Network. *IEEE Conference on Recent Advances in Information Technology.*

Smaragdakis, G., Matta, I., & Bestavros, A. (2004). *SEP: A stable election protocol for clustered heterogeneous wireless sensor networks.* Boston University Computer Science Department.

Sohrabi, K., Gao, J., Ailawadhi, V., & Pottie, G. (1999). Protocols for Self- Organization of a Wireless Sensor Network. *IEEE Pers. Commun., 7*(5), 16–27. doi:10.1109/98.878532

Sohraby, K. (2007). *Wireless Sensor Networks.* Elsevier Inc. doi:10.1002/047011276X

Soliman, & Al-Otaibi. (2011). Enhancing AODV Routing Protocol over Mobile ad hoc Sensor Networks. Sensor Networks, 10(2), 36–41.

Srinivasa Rao, P. C., & Banka, H. (2017). Novel chemical reaction optimization based unequal clustering and routing algorithms for wireless sensor networks. *Wireless Networks, 23*(3), 759–778. doi:10.100711276-015-1148-0

Suh, Y. H., Kim, K. T., Shin, D. R., & Youn, H. Y. (2015, August). Traffic-Aware Energy Efficient Routing (TEER) Using Multi-Criteria Decision Making for Wireless Sensor Network. In *IT Convergence and Security (ICITCS), 2015 5th International Conference on* (pp. 1-5). IEEE.

Su, H., Qiu, M., & Wang, H. (2012, August). Secure wireless communication system for smart grid with rechargeable electric vehicles. *IEEE Communications Magazine, 50*(8), 62–68. doi:10.1109/ MCOM.2012.6257528

Suhonen, J., Kuorilehto, M., Hannikainen, M., & Hamalainen, T. D. (2006). Cost-Aware Dynamic Routing Protocol for Wireless Sensor Networks - Design and Prototype Experiments. In *Personal, Indoor and Mobile Radio Communications, 2006 IEEE 17th International Symposium on.* IEEE.

Sun, G., Yu, M., Dan, L., & Chang, V. (2018). Analytical Exploration of Energy Savings for Parked Vehicles to Enhance VANET Connectivity. *IEEE Transactions on Intelligent Transportation Systems*, 1–13.

Suthaputchakun, C., & Sun, Z. (2011, December). Routing Protocol in Inter-vehicle Communication Systems: A Survey. *IEEE Communications Magazine, 49*(12), 150–156. doi:10.1109/ MCOM.2011.6094020

Taha, R. B., El-Kharbotly, A. K., Sadek, Y. M., & Afia, N. H. (2011). A Genetic Algorithm for solving two-sided assembly line balancing problems. *AIN Shams Engineering Journal*, *3*(4), 227–240. doi:10.1016/j.asej.2011.10.003

Talbi, E. G. (2009). *Metaheuristics: from design to implementation* (Vol. 74). John Wiley & Sons. doi:10.1002/9780470496916

Tang, Q. H., Li, Z. X., Zhang, L. P., Floudas, C. A., & Cao, X. J. (2015). Effective hybrid teaching learning-based optimization algorithm for balancing two-sided assembly lines with multiple constraints. *Chinese Journal of Mechanical Engineering*, *28*(5), 1067–1079. doi:10.3901/CJME.2015.0630.084

Tang, Q., Li, Z., & Zhang, L. (2016). An effective discrete artificial bee colony algorithm with idle time reduction techniques for two-sided assembly line balancing problem of type-II. *Computers & Industrial Engineering*, *97*, 146–156. doi:10.1016/j.cie.2016.05.004

Tapkan, P., Ozbakır, L., & Baykasoglu, A. (2016). Bee algorithms for parallel two-sided assembly line balancing problem with walking times. *Applied Soft Computing*, *39*, 275–291. doi:10.1016/j.asoc.2015.11.017

Taruna, S., Jain, K., & Purohit, G. N. (2011). Application domain of wireless sensor network:-a paradigm in developed and developing countries. *International Journal of Computer Science Issues*, *8*(4), 611.

Taşpinar, N., Karaboğa, D., Yildirim, M., & Akay, B. (2011). PAPR reduction using artificial bee colony algorithm in OFDM systems. *Turkish Journal of Electrical Engineering and Computer Sciences*, *19*(1), 47–58. doi:10.3906/elk-1003-399

The Internet of Things (IoT) - essential IoT business guide. (n.d.). Available: https://www.i-scoop.eu/internet-of-things guide/ #The_growing_role_of_fog_and_edge_computing_in_IoT

The Internet of Tings. (n.d.). Available: https://www.itu.int/itunews/manager/display.asp?lang=fr&year=2005&issue=09&ipage=things&ext=html

Thulasiraman, P., & White, K. A. (2016). Topology control of tactical wireless sensor networks using energy efficient zone routing. *Digital Communications and Networks*, *2*(1), 1–14. doi:10.1016/j.dcan.2016.01.002

Top 50 Internet of Things Applications. (n.d.). Available: http://www.libelium.com/resources/top_50_iot_sensor_applications_ranking/

Toutouh, J., & Alba, E. (2012). Green OLSR in VANETs with Differential Evolution. GECCO'12 Companion, 11-18. doi:10.1145/2330784.2330787

Toutouh, J., & Alba, E. (2011). An Efficient Routing Protocol for Green Communications in Vehicular Ad-hoc Networks. *13th Annual Genetic and Evolutionary Computation Conference, GECCO 2011*, 719-725. 10.1145/2001858.2002076

Toutouh, J., Nesmachnow, S., & Alba, E. (2012). Fast energy-aware OLSR routing in VANETs by means of parallel evolutionary algorithm. *Cluster Computing*.

Tripathi, M., Naidu, K., & Biswas, M. (2017, March). Energy efficient semi grid based clustering in heterogeneous Wireless Sensor Network. In *Wireless Communications, Signal Processing and Networking (WiSPNET), 2017 International Conference on* (pp. 278-282). IEEE. 10.1109/WiSPNET.2017.8299762

Tsitsigkos, A., Entezami, F., Ramrekha, T. A., Politis, C., & Panaousis, E. A. (2012, April). A case study of internet of things using wireless sensor networks and smartphones. In *Proceedings of the Wireless World Research Forum (WWRF) Meeting: Technologies and Visions for a Sustainable Wireless Internet, Athens, Greece* (Vol. 2325). Academic Press.

Tuncel, G., & Aydin, D. (2014). Two-sided assembly line balancing using teaching–learning based optimization algorithm. *Computers & Industrial Engineering*, *74*, 291–299. doi:10.1016/j.cie.2014.06.006

Uhrig, R. (2006). Greenhouse gas emissions from gasoline, hybrid-electric, and hydrogen-fueled vehicles. *Proc. IEEE EIC Climate Change Technology*, 1–6. 10.1109/EICCCC.2006.277196

Van Nunen, E., Kwakkernaat, M., Ploeg, J., & Netten, B. D. (2012). Cooperative competition for future mobility. *IEEE Transactions on Intelligent Transportation Systems*, *13*(3), 1018–1025. doi:10.1109/TITS.2012.2200475

Vinutha, Nalini, & Veeresh. (2017). Energy efficient WSN using NN smart sampling and reliable routing protocol. *IEEE WISPNET-2017*.

Voigt, T., Dunkels, A., & Braun, T. (2010). On-demand construction of non-interfering multiple paths in wireless sensor networks. *Proc. 2nd Workshop Sensor Networks Informatik*, 277–285.

Wang, X., & Zhang, G. (2007). Decp: A distributed election clustering protocol for heterogeneous wireless sensor networks. *Proceedings of the 7th international conference on Computational Science, Part III*, 105-108. 10.1007/978-3-540-72588-6_14

Wang, Z., Bulut, E., & Szymanski, B. K. (2009). Energy Efficient Collision Aware Multipath Routing for Wireless Sensor Networks. IEEE International Conference on Communications, 91 – 95. doi:10.1109/ICC.2009.5198989

Wang, C., Zhang, Y., Wang, X., & Zhang, Z. (2018). Hybrid Multihop Partition-Based Clustering Routing Protocol for WSNs. *IEEE Sensors Letters*, *2*(1), 1–4. doi:10.1109/LSENS.2018.2803086

Wang, F., Wang, C., Wang, Z., & Zhang, X. Y. (2015). A hybrid algorithm of GA+ simplex method in the WSN localization. *International Journal of Distributed Sensor Networks*, *11*(7), 731894. doi:10.1155/2015/731894

Wang, M., Liang, H., Deng, R., Zhang, R., & Shen, X. S. (2013). VANET based online charging strategy for electric vehicles. *Proc. IEEE Global Telecommunications Conference Workshops*, 4804-4809.

Wang, P., & Wang, T. (2006). Adaptive routing for sensor networks using reinforcement learning. In *Proc. 6th IEEE Int. Conf. on Computer and Information Technology (CIT)*. Washington, DC: IEEE Computer Society. 10.1109/CIT.2006.34

Wang, Y., Chen, W., & Tellambura, C. (2010). A PAPR reduction method based on artificial bee colony algorithm for OFDM signals. *IEEE Transactions on Wireless Communications, 9*(10), 2994–2999. doi:10.1109/TWC.2010.081610.100047

Watfa, M. (2010). *Advances in Vehicular Ad-Hoc Networks: Developments and Challenges*. IGI Global. doi:10.4018/978-1-61520-913-2

Wazed, S., Bari, A., Jaekel, A., & Bandyopadhyay, S. (2007). Genetic algorithm based approach for extending the lifetime of two-tiered sensor networks. *Proc. 2nd Int. Symposium on Wireless Pervasive Computing ISWPC*. 10.1109/ISWPC.2007.342578

Wei, S., Goeckel, D. L., & Kelly, P. E. (2002). A modern extreme value theory approach to calculating the distribution of the peak-to-average power ratio in OFDM systems. In *2002 IEEE International Conference on Communications. Conference Proceedings. ICC 2002 (Cat. No. 02CH37333)* (Vol. 3, pp. 1686-1690). IEEE. doi: 10.1109/ICC.2002.997136

Wen, J. H., Lee, S. H., Huang, Y. F., & Hung, H. L. (2008). A suboptimal PTS algorithm based on particle swarm optimization technique for PAPR reduction in OFDM systems. *EURASIP Journal on Wireless Communications and Networking, 2008*(14). doi:10.1155/2008/601346

Winter, T., Thubert, P., Brandt, A., Clausen, T., Hui, J., Kelsey, R., . . . Vasseur, J. P. (2011). *Internet draft*. Retrieved from http://tools.ietf.org/html/draft-ietf-roll-rpl-18

Winter, T., Thubert, P., Brandt, A., Hui, J., Kelsey, R., Levis, P., & Alexander, R. (2012). *RPL: IPv6 routing protocol for low-power and lossy networks* (No. RFC 6550).

Wixted, A. J., Kinnaird, P., Larijani, H., Tait, A., Ahmadinia, A., & Strachan, N. (2016). Evaluation of LoRa and LoRaWAN for wireless sensor networks. In SENSORS, 2016 IEEE (pp. 1-3). IEEE. doi:10.1109/ICSENS.2016.7808712

Wu, E.-F., Jin, Y., Bao, J.-S., & Hu, X.-F. (2008). A branch-and-bound algorithm for two-sided assembly line balancing. *International Journal of Advanced Manufacturing Technology, 39*(9), 1009–1015. doi:10.100700170-007-1286-3

Xiangning, F., & Yulin, S. (2007, October). Improvement on LEACH protocol of wireless sensor network. In *Sensor Technologies and Applications, 2007. SensorComm 2007. International Conference on* (pp. 260-264). IEEE. 10.1109/SENSORCOMM.2007.4394931

Xiuwu, Y., Qin, L., Yong, L., Mufang, H., Ke, Z., & Renrong, X. (2019). Uneven clustering routing algorithm based on glowworm swarm optimization. *Ad Hoc Networks, 93*, 101923. doi:10.1016/j.adhoc.2019.101923

Xu, Y., Heidemann, J., & Estrin, D. (2001). Geography informed energy conservation for ad hoc routing. *Proceedings of the 7th Annual ACM/IEEE International Conference on Mobile Computing and Networking (MobiCom'01)*. 10.1145/381677.381685

Xue, F., Sanderson, A., & Graves, R. (2006). Multi-objective routing in wireless sensor networks with a differential evolution algorithm. *Proc. IEEE Int. Conf. on Networking, Sensing and Control ICNSC,* 880–885.

Xue, Q., & Ganz, A. (2006). On the lifetime of large scale sensor networks. *Computer Communications, 29*(4), 502–510. doi:10.1016/j.comcom.2004.12.033

Xu, K., & Gerla, M. (2002). A heterogeneous routing protocol based on a new stable clustering scheme. *Proceedings of Military communications conference (MILCOM'02), 2,* 838-843. 10.1109/MILCOM.2002.1179583

Ya, L., Wang, P., Rong, L., Yang, H., & Wei, L. (2014). *Reliable Energy-Aware Routing Protocol for Heterogeneous WSN Based on Beaconing.* IEEE. doi:10.1109/ICACT.2014.6778931

Yang & Kull. (2013). Performance analysis of WSN for different speeds of sink and sensor nodes. *International Conference on Complex, Intelligent and Software Systems Intensive Systems CICIS.*

Yang, H., & Sikdar, B. (2003). A Protocol for Tracking Mobile Targets Using Sensor Networks. *Proc. First IEEE Int"l Workshop Sensor Network Protocols and Applications (SNPA'03),* 71-81. 10.1109/SNPA.2003.1203358

Yan, G., Wang, Y., Weigle, M., Olariu, S., & Ibrahim, K. (2008). Wehealth: a secure and privacy preserving ehealth using notice. *Proc. Int. Conf. Wireless Access in Vehicular Environments (WAVE).*

Yang, X. S. (2010). Firefly algorithm, Levy flights and global optimization. In *Research and development in intelligent systems XXVI* (pp. 209–218). London: Springer. doi:10.1007/978-1-84882-983-1_15

Yang, X. S. (2010). *Nature Inspired Metaheuristics Algorithms.* Luniver Press.

Yang, X. S., & Deb, S. (2009, December). Cuckoo search via Lévy flights. In *2009 World Congress on Nature & Biologically Inspired Computing (NaBIC)* (pp. 210-214). IEEE. 10.1109/NABIC.2009.5393690

Ye, M., Li, C., Chen, G., & Wu, J. (2005). EECS: An energy efficient clustering scheme in wireless sensor networks. *Proceedings of the IEEE Conference on International conference on Performance Computing and Communications,* 535-540.

Ye, M., Li, C., Chen, G., & Wu, J. (2012). EECS: An energy efficient clustering scheme in wireless sensor networks. In *National laboratory of novel software technology.* Nanjing University.

Yin, Y. Y., Shi, J. W., Li, Y. N., & Zhang, P. (2006). Cluster head selection using analytical hierarchy process for wireless sensor networks. In *International Symposium on Personal, Indoor and Mobile Radio Communications, PIMRC2006* (pp. 11–14). IEEE 10.1109/PIMRC.2006.254181

Younis, O., & Fahmy, S. (2004). HEED: a hybrid energy-efficient distributed clustering approach for ad hoc sensor networks. *IEEE Trans Mob Comput, 3*(4).

Youssef, M. I., Tarrad, I. F., & Mounir, M. (2016, December). Performance evaluation of hybrid ACE-PTS PAPR reduction techniques. In *2016 11th International Conference on Computer Engineering & Systems (ICCES)* (pp. 407-413). IEEE. 10.1109/ICCES.2016.7822039

Yu, Estrin, & Govindan. (2001). *Geographical and Energy-Aware Routing: A Recursive Data Dissemination Protocol for Wireless Sensor Networks.*" UCLA Computer Science Department Technical Report, UCLA-CSD TR-01-0023.

Yuan, B., Zhang, C., & Shao, X. (2015). A late acceptance hill-climbing algorithm for balancing two-sided assembly lines with multiple constraints. *Journal of Intelligent Manufacturing, 26*(1), 159–168. doi:10.100710845-013-0770-x

Yuan, B., Zhang, C., Shao, X., & Jiang, Z. (2015). An effective hybrid honey bee mating optimization algorithm for balancing mixed-model two-sided assembly lines. *Computers & Operations Research, 53*, 32–41. doi:10.1016/j.cor.2014.07.011

Yuan, X., Elhoseny, M., El-Minir, H. K., & Riad, A. M. (2017). A Genetic Algorithm-Based, Dynamic Clustering Method Towards Improved WSN Longevity. *Journal of Network and Systems Management, 25*(1), 21–46. doi:10.100710922-016-9379-7

Yu, B., Scerri, P., Sycara, K., Xu, Y., & Lewis, M. (2006). Scalable and reliable data delivery in mobile ad hoc sensor networks. *Proc. 4th Int. Conf. on Autonomous Agents and Multiagent Systems (AAMAS).* 10.1145/1160633.1160825

Yuea, J., Zhang, W., Xiao, W., Tang, D., & Tang, J. (2012). Energy efficient and balanced cluster-based data aggregation algorithm for wireless sensor networks. *Procedia Engineering, 29*, 2009–2015. doi:10.1016/j.proeng.2012.01.253

Yunxia, Z. Q. C. (2005). On the lifetime of wireless sensor networks (Vol. 9). Academic Press.

Zeadally, S., Hunt, R., Chen, Y. S., Irwin, A., & Hassan, A. (2010). *Vehicular ad hoc networks (VANETS): Status, results and challenges.* Springer.

Zeadally, S., Hunt, R., Chen, Y. S., Irwin, A., & Hassan, A. (2010). Vehicular ad hoc networks (VANETS): Status, results, and challenge. *Telecommunication Systems, 50*(4), 217–241. doi:10.100711235-010-9400-5

Zhang, S., & Zhang, H. (2012, August). A review of wireless sensor networks and its applications. In *Automation and Logistics (ICAL), 2012 IEEE International Conference on* (pp. 386-389) IEEE. 10.1109/ICAL.2012.6308240

Zhang, D., Yang, Z., Raychoudary, V., Chen, Z., & Lloret, J. (2013). An Energy-Efficient Routing Protocol Using Movement Trends in Vehicular Ad-Hoc Networks. *The Computer Journal, 56*(8), 938–946. doi:10.1093/comjnl/bxt028

Zhang, J., Wang, F. Y., Wang, K., Lin, W. H., Xu, X., & Chen, C. (2011). Data-driven intelligent transportation systems: A survey. *IEEE Transactions on Intelligent Transportation Systems, 12*(4), 1624–1639. doi:10.1109/TITS.2011.2158001

Zhang, W., & Cao, G. (2004). *DCTC: Dynamic Convoy Tree-Based Collaboration for Target Tracking in Sensor Networks. IEEE Trans. Wireless Comm.*

Zhang, X., Zhang, X., & Gu, C. (2017). A micro-artificial bee colony multicast routing in vehicular ad hoc networks. *Ad Hoc Networks*, *58*, 213–221. doi:10.1016/j.adhoc.2016.06.009

Zhang, Y., & Fromherz, M. P. J. (2006). A robust and efficient flooding-based routing for wireless sensor networks. *Journal of Interconnection Networks*, *7*(4), 549–568. doi:10.1142/S0219265906001855

Zhao, J., Xi, W., He, Y., Liu, Y., Li, X. Y., Mo, L., & Yang, Z. (2013). Localization of wireless sensor networks in the wild: Pursuit of ranging quality. *IEEE/ACM Transactions on Networking*, *21*(1), 311–323. doi:10.1109/TNET.2012.2200906

Zhou, H., Wu, Y., Hu, Y., & Xie, G. (2010). A novel stable selection and reliable transmission protocol for clustered heterogeneous wireless sensor networks. *Comput. Commun.*, *33*(15), 1843-1849.

Zhou, J., & Yao, X. (2017). A hybrid approach combining modified artificial bee colony and cuckoo search algorithms for multi-objective cloud manufacturing service composition. *International Journal of Production Research*, *55*(16), 4765–4784. doi:10.1080/00207543.2017.1292064

Zhu, X. (2007). Pheromone based energy aware directed diffusion algorithm for wireless sensor network. In Advanced Intelligent Computing Theories and Applications. With Aspects of Theoretical and Methodological Issues (pp. 283-291). Springer Berlin Heidelberg. doi:10.1007/978-3-540-74171-8_28

Ziyadi, M., Yasami, K., & Abolhassani, B. (2009, May). Adaptive clusteringfor energy efficient wireless sensor networks based on ant colonyoptimization. In *Communication Networks and Services Research Conference, 2009. CNSR'09. Seventh Annual* (pp. 330-334). IEEE

Zohre & Khodaei. (2010). HERF: A Hybrid Energy Efficient Routing using a Fuzzy Method in Wireless Sensor Networks. *International Journal of Distributed and Parallel Systems, U*(1).

Zou, Y., & Chakrabarty, K. (2003). Sensor deployment and target localization based on virtual forces. In *INFOCOM 2003. Twenty-Second Annual Joint Conference of the IEEE Computer and Communications. IEEE Societies* (Vol. 2, pp. 1293-1303). IEEE. 10.1109/INFCOM.2003.1208965

Zuniga, M., & Krishnamachari, B. (2004). Analyzing the transitional region in low power wireless links. In *Sensor and Ad Hoc Communications and Networks, 2004. IEEE SECON 2004. 2004 First Annual IEEE Communications Society Conference on* (pp. 517-526). IEEE. 10.1109/SAHCN.2004.1381954

About the Contributors

Govind P. Gupta is currently working as Assistant Professor in National Institute of Technology, Raipur. He has done PhD from IIT, Roorkee. His area of interests are Computer Networking, Distributed Algorithms design for Wireless Sensor Networks, Performance Analysis, Big Data Processing, Parallel and Distributed Computing, Design & Analysis of Algorithms.

* * *

Saloni Dhiman has received B.Tech degree from Himachal Pradesh Technical University and completed her M.Tech. from Dr. B.R. Ambedkar, NIT, Jalandhar, Punjab, India. Her research is focused in the area of Wireless Sensor Networks.

Hassan El Alami received the master's degree in electronics and computer science from Mohammed Premier University, Oujda, Morocco, in 2012, and the Ph.D. degree in computer science and telecommunications from the National Institute of Posts and Telecommunications (INPT), Rabat, Morocco, in 2019. His current research interests include the Internet of Things, with a focus on the application of artificial intelligence and optimization algorithms for the Internet of Things. He is a TPC Member of the International Conference on Fuzzy Systems and Data Mining. He is the Student Member of the IEEE Computer Society. He serves as a Reviewer for many leading international journals and conferences.

Vrajesh Kumar Chawra Ph.D. research scholar in the Department of Information Technology from the National Institute of Technology Raipur. He has completed his MTech. from CSVTU, Bhilai in 2010 and B.E. from Pt. Ravishankar Shukla University Raipur in 2007. His research areas of interest are Wireless Sensor Networks, Meta-heuristic Algorithms, Clustering, and IoT.

Gurjot Singh Gaba is currently pursuing Ph.D. in Electronics & Electrical Engineering with Spl. in Cryptography and Network Security of WSN and IoT's. He is working as an Asst. Prof. in Lovely Professional University since 2011. His research interest includes Wireless and optical communications, Computer Networks and its Security. He is an author of 8 monographs, published 80 research papers (co-authored with 74 researchers), and filed 3 patents. He has been awarded with the Research Award for Excellence in the year 2016, 2017 and 2018 and Teacher Appreciation Award in the year 2016 by Union Minister of Human Resource and Development, India. He has reviewed articles of 50+ Journals/conferences. He is associated with 8 technical organizations such as ISCA, IEEE, IAENG, IACSIT, CSI, ISTE, ACM, ISDS Society, GIAN. He is serving as an Associate editor of World Journal of Engineering, Emerald Publishers.

Deepti Kakkar, born in 1982, in Jalandhar, Punjab, India. She did her Bachelor of Technology in Electronics and Communication Engineering from Himachal Pradesh University, India in 2003 and Masters of Engineering in electronics product design and technology from Punjab University, Chandigarh. She did her PhD from Dr. B.R. Ambedkar National Institute of Technology, Jalandhar, India. She has a total academic experience of 14 years and at present she is ASSISTANT PROFESSOR in Electronics and Communication department with Dr. B. R. Ambedkar National Institute of Technology, Jalandhar, India. Earlier, she had worked as lecturer in Electronics and Communication department with DAV Institute of Engineering and Technology, Jalandhar, Punjab. She has guided more than 15 post graduate engineering dissertations and currently supervising 2 Ph.D candidates. Her recent research interests include wireless communications, wireless sensor network, neuro developmental disorders, dynamic spectrum allocation, spectrum sensing, software Defined radios and Cognitive Radios.

Nitika Kapoor has obtained B.E. degree from Sant Longowal Institute of Engineering and Technology in CSE and completed M.tech from Lovely Professional University. She has more than 14 years of teaching experience. Her research area includes Vehicular Adhoc Networks, Machine Learning. She has published her research papers in many SCOPUS indexed Journals.

Asha Karegowda is currently working as Associate Professor, Dept of MCA, Siddaganga Institute of Technology form last 20 years. Have authored few books on C and Data structures using C, currently writing books on Python, Data mining and Data structures using C++. Area of interest include Data mining, WSN, Remote sensing, Bio inspired computing. Have published papers both in international conferences and journals. Guiding 3 research scholars in the area of image processing and remote sensing. Handling subjects for both PG and UG students: Python, Data structures C and C++, Data mining, Data Analytics.

Amanpreet Kaur is pursuing PhD in Computer Science & IT from Jaypee Institute of Information Technology, Noida. She has done MTech from NIT, Jalandhar. Her research areas are Wireless sensor networks, Information Security, Performance Analysis.

Gurjot Kaur graduated in Electronics and Communication Engineering from Guru Nanak Dev University, Amritsar, India and completed her Masters in Electronics from UIET, Panjab University, Chandigarh, India. She is currently pursuing PhD in wireless communication from Dr. B.R. Ambedkar, NIT Jalandhar, India. Her research is focused in the areas of Traffic Management in Real Time Networks, mobility in wireless networks, wireless ad hoc and sensor networks, cognitive networks and advances in mobile computing.

Yogesh Kumar has completed his Ph. D and M.tech in CSE from Punjabi University Patiala. He has around 11 years of teaching Experience. His research areas include Communication Networks, Machine Learning, and Natural Language Processing. He has published his research papers in various reputed Journals including SCI and SCOPUS indexed Journals.

Sangeeta Mittal is currently working as Assistant Professor in Jaypee Institute of Information Technology, Noida. She has done PhD from JIIT, Noida. Her area of interests are Computer Networking, Information Security and Wireless Sensor Networks.

Mohamed Bakry El Mashade was born in Cairo, Egypt, in 1954. He received the B.Sc. degree in electrical engineering from Al Azhar University, Cairo, in 1978, the M.Sc. degree in communication theory from Cairo University in 1982, Le D.E.A. d'Electronique (Specialité: Traitement du Signal) in 1985 and Le Diplôme de Doctorat in optical communications from USTL de Montpellier, France, in 1987. He has been with the Electrical Engineering Department, University of Al Azhar since 1978, where he is currently Professor of Electrical and Optical Engineering. His research interests are in radar CFAR detection, direct sequence spread spectrum communications, generation and transmission of optical solutions, quantum-well optical detectors, and digital signal processing. Dr. El Mashade acts as a reviewer for IEE Proceedings of Radar, Sonar Navigation, IEE Electronics Letters, and IEEE

Transactions on Aerospace and Electronic Systems in the fields of CFAR radar target detection and digital signal processing. He won the Egyptian Encouraging 1998 Award in Engineering Science.

Mohamed Mounir is Assistant Lecturer in Communication and Electronic Department at El Gazeera High Institute (EGI) for Engineering and Technology. He received the M.Sc. degree from Al-Azhar University, in 2017. He is currently working toward the Ph.D. degree. His research interests include OFDM, MIMO, and PAPR reduction.

Abdellah Najid received his PhD in Electronic Engineering and the MSc in Networking and Communication Systems from the ENSEEIHT of Toulouse, France. He has several years of research experience with ENSEEIHT, ENSTA, INRIA and ALTEN. He joined INPT, Rabat, Morocco as a Full Professor of Microwave and Telecommunication Engineering in 2000. He has devoted over 16 years to teaching microwave engineering, wireless networking, network architectures, network modeling courses and directing research projects in wireless network performance analysis, wireless sensor networks, microwave, and antennas design.

Padma Priya received her B.Tech degree from Regency Institute of Technology in 2010 and M.Tech degree in the field of Network and Internet Engineering from Pondicherry University in 2012, India. She is doing research in the area of Wireless Communications at Anna University, Chennai, India. Her area of interest includes Wireless Sensor Networks, Optimization, Internet of Things. She has also published 6 papers in International journal, 6 in International Conference. She is currently working as an Associate Professor in IFET College of Engineering for the department of Computer Science and Engineering.

Aswini Raja has completed her bachelor of Engineering at Kalasalingam Institute of Technology and her masters at Sathyabama University as a gold medallist. She has published five papers in international journals and four papers in SCI and Scopus Indexed Journal and three in IEEE conference. She is currently working as an Assistant Professor in IFET College of Engineering for the department of Computer Science and Engineering.

Index